"Best book on the war in Iraq! . . . It is rare indeed that you will read a book about war that is so absorbing and entertaining; yet, it is as analytical and probing as any great history book can be. Richard S. Lowry has written the definitive accounting of the battles in and around An Nasiriyah. . . . This is good reporting and good storytelling . . . receives the MWSA's TOP BOOK RATING of FIVE STARS! It is destined to become a classic book on the war in Iraq."
                                                                        —Bill McDonald,
                                                        Military Writers Society of America

"Lowry's nuts-and-bolts description of the fight represents his strongest writing. It took immense research to produce such detail."
                                                                —Publishers Weekly

"A stirring tribute to one of the most horrific days in the ongoing Iraq war . . . A rare glimpse into the lives of soldiers in the field and a valuable contribution to the annals of modern war literature." —AbeBooks

MARINES IN THE GARDEN OF EDEN

RICHARD S. LOWRY

BERKLEY CALIBER, NEW YORK

THE BERKLEY PUBLISHING GROUP
Published by the Penguin Group
Penguin Group (USA) Inc.
375 Hudson Street, New York, New York 10014, USA
Penguin Group (Canada), 90 Eglinton Avenue East, Suite 700, Toronto, Ontario M4P 2Y3, Canada
(a division of Pearson Penguin Canada Inc.)
Penguin Books Ltd., 80 Strand, London WC2R 0RL, England
Penguin Group Ireland, 25 St. Stephen's Green, Dublin 2, Ireland (a division of Penguin Books Ltd.)
Penguin Group (Australia), 250 Camberwell Road, Camberwell, Victoria 3124, Australia
(a division of Pearson Australia Group Pty. Ltd.)
Penguin Books India Pvt. Ltd., 11 Community Centre, Panchsheel Park, New Delhi—110 017, India
Penguin Group (NZ), 67 Apollo Drive, Mairangi Bay, Auckland 1311, New Zealand
(a division of Pearson New Zealand Ltd.)
Penguin Books (South Africa) (Pty.) Ltd., 24 Sturdee Avenue, Rosebank, Johannesburg 2196,
South Africa

Penguin Books Ltd., Registered Offices: 80 Strand, London WC2R 0RL, England

The publisher does not have any control over and does not assume any responsibility for author or
third-party websites or their content.

PRINTING HISTORY
Berkley Caliber hardcover edition / June 2006
Berkley Caliber trade paperback edition / June 2007

Berkley Caliber trade paperback ISBN: 978-0-425-21529-6

The Library of Congress has catalogued the Berkley Caliber hardcover edition as follows:

Lowry, Richard S.
    Marines in the Garden of Eden / Richard S. Lowry
      p.   cm.
    Includes bibliographical references.
    ISBN 0-425-20988-1
      1. Iraq War, 2003—Campaigns—Iraq—Nasiriyah. 2. Lowry, Richard S. 3. Authors,
American—Biography. 4. Iraq War, 2003—Personal narratives, American. I. Title.

    DS79.764.U6L69 2006
    956.7044'342—dc22   2005057192

PRINTED IN THE UNITED STATES OF AMERICA

10   9   8   7   6   5   4   3   2   1

This book is dedicated to the memory of
Lance Corporal Donald "John" Cline, Jr.—
son, husband, father, friend, and
most of all—United States Marine

1 NOVEMBER, 1981–23 MARCH, 2003

Contents

Foreword

FOR those of us who fought in the battle of An Nasiriyah, it will be a time in our lives that we will never forget. March 23, 2003 was the costliest day in the Coalition's assault into Iraq. Throughout the following week, Marines from Task Force Tarawa fought a determined enemy intent on stopping our attack toward Baghdad.

I first met Richard Lowry after our return from Iraq at Camp Lejeune, North Carolina, in the fall of 2003. He was one of a parade of authors and journalists who wanted to capture the story of Operation Iraqi Freedom in words or on film. What set Richard apart was his growing interest in the events that took place in An Nasiriyah and the actions of the Marines in Task Force Tarawa. Having set out to write a history of the war in Iraq, he became more and more intrigued with the actions and events that took place in this city on the Euphrates River. An enthusiastic and dedicated researcher, he has interviewed scores of the battle's participants, gained access to official Marine Corps files, and has produced the most accurate, readable, and comprehensive work on the battle of An Nasiriyah. In *Marines in the Garden of Eden*, Richard has described one of the most tumultuous actions following our invasion into Iraq. Commencing with the ambush of the 507th Maintenance Company, Richard covers the ferocious fight to take the bridges over the Euphrates River and Saddam Canal, the isolation and deliberate clearing of the city, the rescue of PFC Jessica Lynch, and the final liberation of An Nasiriyah.

Marines in the Garden of Eden captures the sheer heroism and sacrifice of young Marines fighting against the Saddam Fedayeen, Al-Quds, Republican Guard, and Iraqi Army. An Nasiriyah was the first determined resistance faced by Coalition Forces after entering Iraq. The significance of the battle and defeat of the Iraqi Forces by Task Force Tarawa helped open the door to Baghdad and its subsequent fall two weeks later. This book is a testimony to the indomitable will of the American fighting man, his concern for oppressed peoples, and for those soldiers and Marines who made the ultimate sacrifice for their country. They will not be forgotten.

Richard F. Natonski
Lieutenant General, U.S. Marine Corps

Acknowledgments

FIRST, and foremost, I would like to thank Lieutenant General Richard Natonski. Without his help, this book would not have been possible. I would also like to thank the general's aide de camp, 1st Lieutenant Robert A. Kleinpaste who treated me like a VIP on my visits to Camp Lejeune. Colonel James E. Reilly, Commanding Officer, 2d Force Recon Company, was also a kind and gracious host on my second visit to Camp Lejeune.

I would like to offer my appreciation to all the members of Camp Lejeune's and New River's Public Affairs Offices, including Captain Kelly Frushour, Captain Theresa Ovalle, Lieutenant Christopher Wilson, Gunnery Sergeant Marcus McAllister, Sergeant Harris, and Corporal Theresa Seng. They all work hard every day to tell the Marines' story to civilians like me. Each and every Marine I encountered in the Public Affairs Office treated me like it was important to them that I tell Task Force Tarawa's story. While I am on the subject of PAOs, I would like to thank Mr. Richard Bridges at Fort Carson's Public Affairs Office for his help.

Marine aviators are a special breed. I feel honored that I had the opportunity to speak with some of them. Thank you to the members of Marine Air Group-29, including its commanding officer, Colonel Robert E. Milstead; MAG-29's executive officer, Lieutenant Colonel Darrell Thacker; Lieutenant Colonel Jeff "Huey" Hewlett, commanding officer of HML/A 269; 1st Lieutenant John Parker; Major Eric Garcia (HMM-162), who is one of the finest men I have ever had the privilege to meet; Major John O'Neal; Captain Tod Schroeder; Captain Eric Griggs; Gunnery Sergeant William Hetterscheidt; and Hospital Corpsman 3 Moses Gloria. Gloria exemplifies the sacrifices made by everyday Americans in our war on terror.

He is not only a veteran of An Nasiriyah; he also has served fearlessly in Afghanistan. He may not wear a purple heart, but he has suffered psychological wounds that no man should have ever had to endure.

This is really the story of the brave Marines of Regimental Combat Team-2, many of whom took the time to convey their personal accounts to me. Over the last months, I have had the privilege of interviewing Colonel Ronald L. Bailey—RCT-2's Commanding Officer; Colonel Royal Mortenson; Colonel Glenn Starnes, who helped suggest the title, *Marines in the Garden of Eden;* Lieutenant Colonel Paul (Brent) Dunahoe; Lieutenant Colonel Rickey Grabowski; Lieutenant Colonel Michael Mooney; Major Michael Brooks; Major Dan Canfield; Major John Day; Major Rich Dremann; Major Rob Fulford; Major Scott "Hawk" Hawkins; Major Bill Peeples; Major David Sosa; Major Christopher Starling; Major Jeffrey Tuggle; Major Daniel Wittnam; Captain William E. Blanchard; Captain Romeo Cubas; Captain Gerard Dempster; Captain Scott Dyer, who was also very helpful during the editing of my manuscript; Captain Edward Healy; Captain Jim "Kool Aide" Jones; Captain Ben Luciano, who actually came up with the title *Marines in the Garden of Eden;* Captain Tim Newland; Captain Harold "Duck" Qualkinbush, who provided me with images of An Nasiriyah; Captain Gerald Thomas; Captain Jim Thompson; Lieutenant Brian Waite, USN; Captain Kevin Yeo; Lieutenant Michael (Mike) Dubrule; Lieutenant Melvin Euring; Lieutenant Jonathan Forman; Lieutenant Gregory Nolan; Lieutenant James (Ben) Reid; Lieutenant Kris Southwick; Gunner David Dunfee; Gunner Nick Vitale; First Sergeant Jose Henao; First Sergeant James Thompson Jr.; Gunnery Sergeant Kevin Barry Jr.; Gunnery Sergeant Jason Doran; Gunnery Sergeant Alan Kamper; Gunnery Sergeant William Mackes; Staff Sergeant Jason Cantu; Staff Sergeant Kevin Ellicott; Staff Sergeant Fowler; Staff Sergeant Troy Schielein; Sergeant James Johnson; Sergeant Mark Sarmiento; Sergeant William Schaefer; Corporal Will Bachmann; Corporal Nick Elliot; Corporal John Friend; Corporal Jose Gomez; Corporal Matthew Juska; Corporal Matthew Walsh; Corporal John Wentzel; Corporal Randy Whidden; and last, but certainly not least, Navy Cross recipient, Hospital Corpsman Luis Fonseca. These sailors and Marines have earned my respect and some have become my friends.

The story of An Nasiriyah would not have been complete if I had limited my research to the members of Task Force Tarawa. I have also had the honor of speaking with a few Marines from the 1st Marine Division; Colonel Eddie Ray, commanding officer of the 2d LAR Battalion; Lieutenant

Colonel Lewis Craparotta, commanding officer of the 3d Battalion, 1st Marines; and Major Matthew Reid.

Thank you Tina for helping me get to know John.

Special thanks are due CW3 Marc Nash, Sergeant Curtis Campbell, Sergeant James Grubb, and Sergeant Joel Petrik, U.S. Army. They were the only soldiers who were willing to speak with me about their personal ordeal during the ambush of the 507th Maintenance Company.

I would also like to thank another Marine and fellow military historian, Joe Muccia, who provided me with mounds of information that he had collected. Joe had considered writing an account of the battle for An Nasiriyah. However, as a participant, he felt that he was too close to the event to be able to present an objective account. I am proud to have the opportunity to write in his stead. Thanks, Joe.

There is a piece of each of the above individuals buried in the pages of *Marines in the Garden of Eden*. It is my sincere desire that I have accurately conveyed all of your experiences. Thank you, one and all.

I would also like to thank members of the news media who have taken their personal time to relate to me their experiences while with Task Force Tarawa; Ken Kalthoff, Kerry Sanders, and Joe Raedle, whose photographs captured what no amount of prose could ever describe. Thank you, Eric Larson for the wonderful photograph. You are a magician with the camera. I've never looked better.

I would like to express my gratitude to Susan Hodges and the Marine Corps Heritage Foundation for their generous grant and the untold doors that were opened by their recognition.

One of the many reasons that the Marine Corps is the finest fighting force in the world today is that they have an appreciation of their past. When it first became apparent that they would go to war, General Natonski picked up the telephone and called the Marine Corps History Center and requested that a historian be assigned to his unit. They sent Colonel Reed Bonadonna, USMCR, to record the events of the Camp Lejeune Marines. In his personal journal, Colonel Bonadonna provided me a view through the eyes of a professional historian. His running narrative provided body for the story by helping me to understand the personalities of the participants and to add the little details that helped bring the story to life.

I would also like to thank other members of the Marine Corps History Center in the Washington Navy Yard: Chuck Melson; Charles Smith; Chris Doyle, who spent many hours working to provide me with relevant oral histories; and Bob Piehel, who searched the stacks for all of the documents I requested.

Writing can be a lonely, frustrating task. As a perfectionist, my writing never appeared good enough, and the writing was the easy part. To be a successful author, one must also be a marketer. The days, weeks, and months of work required to write and then market a book are filled with disappointments and setbacks. This story would have never made it to print without my good friends, advisors, and supporters at the Orlando Writer's Guild—Marvin Blatt, Dotty Katz, Denise Solis, and John Strelecky; my good friends at the Orlando Economic Development Commission—John Krug and Sally Atkins; and the local community relations manager at Barnes and Noble—Terrie Jordan. Without their support, encouragement, and camaraderie, I would have quit long ago.

Research is a messy, cluttered task. Left to my own devices, I would not have been able to keep track of the thousands of written pages, hundreds of photographs, and dozens of computer files that I have collected over the past two years. I would especially like to thank Ms. Ana Binkley, for without her help I never would have been able to stay organized for more than five minutes.

I would also like to express a special thanks to my wife, Vickye, and my three wonderful sons, Ryan, Jeremy, and Justin. They have been a constant source of help and encouragement throughout the entire project.

I cannot overlook Merry K. Pantano of the Blanche C. Gregory Literary Agency who has worked tirelessly to bring attention to my work and guided me through the minefields of New York's publishing world.

I would also like to thank Natalee Rosenstein and the Penguin Group (USA) Inc. for taking the chance on me and my work. You were all a joy to work with during the publication of this story. Thank you, Michelle Vega for your constant encouragement and support during the production process.

Thank you, Jack Glasgow, for your support at *The Marine Corps Gazette* and Colonel Walt Ford at *Leatherneck* as well as all of the members of the Marine Corps Association who have helped get the word out about my work. Thank you to my friend John Shank at *Military Magazine*.

Over the years, I have been very fortunate to become acquainted with the staffs of several military websites. They have all been gracious enough to publish my work. Thank you to Bill Serra at alwaysfaithful.net, Scott O'Hara at desert-storm.com, Charles Geck at glogalspecops.com, Brian

Williams at militaryhistoryonline.com, Ben Burgess at The History Project, Ho Lin and Christine Vilar at military.com, and Brian King at armchairgeneral .com.

Finally, I would like to personally thank *all* of the men and women of Task Force Tarawa and their families for their individual contribution and sacrifice while working to protect my family and our country.

Semper Fidelis,
Richard S. Lowry

Preface

THIS is a story of heroism and sacrifice—of life and death. This is a story of today's Marine Corps.

The Corps is a young service, the youngest of all the services. The average age of a Marine is twenty-four years old. There are over 26,000 teenagers in the Corps. These guys wear their pants too low and they play their music too loud, but they are just like the seventeen-, eighteen-, and nineteen-year-old kids that landed at Anzio and Normandy, and that landed at Tarawa, Saipan, Tinian, and Okinawa.

One young Marine of the Second Marine Expeditionary Brigade (2-MEB) told his commander that he had fought his father's war, and his father had fought his war. When asked to explain, the young Marine said that his father fought in Desert Storm. Prior to the Desert Storm ground war, the Marines were told to expect stiff resistance. Whereas, for Operation Iraqi Freedom, the Marines were told to expect massive Iraqi surrenders. The father ran into thousands of Iraqis eager to surrender while the son ran into fanatic resistance. And the Iraqis stood and fought at An Nasiriyah.

While the "West Coast" Marines of the 1st Marine Division marched to Baghdad, the Carolina Marines fought, bled, and died in a little-known town on the banks of the Euphrates River.

The battle for An Nasiriyah was the pivotal battle in the invasion of Iraq. American ground forces, the world news media, and, certainly, the American public believed that this ground war would be little more than a road trip through the desert. Everyone expected the real threat to lie at the gates of Baghdad.

On October 27, 2003, I visited Camp Lejeune and had the opportunity to interview then–Brigadier General Richard Natonski and some of the 2nd Marine Expeditionary Brigade staff. I enthusiastically prepared for my visit, hoping that this would be the beginning of my quest to gather details for a sequel to my first book, *The Gulf War Chronicles*. I was told by 1st Lieutenant Robert Kleinpaste, General Natonski's aide de camp, that I should anticipate a forty-five-minute-to-an-hour delay in getting through the main gate during the morning rush hour. When I arrived at my hotel the night before, I inquired about how long it would take to get to Camp Lejeune's main gate at 0700 in the morning, "Oh, at least an hour," the hotel clerk proclaimed. I rose at the crack of dawn so I wouldn't be late and drove through Jacksonville's nearly deserted streets toward Camp Lejeune.

I was at the main gate by 0615, and by 0630 I was driving up to a stately, three-story, redbrick building. The building was set well back from the road. A single lane, semicircular drive led to the front door. There was a small sign at the head of the driveway that read, GENERAL OFFICERS AND GUESTS ONLY. Two Marines, dressed in camouflage, web belts, and brass buckles stood guarding the entrance. I drove up the driveway, stopped at the front door, rolled down my right window, and announced, "I am here to see General Natonski for an appointment at 0800. Where should I park?" One of the young Marines motioned to a parking lot across the street. I thanked him and parked my car.

I was greeted in the lobby by Lieutenant Kleinpaste. He signed me in at the front desk, and we went upstairs to the general's suite of offices. I was invited into Kleinpaste's administrative office. The large room housed four neatly arranged gray metal desks, filing cabinets, book shelves, a few guest chairs, and a small side table, much like you would find in any waiting room. Several outdated magazines were neatly stacked on the table. I sat down next to the table at approximately 0645.

Soon thereafter, a young woman, a Marine captain, came in and introduced herself. "Good morning, sir. I am Captain Frushour. I am with the Public Affairs Office." She asked me if I had any other interviews scheduled for the day, and I told her that General Natonski had mentioned that I could speak with other officers, but I did not have anything firm scheduled. She then excused herself.

What do you do while waiting for an audience with the general? I sat quietly. I tried not to interrupt whatever work was going on, but I also offered a few friendly words to Lieutenant Kleinpaste. He told me that he, too, had been in Iraq, but he had been with the 1st Marine Division. Sometime before

0730, General Natonski stuck his head in the door and introduced himself. He commented that he would be with me soon. To which I replied, "My appointment is for 0800. I can wait."

General Natonski disappeared, and at 0800 sharp he reappeared. He greeted me again and invited me in to his office. Nearly ten hours later, I bid him farewell and left Camp Lejeune with a sense of wonder. I reflected on the day's events as I slowly inched my rental car toward Camp Lejeune's main gate along with hundreds of Marines who were headed home for the night.

I had started my morning with General Natonski. We had moved from his office into a large conference room, and he and I spent the next few hours talking about Task Force Tarawa's contribution to the war effort. Before lunch, Colonel Robert Milstead, the Marine Air Group (MAG-29) commander, dropped in to tell me a little about his contribution to Operation Iraqi Freedom. While we were talking, General Natonski was making arrangements for the rest of my day.

After a short lunch break with Lieutenant Kleinpaste, I returned to the administrative office to wait for my first afternoon appointment. I hadn't been parked back in my familiar guest chair for five minutes when General Natonski appeared again, wearing shorts and a Marine T-shirt, covered in sweat. He saw me and said to Kleinpaste that he was going to change and go home for lunch. Less than five minutes passed again before he was back, this time dressed in a neatly pressed uniform. He called Kleinpaste out to talk, then came back in and asked me if I would like to speak with Captain Michael Brooks, Alpha Company's commander of the Second Marine Regiment. I said, "Absolutely." The general offered the use of his office for the interview and then he headed to lunch.

A short time later, a young Marine captain appeared and introduced himself. We went into General Natonski's office and found a large map of An Nasiriyah opened and laying out on his small round conference table. Captain Brooks and I sat down, and for the next forty-five minutes, I had the privilege of hearing his personal story of leading his men into battle at Nasiriyah.

Next, I was driven out to see General Natonski's command vehicle. I had asked to see the type of vehicle that he used on the battlefield. We drove to a remote area, and several young Marines showed me the general's LAV C3[1].

---

[1]Light Armored Vehicle—Command, Control, and Communications variant.

While I was there, Lieutenant Colonel Glen Harp told me of the general's exploits during the war in this vehicle. My afternoon was then filled with a succession of interviews, first with Colonel Ron Bailey, then Lieutenant Colonel Brent Dunahoe and a few of his battalion staff officers, and lastly with Lieutenant Colonel Royal Mortenson.

Now, as I sat in traffic, I felt a strong urge to focus my energies on writing Task Force Tarawa's story. I was completely awestruck. I had just experienced a day unlike any other in my life and had walked among great American heroes. My train of thought kept shifting as I attempted to absorb the day's experiences. I remembered General Natonski telling me that his only motivation was to tell the story of his Marines. Then I flashed on Colonel Milstead telling me that his Marines did a great job, and that he was proud to have had the opportunity to lead them. Then Mortenson's words flashed through my mind. "I was fighting the fight." Next, Captain Brooks' description of a very dangerous situation at the Euphrates River bridge, "I was starting to get concerned." All the men I had spoken with that day had an air about them that is nearly impossible to describe. They were confident professionals, articulate leaders, fierce warriors, and amicable gentlemen. I had never met men like these.

By the time I reached my hotel, I had decided to tell their story. I returned to Orlando and embarked upon a yearlong research project to collect as much information about Task Force Tarawa's battle for An Nasiriyah as I could. I have personally interviewed nearly one hundred Marines. I have collected thousands of photographs. I have interviewed four soldiers from the 507th Maintenance Company and three embedded reporters. I have made every effort to document the true story for the Marine Corps historical archive.

Regrettably, the story of the 507th Maintenance Company is derived only from the Army's report on the incident, interviews with sergeants Curtis Campbell, James Grubb, and Joel Petrick, Chief Warrant Officer Marc Nash, and accounts taken from Marines who came upon the aftermath of the ambush. I made dozens of requests for additional information and interviews with other members of the 507th. Unfortunately, all either declined or ignored my repeated inquiries, leaving some of the detail of this important part of the battle missing from my work.

Understandably, the United States Special Operations Command also declined to provide detailed information on the operation involving Jessica Lynch's rescue. I have made every attempt to piece together the story of the ordeal of the soldiers of the 507th Maintenance Company on March 23, 2003, and Jessica's rescue.

The story of Task Force Tarawa's battle for An Nasiriyah will go down in the annals of the United States Marine Corps as the first major battle of Operation Iraqi Freedom. Hopefully, *Marines in the Garden of Eden* will serve as the primary reference for this important historical event. Regardless, this is the story of the men and women who were there. To the best of my knowledge, the events are all true and presented in the proper sequence.

Pull up a chair, sit back, and prepare to read the amazing story of America's gallant heroes, brave Marines who fought to free a nation and preserve our way of life. Some never returned home, others returned scarred for life, and all will never forget "The Naz."

Courage is fear hanging on a moment longer.

—Thomas Fuller

CHAPTER 1

Everyday Americans

Never forget where you came from. Never forget what made you and never lose pride in your history. When you do, you have lost your future.

—STAFF SERGEANT TROY SCHIELEIN, USMC
1st Battalion, 2d Marines—2003

DEEP in the heart of Central Command's forward command center in Doha, Qatar, American military staff officers started filling the auditorium. America's finest general officers had been summoned to the Persian Gulf in early December 2002 for a high-level planning session in preparation for the invasion of Iraq. Generals, admirals, and their staffs moved into the room in small groups, greeting old friends and chatting near their seats. As the scheduled meeting time approached, the officers took their seats and the hubbub faded. The lights dimmed, and a field of gently swaying reeds appeared on a large screen. A Roman general, portrayed by Russell Crowe, strolled through the field in the early morning mist. He then approached his troops and said to one of his commanders, "At my signal, unleash hell." The lights came up in the auditorium, and General Tommy Franks appeared.

One of the generals seated in the audience was Brigadier General Richard Natonski. Natonski would soon return to Camp Lejeune to assemble his Marines into Task Force East. Richard Natonski has had a distinguished military career, being one of only a handful of Vietnam veterans who are still on active duty. He is the Marine Corps of the twentieth and twenty-first century. While he would never claim to be a Vietnam vet, as a young lieutenant, he did participate in the final chapter of America's involvement in Vietnam. Lieutenant Richard Natonski was one of the brave Marines who took part in the evacuation of the U.S. Embassy in Saigon. He is also a veteran of the war on terror. He has served in Beirut, Somalia, and Kuwait. Now he represented Camp Lejeune's Marines, as commander of the 2d Marine Expeditionary Brigade (2-MEB).

The general carries an air of leadership. His tall, trim frame displays a lifetime of daily Marine Corps conditioning. His presence fills the room. He is one of those men who are accorded a well-deserved respect wherever he appears. He is confident, amiable, and self-assured. His attitude and personality permeate throughout his staff.

General Natonski returned to Camp Lejeune from the commanders' conference knowing his Marines would soon be going to war. Christmas of 2002 would be a somber prelude to the unleashing of hell.

While the generals planned for war, others continued their training as if nothing was about to happen. Lieutenant Colonel Brent Dunahoe shuffled down the sandy shore of Onslow Beach, shifting his weight to deal with the snow skis he was wearing. He and his entire Battalion (3d Battalion, 2d Marines) were preparing for cold-weather training in the California mountains. Dunahoe, an experienced infantry battalion commander, thought this training was ludicrous. By now, everyone knew that America's next war would be fought in the heat of the Iraqi desert and that his time could be better spent readying for desert warfare.

The Marine Corps is a bureaucratic behemoth. Units are scheduled for special training months in advance. Like a large ship at sea, Marine training schedules can take quite a long time to change course. Dunahoe's battalion had been slated for cold-weather training, so prepare he must until he was directed otherwise.

Brent Dunahoe's rugged appearance is betrayed by a slight upturn in the corners of his mouth. His contagious smile, which never quite disappears, reveals a boyish sense of humor. He has probably been the instigator of many a practical joke over the years, but don't let his charm fool you. He is first and foremost, a ferocious warrior. He is a Marine. His boss, Colonel Ron Bailey, is another no-nonsense Marine.

It is obvious after spending only a few moments with Colonel Bailey that he is the embodiment of Marine Corps professionalism. He is confident, articulate, and unwavering. Bailey does not demand respect. He deliberately works to earn it from the moment he meets you. He leads through motivation and nurture. Bailey, the commanding officer of the 2d Marine Regiment, is tough, disciplined, and intelligent. He is the type of person you want for a friend and pray is never your enemy.

Every year, Ron Bailey journeys home to St. Augustine, Florida, to spend the Christmas holiday with his family. Christmas of 2002 was no different. Except this time he knew that very soon he would be taking his Marines to war. Colonel Bailey had been training and studying for twenty-five years, preparing for this day. Shortly after graduating from college in 1977, he was commissioned second lieutenant. Bailey worked his way up through the officer's ranks to a level that few obtain. On July 2, 2002, he assumed command of the 2d Marine Regiment, an accomplishment limited to only the finest colonels in the Marines.

Lieutenant Colonel Rickey Grabowski, one of Dunahoe's peers, commanded the 1st Battalion of Colonel Bailey's 2d Regiment. Grabowski was an old-school, by-the-book, Marine. He was calm, composed, and always in control. He was tough on his men and on himself.

Rickey Grabowski, a direct descendent of Edward Longshanks, entered the Marine Corps in 1976, just after the Vietnam War. He learned to be a Marine from hardened Southeast Asia combat veterans. As a staff sergeant, he carried that training with him to his job as a Marine Corps drill instructor. Grabowski found that he loved the Corps, so, at the end of his enlistment, he went to college and then returned to the Marines as a second lieutenant. He joined the officer ranks confident with the knowledge that he would end up being surrounded by great Americans. As his career progressed, Rickey found that he loved command. He worked his way up the ladder as a platoon commander, company commander, and then served on many other commanders' staffs. Finally, Lieutenant Colonel Rickey Grabowski was given the command of the 1st Battalion, 2d Marine Regiment. As its leader, Grabowski put his men first. Knowing that his battalion would soon be sent to Iraq, he sent them home on Christmas leave while he stayed in Jacksonville, North Carolina, to continue to plan for war.

Command of a Marine infantry battalion can be a thankless job; Grabowski appeared aloof to some of his men. His younger Marines saw him as an authoritarian, a man who cared little about his troops, but nothing could be further from the truth. Rickey Grabowski cared about every single one of his men. He worried daily about their well-being. The Marines of 1st Battalion were all in his charge; he would work from dawn to dusk to ensure they were prepared for war.

A Hollywood casting department could not have done a better job of finding the perfect commander for "America's Battalion." Lieutenant Colonel Royal Mortenson is outgoing and charismatic. He had a rugged, handsome appearance and confident demeanor. He led his men from the front and felt that he was responsible for their safety and security.

Mortenson's battalion was not part of Colonel Bailey's 2d Marine Regiment. "America's Battalion" was the 2d Battalion of the 8th Marine Regiment. Throughout the summer and fall of 2002, Mortenson's Marines had been planning to fly to Kuwait and become part of the 1st Marine Division. Royal Mortenson's Christmas Eve was interrupted by a cryptic telephone call. A 2-MEB staff officer called to ask, "How many vehicles would you need to bring aboard ship to support command and control of your battalion?" Much to his surprise, it now appeared that his men would be traveling to war aboard ship with the 2d Marine Regiment. In the days to come, Mortenson would learn that Bailey and Natonski had exerted all their available influence to have America's Battalion "chopped[1]" to RCT-2[2].

Bailey was fortunate to have such a fine group of infantry commanders. He saw different strengths in each of their personalities. "Rick was a methodical guy, Royal was a thinking guy, and Brent was this 'tear the doors down' guy."[3] The 2d Marines also brought an artillery battalion, the "King of Battle," along as part of Regimental Combat Team-2. Lieutenant Colonel Greg Starnes commanded the 1st Battalion, 10th Marines. Starnes was a go-getter and a hard-charging Marine. He had just finished a tour with the Central Command (CENTCOM) staff. While at CENTCOM, he spent two years as liaison to the British, helping plan the defense of Kuwait. The men of the 2d Marine Regiment could not have been blessed with a finer set of battalion commanders.

---

1 *Chopped* is a frequently used term meaning "to be reassigned from one's parent unit to a different unit." In this particular case, 2/8 was chopped from the 8th Marine Regiment to the 2d Marine Regiment.

2 Regimental Combat Team-2.

3 Personal interview with Colonel Ron Bailey, 3/25/04.

By the middle of December, Natonski, Bailey, and their commanders were already leaning forward. They were preparing and staging equipment for a rapid deployment. The international political situation that continued to play out on the evening news was still uncertain. Would Saddam back down? Would the United Nations' Security Council vote to authorize military action? Would President Bush act without the UN's approval? No one knew. So, the Marine Corps had to prepare for the worst-case scenario—war with Iraq.

THE Camp Lejeune rumor mill was working overtime as Christmas approached. Of course, all deployment plans were classified, but word continued to circulate that everyone would have new orders by the new year. Everyone at Camp Lejeune expected that they would be headed toward Iraq in the near future. To further fuel the rumor mill, on Thursday, December 19, 2002, Dunahoe's cold-weather exercise was canceled, ending the ski season.

The commanders reasoned that there should be just enough time to shut down for the Christmas holiday. Just like Colonel Grabowski, they, too, let their Marines travel home on leave. The Marines could always be called back early if the plans changed drastically. So Camp Lejeune underwent a normal Christmas slowdown, and Marines headed all over the country to be home with their families during the holiday season.

Dan Wittnam and his entire family (his parents, all of his brothers, his sister, and all of the nieces and nephews) had taken a Disney cruise for the Christmas holiday. Captain Dan Wittnam could not completely forget his work, even in that idyllic environment. As the Charlie Company Commander of the 1st Battalion, 2d Marine Regiment, he knew that he would soon be called to war. So, he telephoned his battalion office daily. Dan hoped that he would not be called back to Camp Lejeune before the cruise ended. It was a special time for him, and he cherished every moment, not knowing what the future would bring. Dan, a ten-year veteran of the Marine Corps and a University of Arizona graduate, knew full well the approaching dangers. Just like his boss, Lieutenant Colonel Grabowski, he, too, had risen from the enlisted ranks to become an infantry officer. On December 28th, a day after he returned to Jacksonville, he received the call. He was ordered to cut his leave short and report in to help plan for the battalion's departure.

Lieutenant James "Ben" Reid and his wife, Susan, went home to Texas for their first Christmas together as husband and wife on December 20th. Ben looked much younger than his years. He had that youthful look of someone barely out of his teens—always the first one to be "carded" when ordering drinks. Here was another Marine whose looks deceive. Ben had the Corps in his blood and was a smart young leader. His father was a retired Marine colonel who had spent many years teaching at staff colleges. Ben, a recent graduate of the U.S. Naval Academy, hoped to follow in his father's footsteps. As they left for Texas, Ben knew he would soon be headed to Iraq. His time at home was not spoiled by the thought of going to war because he had no idea of the horrors that waited in a faraway land.

Major Rob Fulford left for his Christmas leave on December 18th and went home to Georgia. Rob was from another Marine Corps family. As a colonel, his father had commanded Task Force Ripper in the first Gulf War. General Carl Fulford's career took him to one of the top jobs in the Marine Corps. As a "three star," he held the position of commanding general of Fleet Marine Forces Pacific before he retired. General Fulford's son, now midway through his own career, was the operations officer of Colonel Mortenson's Second Battalion of the Eighth Marine Regiment.

FOR some, the only family they had was the Marine Corps. Sergeant William Schaefer, twenty-five years old, from Columbia, South Carolina and a seven-year veteran of Amphibian Assault Vehicles (AAVs) had no real family to visit during the holiday season. So he and a buddy headed off to New Orleans to spend New Year's Eve in the French Quarter. But not all the Marines left Camp Lejeune. Some had already used their allowable leave or were content to remain at home in Jacksonville with their families and friends.

Eric and Bonnie Garcia had bought their first home in May 2002. They only had a few months to ready the nursery before their first son, Kyle, arrived in September. Their new home was nestled in a small development not far from the Marine air station at New River, North Carolina, where Eric worked as a helicopter pilot in HMM-162[4].

---

4 Marine Medium Lift Helicopter Squadron-162.

Eric exemplified Marine aviators. Young and smart, he grew up in Marine Corps artillery, but his true calling was flying. He handled the controls of his multimillion-dollar aircraft with a deftness and precision not often seen. When he flew, it was as if he were playing a fine musical instrument. He became one with his plane. Eric was a quiet man, yet determined. He was a doer, not a talker. Eric was a loving husband and proud father, and the first person you would pick to help you in a pinch.

Bonnie was the daughter of a Navy Chief Petty Officer and had been around the military all of her life. She met Eric when he attended flight school in Pensacola and noticed right off that Eric was not like the other Marine aviators. They quickly fell in love.

Eric and Bonnie's neighborhood was perfect for young families. The modest homes were new, with large backyards. They were set on quiet streets that had little traffic, and most of the homes were filled with the families of junior Marine Corps officers. Chelle and Fred Pokorney lived a few houses down from the Garcia's with their two-year-old daughter, Taylor.

When Chelle found out that Bonnie was home with her new baby, she brought dinner in one of her casserole dishes. Bonnie and Chelle soon became friends. Likewise, Fred and Eric met at a training exercise during the summer of 2002. While they had very different jobs, they knew each other as neighbors. As Christmas approached, Bonnie invited the Pokorneys over for a neighborly Christmas Eve drink and get-together.

Fred was a second lieutenant in the artillery. Like many of his colleagues, Fred Pokorney had come to the officer corps through the enlisted ranks. He was a giant of a man, well over six feet tall with a massive frame. His daughter, Taylor, was the love of his life. Both Chelle and Fred were model parents. Already, Taylor was expected to be polite and considerate of others. She was a gorgeous child, a daddy's girl.

Eric and Bonnie had spent the afternoon cleaning, straightening up their house, and preparing for guests in their home. It was a nice change of pace for Bonnie since taking care of a new baby now filled her days. She was looking forward to Christmas Eve and Fred, Chelle, and Taylor's visit. This was the first time that both families had the opportunity to visit since Chelle and Bonnie had become friends.

Early on Kyle Garcia's first Christmas Eve, Fred and Chelle showed up at the door with their daughter. The two young families spent part of their evening laughing and visiting. After the short get-together, the Pokorneys left to take Taylor to see the town's Christmas decorations. Before they headed out, Bonnie and Eric asked Fred if he would take the first Christmas photograph of the Garcia family. Using Eric's camera, Fred stepped back, "Smile!" he urged, and then flashed the picture. Chelle thanked Eric and Bonnie, wished them a Merry Christmas, then Fred swept his daughter up into his arms and carried her out to see the Christmas lights.

Eric already knew that his squadron would be leaving shortly after the holiday. He had decided to wait until his involvement would be a certainty before he would tell Bonnie. But Bonnie knew. Eric had already prepared a three-ring binder, which contained all the important papers that Bonnie would need.

Gunnery Sergeant William Hetterscheidt, an eighteen-year veteran of Marine aviation, was a divorced father who had custody of his four children. He had been a helicopter crew chief for seventeen and a half years. He was the most senior crew chief in all of Marine Air Group-29 (MAG-29). Because of his single-father status, the Corps would not require him to go on deployments. So, Gunny H was "flying a desk" in Colonel Robert Milstead's air group headquarters. Because of his job, he knew that his unit would soon be headed to Iraq. He also knew in his heart that he had to go. After all, he was a Marine, and this was his job.

Gunny Hetterscheidt spent a quiet Christmas at home with his children. Hetterscheidt was not a touchy-feely kind of guy, so he sat back during the holiday and savored every moment with them, watching them enjoy their Christmas as only children could. He watched them laugh, open presents, and play. He spent as much time with them as he could, knowing that he would be away for many months.

TWO young Marines, Lance Corporal Donald J. "John" Cline, twenty-one and Corporal Will Bachmann, twenty-two, had met on a deployment to Okinawa two years earlier. They could not have had less in common, yet have been more alike. John Cline had grown up in Southern California and gone to high school in the high desert in Nevada; Will grew up in New Jersey. John had recently lost his father; Will and his father were best friends. Will was tall, John short. John was outgoing and boisterous, Will quiet and reserved. John was married and the father of two young boys; Will was single. Yet, Will and John became best friends.

Neatly nestled between the trees and Route 46 in rural New Jersey is the popular Americana Diner. Its glass vestibule shields the customers inside from the harsh New Jersey winters. Its warm coffee and comfortable leather booths were reminiscent of the diners of the fifties and sixties. Life in the small communities of White Township and Belvidere was pretty much the same at Christmas in 2002 as it had been in 1981 when Will Bachmann was born. Will and his friends loved to gather at the diner to talk about who was the prettiest girl in town or who was the worst teacher at Belvidere High. Some nights they would swap their dreams of the future. One night, Will told his friends that he had joined the Marine Corps. Little did he know that the Marine Corps would take him far from that cozy diner and send him to fight America's enemies in faraway lands.

Like Will, John Cline was attracted to the Marine Corps, but from across the country. John was a Nevadan who had volunteered for the Marines at nearly the same moment as Will. John was one scrappy Marine, five-foot, three-inches tall, with large, protruding ears. He was a young father of two small boys: Dakota, two, and Dylan, seven months. He adored his boys and was a loving husband and father.

John and Will, two young American boys, had become men together in the Marine Corps, and now they were living at Camp Lejeune. Both were proud to be part of Charlie Company of the 1st Battalion, 2d Marine Regiment. Bachmann and Cline spent long hours together during the week, and they could talk to each other about anything.

John admired Will and always wanted to become the Marine that Will was. Will was squared away, smart, and always seemed to know the right course of action. He was well liked by his fellow Marines and had a reputation as a "go-to guy." Being single, Will would at times give John money for lunch or help him buy needed uniform accessories before inspections.

John was the youngest father in the battalion. He had no discretionary income, and it was nearly impossible to support a family of four on the pay of a lance corporal. The Clines could just barely afford a family car. On the days that Tina needed to use the car, Will would get up early, drive off base, pick up John, and take him to work.

JACKSONVILLE, normally a sleepy town nestled just outside the gates of Camp Lejeune and New River Marine Air Station, was abuzz. Everyone in town was either related to a Marine or had a Marine as a neighbor. Nightly, the Outback Steakhouse, Chili's, and Logan's were filled with small groups of Marines celebrating a birthday, a promotion, or just getting together for a final beer before shipping out. It was classified, but everyone in town knew that many of their Marines would soon be going to war.

One of those Marines was Staff Sergeant Phil Jordan. Jordan was a Marine's Marine. He had lost his mother at age two and then lost his father and stepmother when he was a young teenager. He lived in foster homes in Texas for the remainder of his school years and then he found a new family when he joined the Marine Corps. Now forty-two, he had spent most of his life in the Corps. He was a veteran of the first Gulf War and Kosovo. Jordan was a "been there, done that" Marine. He had done seemingly everything.

Phil Jordan was a people person. He cared deeply about his Marines and was one of the best noncommissioned officers in the Corps. At 6'3", Jordan could have posed for a recruiting poster. He was trim, handsome, confident, and friendly. Everyone knew and liked Staff Sergeant Jordan.

Jordan had started his own family shortly after Desert Storm, when he married Amanda. As the time to deploy drew near, Phil Jordan moved his wife of nine years and six-year-old son, Tyler, to Connecticut so that they could be closer to her family while he was away at war.

Gunnery Sergeant Jason Doran, father of three and veteran of Operation Desert Storm, had nearly finished his Marine Corps career. He was ready to retire. Doran's life was in a shambles. He had just gone through a divorce from his fourth wife, and he was about to leave his real family, the Corps. When the rumors started circulating that Grabowski's Marines would be headed toward Iraq, Doran asked to delay his retirement so that he could participate.

Jason Doran carefully packed up his belongings from what used to be his Jacksonville home, and loaded them into an old trailer and drove home to Texas. Doran did not have a good feeling about what was going to happen in his life. Crushed from his failed marriage, he probably even fantasized about going out in blazing glory alongside his Marines in battle. He found a storage unit in Dallas and carefully backed the trailer, filled with all his earthly belongings into the storage unit. He unhitched the trailer, rolled down the door, and locked the unit. He was trying to make it as easy as he could on his father if he didn't return from Iraq.

Only days before Christmas, Staff Sergeant Troy Schielein left Camp

Lejeune in his pickup truck. He was on his way home to spend the holiday with his family. But first he had a precious cargo to collect. He drove to his ex-wife's home in Pittsburgh to pick up their two young children, Troy Jr. and Marissa. Then, all three drove on to Illinois to celebrate Christmas with Troy's father and brothers.

Harold "Duck" Qualkinbush was another Marine aviator who called Jacksonville home. Harold loved to take his family out boating and, at least once a week, they would treat themselves to Papa John's Pizza and a visit to Blockbuster. Harold and his wife would rent two movies, one for the kids and one for themselves. They would take the pizza home and have their family movie night. Pizza and movie night was a special weekly ritual in the Qualkinbush household because it was a time when the entire family could just be together.

Captain Harold "Duck" Qualkinbush flew in the backseat of the Marine Corps' EA-6B Prowler, an electronic countermeasures jet. His job was to run the surveillance and countermeasures equipment in this high-tech aircraft. By Christmas, Qualkinbush had just started his ground assignment as the air officer with Colonel Dunahoe's 3d Battalion, 2d Marines.

The Marine Corps is a combined-arms fighting force. Marine aircraft fight over the shoulder of their counterparts on the ground. Close air support (CAS) is just that in the Corps—*close*. To help achieve this dangerous integration of attack aircraft into the combined-arms team, the Marines require that their young aviators conduct a tour of duty with the infantry on the ground. Qualkinbush was just beginning his assignment with the "grunts" on the ground.

The aviators are temporarily assigned to infantry battalions as forward air controllers (FAC) and air officers (AOs). Each infantry battalion has two FAC billets and a single air officer slot. The FACs are assigned to infantry companies within the battalion, and the air officer works on the battalion staff. The idea is that the FACs on the ground have an appreciation for the pilots and they can "talk the talk" of their friends overhead. Also, once they have served on the ground, the aviators return to the skies with a whole new appreciation of the difficulties on the ground. The FAC program brings Marine infantry and aviation closer together and is really what makes CAS work in the Corps.

As is normal, each of the Second Regiment's battalions was allotted two FACs for their three infantry companies. In 1st Battalion, 2d Marines,

Captain Dennis "Mouth" Santare was assigned to Bravo Company and Captain Jim "Kool-Aide" Jones went to Alpha Company. Captain A. J. Greene was Colonel Grabowski's air officer, just as Qualkinbush was Dunahoe's air officer.

AS the year drew to a close, Marines started returning to Camp Lejeune. Troy Schielein loaded his children and their presents into his pickup and started his return road trip. First, he drove his children home to their mother in Pittsburgh. Until this moment, he had not thought about going to war. But as he stood in the crisp winter air, he thought that this might be the last time he would ever see his children. A morbid feeling swept through his body as he let go of his daughter's hand. He actually felt sick. Troy held his emotions together, said good-bye, climbed into his pickup truck, and drove slowly down the road with his children waving a farewell. As soon as he got out of their sight, he pulled over and threw up.

Staff Sergeant Schielein was not afraid of going to war. He was not afraid of dying for his country. But he was terrified that he would never see his beloved children again. He spent many lonely hours driving back to Camp Lejeune contemplating his life in the Marine Corps.

Major Rob Fulford returned from Georgia early on Saturday, December 28, 2002. As soon as he got back in town, he called Colonel Mortenson to check in. Mortenson had no new information about their impending deployment. The colonel told Fulford of the cryptic phone call he had received on Christmas Eve, and they both decided to go to work on Monday morning to try to sort things out.

First thing Monday morning, Colonel Mortenson and Major Fulford called the brigade headquarters. They were told that there was still no firm plan on how their Marines would deploy. Colonel Mortenson decided to recall everyone anyway. He ordered his battalion to cut their leave a few days short and to be back to Camp Lejeune by January 2, 2003.

The next day, Mortenson and Fulford received the official word that they would be deploying on the ships with the 2d Marine Expeditionary Brigade. They were also told that they would be the first battalion to leave town—in less than a week. Going to Iraq was no surprise to Mortenson and Fulford. They had been planning since March 2002. Second Battalion, 8th Marines had been slated to fly to Iraq and be the fourth maneuver battalion in Regimental Combat Team-7 (RCT-7). They had long been planning to be part of the 1st Marine Division. Mortenson still believed that his battalion would take part in the march to Baghdad and that the only thing that had changed was how his men would get over there.

THE personal lives of all of these men and thousands more would soon be interrupted. Soon the streets of Jacksonville would be empty. The men and women that everyone was accustomed to seeing in the churches and movie theaters would be absent. Jacksonville's friends and neighbors, PTA members, little league coaches, and volunteer paramedics would be gone. They would all soon leave family and friends behind and sail off to war. For some, this was a sad and foreboding time, but for others this was an opportunity of a lifetime.

For Lance Corporal Cline, this was a grim time. Outwardly, Cline was full of Marine bravado, but inside he was scared to death. John confided to his wife that he was positive that he would not return from the war in Iraq. He honestly believed that there was some sort of curse on the Cline family. John's father had died young, and he believed in his heart that it was destined that he, too, would not enjoy a long life.

John Cline shared his innermost fears and thoughts with Tina and spent the entire month of December doing as much as he could with his sons. He fed and changed Dylan, and played with Dakota. He would get up in the middle of the night to attend to Dylan. He wanted so much to burn his memory into their being.

Many other Marines had lived for this day. The lot of a peacetime Marine is to train, train, and train. Finally, after years of preparation, these Marines would have the opportunity to prove themselves. Each man wondered if he would be up to the task. Now, it was his turn to take a place in the history of United States Marine Corps.

Just as their predecessors, these young men were from America's households. They were black, brown, and white—rich, poor, and middle class. They were gang bangers, rednecks, city boys, and country boys. Some were U.S. citizens; others wanted to be. Some barely spoke English, and others were college graduates. All loved the United States and believed in what they were doing. Some were model Marines; others came out of the brig. They were typical American youth—a cross section of America. Most were in their teens or early twenties. They liked loud music, pretty girls, and fast cars. Some had girlfriends, fiancées or wives; some had kids or babies on the way. You couldn't tell if they were from a poor family or a rich family. You couldn't tell if they joined the Marine Corps just to get a pair of shoes or to serve their country. Once they put on a uniform, they were all alike. They were simply Marines.

CHAPTER 2

Headed Out

A ship without Marines is like a peacoat without buttons.

—ADMIRAL DAVID PORTER, USN

THERE is only one place on earth that is less hospitable to Marine amphibious operations than Iraq—Afghanistan. Iraq has hardly any access to the sea. The Shat-al-Arab dumps the Euphrates and Tigris rivers into the Persian Gulf on a narrow strip of delta between Iran and Kuwait. Afghanistan, on the other hand, is completely landlocked.

The war in Afghanistan provided the first test of twenty-first-century Marine inland war fighting doctrine. Marines were flown nearly four hundred miles from the *Bataan* and *Peleliu* in the Indian Ocean into combat in a landlocked environment at the rim of the earth. Marine amphibious doctrine needed to be modified yet again for Iraq. Planners spent many painstaking hours rethinking how the United States Marine Corps might be best employed in an invasion of Iraq. Baghdad, the source of Saddam's power, is over five hundred miles from the open waters of the Persian Gulf.

The march to Baghdad would be the deepest penetration in the history of the Marine Corps. Primarily an amphibious force, the Marines needed to drastically modify their concept of employment and logistics. Assault amphibian vehicles, which are usually used to ferry Marines ashore, would now have to be used to carry them all the way to Baghdad. Forward Area Refueling Points (FARPs) would have to be set up so that Marine rotary wing aircraft could leapfrog deep into Iraq, and the Marines would need to borrow logistic techniques from their counterparts in the Army to be able to sustain combat operations so far away from their traditional seaborne support.

While their doctrine needed to be completely reworked, their organization did not. The Marines are organized so that they can easily put together combined-arms fighting forces that are matched to the size of any conflict. The basic Marine Corps building block is the classic infantry battalion. Infantry battalions are the heart of the Marine Corps and are the foundation of a Marine Expeditionary Unit (MEU).

MEUs are comprised of a Ground Combat Element (GCE) and an Air Combat Element (ACE). The ground element is basically a reinforced infantry battalion or Battalion Landing Team (BLT). The Battalion Landing Team is supported by a few tanks, Light Armored Vehicles (LAVs), artillery pieces, and a platoon of AAVs. The air combat element provides a mixture of all the Corps' capabilities. The ACE contains Harriers, Cobras, Hueys, and Sea Knights. The MEU is America's SWAT[1] team. There are always a couple of MEUs at sea, and they can respond to most emergencies around the world on very short notice.

When it comes to larger conflicts, the Corps assembles its infantry battalions into Regimental Combat Teams (RCTs). RCTs will typically have three, or four, infantry battalions, a tank battalion, a Light Armored Reconnaissance battalion (LAR), an artillery battalion and, possibly, an assault amphibian battalion.

RCTs are like the Army's mechanized infantry brigades in size and capability. While, in theory, an RCT could be deployed on its own, the Marine Corps likes to field combined arms teams. A Marine Air-Ground Task Force or MAGTF provides airborne capability to the RCT by adding a Marine Air Group (MAG), which usually consists of a lift and attack squadron. A MAGTF is a powerful combined-arms fighting force able to fight autonomously in virtually any size conflict.

When the Corps is called upon to support major wars like the invasion of Iraq, they call upon their war-fighting division. The 1st Marine Division consists of three RCTs and the logistical support to field a force of more than ten thousand troops. The division is supported by Marine Air Wing 3 which is made up of several MAGs.

Finally, the top level of battlefield command lies at the Marine Expedi-

---

1 Special weapons and tactics.

tionary Force (MEF). I MEF is the West Coast Marine command and II MEF is the East Coast Command. I MEF played an integral role during Operation Desert Storm. Both the 1st and 2nd Marine Divisions had moved in to liberate Kuwait under I MEF's command. I MEF was again preparing to lead Marines into battle against Saddam Hussein.

Since the cessation of hostilities in 1991, Saddam Hussein had been playing a dangerous game of cat and mouse with the United States. By 2002, the U.S. Central Command was planning an invasion of Iraq to finally depose Saddam Hussein. The Marines of the 1st Marine Expeditionary Force would again become an important contributor to the plan.

Hussein and his ruthless cronies had been physically evicted from Kuwait after their attempt to absorb the tiny oil-rich nation into Iraq. Everyone in the world knew that Saddam had not been defeated. He retained his power in Iraq through fear and brutality. But the world felt safe from his tyranny, knowing that the United Nations had kept strict military embargoes in place. Saddam was contained in his little box within his little corner of the world.

As the years passed, leaks appeared in the box, then cracks and gaping holes. By the turn of the century, Saddam was bribing world leaders and U.N. officials. He was reaping profits from the sale of Iraqi oil that should have been diverted to his starving people. Worse yet, he was reconstituting his military capability. By 9/11, Saddam was paying bribes to Palestinian suicide bombers and threatening to destroy Israel.

By 2002, President George W. Bush and his advisors feared a complete collapse of the sanctions against Iraq and the release of the modern-day evil from Pandora's box. Left to his own devices, Saddam would surely threaten the stability of the Middle East and possibly the economy of the entire world. America was already locked in a war against terrorism and President Bush saw this threat as an issue that had to be dealt with as a part of the overall struggle.

Under the direction of the national leadership, CENTCOM prepared for war. Marine planners built the Iraqi invasion force around the Marine war fighting division. The 1st Marine Division was made up of elements from all over the Corps. Three reinforced regimental combat teams formed the backbone. Nearly every AAV in the Marine Corps was pressed into action. Second, 3d, and 4th AAV battalions were spread among the division's nine infantry battalions. While the AAVs provided limited protection and transportation to the Marine infantry, the regiments still needed a heavier punch. So, light armored vehicles and M1 tanks were also assigned to reinforce the 1st Marine Division's regiments. Regimental Combat Teams (RCT) 1, 5, and 7 each had a light armored reconnaissance (LAR) battalion assigned, and two M1 battalions were spread among the three RCTs.

Marine commanders spent many hours planning the routes to Baghdad. General Franks had decided to send the Marines straight up the Tigris River while he sent his main effort, the Army's 3rd Infantry Division, west through the Iraqi desert. The Marines' planned routes led through the Euphrates River town of An Nasiriyah, on the edge of the Arabian Desert. Nasiriyah, a critical choke point, was the only viable Euphrates River crossing for a hundred miles in either direction.

If the Iraqi Army chose to stand and fight in Nasiriyah, the entire invasion could bog down and the 1st Marine Division could have their combat power diverted away from their primary objective—Baghdad. Nasiriyah was also the home of "Chemical Ali" and was a known chemical weapons test facility. The worst possible scenario would have been for the Marines to be slowed while crossing the Euphrates River, then hit with chemical weapons.

More Marines would be needed in the invasion force, so the Pentagon called upon Brigadier General Richard Natonski's 2-MEB from Camp Lejeune. A Marine Expeditionary Brigade (MEB) is a funny animal, not often used in today's Corps, but they have been around for quite a while. They are command units, led by a general officer that can quickly become an advance party for a division headquarters or can stand alone to command a complete MAGTF. MEBs are larger than a MEU, yet smaller than a MEF. It is a MEU on steroids. 2-MEB commanded RCT-2, MAG-29, and a large combat service support element.

2-MEB became another of the MEF's assets alongside the 1st Marine Division and the British forces. While Marine Expeditionary Force commanders planned to send the 1st Marine Division to Baghdad as their main effort, the 2d Marine Expeditionary Brigade would secure the bridges through An Nasiriyah, then provide route security behind the main attack on Baghdad. The brigade would also be available as a reserve force. As follow-up forces arrived in theater, two battalion landing teams, a reserve infantry battalion, and several other support units would be added to Natonski's brigade to help him secure nearly one-third of the Iraqi countryside.

The planners put as much of their power as possible up front, with the 1st Marine Division. The Marines of 2-MEB ended up with what was left over. The 1st Marine Division was entirely "meched up," but Camp Lejeune's

RCT-2 was given only a single LAR company, an AAV company, and a tank company. The Corps was simply stretched too thin to fully mechanize four full Marine regiments. So RCT-2 went to war with a Marine Reserve tank company from Fort Knox—Alpha Company, 8th Tank Battalion; Alpha Company, 2d AAV Battalion; and Charlie Company, 2d LAR Battalion.

GENERAL Natonski and Colonel Bailey worked their staffs furiously to scrape together a viable brigade from units throughout Camp Lejeune. Colonel Bailey's 2d Marine Regiment was far from being at full strength. His 2d Battalion had already been committed to the 24th MEU, leaving Bailey with only two infantry battalions. On top of being short an entire battalion, only Rickey Grabowski's 1st Battalion was at full strength. Brent Dunahoe's 3d Battalion was not even close, so the MEB staff reached across the New River to Camp Geiger. With the stroke of a pen, one hundred and four young Marines were graduated two weeks early from the School of Infantry and sent to 3/2.

Finding a third battalion to round out the regiment would be a little more difficult than filling 3/2's ranks. General Natonski would have to dig deep to get an entire operational battalion assigned to RCT-2. The solution to their problem was right there at Camp Lejeune. Lieutenant Colonel Royal Mortenson's 2nd Battalion of the 8th Marine Regiment was at full strength and had been planning for months to go to Iraq. In the grand deployment scheme, they were going to be part of the 1st Marine Division.

The first order of business would be to find additional sea lift for Mortenson's Marines. If General Natonski could have 2/8 travel aboard the ships in his task force, possession would end up being nine-tenths of the law and his problem would be nearly solved. Fortunately, the brigade's Marine Air Group 29 had a large number of aircraft that needed to be transported. Natonski's staff immediately set out to kill two birds with one stone. If they could talk the Navy into providing a third "Big Deck" amphibious ship, they would have enough room for all of the aircraft and Mortenson's Marines.

By New Year's Day, the Navy had agreed to deploy three "Big Decks" with Task Force East. With the extra ship, eight hundred beds became available. Natonski had offered to bring Mortenson's infantry battalion along for the ride, and this started a chain of events, which would prove quite helpful to Colonel Bailey.

With the new year came a whirlwind of activity throughout Camp Lejeune in preparation for the brigade's deployment. Marines were given immunization shots, wills were filled out, weapons were issued, and last-minute maintenance was conducted on vehicles. It seemed as if the occupants of every building within the camp were all working around the clock to prepare for the deployment.

No one was busier than the Marines in the battalion areas. The battalion commanders and their staffs were trying to get all their equipment together, checked, and prepared for transport. They were working to insure that each of their Marines was administratively ready. Meanwhile the staff NCOs[2] worked to insure that each Marine was ready. They had them lay out all of their equipment on large fields in their battalion areas so that it could be checked. Platoon sergeants and squad leaders inspected each man's personal gear to insure he had everything he needed for the deployment.

By January 2nd, there was a flurry of activity at 2/8's battalion headquarters as its Marines continued to return to Camp Lejeune. They needed to hurry, as they would be the first to leave. The Marines of "America's Battalion"[3] worked for six long days from four in the morning to nine at night, completely reorganizing for their embarkation aboard ship. Everything had to be packed for sea along with the myriad other tasks that accompany preparation for deployment. On January 5th, the battalion's advance parties headed out to USS *Saipan,* which was still preparing for sea in Norfolk.

Ben Reid recognized Fred Pokorney when he appeared at Charlie Company's offices. They had met before. Reid and Pokorney could not have been more different. Reid was a slender young Naval Academy graduate from Texas; Pokorney was an ex-football player from the far west and a Mustang.[4] First Lieutenant James "Ben" Reid, Charlie Company's fire support team (FiST) leader, had been working for several days to prepare his weapons platoon for war. There was a lot of paperwork that needed to be completed prior to shipping out, and Fred had come to the Timberwolves[5] Charlie Company office to report and make his contribution to the pile of

---

2 Noncommissioned officers.

3 Each Marine battalion has a nickname. The 2d Battalion of the 8th Marine Regiment is known as "America's Battalion."

4 *Mustang* is a term used to describe an officer who started his military career as an enlisted man.

5 The 1st Battalion of the 2d Marine Regiment is known as the "Timberwolves."

papers. Second Lieutenant Pokorney, an artillery officer with the 1st Battalion, 10th Marines had been assigned to Charlie Company of the 1st Battalion, 2d Marines.

Pokorney and his small cadre of artillerymen would be Charlie Company's artillery forward observers (FOs)—Reid's lifeline to the regiment's enormous 155mm howitzer batteries. As such, Pokorney would report directly to Reid. Pokorney brought with him a list of all of the serial numbers of the weapons that his team would be bringing to Charlie Company, and he assured Reid that his men were administratively ready to go to war.

EVEN though the Camp Lejeune Marines had been planning for many weeks and working around the clock for many days, it wasn't until January 6th that the Second Marine Expeditionary Brigade was officially activated. Once the activation was official, everyone in Jacksonville, North Carolina, received the word that their loved ones were headed to war. The local television stations and newspapers picked up on the story and started interviewing Marines, their wives and girlfriends, neighbors and friends. The activation order only served to reaffirm what the Carolina Marines and their families already knew. Camp Lejeune's Marines intensified their preparation efforts.

Once the brigade was activated, Colonel Grabowski sent his advance party to Norfolk. They would prepare to load Marines onto the ships that would take them halfway around the world. Captain Dennis Santare led the advance party of junior officers and staff NCOs. Santare, a Marine aviator, was the senior forward air controller in Grabowski's battalion. The group consisted of seasoned Marines—Staff Sergeant Troy Schielein, Staff Sergeant Phillip Jordan, Gunnery Sergeant Jason Doran, and several others.

They arrived at the USS *Ponce* in the afternoon, crossed the gangway, paused, faced aft, saluted the ship's colors, turned to the officer of the deck, saluted again, and repeated the phase that was buried in their memory, "Request permission to come aboard." Without waiting for an answer, each dropped his salute, crossed the quarterdeck and headed for his quarters. They had not been aboard long when one of the gunnery sergeants appeared in Doran's berthing area. "Hey, Gunny, all the staff NCOs and a couple of officers are going to the club on base to go drinking. Do you want to go?"[6]

---

6 Telephone interview with Jason Doran, 9/22/04.

"Hell, yeah!" Doran replied.

Doran, Jordan, Santare, and a couple others dressed and got ready to hit the beach. The Marines got off the ship and grabbed a couple of taxis. At the club, Jordan and Doran spent the night telling sea stories[7] and drinking tequila. They hit it off immediately. They had such a good time that they returned the next night to continue their drinking. From that point on, Phil Jordan and Jason Doran were good friends.

ONE of the most serious shortfalls for the brigade was armor. Camp Lejeune's 2d Tank Battalion had already been assigned to the 1st Marine Division, so the MEB planners had to find tankers to support Colonel Bailey's Marines. They found a Marine Reserve tank company at Fort Knox, and they managed to scrape together fourteen tanks from the 2nd Tank Battalion's inventory.

The M1 Abrams tank has been in use in the Marine Corps since Desert Storm. While all Marine strategy is based on Marine infantry, they have always used a limited number of tanks to support their operations. All marine expeditionary units carry a platoon of four M1 tanks. It is always nice to have a tank, the great equalizer. So, Regimental Combat Team-2 brought fourteen tanks along as their armored punch.

And the M1 packs quite a punch. There is no other tank in the world that can stand up to the M1. Its armor can stop RPGs[8], tank main gun rounds, and most high-caliber projectiles. Its 1,500 horsepower gas turbine engine can propel the tank forward at nearly forty-five miles per hour, and it carries weapons that can defeat any ground threat. Its 120mm main gun can blow holes through any tank ever built. If the main gun weren't enough, it also has a machine gun mounted in tandem with the main gun, as well as another M240 machine gun mounted atop the turret. This king of armor is a 68-ton behemoth getting a half-mile to the gallon of gas. Fourteen fully operational Abrams tanks could defeat most of today's armies.

On January 7th, Bill Peeples was sitting at his desk at work when his phone rang. Bill was a member of the Town of Avon planning commission

---

7 The only difference between a fairy tale and a sea story is that a fairy tale starts with "Once upon a time;" a sea story starts with "This is no shit."

8 Rocket propelled grenades.

in Indiana. Herman Glover from the Marine I&I[9] office at Fort Knox was on the other end of the phone call. He told Bill that his Marine Reserve tank company, Alpha Company, 8th Tank Battalion, had just been activated. Everyone had to report to Fort Knox by January 10th. Major Peeples had less than three days to get everything in order and report for war.

Even though the Navy's deployment order had not yet been signed by the secretary of defense, General Natonski wanted to get a jump on the embarkation. The Marines of Task Force East started loading 7,100 troops, eighty-one aircraft, along with equipment and vehicles on January 9th. The ships could not yet come to North Carolina, so the Marines went to Norfolk to load up.

MORTENSON'S Marines were the first to leave Camp Lejeune at the head of a steady stream of buses that trickled north on the Carolina highways for days. They were bused to the naval station in Norfolk to get an early start on boarding *Kearsarge* and *Saipan*. Four-fifths of the battalion loaded onto USS *Saipan* while Echo Company boarded USS *Kearsarge*. There was room for the Marines of 2/8, but most of their equipment would have to be sent over on a "Black Bottom"[10] ship.

Throughout Camp Lejeune and Jacksonville, Marines rose at zero-dark-thirty to prepare for their departure. They had been ordered to report to the Camp Lejeune armory at 0500 to draw weapons. Each family handled this morning differently. The wives of some of the older Marines climbed out of bed, showered, and dressed as if the day was like any other day in the life of a Marine wife, while other younger wives fell apart.

Marines were on the road well before 0500, headed through the nearly deserted streets of Jacksonville with their wives or girlfriends. It was well below freezing in the predawn darkness, and each drove through the main entrance to Camp Lejeune, then down the tree-lined highway leading into the base. Traffic was heavier than normal for this time of morning. Each Marine received two meals-ready-to-eat (MREs)—the military equivalent of a boxed lunch for their day's journey.

A senior staff NCO returned to his car and sat with his wife to spend their last few moments alone before his departure. Muster was at 0600, so

---

9 I&I—Inspector and Instructor.

10 "Black Bottom" is a term used to describe USNS transport ships.

at 0555 he kissed her good-bye and told her he loved her. "I love you, too. I will pray for the fighting angels to protect you." she replied.

The gunnery sergeant smiled, then turned and got out and unloaded his equipment. His wife reached down deep within her soul to muster up a smile and drove off into the frozen Carolina morning. The sergeant was buoyed by his wife's strength. He knew that she would be fine while he was away at war. Then the Marine waited.

Other Marines hated good-byes. Lieutenant Kris Southwick's family had ventured down to Jacksonville to see their son, their brother, off to war. But Kris said his good-byes the night before and rose in the early morning and drove himself to work.

The story of Marines leaving for war was repeated over and over as each bus headed out of Camp Lejeune's gate. Uniformed Marines sat quietly for the beginning of their journey into uncertainty as family and friends waived good-bye—some were stoic, others broke into tears.

At their destination, the buses pulled onto a bustling pier, filled with trucks, forklifts, and sailors busy loading supplies. Each bus rolled up next to a metal staircase and gangway, which led to a giant gray ship. The Marines got off the bus, stretched their legs, snatched up all their gear, and climbed the metal stairs.

Just a day before they would move to the ships, two military buses arrived at the 3d Battalion's area. More than a hundred young Marines, most still teenagers, clambered off the buses. They had been graduated early from the School of Infantry, and then quickly loaded onto the buses for the short journey from Camp Geiger over to Camp Lejeune. The new Marines were assigned throughout the battalion to help fill out the ranks of the "Betio Bastards."[11] Captain John Day was assigned mortar men who had never fired a round out of an 81mm mortar. The young men barely had time to get settled. They slept in the battalion barracks for one night, and then climbed back on buses to be taken to the ship.

At midnight on January 9th, Marine Reserve tankers began to show up at Fort Knox, Kentucky. Because of their orders and travel insurance rules within the Marine Corps Reserve, the men of Alpha Company were not allowed to start their travel to Fort Knox until after midnight, in the early

---

11 Ever since the World War II battle for Tarawa, 3d Battalion, 2d Marines have been known as the "Betio Bastards."

hours of January 10th. Some had short journeys to the muster, others had several-hour drives. By 0300, over 90 percent of the company had reported for duty. The remaining tankers continued to report in all night. By morning, most of the company had arrived. They spent the entire day, and half of the next night making the final preparations for their departure.

Major Bill Peeples, a soft-spoken, middle-American public servant, would soon lead his Marine Corps Reserve tank company into battle. His transformation from weekend warrior to active-duty Marine had already begun. Little did he know that soon he would be saving lives and risking his own on a dusty battlefield halfway around the world.

These Reserve Marines of Alpha Company were more than weekend warriors. They were a close-knit family, members of a very small Marine contingent, stationed at the home of the U.S. Army's School of Armor. Most lived in America's heartland and came from all walks of life.

Captain Jim Thompson, the senior captain in the company, was 1st Platoon's commander. Thompson's friend Captain Scott Dyer was Alpha Company's executive officer.

Major Peeples was short several officers in his unit so two gunnery sergeants commanded his other two platoons. The 2d Platoon leader, Gunnery Sergeant Randy Howard was an independent general contractor, and Alan Kamper was his 3d Platoon leader.

No tank company would be able to get to the battle without the support of its maintenance personnel. Alpha Company was blessed with a talented group of Marines in its maintenance section. They were led by one of the best maintenance chiefs in the Corps, Staff Sergeant Charlie Cooke. He was a by-the-book Marine and a great guy.

Lance Corporal Randy Whidden had entered the Marines late in life. He had served a short time as an active-duty Marine, but was now a thirty-four-year-old reserve and was not part of Alpha Company's family. He was a master electrician from Fort Meyers, Florida. Whidden belonged to a TOW[12] Scout Platoon reserve unit in Hialeah, Florida. Peeples needed an electro-optics ordinance repairman, so Whidden was yanked from his Florida unit and quickly shuffled off to Camp Lejeune to join Alpha Company, 8th Tanks.

The men of Alpha Company, 8th Tanks were America's neighbors and coworkers. They were the guys who coached little league, the mechanics who

---

12 Tube-launched, optical-tracked, wire-guided missile.

fixed your car, or the guys on the volunteer fire truck. They were just like the tens of thousands of other Reserves who were reporting all over the country. Yet, Marine Reserves are not like Army Reserves who need weeks of workups prior to deployment. They stay ready and come when called. Peeples' tankers would be on their ships in less than a week.

General Natonski had called upon the 2d Force Reconnaissance Company to deploy with his MEB. Force Recon is the commanding general's eyes, ears, and fists. Lieutenant Colonel James E. Reilly III was the recon company's commanding officer. He was tough, yet friendly—with a disarming smile. Just like the 2d Tank Battalion and the 2d AAV Battalion, most of Reilly's recon Marines had already been assigned to the 1st Marine Division and I MEF, So he also had to utilize Marine Reserves. He called upon the Marine Reserves of Company C, 4th Recon Battalion, in San Antonio, Texas.

Almost immediately, telephones started ringing in Texas homes and businesses. Within seventy-two hours of the first phone call, three complete reconnaissance platoons and Charlie Company's headquarters element were aboard USS *Bataan*, sailing with Task Force East.

Donald "John" Cline was the youngest father in Captain Wittnam's Charlie Company, and he would read to his oldest son every night. As their deployment approached, his wife, Tina, walked in on the end of the night's bedtime story. John had finished reading, and he was talking with Dakota, his oldest son.

"Daddy's going to be at work for a while. You need to take care of Mommy and Dylan, while Daddy is away. Just remember, I'll be thinking of you every day, and I'll see you as soon as I can."[13]

NAVY AMPHIBIOUS GROUP 2:
THE MAGNIFICENT SEVEN

Once the deployment order was signed, Navy Amphibious Group 2, the Magnificent Seven, set sail from Norfolk, under the command of Rear Admiral Michael P. Nowakowski, on January 11th and 12th. The group of

---

13 Telephone interview with Tina Cline, 3/13/05.

seven ships sailed south to Moorhead City, North Carolina, and continued loading General Natonski's Amphibious Task Force East.

USS *Kearsarge* (LHD-3[14]), one of the Navy's newest Big Deck amphibious carriers, became the flagship carrying Admiral Nowakowski and General Natonski. *Kearsarge* is the fourth ship in the U.S. Navy to have been named for Kearsarge Mountain in New Hampshire. The Civil War–era sloop named *Kearsarge* defeated the CSS *Alabama*. The turn-of-the-century battleship, *Kearsarge*, sailed as part of Theodore Roosevelt's Great White Fleet. The post–World War II aircraft carrier, *Kearsarge*, picked up Allen Shepherd after his Mercury space flight. Now the modern-day amphibious assault ship, *Kearsarge*, was sailing into history again.

Being the Task Force flagship and floating brigade headquarters, *Kearsarge* was loaded down with staff officers. The only officers allowed to live on the 02 level were commanders and pilots. All of the other officers were cramped into NCO quarters. In addition to most of Task Force Tarawa's staff, *Kearsarge* carried nearly all of Dunahoe's 3d Battalion, 2d Marines, Echo Company of 2d Battalion, 8th Marines, and Charlie Company of the 2d LAR Battalion. *Kearsarge* was packed from stem to stern; nearly every bunk was filled.

The second Big Deck of the Magnificent Seven, USS *Saipan* (LHA-2[15]) displaced 14,000 tons and was over two football fields long. *Saipan* had a crew of sixty-five officers and over a thousand sailors. It could carry over 1,800 Marines and, on this trip, nearly every bunk would be filled. *Saipan* also carried most of MAG-29s helicopters and most of the 2/8's Marines.

USS *Bataan* (LHD-5) was the third Big Deck in the task force and one of the largest of all amphibious warships. It would carry the majority of the brigade's Harriers and six giant CH-53 helicopters.

Four more ships of the "Gator Navy" rounded out Task Force East: the USS *Ashland* (LSD-48), USS *Gunston Hall* (LSD-44[16]), USS *Portland* (LSD-37), and the USS *Ponce* (LPD-15). Typically, a MEU goes to sea aboard one Big Deck and one LSD. Task Force East was an impressive flotilla, carrying the entire brigade to war.

Ponce, Portland, and *Gunston Hall* pulled into Moorehead City and tied up along the pier on January 11th. First Battalion Marines climbed

---

14 Landing helicopter dock ship.

15 Landing helicopter assault ship.

16 Landing supply dock ship.

aboard buses for their short journey to Moorehead City. Grabowski's Bravo Company boarded USS *Gunston Hall* while Alpha Company boarded *Portland,* then they sailed south to Onslow Beach to load vehicles via LCAC[17].

USS *Ponce* would carry the remaining Marines of Grabowski's 1st Battalion. In all, there were approximately 750 Marines on *Ponce.* Charlie Company moved out to the USS *Ponce* on January 11th, and they were followed by Weapons Company, a platoon of AAV Marines, the battalion staff, and seven Cobras with their pilots and a maintenance crew. They were all packed into *Ponce's* berthing quarters from deck to overhead. Charlie Company's platoon leaders; Swantner, Lapinsky, Seely, Reid, Tracy, and Pokorney all shared the same small stateroom.

Major Peeples' one hundred and six reserve tankers were scheduled to leave in the afternoon, but little delays caused the Marines to get on and off the bus several times. Parents, brothers, sisters, sons, daughters, wives, and girlfriends went through hell as they repeated their tearful good-byes several times. Finally, after hours of false starts, the small convoy pulled away and disappeared from the small crowd's view. The Marine reserves of Alpha Company, 8th Tank Battalion began their long trek to war in two chartered buses and a handful of government automobiles. They traveled all night from Fort Knox, Kentucky, to Camp Lejeune. Major Bill Peeples and his Marine Reserve tankers arrived at 0700 on January 11th, just as Lieutenant Colonel Grabowski was headed out the door on his way to move out to the ships. Colonel Grabowski quickly greeted Major Peeples and told him he would talk to him at sea.

Alpha Company's tankers immediately started drawing their equipment. They drew trucks, Humvees, tank retrievers, and fourteen M1A1 tanks. Major Peeples' maintenance Marines quickly reviewed the records of their tanks. Everything looked in order, so Major Peeples signed for the tanks, and his men moved them to Onslow Beach.

Lieutenant Colonel Grabowski was in the last group of Timberwolves to board the ship. Just as each Marine before him, he labored as he walked the metal bridge that took him from shore to ship. The last few steps are always tricky when boarding. The brow is lashed to the ship so that when the tide ebbs and flows, the brow remains in place. Depending upon the tide and the

---

17 Navy hovercraft, or landing craft air-cushioned (LCAC), are used to ferry Marines ashore from Navy amphibious ships.

angle of the brow, the last step onto the ship can be straightforward or hazardous.

One of the Marines ahead of Grabowski faltered as he took that last
step, nearly falling. Two sailors standing on either side of the brow, waiting
for this very occurrence, grabbed the Marine just before he lost his balance,
"Hey, Devil Dog! We got you."

This would not be like a standard peacetime deployment of Marines.
The ships' crew knew full well that they were taking Marines to war. Gone
were the jokes about Marines, replaced with a respect and a true desire to
help their comrades in arms.

Once the Marines were aboard, *Ponce* set sail and moved south to the
open waters off Camp Lejeune's Onslow Beach, where she commenced
loading most of the battalion's AAVs. Captain Blanchard loaded up his tractors at Courthouse Bay, drove them down the ramp into the water and swam
them out to *Ponce, Gunston Hall,* and *Ashland.* Peeples' heavier tanks and
all the brigade's trucks would have to be ferried to the ships on LCACs.

ON Sunday, January 12th, *Kearsarge* set sail. She sailed down off the coast
of Camp Lejeune and proceeded to load vehicles and aircraft. Her well deck
was flooded and opened to the sea, and her amphibious landing vehicles
spent the day ferrying back and forth to Onslow Beach, filling her well deck
with vehicles. Seven CH-46s, six CH-53s, and ten Harriers were flown
aboard along with a third of New River's HMM-162 helicopter squadron
personnel, completing the loadout. Every inch of space was filled.

The M1 Abrams tank was originally designed for the Army to replace
the M60 Patton tank. The Marine Corps had used the smaller M60 for
years, up until Operation Desert Storm. After several fights in Kuwait, Marine tankers decided that all of their M60s should be replaced with the
newer M1. The M1 was not designed for Marine amphibious deployment; it
is heavy and bulky. But Marines are resourceful, and they found a way to
load a single M1 onto an LCAC and transport the heavy tank to and from
their amphibious ships. Because of their size, Major Peeples would have to
spread his fourteen tanks among most of the task force's ships.

The USS *Ashland* (LSD-48) was the newest of the amphibious transports, yet its name had the most history. In a strange example of history repeating itself, *Ashland* would be carrying Marines of the 2d Regiment to
war for a second eventful time. The USS *Ashland* (LSD-1) had carried 2d

Marine Division tanks to the invasion of Tarawa in World War II. Now, Major Bill Peeples loaded his command group and 3d Platoon of Alpha Company, 8th Tank Battalion onto her modern-day namesake. Peeples loaded his second Platoon onto USS *Gunston Hall* and his 1st Platoon onto USS *Portland.*

Loading the ships was like packing the family car for a summer vacation. The ships of Amphibious Group 2 were filled to the rails, so A Company, 8th Tank's field trains had to be loaded on the Black Bottom, USNS *Watson.*

Colonel Bailey still had only two infantry battalions assigned to Regimental Combat Team Two (RCT-2); Grabowski's 1st Battalion and Dunahoe's 3d Battalion. He also had Lieutenant Colonel Starnes artillery battalion, the M1 tanks, AAVs, and a light armored recon company. America's Battalion was traveling with the brigade but was still not assigned to the 2d Marine Regiment, though Natonski continued to lobby for Mortenson's assignment to Bailey's regiment. If 2/8 could be chopped to the regiment, Colonel Bailey would have a viable fighting force.

Again, a sense of déjà vu brought the spirits of World War II Marines along with Colonel Bailey's men. At the invasion of the small Pacific atoll, Tarawa, the 2d Battalion, 8th Marines reinforced the 2d Marine Regiment, and 1st Battalion, Tenth Marine's artillery supported the landings. They all fought a bloody, three-day battle for control of the South Pacific atoll. The Second Marine Regiment and 2/8 sustained heavy casualties in one of the first large-scale amphibious operations of the war in the Pacific. Almost eight hundred Marines were killed and nearly 2,300 were wounded in those three days of hell on Tarawa.

Tarawa was the first amphibious landing of World War II in which the Marines used amphibious tractors. They were needed to get the first three waves of infantry safely across Betio's coral reefs and onto the beaches. Now, Natonski would get his lead infantry battalion across the Iraqi wasteland in forty-six modern-day AAVs.

Alpha Company, 2d AAV Battalion's "Tracks" were commanded by Captain William E. Blanchard. His tracks would allow Colonel Bailey to "mech up" only one of his infantry battalions. Grabowski's Timberwolves had recently returned from Combined-Arms Exercise (CAX), so, Bailey assigned the AAVs to his 1st Battalion.

The AAV is unique to the Marine Corps. This vehicle is the "grandson" of the World War II armored amphibious tractors that first carried Marines ashore at Tarawa. The amphibious vehicle has been continually improved to meet the special needs of the Marines. It is one of only a handful of vehicles in the U.S. inventory that is specifically designed to carry Marines ashore from their naval transport ships.

For years, the Navy and Marines have worked together to develop the world's finest amphibious capability. The Navy has spent billions of dollars to design and field ships that support the Marine Corps. LHDs, LHAs, LSDs, and LPDs all have what is known as a well deck. The well deck is a large cargo area at the stern of the transport ship that can store Marine vehicles like the AAV. These ships can carry Marines and their equipment anywhere in the world. Once on station, the well deck can be flooded, the entire aft end of the ship can be opened, and then AAVs and LAVs can swim out of the ship and carry Marines ashore. Once ashore, AAVs can support ground combat operations.

The engineers who have made the AAV what it is today have constantly struggled to produce a vehicle that is both armored and fast moving. Previous attempts to add armor made the tractors so slow that they were literally sitting ducks. Larger power plants and aluminum alloy hulls provided a compromise in capability. Today's AAV is nearly thirty tons when fully loaded (thus the nickname "Hog"). Its box-shaped silhouette looks like no other vehicle on the battlefield. It can carry twenty-one combat equipped Marines along with a three-man crew. Maximum speed on land is forty-five miles per hour and a little over eight miles per hour in the water. Its aluminum alloy hull can protect its occupants from small arms fire and shrapnel from air bursts, but little else.

RPGs and .50-caliber rounds will go right through the AAV's light armor. The designers never envisioned these vehicles in an urban combat role, hundreds of miles inland. In an effort to beef up the vehicle's armor, an External Appliqué Armor Kit (EAAK) was developed to provide additional protection to the Marines. Unfortunately, Blanchard's tracks did not have the appliqué armor.

With their M1 tanks, artillery, and AAVs, these twenty-first-century Marines prepared to travel into history and take their place alongside their WWII counterparts in a battle completely different from the amphibious landings of sixty years ago. The enemy was a different enemy, and the battlefield couldn't have been more different, but the young Marines were hauntingly the same. They were eager, naive, courageous, but also apprehensive.

THE entire brigade was aboard ship by January 15th. The Magnificent Seven sailed east over the horizon with 13,000 sailors and Marines and enough equipment to fight a small war. As the journey started, Commander Andy Pachuta picked up his ship's 1MC[18] microphone to deliver his traditional getting-underway message to the crew and his newly loaded passengers. "We are taking Marines to war . . . some of these men will not come back to see us."[19]

This would be no leisurely cruise. The Marines' days aboard ship would be filled with planning, training, and equipment maintenance. They would be up all day and most of the night. Aboard *Kearsarge,* the chow line ran nearly continuously from 0500 to midnight, feeding three thousand sailors and Marines each day.

Most of the trip was uneventful, but General Natonski worried about the four narrow passages that the task force would encounter in its journey. As the days at sea stretched into weeks, the Magnificent Seven would first pass through the Straits of Gibraltar into the Mediterranean Sea. The next narrow passage would be through the Suez Canal. After transiting the Red Sea, Task Force East would have to negotiate the Straits of Bab el Mandeb, near the port of Aden, Yemen. Finally, Natonski's sailors and Marines would enter the Persian Gulf through the Straits of Hormuz. These four choke points would be where Natonski and his men would be most vulnerable to terrorist attack.

Colonel Dunahoe's right-hand man, Major Christopher Starling was the executive officer of the 3d Battalion, 2d Marines. He was another steely Marine—handsome, smart, and dedicated to his job. Before coming to the 3d Battalion, Major Starling had served as an assistant professor of military science at the U.S. Military Academy, West Point, New York. He was the lone Marine representative at the national landmark that has produced Army officers since 1801. He likened his position to that of the Protestant chaplain at Notre Dame. In that role, he felt obligated to impress Marine Corps heritage and traditions upon the cadets at every opportunity.

---

18 All Navy ships have a ship's announcing system (IMC). Announcements made on the IMC can be heard throughout the ship.

19 Telephone interview with Lieutenant Colonel Rickey Grabowski, 1/5/05.

Just after the 9/11 attacks, the small Army military police garrison at West Point became overworked with increased security requirements. In an effort to relieve their fatigue, the Commandant of Cadets ordered that officers on the staff pitch in and take their turn at guard duty. One Friday afternoon in November, Major Starling received an order via e-mail to stand a twelve-hour guard shift beginning that Sunday evening. Surely, the intent of the order was not to have members of sister services guarding the entrance to one of the Army's most hallowed institutions. There had to be some mistake.

Confident that this order was erroneous, Starling inquired with his immediate superior, who granted no reprieve. The Director of the Department of Military Instruction had endorsed the order. The Marine Corps representative would be required to report "at 1700 hours, uniform: BDUs[20], black beret, and cold-weather gear."

Major Starling reported for duty in his Dress Blue Bravo uniform, equipped with ribbons, badges, Sam Browne belt, and his Mameluke sword. When confronted by the Army major who had published the order, he explained: "I don't have BDUs, I don't have a beret, and I knew you wouldn't be providing me with a side arm. Since Marines don't stand post unarmed, I have decided to bring my sword. In order to legally wear the sword, I need to be in dress blues. It's a service culture thing, I'm sure you guys can understand that."[21]

As their weekend passes expired that Sunday evening, cadets rolled through Thayer Gate in a long line of vehicles, welcomed back on post with a snappy salute and a dose of pomp and circumstance that is an institutional characteristic of American Marines.

Now, as his battalion sailed toward Iraq, Major Starling devised a plan to use his Marines to supplement the ship's defenses as they traveled through the four potentially dangerous passages in their journey. The Regiment's Avenger antiaircraft Humvees were lashed to the flight deck of *Bataan* and *Kearsarge*. Infantry machine gun and sniper teams, equipped with spotting scopes and night-vision devices, were distributed along the ships' rails for additional protection against small boats. It would be interesting to know if any of these modern-day Marines ever imagined that they would be protecting their naval warships like their first ancestors who

---

20 Battle dress uniform, Army terminology, camouflage utilities for Marines.

21 Personal Interview with Major Christopher Starling USMC.

swung through rigging of *Bon Homme Richard* in the 1700s, and repelled British borders with their pikes and swords.

JASON Doran was lying in what he called his "coffin rack," in the NCO berthing aboard *Ponce* when the door burst open and Staff Sergeant Jordan sauntered into the berthing area. Doran's bunk was his only private space on the ship. The berthing area had bunks stacked three high. Unlike the open racks from World War II, these beds provided some privacy. Doran's thin mattress sat in a stainless steel tray. On the side exposed to the passageway, a long curtain closed off his space, much like a berthing car on a train. On the opposite side of his mattress was a solid, Formica-covered wall, and less than three feet above his mattress was a metal tray that held the rack above.

When the curtain was closed, it felt like he was buried in a coffin. Attached to the underside of the rack above, was a small fluorescent reading light at the head of the rack. Doran was writing a letter to his girlfriend under the quiet buzz of the light when Jordan ripped open Doran's curtain.

Jordan, who never smiled, was grinning from ear to ear. He had just finished talking with his son on the telephone. "When you see the bad guys, make them stand in the corner a really long time."[22] His son had told him. Jordan spent a half hour telling Doran about his conversation and what a great son he had. Doran recalled later, "That was the first and last time I saw him really smile."

Until the time he came home one day, after the tragedy of 9/11, and announced to his family that he had joined the Marine Corps, Michael Williams had not found how to direct his energies in a positive way. Mike waited much longer than most to join the Corps. So, now he was a thirty-one-year-old corporal who was older than most of the young officers in the battalion. Mike was a people person who found his calling in the ranks of the Marine Corps.

During the long days at sea, Corporal Michael Williams would send frequent e-mail messages home to his family in Phoenix, Arizona. Most of the messages were sent to his girlfriend, Heather. On January 26th, Heather received a special message:

---

22 Telephone interview with Gunnery Sergeant Jason Doran, 9/22/04.

"I will formally ask you when I get back, but for now I have to use e-mail. Will you marry me babe? I love you and want to spend my life with you. We can plan the wedding when I get back. I miss you in a bad way."

Life seemed to be coming together for Williams. He had a career—work that he loved—and now he would soon have a chance to start a family with the girl of his dreams. What more could a man ask for?

Peeples' tankers had a rude awakening when they started inspecting their tanks. The vehicles were in horrible condition, laden with rust and long lists of maintenance issues. They would spend their entire month at sea working on the tanks in the well decks. They worked hard from dawn to dusk to prepare their newly acquired tanks for war. The company's maintenance checks produced a long list of badly needed repair parts.

Randy Whidden offered the ship's machinist mates tours of the tanks in exchange for the use of their onboard machine shop. Whidden was a regular "MacGyver." He worked hard to get Gunny Howard's tank working. If he needed a part, he went to the machine shop and made one. Word spread quickly about Whidden's resourcefulness and talent for fixing just about anything.

Several tanks had problems with their External Auxiliary Power Units (EAPUs). These were nothing more than a generator that the tankers could use to keep the systems in their tank powered when the engine was not running. Judicious use of the EAPUs could conserve many gallons of fuel. An idling M1 tank engine is a horrendous gas guzzler. The M1 parts were quickly ordered, but were not received until long after the Marines had charged into Iraq.

The Magnificent Seven steamed across the Atlantic for twelve days before reaching the Straits of Gibraltar. As January was nearing its end, they moved through the straits and into the ancient shipping lanes of the Mediterranean. They continued to sail east, moving farther from home and closer to an uncertain future.

Somewhere in the Mediterranean, General Natonski called Colonel Bailey and each of the battalion commanders over to *Kearsarge* for a briefing on Nasiriyah. Natonski wanted his officers to discuss a possible mission to seize the eastern bridges through the city. Colonel Ron Johnson, the brigade operations officer, conducted the briefing on the potential mission. Johnson presented a large aerial photograph of An Nasiriyah to the officers of the brigade. The photo should have been in the back of a Marine Corps gazette. The city's location and topography would provide a tough challenge to any military planner.

THE ancient city of An Nasiriyah is built in the Euphrates River delta within only a few miles of Ur, the birthplace of Abraham. It is located on slightly raised ground in the midst of a web of rivers, marshes, and canals. The Euphrates River runs from west to east, almost perfectly bisecting the city. A large man-made canal runs along the north side of the city. An Nasiriyah is also a crossroads on the edge of the Arabian Desert. Three major Iraqi highways and several other small thoroughfares intersect in and around the city. Highway 1, which connects Basrah in the east with Baghdad in Iraq's heartland, skirts An Nasiriyah to the south and west. Highway 8 runs along the south bank of the Euphrates. It connects Basrah with Karbala in the west and eventually, it heads to Baghdad. Highway 7 originates about thirty kilometers south of An Nasiriyah, runs through the center of the city and heads north to Baghdad, paralleling Highway 1 to the east. In Iraq, all roads lead to Baghdad.

Marine planners were still working at selecting routes for the 1st Marine Division to use on its attack toward Baghdad. Once north of the Euphrates River, they planned to attack up both Highway 1 and Highway 7. The first plan was to move the entire division up Highway 1 and, once north of the Euphrates River, some of the division would move east to Highway 7. Just in case there was a problem with Highway 1, I MEF told the Marines of 2-MEB to be prepared to seize a route through the middle of An Nasiriyah. Natonski's Marines picked the most expeditious route into the city on the east-side road.

Army planners had nicknamed the east-side road "Ambush Alley" because it went through a highly populated urban area, an area rife with opportunity for ambush. Noticing a haunting resemblance to another Third-World urban environment, Sergeant Joe Muccia called the road, "the Mogadishu Mile." Colonel Johnson said, "We are not going to call this Ambush Alley, because we are not going up this road. We are going to find a way around it."

Bailey agreed. He did not want to get his only mechanized battalion decisively engaged in a city fight. So the combined staffs searched for a plan. They contemplated fording the Euphrates River and the Saddam Canal east

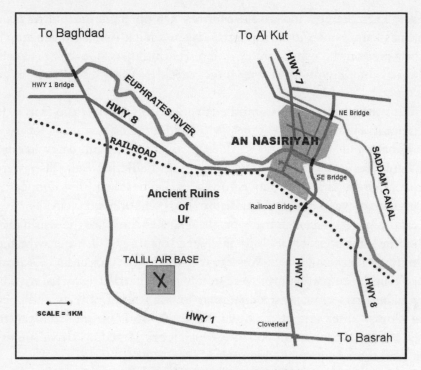

Nasiriyah—Gateway to Baghdad

of Nasiriyah, but no suitable approach could be found. Eventually, they planned to assault the southeast bridge. Once across the Euphrates, 1st Battalion would sidestep to the east of the city and attack north to the Saddam Canal bridge.

AFTER a six-day journey through the Mediterranean, Task Force East began preparations for their transit through the Suez Canal. Marine snipers and machine gun teams took up their positions along the rails while the ship's crews manned their battle stations. Task force ships moved into a single file and moved slowly through the narrow channel that had been dug through more than one hundred miles of desert. This was the first time that many of the Marines had seen land in two weeks.

The Marines could nearly reach out and touch Egypt as their giant ships negotiated the narrow canal. Mortar teams drilled at quickly setting up their tubes on the flight decks. At one point, a screaming Egyptian began making obscene hand gestures toward the Marines. On the flight deck of *Kearsarge*, a mortar team from 3/2's Weapons Company quickly focused the attention of their drill on the protesting Egyptian. Fearing the worst, the man ashore fled for his life. Egyptian security forces quickly chased him down and took him away.

The young Marines of Camp Lejeune were unique in many ways. They were twenty-first-century Marines. Most did not know what it was like to live without cell phones, DVDs, video games, and e-mail. They barely remembered Desert Storm, the Soviet Union, or the Berlin Wall. They weren't even born when Americans landed on the moon or when John Kennedy was shot. Vietnam was a war they studied in high school history classes.

As they passed through the Suez, the Marines could see the world changing before their eyes. Their ships navigated this thread of water, which carried them from the high-tech Western world into the ancient land of Arabia. These young men and women were slowly being carried away from a familiar land of prosperity and freedom to an exotic land of poverty and oppression. On the other side of the canal, the uniform of the day changed from green BDUs to desert camouflage, which only served to drive home the point that these Marines had journeyed into another world.

Task Force East moved uneventfully through the Red Sea. They continued to plan, train, and hone their fighting skills. On the way across, every Wednesday and Saturday, Captain Karl Rohr would hold fire support team (FiST) training for the Timberwolves in *Ponce*'s well deck. Reid, Pokorney, and Charlie Company's entire FiST attended every session. Rohr, the 1st Battalion's Weapons Company commander had made up a game board for training. Reid, Pokorney, and the others would practice calling in air strikes and artillery on enemy positions on the game board, and Rohr would mark the effects on their simulated targets. The well deck was a noisy warehouse—a metal box. Marines and sailors scurried about conducting maintenance on their vehicles while other small groups conducted training of their own. It was a perfect place to practice radio communication. The noise and confusion in the well deck helped prepare Reid's men for the chaos of battle.

In these close quarters, Reid and Pokorney became friends. They trained together, they ate together, they roomed together, and during the long hours of boredom, they talked. They talked about their jobs. They had endless discussions on how Iraq would be different than their training. They talked about how they would divide up the responsibilities on the FiST team. They developed a plan for the employment of their weapons. They always ended up talking about their families and home. Pokorney's conversation always turned to his daughter—Taylor.

Just as Rohr had done with his Weapons Company officers, Captain Santare conducted training of the battalion's tactical air control party (TACP) teams, continually covering close air support procedures with his officers and NCOs. Santare, a Marine pilot, had been with the Timberwolves since November 2002. He was in the middle of his six-month rotation and had been assigned as Bravo Company's forward air controller (FAC).

Staff Sergeant Troy Schielein met with his CAAT[23] Marines every day. During one of their meetings, he told them that they needed to learn from the lessons of Vietnam. "Study your history and learn from it." He went on to counsel his men, "Don't underestimate this enemy. If they have the heart, the desire, and the motivation that they do to hate Americans, we're in a dangerous situation."[24]

Captain Timothy "Rich" Dremann was Colonel Mortenson's Fox Company commander. Dremann was young and confident—a true professional. Dremann had been with the battalion for over nine months, but he had only been Fox's commander for a few months. He learned quickly that the company NCOs were some of the best the Corps had to offer. While at sea, he regularly took tours through the ship to speak with his Marines. He was repeatedly amazed at their dedication.

He would always find his NCOs conducting training of their younger Marines. They hung out in small groups wherever they could find room and trained on everything. They trained one day on weapons. The NCOs would show the younger Marines how to break down a weapon, then they would make them repeat the operation, and then they would repeat the task over and over until it was second nature.

They drilled on everything—land navigation, clearing buildings in an urban environment, MOPP[25] suit drills, casualty handling, and even crash courses in handy Arabic phrases. The Marines worked tirelessly every day, with a sense of urgency brought on by the realization that they would all soon be in combat.

---

23 Combined anti-armor team.

24 Telephone interview with Staff Sergeant Troy Schielein, 9/14/04.

25 Mission-oriented protective posture.

The Marines sailed for several more days before reaching their next dangerously narrow passage on February 7th. The Magnificent Seven exited the Red Sea and entered the Arabian Sea through the Straits of Bab el Mandeb (Gate of Tears), near the port of Aden, Yemen. Aden is where terrorists had attacked the USS *Cole* in October 2000, killing seventeen American sailors. Task Force East passed by this grim reminder of the enemy they would soon face. Ill-equipped yet fanatic and resourceful, this enemy was eager to die for their cause. Victory, in their eyes, would be a single Marine killed, even if dozens of their own would die in the process.

MARINE AIR GROUP-29

The Big Deck ships of Task Force East carried Marine Air Group-29, but they would soon be part of the MEF's 3d Marine Air Wing. MAG-29 was a one-stop-shopping, composite air group. Unlike its West Coast cousins, MAG-29 was made up of all of the Marine Corps' aircraft types. It had Harriers, Cobras, Hueys, Sea Knights, and Sea Stallions. The West Coast MAGs were more specialized, either containing lift or attack planes, but not both.

Colonel Robert Milstead Jr. was the group commander; and, as such, he was the Air Combat Element (ACE) commander for the 2d Marine Expeditionary Brigade. Milstead had spent nearly all of his life in Marine aviation. He was married, with four children. Milstead, an English Literature major in school, looked much younger than his age. He was articulate and intelligent, and he was the epitome of a twenty-first-century Marine Corps officer. He had both a sense of where he came from and a vision of where he was going.

Milstead was certainly a leader of men. He believed that command is a position of service. He served his men: they didn't serve him. He felt a deep responsibility for each and every one of the Marines in his command.

Lieutenant Colonel Darrell Thacker, a soft-spoken Cobra pilot, was Milstead's executive officer. As the XO[26] of the only composite air group,

---

26 Executive officer.

Thacker was assigned the job of air mission commander for the raid on Safwan Hill. The hill was centrally located along the Iraqi/Kuwaiti border. Even at this early date, the Marines had identified Safwan Hill as the first target of the invasion.

Colonel Thacker began to plan the attack immediately. Milstead told him that HMM-162 would provide the CH-46s for the mission and HML/A-269[27] would provide the "Skids."[28] As the days passed, Thacker's plan changed several times. "The plan evolved, it morphed, it changed."[29] Everyone finally agreed that an F/A18 strike on Safwan Hill would be the tripwire for G-Day, because it would be easy for everyone along the front to see the jets' large bombs exploding atop Safwan Hill.

The F/A-18 bombing would be followed by several Cobras. They would swoop in and rake the hill with rockets and cannon fire. Other Cobras would move to the northern frontier and take out a half dozen more guard towers along the border. Then Thacker's 46s would move in and drop two dozen recon Marines on the hill. By the time Task Force East reached the eastern end of the Arabian Sea; Thacker's plan was pretty much confirmed.

On February 8th, RCT-2's forward air controllers practiced close air support with the brigade's Harriers, Cobras, and Hueys launched from *Kearsarge, Saipan, Bataan,* and *Ponce,* running thirty air strikes in a live-fire range in Djibouti. 3/2 took this opportunity to provide training to some of the newly acquired Marines.

NAVY AMPHIBIOUS GROUP 2: THE MAGNIFICENT SEVEN

For the entire trip, Major Day trained his new Marines. They trained from the flight deck to the well deck, any place they could find a suitable space to set up a mortar. He trained his newly acquired Marines every chance he got. Day's NCOs ran their men through repeated gun drills, until the mortar

---

27 Marine light attack helicopter (squadron).

28 Skids—nickname for Cobra and Huey helicopters.

29 Personal interview with Lieutenant Colonel Darryl Thacker, 1/12/04.

crews could seemingly do their job in their sleep. Now that they had reached the Horn of Africa, Day took his mortar crews ashore for live fire training. He took a mixture of experienced Marines and all of his new Marines so that the seasoned mortar men could train the young men who had never fired a round. They fired more than 120 rounds as part of the combined arms exercise.

USS *Portland,* the oldest of the Magnificent Seven, had been limping along on a single boiler for several days. Another serious breakdown left *Portland* floating adrift with no propulsion. USS *Ponce* was ordered to remain with *Portland* while her sailors worked furiously to get propulsion back in one of the engines. As *Portland* sat dead in the water, the two ships became separated from the other five. The main body of the task force steamed ahead, leaving *Ponce* and *Portland* to finish the journey on their own.

The first five ships of the Magnificent Seven sailed past their final landmark, moving through the Straits of Hormuz and into the waters of the Persian Gulf on February 13th. Once in the Persian Gulf, the demeanor of the Marines changed. General Natonski's Marines were prepared to go directly from ship to combat. The "smoking and joking" was over. Most Marines became deadly serious. Some began wearing their gas masks while involved in everyday tasks. If the threat weren't so real, the scene of Marines wearing their gas masks while watching training films or running on the treadmill would have been comical. The ships' crew began looking upon their cousins with a sense of awe and respect, knowing that they would soon be facing the enemy in a fight to the death.

IRAQ

Saddam Hussein was a master when it came to dictatorship and staying in power. He never put too much power in the hands of any individual or organization. He compartmentalized both his military and his government. In Saddam's Iraq, spies and informants were behind every door and every curtain. He had military, police, and civilian organizations whose specific charter was to keep watch on other military units or the civilian government.

Possibly, the most powerful organization in Iraq was the Ba'ath Party. It was Iraq's only political party. All other opposing parties had been eliminated by Saddam Hussein, and dissent in Iraq was not allowed. Saddam's political opponents would either find themselves in prison or a grave. The Ba'aths ruled with an iron fist throughout the country and especially in Shiite cities like An Nasiriyah. Most of Nasiriyah's Ba'ath officials were Sunni Muslims who had been moved to Nasiriyah from Iraq's heartland. Some were local Nasiriyans who had gone over to the dark side. The Ba'ath Party leaders lived a luxurious life, while the local Shiite inhabitants scratched out a living as some of the poorest inhabitants of Iraq.

Saddam had also formed a national militia. The Al-Quds were locals who had been recruited to maintain order in the outlying provinces. They were ragtag and poorly equipped, but some were willing to fight and die for Saddam.

The primary source of Saddam's power was the regular Iraqi Army. Some were veterans of Desert Storm, and they were equipped with almost limitless stockpiles of weapons and ammunition. The Iraqi 11th Infantry Division was responsible for the territory in, and around, An Nasiriyah. CENTCOM hoped that the regular Army would pack up and go home as soon as Coalition ground forces rolled into Iraq.

The Saddam Fedayeen[30] were a group of young zealots. They were the worst of the worst. They were murderers, butchers, and thugs. These fanatics, Uday Hussein's personal gang of henchmen, had everything to lose with the fall of Saddam Hussein. They would surely fight to the death.

KUWAIT

Mortenson's eighty-man advance party was the first to arrive in Kuwait. They were flown directly from Camp Lejeune to meet the Black Bottom that had carried the battalion's equipment. As soon as they arrived, they were bused to the pier, where they collected the battalion's vehicles and drove them north, into the Kuwaiti Desert. Per the original plan, 2/8's convoy drove to RCT-7's assembly area. They arrived to find that 2/8 had been chopped to Task Force Tarawa and the 2d Marine Regiment.

The Marines of RCT-7 were gracious hosts. They fed Mortenson's men and gave them a place to rest for the night. In the morning, Mortenson's

---

30 *Saddam Fedayeen* translates to *Saddam's Martyrs*.

convoy set out for its new home, Camp Shoup. When they arrived at the designated coordinates, Camp Shoup was nothing more than a patch of sand in the Kuwaiti Desert. The advance party of America's Battalion quickly began to transform this spit of desert land into a home for the entire regiment. They started constructing a defensive berm around the perimeter, pitching tents, digging latrines, and setting up communications.

CHAPTER 3

Kuwait

I have just returned from visiting Marines at the front, and there is
not a finer fighting organization in the world.

—GENERAL DOUGLAS MACARTHUR, U.S. ARMY

ON February 15th, 2003, after more than thirty long days of confinement
aboard their transport ships, the Marines of the Second Marine Expeditionary Brigade arrived at Kuwait Naval Base. They were itching to vacate
their cramped quarters and get ashore. A month of Formica, stainless steel,
and no skid decks had made them eager to live in the desert sand. At least,
in the desert, they would have all the space, fresh air, and sunshine they
wanted.

Just offshore, the order, "Land the landing force," echoed through each
of the task force's ships. Five of the Magnificent Seven's gray behemoths
opened their well decks to the sea, and the Marine's AAVs and LAVs came
ashore. LCVs and LCACs began ferrying troops, equipment, and vehicles.
Sailors and Marines worked around the clock for five days moving everything ashore.

As soon as Natonski's brigade was ashore, Colonel Milstead's Marine
Air Group 29 was chopped to the 3d Marine Aircraft Wing, dramatically
reducing Natonski's war fighting capabilities. The MEF headquarters
wanted to combine all of its aircraft into a single wing. All air missions
could then be controlled from a single command, hopefully reducing command redundancy and streamlining Marine air operations.

For the next few days, helicopters and men were shuffled among ships so that each squadron was united on a single ship. HMM-162's Sea Knight squadron and HML/A-269's Cobras and Hueys congregated on USS *Saipan*. USS *Kearsarge* became the consolidated heavy-lift ship—home to sixteen CH-53 Super Sea Stallions. USS *Bataan* joined with USS *Bon Homme Richard* as Task Force 51's floating airbase for the Marine Harriers.

Now, with a regimental combat team, a combat service support battalion, and a few other small units in his command, the general officially designated his unit as Task Force Tarawa. Natonski wanted to provide some sense of identity to his East Coast Marines who were now part of a West Coast MEF, so he picked a name out of the Marine Corps' illustrious past that could only be associated with the 2d Marine Regiment. Every Marine at Camp Lejeune is familiar with the name—Tarawa. The Second Marine Regiment had fought an historic and bloody battle there in World War II. It was only fitting that General Natonski would associate the men of the 2d Marines who fought and died for that speck of land in the middle of the Pacific with Bailey's modern-day 2d Marine Regiment.

The Marines of Task Force Tarawa moved ninety-two miles from Kuwait Naval Base to Assembly Area (AA) Coyote. Coyote, sprinkled with Army and Marine camps, was a barren desert expanse that straddled the road leading north out of Kuwait. Task Force Tarawa moved into its camps at the southern extremity of Coyote, Ryan, and Shoup.

Camp Shoup was named after Colonel David M. Shoup, who had commanded the 2d Marine Regiment at the Battle of Tarawa. Now, Camp Shoup became the home of more than four thousand Marines of Colonel Bailey's Regimental Combat Team-2.

Camp Ryan, General Natonski's headquarters, was named after Major Michael P. Ryan, the Lima Company commander who had commanded scattered elements on Betio Island in the remote atoll of Tarawa. Major Ryan was awarded the Navy Cross "for extraordinary heroism" when he took command of the men on the beach after the 3/2 battalion commander failed to make it ashore. Most of Ryan's Marines were part of 3d Battalion, 2d Marines. To this day, the 3d Battalion, 2d Marines are known as the "Betio Bastards."

Camp Ryan, Task Force Tarawa's headquarters in Kuwait, was just a kilometer south of Camp Shoup; approximately thirty miles from the Iraqi Border. Soon one hundred general-purpose (GP) tents quickly rose in the dry, khaki-colored sand, and two ten-foot-tall earthen berms surrounded a 1000-by-800-meter compound. A section of the tents housed Marines. The Brigade's Command Operations Center (COC) was housed in a group of tents covered with cammo netting at the center of the camp. Other tents contained the headquarter group offices and finally, there was a mess tent. Showers and latrines were being erected, and most tents had electricity, supplied by constantly humming portable generators. Camp Ryan quickly became the MEB headquarters and home to another eighteen hundred Marines.

TASK Force Tarawa's Marines began pouring ashore. Infantrymen who arrived on the Big Decks were shuttled directly from sea to camps Ryan and Shoup in Marine helicopters. Captain Kevin Yeo's Echo Company Marines were some of the first to fly from *Kearsarge* to Camp Shoup. Yeo was a calm and deliberate company commander. He was slow talking and not easily excited.

Echo Company had traveled across with Dunahoe's Marines on *Kearsarge*, while the rest of America's Battalion was on *Saipan*. Colonel Dunahoe's Betio Bastards were not far behind Echo Company, as waves of helicopters landed in the Kuwaiti Desert.

Infantrymen who arrived on *Gunston Hall* and *Ashland* were moved ashore, then picked up and flown to Shoup. Some Marines stayed behind with the regiment's vehicles. The smaller vehicles were driven in convoy into the barren Kuwaiti desert while Peeples' tanks and Blanchard's AMTRACs[1] waited on the dock for flatbed Heavy-Equipment Transporters (HETs) to haul them north to Camp Shoup.

Convoy after convoy began traveling cross country for more than eighty miles from their landing at the Kuwait Naval Base to their remote camps in northern Kuwait. Captain John Day left the Kuwaiti Naval Base with the first convoy. He led 3/2's Weapons Company CAAT Humvees through the desert to Camp Shoup. When Day and his CAAT vehicles arrived at Shoup, it was just a piece of dirt with a ten-foot berm around its perimeter. They were still hammering in the tents, which had no floors or

---

1 Amphibious tractor.

cots. Second Marine Regiment Marines would spend the next month sleeping in the Kuwaiti sand.

Like his boss, Colonel Dunahoe, Captain John Day was a no-nonsense Marine. Day was spit-and-polish and gung ho. He was enterprising and confident, with a balanced mixture of intelligence, aggressiveness, and common sense.

Two days behind the main flotilla, *Portland* limped into the Kuwaiti Naval Base with *Ponce* and *Regulus*. After thirty-seven days at sea, Sergeant Schaefer and the other AAV crewmen of Alpha Company, 2d AAV Battalion brought their remaining vehicles ashore from the flooded well decks of their ships. Once ashore, 1st Battalion's armored amphibious vehicles were loaded onto flatbed trucks and transported to Camp Shoup.

The last of Major Peeples' tanks drove on to giant LCACs squeezed into the well decks of their ships. The modern-day Navy landing craft ferried the 68-ton Abrams tanks ashore one at a time. They were loaded onto more Army transporters to be driven to Camp Shoup. The convoy moved through Kuwait at a snail's pace, never exceeding twenty-five miles per hour. The eighty-mile trip took fourteen hours.

Meanwhile, USNS *Regulus* began to unload Lieutenant Colonel Eddie Ray's 2d LAR vehicles. For the next two days, the "Barbarians" convoyed their armored vehicles to Camp Commando, the MEF headquarters.[2]

Marine Lieutenant Colonel Eddie Ray (Barbarian 6) was a decorated veteran of Operation Desert Storm. On the second day of the ground war in 1991, Ray repelled an enemy attack on the 1st Marine Division's forward command post in Kuwait. He not only protected the command post but his fearless counterattack completely destroyed a mechanized Iraqi brigade. Captain Ray received the Navy Cross for his courage under fire that day. Ray was one of a handful of Marine officers who would bring combat experience to the invasion of Iraq.

Second Force Recon also moved into Camp Commando. Commando was located just north of Jahra. The camp was nearly at the same location as the infamous "Highway of Death," where coalition aircraft pounded fleeing Iraqis in the closing days of Operation Desert Storm.

---

2 Colonel Eddie Ray's call sign war Barbarian 6, giving the nickname "Barbarians" to his entire unit.

REGIMENTAL COMBAT TEAM-2

Within days, tent after tent sprouted from the desert floor at Camp Shoup. The tents were pitched with Marine Corps precision in row upon row, within a perimeter defensive berm. Soon a canvas and plywood city burgeoned in the Kuwaiti desert. There were no trees, no shrubs, not even a weed in sight. An occasional sand-colored tent pitched among a sea of army-green hooches provided the only variety. This city of canvas, plywood, and sandbags would be RCT-2's home away from home for more than a month.

Marines set up homemade street signs and mileage markers to help them find their way through the sea of canvas. These signs had almost become a tradition in the American military. Makeshift stanchions were adorned with almost more signs than they could hold—ALLENTOWN, PA—11,450 KM; DENVER—14,100 KM; TOKYO—8,499 KM; NORTH HOLLYWOOD, CA—9,767 MILES; and topped with BAGHDAD—400 MILES.

Camp Shoup was twice the size of Camp Ryan, but it was undoubtedly the least improved camp in all of northern Kuwait. The East Coast Marines had to scrounge for everything. At first, the camp only had twelve porta-potties spread among four reinforced battalions.

Marines are known throughout the world for their resourcefulness. The Marines' position within the U.S. military family has always been that of the little brother who gets all the hand-me-downs. Only six cents of every DOD[3] dollar is spent on the Corps. This stems from the fact that the Marine Corps is under the umbrella of the Navy Department. The Army fights for its budget for ground warfare equipment; the Air Force lobbies for cutting-edge airplanes, and the Navy spends most of its energy lobbying for ships.

So the Marines have all grown up in a culture where they never really have all they need. This has fostered a talent for making the most of what they do have and a knack for finding what they need, when they need it. The Marines of Task Force Tarawa excelled in creative acquisition of supplies.

---

3 Department of Defense.

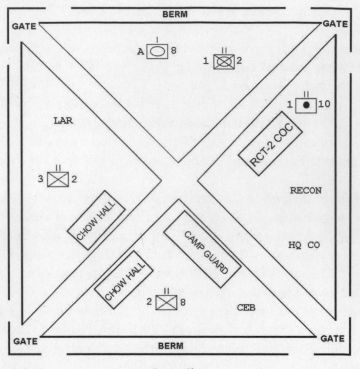

Camp Shoup

Spare parts were nonexistent at camps Shoup and Ryan. Almost daily, groups of Tarawa Marines would visit nearby camps to scrounge, cajole, beg, borrow, and steal needed supplies. Warrant Officer Mark A. Toenniges, the AAV maintenance officer, made daily field trips across the desert to other camps to scrounge repair parts from his 1st Marine Division counterparts. Major Peeples' maintenance chief, XO, and tank leader visited the 1st and 2d Tank Battalions. Ninety percent of their needed parts were acquired on these trips. Sometimes they would visit Army camps, and while two of the Marines visited with the supply clerk, others would scramble to the rear of the compound and load up everything that wasn't nailed down.

Other Marines found plywood and empty supply boxes. The Betio Bastards made a complete MOUT[4] training facility out of discarded materials.

---

4 Military operations in urban terrain.

Everything imaginable was used for tables and chairs. Some lucky Marines managed to abscond with a few sheets of plywood, which they used as flooring for their tents. There was never enough to cover the entire floor, so they were strategically laid down in the Kuwaiti sand like kitchen throw rugs.

1ST BATTALION, 2D MARINES: THE TIMBERWOLVES

As they arrived, the Marines of the 1st Battalion tried to make the camp as livable as possible, but it was hard to get comfortable with so few resources. Staff Sergeant Jason Cantu, a gravel-voiced Texan and close friend of Troy Schielein, had been pretty much everywhere in the Corps, but he had never been to Kuwait. When he first saw Camp Shoup, he exclaimed in typical Marine Corps fashion, "This place sucks."[5] Cantu was Alpha Company's 3d Platoon sergeant; so he shared a tent with the company's NCOs. With no floors and no cots in his tent, he ended up sleeping in the sand.

Over at Charlie Company, the junior officers and the NCOs also shared a tent. Lieutenants Reid, Pokorney, Seely, Lapinsky, Swantner, and Tracy all lived together in the same GP tent with sergeants Crosby, Jordan, Pompos, and Parker.

Seely and Jordan were both veterans of the first Gulf War. Seely had been a recon Marine during Desert Storm. He had received a Purple Heart for being injured in a mistaken attack by an Air Force A-10. Jordan had also learned firsthand about the dangers of having A-10s overhead. He warned the other sergeants not to trust the A-10s. Parker was a laid-back, ex-Recon Marine, who would give one the shirt off his back.

Swantner, like Reid, was a Naval Academy graduate. He was a mountain of a man. At 6' 4" and nearly three hundred pounds, he had played offensive tackle for his alma mater. In contrast, Lapinsky was small, quiet, and reserved.

In Camp Shoup, Pokorney and Reid spent many more hours talking of work. They talked about how they could best split the workload to supply timely supporting fires to the company. They worked out how to keep each other and Captain Wittnam informed, and they spent hour after hour talking

---

5 Telephone interview with Staff Sergeant Jason Cantu, 10/1/04.

of home and family. Their conversation always seemed to lead to Chelle and Taylor, Fred's wife and daughter. During those long days in the desert, Fred and Ben became even closer.

While at Camp Shoup, Fred Pokorney wrote home as often as he could. He would send letters to both Chelle and his daughter. One night, he sat quietly and wrote one of his last letters before leaving Kuwait. The letter was to his daughter.

Dear Taylor,
Are you taking care of Mommy? How is she doing? I know you are doing your best to help her with everything. Please give her a big hug and kiss for me and tell her I love her, okay? I love you very much and miss you so much, my heart hurts . . . I hope I get home to you and Mommy soon.

Love,
Daddy[6]

TASK FORCE TARAWA

CENTCOM was planning for the U.S. Army's 3d Infantry Division (ID) to make a mad dash toward Baghdad. The soldiers of the 3d ID were to sprint northwest from Kuwait, remaining south of the Euphrates River. They were to get as close to Baghdad as possible before moving out of the open desert. Their path of advance took them around Iraqi population areas in the hopes of avoiding detection and/or major combat until they were within striking distance of the Iraqi capital.

While the 3d ID charged through the open desert, the 1st Marine Division would attack straight up highways 1 and 7. Their mission would be to divert attention away from the Army. The Combined Forces Land Component Command (CFLCC) hoped that the Iraqis would shift the majority of their resources toward the Marines, as they moved deliberately toward Baghdad. As far as CFLCC was concerned, the 1st Marine Division was the pretty girl of the magic act. While the Iraqi military command watched the Marines advance, General Tommy Franks would take the opportunity to move the 3rd ID into attack position.

---

6 Brian Cabell, "Family honors Marine's sacrifice" (CNN, May 26, 2003).

Regardless of the intent of the high-level planners, the Marine commanders believed that a quick thrust into Iraq's heartland could be decisive as well as the safest course of action for the Marines on the ground. "Speed, speed, speed," was the phrase of the day at MEF headquarters. A rapid advance would keep the enemy off balance and unable to react. The Marine commanders also considered their effort to be a competition with the Army. All of their planning centered on a quick thrust into Saddam's heartland. The Marine offensive was characterized by a senior officer as:

> *Hey, diddle diddle*
> *Right up the middle*
> *Last one to Baghdad eats shit!*

The attack toward Baghdad was to be entirely a 1st Marine Division effort. General Natonski and the 2d Marine Expeditionary Brigade would provide the East Coast contingent of Marines from Camp Lejeune. While the California Marines planned for the fastest, longest Marine attack in history, I MEF commanders stripped the brigade of its 2d LAR Battalion, its 2d Tank Battalion, most of the 2d AAV Battalion, almost half of its reconnaissance resources in 2d Force Reconnaissance Company, and all of its MAG-29 aircraft, and then relegated the remaining Task Force Tarawa to mop-up work. Their orders were:

> *On order, Task Force Tarawa secures MEF OBJ C (JALIBAH) in order to facilitate establishment of LSA VIPER. On order, conduct relief in place with 3ID at western crossing site vicinity Hwy 1 and Euphrates River. Be prepared to secure crossing sites on the eastern side of An Nasiriyah and continue attack north to seize MEF OBJ E (QALAT SIKAR) in order to facilitate the main effort's rapid attack toward Baghdad.[7]*

Task Force Tarawa was to move across the southeastern Iraqi Desert, while the 1st Marine Division conducted the important operations of securing the oil fields. Like a pulling guard clearing the way for the team's star

---

7 Richard Natonski, "Task Force Tarawa Battle of An Nasiriyah PowerPoint Presentation" (USMC 10/27/03).

running back, Regimental Combat Team-2 had orders to secure Jalibah Airfield, which was virtually out in the middle of nowhere.

Task Force Tarawa was to fight its way up Highway 1 through massive 3d ID traffic jams and guard a bridge that had already been secured by the Army. The original orders were clear. This was Tarawa's mission. Once these two objectives had been secured, RCT-5, RCT-7, and RCT-1 would pass RCT-2 and move forward to attack toward Baghdad.

Over a half century ago, Colonel Shoup's Marines had been ordered to take the atoll of Tarawa to, ". . . improve the security of the lines of communication" in the Pacific Theater. Amphibious tractors carried the 2nd Marine Regiment across coral reefs to assault the enemy on Betio Island. Now, AMTRACs would carry the Timberwolves of Task Force Tarawa across a sea of sand to meet the enemy at a fertile island in the barren Iraqi desert.

While all of Colonel Milstead's MAG-29 had been chopped to the 3d Marine Air Wing, the East Coast pilots and their commanders paid close attention to the needs of their comrades in RCT-2 and made every effort to be around when they needed assistance. After all, they were still part of the Carolina MAGTF, and Task Force Tarawa's grunts on the ground were their friends and neighbors.

By the end of February, all of Task Force Tarawa had closed on Camp Shoup. While spartan, every day brought more comfort to the camp. Showers and latrines were constructed, field kitchens were set up to provide warm meals, and mail began to arrive. All the Marines knew that Camp Shoup was only a temporary way station on their road to war, and they knew that the road home would be through Iraq.

NBC NEWS

As the invasion of Iraq grew near, Marine Public Affairs Officers sent e-mail invitations to three teams of reporters. The reporters were invited to camps Ryan and Shoup to interview different units within Task Force Tarawa. One of the three crews was from NBC's *Today Show*. Purely by chance, Kerry Sanders was assigned to the Marines of 2d Battalion, 8th Marines. He and his crew were invited to spend four days and five nights with the Marines of America's Battalion.

Kerry, one of NBC's veteran reporters, was not part of the embedded-reporter program. He had not attended the military's special training sessions in the United States before his departure to the Middle East. He had not been selected to travel with any specific unit. But Kerry Sanders was a seasoned reporter of world news and one of the few NBC reporters who had taken the time to familiarize himself with the new technological tools of his trade.

Kerry was a valuable asset that NBC could not afford to leave out of the war, which was why he was at Camp Shoup with his cell phone and laptop computer. Kerry and his crew could have introduced themselves to Colonel Mortenson, interviewed a few Marines, taken a quick tour of the camp, and been back in Kuwait City before they turned down the sheets in the Sheraton Hotel. Instead, Kerry thought that he would get a better feel for his story if he stayed for all five nights with the Marines of America's Battalion. Besides, adventures like this were part of the excitement of being a reporter.

Spending five nights in barren Camp Shoup certainly gave the NBC crew a better appreciation of the hardships these Marines were enduring out in the Kuwaiti Desert, but it also had another effect. The Marines took notice that these "news" people were willing to sacrifice, too. They didn't take a few minutes of film, talk to the CO, and leave to go back to a hot meal and a warm bed. These guys were okay. Kerry found that the khaki-clad Marines were not just trained killers; they were a sampling of America. They were courteous, smart, and compassionate. And, they were very young.

Royal Mortenson and Kerry Sanders got to know each other in those four days. Kerry felt that he had connected with this battalion commander more than anyone else he had interviewed in Kuwait. Kerry had not only gotten his story, he had made a friend.

REGIMENTAL COMBAT TEAM-2

In early March, planning focused on Task Force Tarawa's primary mission—defense in sector, south of An Nasiriyah, to protect Highway 1. Planning also continued for the possibility that Task Force Tarawa would be ordered to seize the two eastern bridges across the Euphrates River, in An Nasiriyah.

Brent Dunahoe's battalion would move to secure the regiment's primary objective. The Betio Bastards planned to race up Highway 1 to the Euphrates River, set in defensive positions, and protect the Highway 1 bridge and the intersection of highways 1 and 8, just south of the river. Bailey's 3d Battalion would be far beyond the protective umbrella of the regiment's artillery, so Bailey decided to send his company of LAVs with Dunahoe. Dunahoe's Marines would need the extra firepower if the Iraqis attacked.

As the 3d Battalion moved up Highway 1, the mechanized 1st Battalion would move up Highway 7 toward the outskirts of An Nasiriyah. They, too, would set into defensive positions to further protect Highway 1. Colonel Mortenson's motorized 2d Battalion, 8th Marines, and Colonel Starnes' artillery battalion would move up behind the Timberwolves and be prepared to support Grabowski in the defense of Highway 7 or in his advance into the city.

Grabowski and his officers developed a plan to take the eastern bridges in case the order came down to move into An Nasiriyah. If the Timberwolves were ordered to secure the bridges, Bravo Company would first move to establish a support-by-fire position on the southern bank of the Euphrates River. Next, Alpha Company would move quickly to secure the first bridge.

Once in the city, the Timberwolves planned for two possible courses of action. If, as expected, the resistance was light, Bravo Company would head straight up Ambush Alley for the northern bridge. If, however, Grabowski ran into armed resistance, Bravo and Charlie companies would race across the Euphrates River and immediately turn east to skirt the built-up sections of the city, thus avoiding Ambush Alley.

By moving out to the east, the Timberwolves would avoid the potential perils of Ambush Alley. Tim Newland would move Bravo Company to a second support-by-fire position on the southern bank of the Saddam Canal, and then Dan Wittnam would rush across the canal bridge with Charlie Company.

Rick Grabowski believed the eastern movement to be the best course of action for securing the bridges through An Nasiriyah. The plan enabled his companies to provide mutual support in a coordinated advance to secure the bridges, and it exposed his men to the smallest possibility of harassing fire. After all, everyone's expectation was that any Iraqis in the city would fire a few shots and then surrender. *Capitulation* was the word of the day at CENTCOM and CFLCC headquarters.

Royal Mortenson planned for one of his motorized companies to drive into Ambush Alley behind the 1st Battalion. The conventional thinking was that once Grabowski had taken the bridges, the enemy would either fade away into the city or surrender; minimum resistance was expected. Mortenson's men should be able to move into the city uncontested. They would immediately start to secure the new Main Supply Route (MSR) and to establish order.

So, 2/8 and 3/2 trained in their brand-new seven-ton Osh-Kosh trucks. Both battalions would be going into battle for the first time in these large vehicles. They had trained to deploy in helicopters, they had trained to deploy in AMTRACs, but they had never trained to advance on the enemy in trucks. Colonel Dunahoe and Colonel Mortenson worked their staffs hard to define configurations that would best protect their Marines.

They organized their companies much like they would if they were to be traveling in AMTRACS. Each squad had its own truck, and there were three trucks to a platoon. They sandbagged the beds, and then loaded a layer of supplies on top of the sandbags. The trucks were loaded with cases of water and MREs. Then more sandbags were used to build up a protective wall on each side of the truck's bed.

The Marines spent several days filling and carefully placing the sandbags in their trucks. Captain Dremann was right there among his lance corporals filling sandbags. Another group carried the filled bags to each truck, while others meticulously stacked the sandbags in the beds. They mounted either a .50-caliber machine gun or a MK19 automatic grenade launcher in the cab. By the time they were finished, there was barely room for the Marines inside these mobile fighting positions.

1ST BATTALION, 2D MARINES:
THE TIMBERWOLVES

Staff Sergeant Alan Kamper commanded Major Peeples' 3d Platoon. The reserve tank company had left Fort Knox short of officers, so Kamper had kept his job as platoon leader. When Kamper arrived in Camp Shoup, he decided that he would sleep with his tank, instead of in the platoon tent. Kamper picked a spot atop his tank's turret and slept under the stars almost every night. Kamper's gunner slept on the tank, too. After a few nights, Kamper actually found it comfortable.

During one of their forays for spare parts, Staff Sergeant Jeffrey Filip-kowski and Kamper traveled to Camp Commando. The two sergeants found that they could get pizza there, so they brought enough pizza and sodas back to Camp Shoup for the entire platoon. That night, the 3d Platoon had a party. They ate cold pizza, joked and laughed through a large rainstorm, and then all fell asleep inside the tent.

That same week, Lance Corporal Mike Williams was standing guard duty in the battalion area in Camp Shoup in the middle of the night. Colo-nel Grabowski had been extremely concerned about terrorist infiltrators, so he had ordered that the battalion use a challenge/password check of every-one who approached a guard post. Williams diligently followed his orders and issued his challenge to everyone who walked by. Most would reply with some wisecrack like, "What are you going to do, shoot me?" and continue past his post without responding to the challenge.

Toward the end of Williams's watch, Lieutenant Colonel Grabowski awoke. He needed to make a head call. Grabowski rose and pulled on a min-imum of clothes and walked the short distance to the head located near his tent. As he was returning, he ran into Williams. Williams issued the ordered challenge, and Grabowski stopped dead in his tracks. His mind went blank. He could not remember the password for the day.

After a few nervous seconds, Grabowski said, "You got me son. I can't remember the password."

"Advance and be recognized!" The Marine sentry commanded.

Grabowski slowly walked forward until he moved into Williams's nar-row flashlight beam.

"I know who you are, sir. You may pass."

As Grabowski started toward his tent, the Marine interrupted, "Excuse me, sir. Could you do me a favor, sir?"

Feeling obligated to Williams for not shooting him on the spot, Grabowski agreed. "Sure, son, what can I do for you?"

"I have been standing this watch most of the night, and almost everyone is ignoring my challenge," Williams complained

"Who ignored your challenge?" Grabowski inquired.

"I don't want to name names, sir, but it's been enlisted guys and officers, too. Do you think you could do something?"

Grabowski assured the young Marine that things would be different the next night, and he went back to bed. First thing in the morning, he called his officers and NCOs together and made it quite clear that he would check, and if he found anyone ignoring sentry challenges, they would be standing sentry duty, no matter who they were.

REGIMENTAL COMBAT TEAM-2

Fortunately, the oppressive desert heat of summer had not yet set in, the days were still pleasant and the nights cold, but there were sandstorms three times a week. The temperate weather could not keep moods in Camp Shoup from getting tense. There was a sense of dread and uncertainty among the Marines. Nerves were getting raw—tempers short. War was on the horizon.

A shock trauma platoon is a mobile ER. They have the personnel and equipment to treat life-threatening injuries and to keep casualties alive long enough to get them to a surgical unit. Members of the shock trauma platoon assigned to RCT-2 gave a briefing at Camp Shoup on the 5th of March. They told the Marines about their capabilities and their charter—"No one dies alone. No one dies in pain." They assured the Marines that even the dying would get morphine.

MARINE AIR GROUP-29

On a clear day, Safwan Hill commanded a view for miles in all directions. In southern Iraq, along the border with Kuwait, it was the only high point on an otherwise flat terrain. Atop the hill, the Iraqis had built a radio relay station and observation post. They had sprinkled smaller observation towers in both directions along the border. Safwan had to be the first site taken out in the ground attack.

The Marines planned for the attack on Safwan Hill to be the centerpiece of the attack into Iraq. As the air mission commander, Lieutenant Colonel Darryl Thacker was responsible for the raid. The lead attack would come from fixed wing aircraft—F/A-18s. They would sweep in and bomb the hill. Exploding bombs would signal hovering Cobra helicopters to attack all along the border. Four HML/A-269 Cobras would sweep in and rake the hill with rockets and 20mm cannon fire.

After the devastating air attacks on the facilities on Safwan Hill, two Sea Knight helicopters would sweep in and drop two dozen recon Marines. They would move quickly to secure the hill. The commanders hoped that the operation would be swift and successful. Any Iraqi relegated to border post duty was at the bottom of the food chain and would certainly fold quickly. Once attacked, they would either flee or surrender.

TASK FORCE TARAWA

All the Marines of Task Force Tarawa knew that "G" Day was rapidly approaching when they were served the traditional "warrior's" dinner, on March 9th. Compared to what they usually ate, they were served a feast; steak, potatoes, peas, cake, and Coke.

On March 10th, a Rehearsal-of-Concept (ROC) drill and briefing was conducted at Camp Shoup to coordinate the handover of key terrain at An Nasiriyah from 3d Infantry Division to Task Force Tarawa. The Army's 3d Brigade Combat Team (BCT) commanding officer, Colonel Dan Allen, announced during the briefing that he was planning to move a company/team to the Highway 1 Euphrates River bridge and another company/team was going to move up Highway 7 to the edge of Nasiriyah and defend in sector. On the 23d, Task Force Tarawa Marines would move in behind the 3d Infantry and relieve them in place at the western bridge and on the southern edge of town along Highway 7.

In anticipation of the invasion into Iraq, twenty-one media representatives from all over the world arrived at Camp Ryan on March 11th. General Natonski welcomed the large group of reporters. These were the men and women who had been selected to be embedded reporters in Natonski's 2d Marine Expeditionary Brigade, and there was a wide range of representation. Mark Franchetti and Art Harris represented CNN. Ken Kalthoff was an announcer for NBC's Dallas local affiliate. Joe Raedle was a photographer from Getty Images, and Mike Wilson was a young writer from the *New York Times*.

After Natonski's greeting, they were all sent throughout the brigade to their assigned units. Ken Kalthoff and his crew ended up with the brigade's artillery. Art Harris went to the Betio Bastards, and Joe Raedle was assigned to Charlie Company of the Timberwolves.

REGIMENTAL COMBAT TEAM-2

The newsmen assigned to the combat units within RCT-2 were taken to Bailey's COC. Inside the command center, the regimental staff had built a sand table of all of southern Iraq—Kuwait to Baghdad. There were little cards and flags scattered all over the map. On the other side of the room was an easel with a map that contained the entire battle plan. The reporters were welcomed, cautioned about security issues, and then given a briefing about what was about to unfold. One of the photographers in the news pool pointed his camera in the direction of the map and snapped a picture of the briefing room.

Later the reporter broke out his laptop computer and showed tiny thumbnail images of his work to public affairs Marines. Unaware that he had shots that were several mega-pixels each and that once blown up, all the detail on the map would be legible, they approved the release of his work. The next day, the photo of the entire attack plan appeared on the front page of the *New York Times* and other newspapers around the world.

Political wrangling in the UN and Turkey's hesitation in joining the Coalition continued to add to the uncertainty for the future. The Marines were ready to move into Iraq; they had been ready for quite some time. Now all that was left was to hurry up and wait. Another week had passed with no firm news on what would happen, so Colonel Bailey ordered his commanders to schedule another week of training.

1ST BATTALION, 2D MARINES: THE TIMBERWOLVES

Sitting in Camp Shoup and waiting for word of a decision to invade would have been the worst thing that the Timberwolves could have done. Colonel Grabowski's Marines moved back out into the Kuwaiti desert to continue their practice for the invasion of Iraq. They practiced radio communications, convoy movement, and MOPP drills. Grabowski kept working his men.

On March 16th, Grabowski brought his staff together to conduct a Tactical Exercise Without Troops (TEWT). This would be the Timberwolves' last opportunity to practice command and control of the battalion. Grabowski had an excellent set of officers to help him run the battalion. Major Jeff Tuggle, 1/2's executive officer, was another Marine who looked much younger than his years. Grabowski's operations officer, Major David Sosa, originally from Brooklyn, was a man who was always frank with his men and was always in control. He never sugar-coated any news just to make his Marines or his boss feel better. As the S3[8], Sosa was Grabowski's right-hand man.

Gunner David Dunfee had been in the Marine Corps for nearly twenty-five years. Dunfee grew up in Florida, and as soon as he finished high school, he entered the Marines. He was married, with an eighteen-year-old son in college. As the battalion gunner, Dunfee reported directly to Colonel Grabowski as a special staff and operations officer. His primary job was to advise Grabowski on weapons employment and to convey his commander's intent to the Marines within the 1st Battalion.

Sergeant Major Charles Arrick was the senior enlisted Marine in the battalion and had already spent twenty-five years in the Marine Corps. As the senior NCO, Arrick was responsible for every Marine in the battalion. Major Sosa rode in his own vehicle, but Arrick and Dunfee would ride in Grabowski's Humvee and remain at his side wherever he went on the battlefield.

In addition to his close advisors, Grabowski was fortunate to have three extremely competent infantry commanders and staff NCOs. Captain Michael Brooks, Alpha Company's commander, was a sandy-haired young Marine captain. He was confident, intelligent, and a family man. Bravo's commander, Captain Tim Newland was a tall blond-haired Marine from the Midwest. Newland who was quite muscular, was a model Marine company commander—a deliberate man, always in control of his words and actions. His first priority was to bring all of his Marines home alive. Finally, Charlie Company was led by Captain Dan Wittnam, who was idolized by his men. He led through example. His Marines knew they were in good hands with Captain Wittnam as their leader.

James Thompson Jr. grew up in Birmingham, Alabama. His father passed away while he was in high school, and he lost his mother soon after he graduated. With no family left to keep him in Alabama, young Jim Thompson decided that anybody could be in the Army. Jim wanted to be

---

8 The S3 is the battalion's operations officer.

someone special, so he joined the Marine Corps. Now, twenty-one years later, 1st Sergeant James Thompson Jr. was married, with three children, and he was Alpha Company's senior enlisted Marine. He was also Captain Brooks' right-hand man, responsible for all of Alpha Company's young Marines.

The Timberwolves' staff moved out into the desert to test their organization and plans one last time. Grabowski had molded his infantry battalion into a reinforced, mechanized fighting force. This would be his last chance to pull the different resources together into a coherent unit.

Colonel Grabowski had two specially outfitted tracks (AAV-C7s). The command variants carried the communication gear needed to command a battalion. Grabowski took two more standard tracks (AAV-P7)[9], which he paired with each of his command tracks. Each command pair had the same resources. The first pair was dubbed Alpha Command and would travel with Grabowski. The second pair of tracks would be Bravo Command and would stay with the battalion executive officer, Major Jeffery Tuggle, at the rear of the battalion formation.

Captain William Blanchard's AAV company would provide the lift for Grabowski's infantry, and Major Peeples' fourteen main battle tanks would provide the armored support. Having the only mechanized battalion in Task Force Tarawa, Colonel Grabowski shuffled his resources to configure the Timberwolves into a lethal fighting force.

Grabowski spread his remaining thirty-six AAVs among his three infantry companies. Each company would have twelve tracks to carry its Marines, and each track was designed to carry seventeen Marines and three crewmen. Coupled with its infantry, an assault amphibian vehicle became a lethal weapons system capable of fighting as an autonomous unit on almost every type of battlefield. Putting three manned AAVs together into an infantry platoon exponentially increased their capabilities, and combining three mechanized infantry platoons produced a nearly unstoppable battlefield machine.

Each of Grabowski's infantry companies needed nine tracks to carry their infantry, leaving three additional tracks. The tenth track carried the

9 The AAV-C7 is the command variant of the vehicle, crammed with the communications gear to command a battalion. The AAV-P7 is the personnel variant, outfitted to carry a Marine rifle squad.

company 1st sergeant and a medical team serving as the company's armored ambulance. Another track carried part of the mortar platoon and the company fire support team with FAC and FOs and the FiST team leader. The twelfth track was the company commander's track, the heart of the mechanized company, carrying the company command element, with all its radios and the other half of the company's 60mm mortar section.

The company commander would ride in the troop commander's hatch of the company command track. The AAV platoon commander would ride in the vehicle commander's position in the tractor's turret. The mortar track would carry the rest of the company command element. The weapons platoon leader would be the mortar track's troop commander (TC), and all of the supporting arms controllers and observers would ride in the back, each with their own radio operators.

In the infantry tracks, the lead track's TC would be the platoon leader, and sitting in the vehicle commander's position would be the AAV section leader. Another of the platoon's tracks would carry the platoon sergeant in its TC position. As the mechanized infantry company moved across the battlefield, the company commander, weapons platoon leader, three infantry platoon leaders, and three platoon sergeants all had a position perched on their mighty steeds. They could each fight separately or in threes, as a platoon, or all together as a company.

The AAV itself was mobile and deadly. The AMTRAC's turret, known as the "up gun," provided each vehicle with its protection. The electric turret housed a .50 caliber machine gun and a MK19, 40mm automatic grenade launcher. The gunner could lay down a massive amount of fire with his .50-caliber machine gun and could hurl grenades in nearly any direction with impressive accuracy. The entire back wall, or ramp, of the AAV could be lowered for quick deployment of the infantry. The Marine infantry squad could take and hold ground, clear buildings, and maneuver separately against enemy positions. There was a smaller door built into the ramp that could be used as an emergency exit if the ramp became inoperable. There were also two large hatches that ran the length of the troop compartment's roof. When open, the infantry inside could stand on the benches and provide covering fire from atop the track. The hatches could also be "buttoned up" to provide a modicum of protection from indirect fire.

There were three crew positions in the front of the track. The forwardmost hatch provided access to the driver's compartment on the left side of the vehicle. The troop commander's compartment was directly behind the driver, and the vehicle commander/gunner's position was in a turret on the right front of the AAV. The massive engine, which was mounted in the center of the track at the front of the troop compartment, separated the TC and vehicle commander from one another.

In addition to his newly mechanized infantry, Grabowski commanded a weapons company that had two CAAT sections and an 81mm mortar platoon. Each CAAT section was made up of eight "hard back" or armored HMMWVs[10]. Four trucks carried a TOW missile launcher, and the other four carried either a .50-caliber machine gun or a 40mm automatic grenade launcher, the same weapons as in the AAV's up-gun. CAAT was fast, mobile, and deadly.

Colonel Grabowski shuffled his resources to organize all of his assets into an unstoppable juggernaut. He moved one of Peeples' four-tank platoons, Diablo, to Bravo Company. In return, he moved one of Bravo Company's infantry platoons, Green Platoon, into Major Peeples' tank company. This gave Grabowski four maneuver elements and a supporting weapons company with CAAT and mortars.

Team Tank would lead the battalion with two tank platoons, the tank command group, and one of Bravo Company's mechanized infantry platoons. Team Tank was comprised of ten tanks and an infantry platoon riding in three AAVs. Team Mech would follow directly behind Team Tank with Bravo's two remaining mechanized infantry platoons, Bravo's weapons platoon, the Bravo company commander and a platoon of M1 tanks. Team Mech was slightly lighter than Team Tank, with only four tanks and nine tractors.

Alpha and Charlie companies each had one weapons platoon and three mechanized infantry platoons, riding in twelve AAVs. Lieutenant Clayton's 81mm mortar teams would stay close to Colonel Grabowski in their eight Humvees, and Lieutenant Letendre's CAAT vehicles were left free to provide support to the battalion wherever they were needed. Finally, the headquarters and support (H&S) company rounded out the battalion with the Alpha and Bravo command groups and the ALOC[11]. First Battalion was a formidable force, numbering nearly five hundred Marines in seventy armored vehicles.

---

10 High mobility multi-purpose wheeled vehicle: commonly known as a Humvee or Hummer.

11 Administration and logistics command.

The Timberwolves were the most heavily armed battalion in Task Force Tarawa. They would lead the 2nd Marine Regiment into Iraq. If there was going to be a fight, Grabowski's Marines would certainly be involved. They had planned, trained, and prepared their vehicles for any eventuality. They were ready for battle, but Colonel Grabowski continued to worry about his men's well-being. He knew that some of his men might die in battle, but, more likely, they would die in accidents and friendly-fire incidents.

Grabowski's biggest concern was friendly fire. At every opportunity, he would warn his men that he feared Marines shooting Marines more than he feared Iraqis shooting Marines. He voiced this concern so often that some of his men were insulted. They believed that he did not have confidence in his own men's training and ability to tell the difference between Marines and the enemy.

Colonel Grabowski had every confidence in his men, but he knew from history that the likelihood of friendly-fire incidents was high. He was most concerned about his close air support (CAS). His first concern about the air support came when he learned that Type 2 and Type 3 CAS had been authorized and the battlefield would be patrolled by aircraft from all the services. Marines only train using Type 1 CAS, and even his air officer and forward air controllers had to look up what Type 2 and 3 CAS actually were.

The different types of CAS define the rules for employment of the supporting aircraft's weapons. Type 1 rules state that the aircraft can only fire at a target on the ground if the forward air controller can see the target and the aircraft. Type 2 and 3 CAS procedures are for the employment of intelligent weapon systems like laser- or GPS-guided[12] bombs. In a Type 2 engagement, the FAC does not need to have eyes on the target. The FAC can see the aircraft, but he relays a GPS coordinate for the target, which he may not actually be able to see. The incident in Afghanistan when Hamid Karzi was almost killed by an American bomb was the result of a Type 2 CAS mission. Type 3 CAS is used to attack the enemy in deep battle space. In a Type 3 CAS situation, it is possible that the FAC will not be able to see either the aircraft or the target.

Marines had a good understanding of what "close" was in close air support. The MAGTF constantly practiced the employment of combined arms. Each ground unit had embedded forward air controllers who themselves were

---

12 Global positioning satellite.

Marine pilots and F/A-18s, Harriers, Cobras, and Hueys were part of the ground commander's assets. FACs fought the airborne fight in concert with the artillery and ground forces. Marines had become proficient in Type 1 close air support. Marine air truly fought from over the Marine infantry's shoulder.

Now that Type 2 and 3 CAS had been authorized, Colonel Grabowski became very concerned about friendly fire from above. He wanted his men to stick to the basics; he ordered that Type 2 or 3 CAS could only be employed with his direct knowledge and express permission. He issued orders to his battalion stating that Type 2 CAS required the express permission of the battalion air officer, and Type 3 could only be authorized by him.

Grabowski's battalion had been allotted two forward air controllers, which he attached to two of his three infantry companies. These specially trained controllers were the forward-most controllers on the ground, and they supplemented the battalion's air staff, which usually traveled with the battalion Command Post (CP)[13]. Grabowski's FACs were assigned to Alpha and Bravo Company. Captain Jim "Kool Aide" Jones was assigned to Alpha Company, and Captain Dennis "Mouth" Santare to Bravo Company.

When Alpha Company, 8th Tanks was activated, they were short on officers. They had no FAC, and two of their platoons were commanded by gunnery sergeants. Just as with Randy Whidden, the reserve commanders scrambled to fill the empty billets. While they searched, Major Scott Hawkins volunteered to fill the FAC position, and a newly promoted captain, Romeo Cubas, had also asked to be assigned to a frontline tank unit.

Both wanted to take part in Operation Iraqi Freedom. When the reserve tankers found out about Hawk and Cubas, orders were cut to send them to the Timberwolves. By the time Hawk and Cubas were ready to go, Task Force Tarawa's Marines were already in Camp Shoup.

Major Hawkins and Captain Cubas were flown directly to Kuwait. Captain Cubas, an active-duty Marine, arrived first. He reported to Major Peeples, who assigned him to the 3d Platoon with Gunny Kamper. Hawkins arrived with only days remaining until the invasion. He stepped off the airplane in Kuwait and into a new Crown Victoria and was driven from Kuwait City directly to Camp Shoup. The Crown Vic rolled up right next to his tank, he got his gear out of the trunk and announced his arrival with, "Hey, anybody order a FAC?"[14]

---

14 Telephone interview with Major Scott Hawkins, 6/4/04.

This gave Colonel Grabowski an unexpected third FAC for the battalion and the men of Alpha Company a story that they would never let Hawk forget. "Couldn't come over with the rest of us, huh? Had to get your forty-two-year-old ass chauffeured out to us in a Crown Vic." Scott Hawkins, a religious man, had proudly served his country and returned to civilian life, but was called back to the Corps after 9/11. He was told, "We need FACs" and was reactivated as a major. Now, Major Scott Hawkins was about to head to war.

As the invasion drew closer, only one of Grabowski's four maneuver elements lacked a FAC—Charlie Company. But Grabowski's plan had taken that into account. Team Tank and Team Mech would always be in the lead. Charlie would travel close behind Team Mech. Alpha would take the Euphrates River bridge and Charlie Company would not bound forward to the Saddam Canal bridge until Team Mech had set into a support-by-fire position on the southern bank of the canal. There would always be one FAC with "eyes-on" the forward line of troops.

Just like the FACs controlling the air assets, the Timberwolves had artillery Forward Observers (FO) spread throughout the battalion to call in artillery from Glenn Starnes' 155mm howitzers. Each company, including Team Tank, had an artillery FO. Lieutenant James Carter, Team Tank's FO, rode with Major Peeples in his tank, and Lieutenant Fred Pokorney rode in the mortar track with Lieutenant Reid as part of Charlie Company's Fire Support Team (FiST). Team Mech, Alpha Company, Alpha Command, and Bravo Command all had their own FOs as well.

The plan was for the 1st Battalion, 10th Marines' artillery to follow close behind the Timberwolves. Colonel Starnes' artillery would set up south of the city and stand ready to provide supporting fire if Grabowski ran into trouble. Carter, Pokorney, and the others would call in the artillery, if needed.

AFTER a long day of training in the desert, Gunnery Sergeant Jason Doran had parked his Humvee for the night. Doran was one of the "old men" of the battalion. He had postponed his retirement to go to war with his men. Gunny Doran was a Marine's Marine: loud, crass, and always outspoken, he was liked by nearly everyone.

There is only one thing Doran loved more than the Corps—his two young daughters, and they both loved Scooby-Doo. Hoping that his daughters would find out someday, he affectionately named his HMMWV "the Mystery Machine," after the cartoon's colorful van. Everyone knew the Mystery Machine when they saw it, because nearly everyone in the battalion knew Gunny Doran.

Doran's Mystery Machine carried combat supplies and one of the battalion's Navy corpsmen. Corporal Aaron Day, Doran's driver, and a young Navy corpsman from the Dominican Republic, Doc Sabilla, had been assigned to Doran's Humvee. They were constantly razzing each other, but Day and Sabilla loved each other like brothers. Day would constantly harass Sabilla about his heavy Spanish accent, and Sabilla would insult Day's driving, choice of music, taste in women, and anything else he could think of.

Once settled in for the night, Gunny Doran mixed up a brew of coffee and cocoa, and offered some to Day and Doc Sabilla. Both gladly accepted, but Sabilla did not have a cup. He grabbed an empty plastic water bottle out of their Hummer, and using his surgical scissors, Sabilla cut the bottom off the bottle, making a nice-size coffee cup. He threw the top half back into the front seat and offered up his newly fashioned cup for a taste of Doran's brew.

The three men finished their Starbucks break and collected up their things before trying to get some much-needed sleep. Gunny Doran, being the senior of the three, took the nicest sleeping accommodations. He would sleep in the HMMWV's trailer, on top of the MREs. Sabilla took the front seat, and Day was left with the cold metal floor in the back of the Mystery Machine. It didn't take long for the three men to fall into a restless sleep.

Later, Doc Sabilla awoke in the middle of the night. Doran's coffee had traversed his system and now he had to pee. The Iraqi desert is not a very hospitable place. It is filled with scorpions, snakes, and all sorts of nocturnal creatures that one would not want to step on. A midnight trip to the outhouse would require socks and boots. It was cold outside the vehicle, too. So Doc Sabilla opted for Plan B.

He rummaged around in the front seat, hands groping in the dark, searching for an empty water bottle. Just as he had done many nights before, Doc found the bottle, turned his body, placed it between the seats, and carefully peed into the neck. Day immediately awoke. He jumped up and asked, "What the fuck are you doing?"[15] Doc Sabilla had picked up the

---

15 Ibid. Doran.

bottle he had cut the bottom out of earlier and was spraying pee all over Day's feet. When Doc Sabilla and Day realized what Doc had done, they both broke out laughing.

The Marines tried to fill their spare time with sports and physical training. They played football and even fashioned a softball out of paper and masking tape. They built pull-up bars and used sandbags for weight lifting. They even held evening boxing and wrestling matches. Corporal Randal Rosacker, the son of a Chief of the Boat (COB) on a nuclear submarine, won the last evening wrestling match.

NBC NEWS

Shortly after his return from Camp Shoup, Kerry Sanders was sitting in his Kuwait City office with a young producer and NBC's executive management team, who had flown over from New York to get a firsthand look at their operations in Kuwait. The NBC office was filled with high-tech communication and editing equipment, telephones, laptops, and television sets. There was a constant feed of all the major TV outlets on the sets—ABC, CBS, CNN, and FOX constantly flickered in the background.

As the executives were touring the offices, a FOX News reporter came on the screen, reporting live from Camp New York.

"Why aren't we out there?" One of the executives inquired.

The young producer offered, "Jim Avila and his cameraman are out right now. They are shooting a story for *Nightly News*. Maybe we can get them to shoot a couple live shots for MSNBC using their videophone."

The executives thought that was a good idea, so the young producer picked up her phone and called Jim Avila.

"Could you guys shoot some film for MSNBC?" she asked.

Jim and his crew would have to set up again and break down. There would be a significant amount of work to satisfy the request.

"But, you don't understand. Yes . . . But . . ." It was clear to all listening that the crew in the field was not taking to the young producer's request, so she handed the phone to one of the executives, who said, "Look, Jim, we need you to do this."

Jim still refused to help, and the next day he was on an airplane back to the United States. This was quite fortuitous for Kerry Sanders. Jim Avila had been outfitted with a state-of-the-art satellite uplink. NBC had purchased a civilian Humvee that had been left in Kuwait after Desert Storm, and they had installed the satellite equipment so that they could have live feeds from the battlefield.

The next day, Sanders was called into the office and told, "You got this satellite equipment and this Humvee. We'll have you go do some stuff." The storm was gathering, and Kerry had just been given the opportunity to report live from the battlefield, but he was not a sanctioned embed. Kerry began to wonder how he could use his newly acquired equipment. Without a military unit to help, it was possible that he would never get out of Kuwait.

That evening, Kerry talked with one of his colleagues in the Sheraton Hotel who was a producer with a sanctioned embed team. He asked, "Why don't you do what everybody else does? Why don't you cut a 'Drug Deal'?"[16]

"What are you talking about?" Kerry responded.

"That's what the military calls it—cutting a drug deal. You go out and make up your own thing, make up your own embedded position. Just do it."

Kerry was flabbergasted. "It sounds so simple. I can't imagine you can just do that." Kerry knew that the Pentagon and NBC's Washington Bureau chiefs had been negotiating for a long time over these things. "I can't just show up and do it myself."

His friend sat silent as Kerry contemplated how he was going to lose his job. It didn't take long for the reporter in Kerry Sanders to win the internal struggle. "What the hell. I'll try."

Kerry immediately thought of Royal Mortenson.

2D BATTALION, 8TH MARINES: AMERICA'S BATTALION

The entire northern portion of Kuwait was now cordoned off, and civilians were not permitted in the area. Military checkpoints littered the few roads leading into the Kuwaiti frontier with Iraq. If Kerry Sanders were to cut a "drug deal" with Mortenson, he would have to speak with him first. So, Kerry came up with a plan and immediately went to work on his laptop.

---

16 Personal interview with Kerry Sanders, 1/27/04.

Kerry sifted through his e-mail folders until he found the invitation that he had received weeks earlier. He spent a few minutes doctoring the old e-mail, and when he had finished, Kerry Sanders and his NBC crew had a new invitation to visit the Marines of America's Battalion in their desert camp. As the icing on the cake, Sanders added, "Challenge codes will be provided verbally."

With their bogus e-mail invitation in hand, Kerry Sanders, cameraman Sebastian Rich, and engineer/driver Danny Miller loaded their gear into the high-tech mobile TV satellite station and climbed into the ancient Humvee, which they had christened "Goldfinger,"[17] and headed north into the Kuwaiti wasteland.

NBC had purchased the metal-flake-gold civilian Humvee in Kuwait City to be used for transportation of an embedded reporter team. The Humvee had been salvaged by a local Kuwaiti and repainted. Goldfinger was outfitted with the latest in satellite technology so that the war could be beamed live back into America's living rooms.

The NBC news crew had no trouble making it through the military checkpoints, and they soon arrived at Camp Shoup. Sanders went straight to Lieutenant Colonel Mortenson and said, "I am not an embed. I have no authorization to cross the border, but this is an amazing organization, and I want to trace this battalion through the war. I want to be your embed."

Sanders could become Mortenson's best friend or his worst enemy, but Mortenson had a good feeling about Kerry. He honestly believed that he was there to tell the Marines' story. Mortenson wryly shot back, "Are you trying to cut a drug deal?"

"Yes, I am." Kerry responded.

Kerry showed the ugly Humvee and his equipment to Mortenson. Then he introduced his small crew. Mortenson liked Kerry Sanders, and he knew that having him with his battalion would help keep the families back home up to date on their loved ones' plight in the war. "Yeah, I think we can do this," Mortenson told Sanders. "But don't let this get out."

He told Sanders that he could stay, but first he needed the idea cleared by his superiors. Mortenson went off in search of permission to bring Kerry and his crew along with America's Battalion. Mortenson told Bailey, Bailey told Natonski, and Natonski asked Conway for permission to add the NBC

---

17 Ibid. Sanders.

news team. Unbeknownst to Kerry, everyone agreed that he should be allowed to tell 2/8's story.

Meanwhile, Mortenson sent Goldfinger to his motor T[18] guys to transform Sanders' truck into a military-looking vehicle. Working for two days and nights, through a blinding sandstorm, they completely stripped and rebuilt the ancient HMMWV.

REGIMENTAL COMBAT TEAM-2

As each day passed, war with Iraq became more certain. On March 17th, Bailey recalled his units from training and issued orders for the final preparations. There was a new flurry of activity in the camp as Marines unpacked their MOPP suits and started packing their personal gear into their sea bags. Anything not needed for combat would be left behind in Camp Shoup.

Each vehicle was topped off with supplies. Grabowski's AMTRACs and all of the regiment's trucks and Hummers were filled with food, water, batteries, and ammunition. Vehicles, radios, and weapons were checked again, and each NCO checked his Marines' gear to make sure that each man had what he needed. Ammunition was issued.

With war now certain, each Marine sat alone and prepared a final good-bye to his loved ones. Some just wrote their final letter from Camp Shoup. Some recorded audio tapes, while most wrote letters to say farewell.

Lance Corporal Donald "John" Cline Jr. called his friend aside and handed him a package. "There are some things in here that I want you to give to my wife if I don't make it,"[19] Cline told Bachmann. There were photographs that Cline had taken on the ship and in Kuwait, and there were two letters. One of the letters was addressed to Tina, and the other to Cline's two sons:

Dear Dakota and Dylan,
Well, boys, I have some things that I want you to know. First, before anything, you two make me so damn proud. I look at you two and all I see is love.

---

18 Motor transport.

19 Quote and letter from telephone interview with Tina Cline, 3/13/05.

Dakota, you are my first son, and me and you have had a lot of time together. You are going to be the oldest man now. I want you to take care of your mom and your brother. You are such an incredible little boy. You have so much potential . . .

You two have been such an inspiration to me . . . Me and your grandpa will always be there to watch over you. I am so sorry that I can't be there for your first days of school, to teach you both to drive, to watch you graduate, marry and have kids of your own, but I will always be there to watch over you and keep you safe . . .

Cline went on to tell his boys that they should always put their family first, strive to be honest, and that they should try to stay happy. His letter ended abruptly, almost cut off in mid-thought, with no closing or signature.

Another young Charlie Company Marine, Corporal Jose Garibay, was from Costa Mesa, California. He had moved to the United States from Mexico when he was a child and was not yet a citizen. Garibay loved the United States and the Corps. Before pushing off, Garibay sat alone and quietly recorded a message for his uncle who had been the family's benefactor and had helped them when they first came to America. Garibay thanked his uncle for everything he had done for the family, then he sealed the small cassette in an envelope and dropped it in the mail.

On the morning of March 18th, Major Scott "Hawk" Hawkins visited Reed Bonadonna's tent right before the regiment started to break camp. Hawk's daughter was a student of Bonadonna's back at the Merchant Marine Academy at King's Point. Hawk spent the first few minutes engaged in small talk with Bonadonna. Then, just as he was about to leave, Hawk got to the point of his visit. He told Bonadonna that he had written "the letter" to his wife, and he asked if Bonadonna would tell his daughter to "stay focused" if he didn't make it back. Bonadonna assured Hawkins that he would relay his message, and the two Marines parted.

Marines could be seen in every secluded corner of the camp—contemplating their future, trying to write something that would make their death easier to handle—trying to leave their thoughts for posterity.

Some Marines turned to their God. The chaplains were busy in those last days at Camp Shoup. They talked with Marines who were familiar to them, and they spoke with men whom they had never seen before.

MARINE AIR GROUP-29

Saipan's flight deck was abuzz with activity on the afternoon of the 18th. Colonel Thacker's attack force was preparing to move ashore. Some of the flight deck crew moved aircraft into position while others worked at fueling and arming the birds. Sailors and Marines scurried in every direction in a fine-tuned choreography that, to the untrained eye, looked like chaos. Everyone worked with the knowledge that a missed lanyard or loose bolt could have catastrophic consequences—someone could die. This was not a drill. The Marines were going to war.

By mid-afternoon, the preparations were complete. Hueys, Cobras, and Phrogs[20] began taking off from *Saipan*'s gently heaving deck. The small attack force of eight Cobras, three Hueys, and three Sea Knights took to the air and headed inland to Joe Foss Field. Joe Foss was an American airfield carved out of the northern Kuwaiti desert, little more than a sand-swept tarmac and some GP tents. Thacker found Lieutenant Colonel A. J. Cox waiting at Joe Foss with twenty-four of his recon Marines. Cox and Thacker started their final planning while their Marines readied their aircraft and equipment.

Soon, Thacker, Cox, and their men would kick off the invasion of Iraq. They would fire the first shots in anger at Iraqi border positions. Their attack would signal the start of the ground war and would quickly be followed by soldiers and Marines racing across the frontier toward their first objectives.

Thacker's pilots had just settled in when a sandstorm from hell blew in. First, the wind picked up, and then the Marines could see a wall of sand blowing toward the field. It quickly blew in and engulfed the Marines. By evening, the Kuwaiti desert had consumed all of the military camps in northern Kuwait. The storm was horrendous, pulling up tent pegs, breaking supports, and hurling anything that wasn't lashed down through the air. One by one, GP tents began to collapse on their occupants.

NBC NEWS

The storm covered Camp Shoup in a blanket of red dust. That night, Kerry climbed into his two-man pup tent to escape the sandstorm and try to get

---

20 "Phrog" is the Marine nickname for the CH-46, Sea Knight helicopter.

some sleep. Kerry, a Floridian, likened the sandstorm to a hurricane in the desert. The wind was so strong that his tent collapsed in the middle of the night. His small tent rolled across the battalion area like a large piece of tumbleweed in the Arizona desert, with Kerry inside.

Two days after Sanders' and Mortenson's conversation, Kerry was sitting on a bench in the middle of the desert, wearing an NBC cap. A tall guy walked up, and a loud confident voice boomed, "So, the *Today* show is here?"

Kerry responded before he looked up, "Yeah." Then Kerry looked up, and as he would always do, he glanced at the name tag on the Marine's chest, and then his eyes shot right to his collar. A star adorned each lapel. Natonski thrust out his hand and greeted Sanders. He introduced himself as "Rich Natonski" while he vigorously shook Kerry's hand.

Natonski took Sanders on a long walk. As they walked around the camp, Kerry learned that the general was from the same town in Connecticut as Tom Brokaw. They walked up to and around the general's helicopter, and Natonski introduced Kerry to his pilot. Then they walked over to Goldfinger, and Sanders asked, "Can we take it?" Natonski told Sanders that he did not have a problem with that, but he should check with Colonel Bailey, too.

Captain Kelly Frushour, the public affairs officer had been listening to Sanders and Natonski's conversation. As soon as Natonski left, Frushour escorted Sanders off to find Bailey. When they found Colonel Bailey, Frushour wasn't quite accurate as she conveyed the previous conversation. She told Bailey that General Natonski had said, "If it's okay with Bailey, its okay with me."

Bailey was not pleased. He thought that Natonski had placed the decision in his hands so that if something went wrong, Bailey would be stuck with the responsibility. In fact, Natonski had given Sanders permission. He just wanted to insure that Bailey was kept informed. Bailey grumbled but did not give Sanders a definitive answer.

Sanders and his crew sat in the camp all day long, waiting on Bailey's answer. Those eight hours felt like the slowest in Kerry Sanders' life; he could feel each second go by. This could either be the biggest story Kerry would ever cover, or he could be told to return to Kuwait City and be relegated to reporting Scud scares.

The Marines were starting to line up their vehicles. Kerry began to freak out as the hours wore on, so he went in search of Colonel Mortenson to see if he had heard anything, and Mortenson immediately checked with Colonel Bailey. Bailey's response was short, "I thought it was already decided. Sure it's okay."

The motor T guys delivered NBC's renovated HMMWV to Sanders. Goldfinger was dead. Kerry's vehicle was now painted desert-tan with large black H2/8 identification markings on its back doors. The NBC crew now called their traveling TV station "Down and Dirty 2." In the television news world, this was the fastest, most rudimentary piece of television equipment that had ever come together to broadcast live from the battlefield. This was the first time the satellite gear had ever been used. It had been tested once in a parking lot in Long Island City, but that was it. This was experimental, cutting-edge technology that no other news agency possessed. Sanders was thrilled that he was about to get the opportunity to go to war with this equipment.

Everything had finally come together for Sanders. Besides having live television uplink capability, Sanders had satellite Internet connections and five satellite telephone lines. Just before pushing off, they set all five phones out on a table and let every Marine in the battalion make a five-minute call home. With nearly one thousand men in America's Battalion, Kerry imagined there would be an enormous phone bill that he would have to explain to his bosses. Oddly, the way the satellite was set up, the Marines got a New Jersey dial tone. Coupled with NBC's discount telephone rates, the total bill was less than $100.

Kerry couldn't help overhearing some of the conversations. Some of the Marines had newborns. Some of them had pregnant wives. Some just wanted to say hi to their moms. Some just wanted to say, "I love you." Half would say, "We're here with the NBC News guys. So, if you're watching NBC, you'll see me on TV," or "Did you see me? I was on TV." When Ben Luciano got his turn on the satellite phone, there was no answer at home, so he called his wife's cell phone. She was at dinner at the Outback Restaurant with Bonnie Garcia and Chelle Pokorney.

1ST BATTALION, 2D MARINES: THE TIMBERWOLVES

Major Peeples' tankers had been working hard since they started their efforts to get their fourteen tanks in order. At one point early in the float,[21] ten

---

21 Float is Marine Jargon for traveling at sea. In this case, their trip from North Carolina to Kuwait aboard the magnificent 7.

of the fourteen tanks were "deadlined," or not ready for combat. As they staged for war, all fourteen of Major Peeples' tanks were finally running. The maintenance Marines had worked tirelessly through the dark of night and raging sandstorms to prepare the vehicles for war.

When they first arrived in Kuwait, Gunny Wright, the tank leader, would not let Whidden work on the tanks because his real job was to repair sophisticated night-vision and other electronic equipment. Once Gunny Howard told of Whidden's work aboard ship to get his tank running, Wright immediately relented. Whidden worked his magic almost nightly, creatively fixing seemingly unsalvageable systems aboard all the tanks. He had become so valuable that he was assigned to ride with the maintenance chief, Staff Sergeant Cooke, in his Humvee as part of the combat trains. Not only could he fix just about anything, he was an expert SAW[22] gunner. Cooke was more than happy to have Whidden and his SAW riding with him in the vehicle.

The Timberwolves parked their seventy armored vehicles in a tight rectangular formation on a spit of Kuwaiti desert that was smaller than a football field. This armored phalanx looked like the modern-day equivalent of the starting line at the Oklahoma land rush. Grabowski's vehicles had dug parallel ruts in the sand as they pulled into the formation. The vehicles were meticulously staged with the CAAT Humvees, Team Tank, and Team Mech in the front of the formation.

As they were making their final preparations to head into Iraq, Schielein told his Marines, "Boys, if you think we are going to come into somebody's backyard and we're not going to see a fight, you're retarded."[23]

2D BATTALION, 8TH MARINES: AMERICA'S BATTALION

Mortenson's Marines staged their seven-ton trucks with equal precision. The Marines of America's Battalion congregated between the lines of their large vehicles. Again, Mortenson's CAAT vehicles waited at the front of the battalion.

---

22 Squad automatic weapon.

23 Ibid. Schielein.

The entire regiment was getting ready to go to silence, so Kerry Sanders called his boss in Kuwait City to tell her, "You're not going to hear from me for a while. Everything is okay. When you hear from me, you hear from me."[24] Down and Dirty 2 was now in the lineup of vehicles; Kerry was in— the drug deal had worked. The only thing left was to start the engine and move north.

After a whirlwind of preparation, a month of sailing halfway around the world, and another month of waiting in the desert; the men of Task Force Tarawa were ready to move into combat. All that remained was for the order to be given.

Kerry thought, "This is it. The war is starting."

---

24 Ibid. Sanders.

CHAPTER 4

Lightning! Lightning! Lightning!

People sleep peaceably in their beds at night only because rough
men stand ready to do violence on their behalf.

—GEORGE ORWELL

3D BATTALION, 2D MARINES:
THE BETIO BASTARDS

Lieutenant Colonel Brent Dunahoe's Marines staged in a unique triangular
formation. Each of Dunahoe's three companies parked their seven-ton
trucks in a line, which made up one leg of an equilateral triangle. The battalion's CAAT sections manned each of the three points of the triangle. As
his Marines prepared to move to the Iraqi border, Dunahoe sat down and
wrote a one-page Commander's Guidance to his men:

> . . . 1st Marine Division is the MEF's main effort. TF Tarawa is a sup-
> porting effort. Within RCT-2, initially, our task as a supporting effort
> will be to facilitate 1st Marine Division's rapid movement north by pre-
> venting the enemy from interdicting the lines of communication. As a
> battalion, we must be prepared to conduct a variety of missions and tac-
> tical tasks ranging from urban warfare to humanitarian relief. Our focus
> in 3/2, however, will be high-intensity combat; locating and killing the
> enemy wherever and whenever he chooses to resist.
>   If the enemy resists, attack and overwhelm him with absolute force

and resolution. Surprise, shock, and violence of action at the point of contact are the keys to our success . . .

Colonel Dunahoe went on to say:

Our enemy is not the Iraqi people. We will conduct ourselves as liberators, not conquerors. Civilians should be treated as you would desire your family to be treated in a similar circumstance . . .

He concluded with:

We must remain physically, mentally, morally, and spiritually hard. We are expected to do that which others cannot or will not do. Common sense and initiative at all levels are essential throughout this campaign. No one can predict or explain every situation we may encounter on the battlefield. Small unit leaders and individual Marines will make decisions that impact not only the tactical situation, but also the political and strategic situation. Do what is right. Remember the Marines from our battalion who landed on Betio Island during the Second World War. Their courage and sacrifice is our legacy and will be the measure to which we are compared. Uphold your personal honor, the standards of our Corps, and take care of each other as we attack and defeat hostile forces in Iraq.
    Non conjuge nobiscum
    P. B. DUNAHOE
    Commanding[1]

Once completed, he called each of his companies together for what would turn out to be his last opportunity to speak with all of his men prior to going into battle. Dunahoe brought the battalion colors to each of the company musters. Before Colonel Dunahoe spoke, he solemnly removed the Tarawa Presidential Unit Citation streamer from the flagstaff and passed it around for every Marine to hold. He explained that it was now their turn to continue the battalion's brave tradition. He went on to tell his men, most barely out of their teens, that they were just as good Marines as the young men who fought at Tarawa so long ago.

---

1 P. B. Dunahoe, *Commander's Guidance* (USMC, 2003).

MARINE AIR GROUP-29

Just as Dunahoe had done, Colonel Milstead called his MAG-29 staff together for his last-minute briefing. They went over the Safwan Raid and all of the other tasks planned for MAG-29 aircraft. They talked about the close air support for the 1st Marine Division and Task Force Tarawa. They discussed the plans for setting up FARPS that would allow their pilots to leapfrog to Baghdad. And they talked about the casualty evacuation support. At the end of the briefing, Colonel Milstead reminded his Marines, "We are not going to cut any corners. We have trained the way we fight; now we are going to fight the way we trained . . . Every one of your Marines is somebody's son or daughter. We owe it to the parents of America to do it right."[2]

On the morning of the 19th, there was another flurry of activity on *Saipan*. HMM-162's Golden Eagles were preparing to send out two helicopters to each Marine regiment to support casualty evacuations. In one of the cockpits, Captain Eric Garcia and Lieutenant Tod Schroeder were an unlikely match. Tod was 6' 4", blond-haired and blue-eyed. Eric, on the other hand, was well under six feet tall with dark eyes and hair, and perpetually tanned skin. Being the most senior crew chief, Gunny Hetterscheidt was involved in the scheduling of aircrews for the squadron's missions. When he saw that Captain Garcia and Lieutenant Schroeder had been teamed together, he immediately assigned himself to their crew. Hetterscheidt had known Garcia since he was a young pilot, and he had been Schroeder's instructor in crew chief school in 1995–96, before Schroeder had become an officer and a pilot. Garcia and Schroeder were the best in the squadron. If Hetterscheidt were going to war, he wanted to fly with them.

Corporal Lewis, however, was nearly the squadron's youngest crew chief. Because of his lack of experience, others did not want him on their crew, so Hetterscheidt took Lewis under his wing. Corporal Lewis would now round out the crew. Two Navy corpsmen were brought along to take care of any casualties. By midmorning, Captain Garcia was setting his airborne ambulance down at Task Force Tarawa's headquarters at Camp Ryan.

---

2 Personal interview with Colonel Robert Milstead, 10/27/03.

As HMM-162s cas-evac[3] birds fanned out to all the regiments, Colonel Thacker and the recon battalion commander drove to the MEF headquarters from Joe Foss Airfield for their final update. They drove through blowing sand, crawling along at twenty miles per hour. Their miserable trip south to Camp Commando provided no new intelligence and now they had to grope their way home, back up the road through the same sandstorm. They returned to Joe Foss by late afternoon. Colonel Thacker went directly to his CP and found that the war had already started.

CENTCOM had acted on what they believed to be accurate intelligence as to the whereabouts of Saddam Hussein. General Franks had ordered a decapitation strike. The Navy had hurled forty-two cruise missiles at Baghdad, and two Air Force F-117s had dropped bunker-buster bombs on Saddam's suspected hideout. When Thacker heard the report of the attack on Baghdad, he turned to his staff and said, "This might change things a little bit."[4]

2D MARINE EXPEDITIONARY BRIGADE: TASK FORCE TARAWA

Task Force Tarawa's lead elements moved out on March 19th, to be followed by the rest of the brigade on March 20th. There would be a steady stream of vehicles leaving Camp Shoup and Camp Ryan for the next two days, as Task Force Tarawa moved toward its attack positions in the northwest corner of Kuwait. Natonski's Marines had a narrow corridor through which to move into Iraq. They were sandwiched between the 3rd Brigade Combat Team of the Army's 3rd Infantry Division on their left and RCT-5 of the 1st Marine Division on the right. The East Coast Marines didn't even have their own battle space; they would travel behind 3 BCT, in the Army's territory.

As they moved closer to war, the 2d Marines received word that the Iraqis in Nasiriyah were fishing off the bridges. No other timely intelligence appeared to be available. There was no current satellite imagery, no imagery from UAVs, no updated reports on the state of the defenses around the city. There was just the message that indicated that Nasiriyans liked to eat fish.

---

3 Casualty evacuation.

4 Ibid. Thacker.

REGIMENTAL COMBAT TEAM-2

Colonel Bailey sent Charlie Company of 2d LAR forward first. Captain Gregory Grunwald's LAVs raced across the desert to the Kuwaiti border to screen Task Force Tarawa's movement into its attack positions. Bailey's combat power moved behind LAR's screen. Bailey sent the lead elements of his mechanized battalion to the frontier behind Grunwald's screen first.

The rest of the regiment would move to the border on March 20th. Colonel Starnes' artillery would follow Grabowski's Timberwolves, followed by Bailey's regimental command group. Dunahoe's and Mortenson's motorized battalions would take up the rear of the regiment's column.

1ST BATTALION, 2D MARINES:
THE TIMBERWOLVES

The Timberwolves moved out from Camp Shoup to AA Hawkins as the lead battalion of Task Force Tarawa. The Battalion Main, CAAT, Team Tank and Team Mech departed Camp Shoup on the evening of March 19th for AA Hawkins.

As CAAT pulled out of Camp Shoup at the head of 2d Marines, Staff Sergeant Schielein switched his radio to the CAAT platoon net, which only his men could hear. "Net clear! Net clear!" He announced, and the net went quiet. Then he kicked control of the net to Sergeant James Johnson, who went on, "The Lord is my shepherd, I shall not want . . ."[5] Once Johnson completed the Lord's Prayer, the platoon net returned to the normal radio traffic of a CAAT platoon leading a regiment to war.

The CAAT platoon had sixteen armored HMMWVs. Each Hummer had a ring mount on its roof. Eight of the vehicles carried TOW missile launchers and a small machine gun. The other eight carried .50-caliber machine guns and MK19 automatic grenade launchers.

The platoon was structured so that it could be broken up into two sections of eight vehicles, four TOW and four machine gun vehicles. Each section could be split again into two squads of four vehicles.

---

5 Ibid. Schielein.

First Lieutenant Brian S. Letendre was the CAAT platoon commander. He was also the CAAT 2 section leader. Schielein was Letendre's second in command and the CAAT 1 section leader. Letendre rode in a machine gun vehicle with his driver, Private First Class S. A. Torrey, and gunner, Corporal Daniel Strong.

Captain Brooks led Alpha Company from his command track. Each of Brooks' platoon leaders commanded tracks, as did their platoon sergeants. Lieutenant Matthew Martin commanded one of 3d Platoon's tracks. Staff Sergeant Cantu was perched atop another 3d Platoon track. First Sergeant Thompson took up the rear of the company formation in the medical track. They all drove forward with their troop compartment hatches closed to protect the Marines in the rear from NBC[6] attacks.

Corporal Jorge "Gonzo" Gonzales was riding with Charlie Company's mortar team across the desert. After a rocky start in the Marine Corps, Gonzales ended up in Staff Sergeant Jason Cantu's squad. Cantu, from a Marine Corps family, was an even-handed leader who only wanted to make his Marines the best they could be. In 2002, Cantu ended up with several Marines who had been in trouble. He molded them into one of the finest infantry squads in the Corps. His "Dirty Dozen" won the 2d Marine Division Super Squad competition that year. Gonzalez had turned his life around as a part of Cantu's Dirty Dozen. He had gotten married and been promoted to corporal. He was even talking of reenlisting. Cantu's "Dirty Dozen" had been broken up before deployment, and Gonzales was now part of Charlie Company' weapons platoon, working for another great leader, Staff Sergeant Phil Jordan.

A couple of hours after they left Shoup, the Timberwolves had their first SCUD alert and MOPP warning. The entire column ground to a halt while all the Marines donned their MOPP gear—gloves and gas masks.

1ST BATTALION, 10TH MARINES

Colonel Starnes' attitude was "Damn the SCUDS full speed ahead," as he continued to press forward with his artillery battalion. The SCUDs were impacting south of his Marines, and the prevailing winds were blowing from northwest to southeast. If the Iraqi weapons were loaded with deadly gas, it

---

6 Nuclear, biological, and chemical.

would be blown away from the artillerymen. Starnes did not stop or order a MOPP alert. Instead, he took the opportunity to charge forward ahead of Marine and Army units that were continually stopping to either don their gas masks or to remove them. They moved forward in a battalion wedge, three battery columns abreast. The artillery battalion was moving independently. At times, the wedge raced ahead of Colonel Grabowski's Marines.

MARINE AIR GROUP-29

At 0900 on the morning of the 20th, Thacker was standing outside the Joe Foss Field's CP, talking with the Forward Armament and Resupply Point (FARP) operations officer, when he heard a really loud noise. It continued to get louder, like a jet aircraft making a low-level pass. Thacker quickly looked toward the noise and saw a cigar-shaped object fly over the airfield at about five hundred feet—going the speed of heat.

"That wasn't good!" Thacker offered to his companion. "It was too low, too fast, and headed in the wrong direction. I don't think that was one of ours."[7]

A radio operator rushed out of the CP and Thacker, "Hey, sir. What does 'Lighting! Lighting! Lighting!' mean?"

Everyone ran toward the bunkers as the air raid and chemical alarms started to wail. This would be the first of many alarms, which continued throughout the day. The Safwan Raid force knew they would be going that night, so they struggled to prepare through interruption after interruption of running for shelter and donning their gas masks. They were in and out of NBC alerts all day.

REGIMENTAL COMBAT TEAM-2

RCT-2's command post broke camp around noon on March 20th. Colonel Bailey and his entire command group drove north across the Kuwaiti desert, stopping several times to don gas masks. They arrived at AA Hawkins along the Kuwaiti berm long before sunset. Hawkins was only an assembly area,

---

7 Ibid. Thacker.

a bare patch of sand identified by a GPS coordinate. The regiment's Marines unpacked what they would need for the night and set up a hasty defense.

The regiment was standing on the edge of invasion. Only a couple of berms and a ditch separated Task Force Tarawa from Iraq. Sunrise would bring the long-awaited moment; tomorrow, the invasion of Iraq would start. Most of the men tried to sleep, but many were too excited.

3D BATTALION, 2D MARINES: THE BETIO BASTARDS

Dunahoe's Marines started moving across the Kuwaiti desert to their tactical assembly area (TAA Hawkins) behind 1/2, Starnes' artillery, and the regimental command group. There were no roads. Sand and dust was everywhere.

Once the Betio Bastards had assembled at Hawkins, Lieutenant Colonel Dunahoe called a battalion staff meeting to go over final preparations for movement into Iraq and to issue a short commander's intent to all of his company commanders and staff:

> *I see the enemy initially attempting to delay and defend the southern approaches to An Nasiriyah in order to allow the current regime time to affect a political solution. I see the enemy's main source of strength in the vicinity of An Nasiriyah as the organized militias and paramilitary forces, such as the Ba'ath Party Militia, the Saddam Fedayeen, and others loyal to Saddam Hussein. They have the most to lose in a regime change. They may attempt to attrite our forces through the use of obstacles, ambush, the employment of weapons of mass destruction (WMD), or asymmetrical attacks. We will initially occupy strong points in sector to prevent enemy forces from interdicting the lines of communication leading to the Highway 1 bridge crossing west of the city. We will ensure 1st Marine Division's unimpeded movement over the Euphrates River as they continue to attack north. I want an aggressive defense. Don't become a target. I want our Marines to stay out of the built-up areas to the greatest extent possible. I do not want to get sucked into an urban fight unless absolutely necessary. I want an aggressive patrolling plan and a defense in depth to keep the enemy off balance and unsure of our intent. I want a mobile reserve capable of responding to any penetrations and conducting limited objective attacks as directed.*

My end-state for this phase of the operation is the battalion posi-
tioned to secure designated lines of communications and prevent enemy
interdiction of the Highway 1 bridge over the Euphrates River. Further-
more, the battalion is poised to execute assigned "be prepared to" mis-
sions and ready to cross the Euphrates River over either the Highway 1
bridge or Highway 7 bridge to continue the attack to the north.

Air raid sirens wailed their warning of another Iraqi missile attack as
Dunahoe delivered his intent to his officers. The fighting had started, and the
Bastards of 3d Battalion, 2d Marines were ready to go to war once again.

507TH MAINTENANCE COMPANY

Captain Troy King, a stocky thirty-seven-year old, had been in the Army
for several years but had never seen combat. As a matter of fact, he wasn't
even trained as a combat officer. He had entered the Army as a dental assistant and worked his way into the command of the 507th Maintenance
Company. He commanded an organization of mechanics, cooks, computer
technicians, and clerks, most lacking basic military skills. Each of the soldiers of the 507th Maintenance Company was very good at his or her assigned job, but they were not riflemen or infantrymen. They were drivers
and technicians.

King's 507th Maintenance Company was part of the Army's giant logistics team. Their primary function was to provide maintenance, supplies, and
support to a Patriot missile battery that would advance toward Baghdad
with the 3rd Infantry Division. They carried the critical spare parts for the
Patriot missile and its state-of-the-art fire control electronics. These were the
soldiers who provided the vital everyday support to the missile battery. They
fed the soldiers, maintained their vehicles and the sophisticated electronics,
and made sure they had the spare parts they needed. Like the 507th, more
than half of the soldiers in Kuwait had unglamorous jobs. These soldiers
would keep the combat troops equipped, fueled, and fed. None were ever
expected to see combat.

As a leader of a support company, Captain King lacked the basics of
combat leadership. The Army never intended his soldiers to get anywhere
close to the front lines, and Captain King was so certain that he would not

see action that he had his soldiers' hand grenades and AT-4 antitank weapons collected and locked up prior to their departure.

At thirty-eight, 1st Sergeant Robert Dowdy was the old man of the outfit. He had just been promoted from master sergeant and had been awarded the coveted job of company first sergeant. Dowdy, a native of Cleveland, Ohio, was a career NCO. He had served his country for nearly twenty years and was one of the best leaders the Army had to offer.

Dowdy grew up in the Midwest, surrounded by a large network of family and friends. He was a loving husband, good friend, and father of a teenage girl. Robert Dowdy was cut from the fabric of America's heartland. He was kind, honest, and friendly. Most of all, he was dedicated to his job. He gladly accepted the responsibility for the well-being of all the soldiers of the 507th. His soldiers had not had a very long time to get to know him; yet, most liked and respected him immediately.

Chief Warrant Officer Marc Nash had spent his entire adult life in the Army. He had enlisted right after he graduated from high school in the Bronx and had since received a wide range of training. Earlier in his career he had served in the 82nd Airborne Division and been an enlisted infantryman before becoming a Patriot missile technician.

The American military walks a fine line between equal opportunity and an age-old idea that women should be shielded from the horrors of combat. Throughout history, men have gone off to fight the wars, while women have stayed behind to care for the family. In twenty-first-century America, and a handful of other enlightened nations, women have become an integral part of the military. But, still, the American military does not allow women to be placed in combat roles.

Three of the young women of the 507th Maintenance Company were: Shoshana Johnson, Lori Piestewa, and Jessica Lynch. These young soldiers contributed as equals with the other soldiers in the unit. They were all good at their jobs and worked hard alongside the men of the unit.

Jessica Lynch was a young supply clerk from the backwoods of West Virginia. Her family had not ventured out of those green rolling mountains for generations. Lori Piestewa was born and raised a Hopi Indian on a Navajo reservation in New Mexico. Her grandfather was a World War II veteran, and her father was a Vietnam vet. Piestewa had married very young and had two small children from her failed marriage: Brandon, four, and Carla, three.

Lori Piestewa and Jessica Lynch had been roommates at Fort Bliss and had become best friends. Like Will Bachmann and Donald Cline, and Pokorney and Reid, the military had brought these two young women together from backgrounds that could not have been more different—Piestewa from the high desert of New Mexico, Lynch from the Appalachian Mountains.

Jessica Lynch had enlisted in the Army to earn money for a college education and to see the world outside her sleepy hometown. Lori Piestewa had left her children in the care of her parents and had joined the Army to provide for her family. Lynch was petite, and Piestewa was outgoing and determined.

Shoshana Johnson a black woman from Georgia and a native of the Republic of Panama, joined the Army in 1998 to learn how to become a cook. She, too, was a single mother trying to provide for her two-year-old daughter, Janelle. Shoshana Johnson's father was an Army retiree, and she knew that she could get a good start in life in the Army.

Blond-haired and trim, Don Walters was one of the few war veterans in the company. He had grown up in Colorado but had moved west in his teens and graduated from high school in Salem, Washington. After high school, he joined the Army and served in Desert Storm. In 1992, he moved to the reserves and became a police officer. After marrying his second wife, Stacie, he returned to the Army to help build a stable life for his three daughters.

Specialist James Grubb was a mechanic. His fuel truck was built in 1984 and still had its original motor. Grubb worked all day to maintain the 507th's vehicles. He always paid a little extra attention to his fuel truck. His engine compartment was a little cleaner, his oil filters were a little newer, and his carburetor was a little more finely adjusted. Grubb wanted to make sure that his own transportation would carry him across the Iraqi wasteland.

Sixty-four soldiers of the Army's 507th Maintenance Company left Camp Virginia at approximately 1400. Their thirty-three vehicles were part of a larger convoy that was headed for Objective Rams, deep in the heart of Iraq. According to King's orders, the 507th would be directed from Route Blue to Route Jackson by soldiers at a manned tactical control point (TCP) at a Cloverleaf intersection, south of An Nasiriyah. The 3rd FSB[8] operations officer gave King a CD ROM that contained orders and route information. King was also issued a global positioning satellite receiver and 1:100,000

---

8 Forward support battalion.

scale maps of the area. King's almost-three-dozen vehicles pulled out onto the dusty desert in a line of vehicles that stretched out to the horizon.

MARINE AIR GROUP-29

By 1700, Colonel Thacker's aircrews were conducting their final weapons cleaning, preflight checks, and crew briefings. Thacker was still with the recon Marines because they had established direct communications with the MEF. General Conway came up on the radio and asked Thacker, "Can you move the attack up?"[9] Conway was worried that now that Baghdad had been bombed, the Iraqis would start blowing up the oil wells and pumping facilities in southern Iraq.

Thacker asked, "Move it up to when?"

"Can you go in thirty minutes?" the MEF commander asked.

There was no way that Thacker could recalculate the time line, race to the other side of the field, load the recon Marines, back-brief the mission, and get airborne in thirty minutes. He responded, "Let's shoot for 1830."[10]

Thacker's nine planes took off around sunset, as another sandstorm started to blow into northern Kuwait. Once in the air, the weather got even worse. The visibility rapidly started to drop with the fading light and the swirling sand, but Thacker and his small attack force pressed forward toward Safwan Hill. Thacker ordered his pilots to spread their positions to insure they didn't fly into one another in the limited visibility.

When MEF put the call out to go ahead of schedule, it was like someone had thrown a rock into a school of minnows. Everyone all along the border was jumping through hoops to move up their time line. As they flew north, they could see the ground forces moving up under them.

Thacker's four Cobras led the attack through the swirling sand. Three Phrogs followed safely behind, and the two Hueys took up the rear of the loose formation. Thacker and his force arrived on station, but the F/A-18 guys were late, forcing the helicopters to loiter in the increasingly poor flying conditions. Thacker recalled later, "I can safely say, this was the worst weather I have ever flown in." Riding in the back of his C3 Huey, Thacker

---

9 Ibid. Thacker.

10 Ibid. Thacker.

had no way to control his own destiny. He kept thinking, "Good pilot. Good pilot." He tapped the pilot, Captain Andy Dyer, on his head and said, "It's okay Andy, keep it straight and level. Don't do anything stupid."

After twenty minutes of waiting, the F/A-18s finally arrived on station and dropped twenty-four JDAM[11] bombs on the hill. The ground war had officially started. Due to the terrible visibility, no one saw the Hornet's attack on the Hill, and few Cobras along the border could find their targets. As the Hornets rolled off their target, Thacker got on the TAD and told his pilots, "We've got one chance to do this right. Then, we're running for gas."[12]

The Cobras moved in and laid down their rockets on the hill. Because of the horrible visibility, Lieutenant Colonel J. S. O'Meara led his two Phrogs up to the base of the hill and began to follow a winding road up to the objective at the top. O'Meara managed to make it to the top of Safwan Hill, but each time he attempted to land, blowing sand obstructed his view of the landing zone. Colonel Thacker sat in his command helicopter, helplessly listening to his Phrog pilots:

"Dash One: waiving off."

"Dash Two: waiving off. Dust is bad. Dust is bad."

The forty-six pilots made three attempts to land before Thacker called off the landing.

The trip back to Joe Foss was more dangerous than the attack on the hill. Colonel Thacker ordered all of his pilots to increase their separation. The last thing in the world he wanted was for his Marines to be killed in a mid-air collision. It was hard enough for the pilots to avoid hitting the ground. Visibility was absolutely zero, and each pilot had to depend on his instruments to stay on course and altitude.

One pilot came up on the radio with a bit of panic in his voice. He reported that he was breaking out of the formation and moving to a higher altitude. He had been overcome by vertigo. Fortunately, he got high enough to gain some visibility and regain his equilibrium. After this close call, all of Thacker's aircraft made it safely home.

Once they were safely on the ground, Thacker got into a radio conversation with the MEF headquarters. They wanted him to refuel and to go

---

11 Joint direct attack munitions.

12 Ibid. Thacker.

back to the hill immediately. Thacker reasoned with the MEF command that it was really too dangerous to return that night. The visibility was well below the acceptable minimums. "In aviation terms, it was absolute dog shit."[13] MEF finally agreed that Thacker should wait and launch again at first light.

The weather was so bad that night that a Marine CH-46 carrying British commandos went down, killing all aboard. When Colonel Milstead woke up the next morning, he turned on his computer. There was an e-mail waiting for him from his wife, Suzanne. The e-mail was short and to the point. "Would like to know everything is okay."

The colonel's wife had an entire air group's worth of wives who were worried that their husbands might have been involved in the CH-46 crash. Milstead sat down and typed a carefully worded encouragement, "It wasn't one of ours."[14]

Within two minutes, Milstead's computer chimed the receipt of an incoming message. "Can I share that with the wives?" Colonel Milstead typed a single word reply, "YES!"

Technology had brought the news of the doomed Sea Night helicopter into America's living rooms within hours of the crash. Every wife and mother of every CH-46 crewmember in the theater was gripped in the fear that her husband or son was dead. But, technology quickly brought relief to Bonnie Garcia and the wives of HMM-162 and HMM-365. After the quick e-mail exchange, Suzanne started making phone calls to reassure the Carolina wives that all was well with their loved ones.

2D MARINE EXPEDITIONARY BRIGADE: TASK FORCE TARAWA

The 1st Marine Division headed north to seize the strategic Iraqi oil fields. CENTCOM and the MEF commanders did not want a repeat performance of Desert Storm, where most of the oil fields had been set ablaze. Even a temporary loss of the flow of oil to world markets could be catastrophic to the Iraqi economy. Task Force Tarawa moved to the northwest, in a small

---

13 Ibid. Milstead.

14 Ibid. Milstead.

corridor, behind the 3rd Infantry Division. After RCT-1's movement north, they were to turn west and follow in trace of Task Force Tarawa. Once Task Force Tarawa had secured the bridges through An Nasiriyah, RCT-1 would turn north toward Baghdad along with the division's other two regimental combat teams.

IRAQ

In Operation Desert Storm, the Iraqi commanders learned that they could not stand toe-to-toe in open land warfare against the American military. Iraqi forces that managed to survive the relentless air attacks were rolled up by the Army and Marine Corps' high-tech juggernaut. This war would have to be fought differently if the Iraqi Army would have any chance at victory. This war would have to be waged in the streets of Iraq's cities.

The seat of Saddam's power was Baghdad. American ground forces would have to move to Baghdad to unseat Saddam, so Iraqi generals prepared to defend the most obvious approach from the south—from Kuwait.

The Arabian Desert covers the first hundred miles of the approach from Kuwait. It was on this same desolate landscape that the U.S. Army's VII Armored Corps decimated the Republican Guard in 1991. Saddam would not make this mistake again. He would not face the American onslaught in the open desert.

The Iraqi generals carefully picked their first location to take a stand. An Nasiriyah, home of the 11th Infantry Division, was the logical choice. It is Iraq's fifth-largest city and the first on the road to Baghdad. It could provide cover from American air strikes; the generals doubted that the Americans would bomb the civilians of An Nasiriyah.

Knowing that his national communication lines would be severed during the opening moments of the war, Saddam sent his most trusted confidants out from Baghdad to command the defense of outlying regions. Saddam's cousin and chief henchman, Ali Hassan al-Majid al-Tikriti, "Chemical Ali," was dispatched to the lower Euphrates region to command the defense of the Shia territory south and east of Baghdad.

Chemical Ali was well known and feared in An Nasiriyah. During the Iran-Iraq war, he gassed the Kurds to suppress their revolt in the north. Then Saddam anointed him governor of Kuwait during the occupation in 1990. In Kuwait, Ali oversaw the murder, torture, rape, and kidnapping of

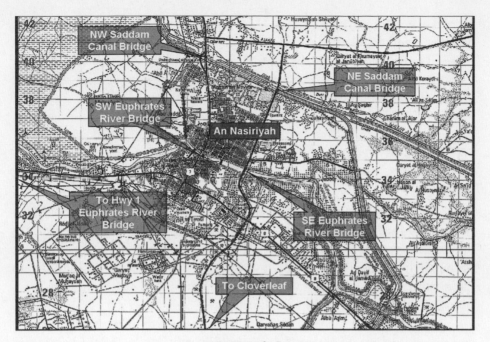

An Nasiriyah, Iraq

Kuwaiti civilians. Then he fled north to control the Shia provinces where he slaughtered dissenting Shiites in southern Iraq. Now, as a presidential advisor and member of the Revolutionary Command Council, Chemical Ali would command the first line of defense from his stronghold in Nasiriyah.

Iraqi highways 1, 7, and 8 converge at this primarily Shia city on the edge of the Arabian Desert. The city center sits on a fertile delta strip of land bordered on the north by the man-made Saddam Canal and on the south by the meandering Euphrates River. Four large bridges provide access to the city center, and impassable marshes flank the city on the east and west. Nasiriyah would be an easy place to defend.

There were myriad places to hide in the city and an entire civilian population of 500,000 to hide behind. Two main roads ran north-south through the city, and each of the four bridges connected the isthmus with the desert in the south and the Fertile Crescent in the north. About twenty kilometers west of the city center, Highway 1 crossed the Euphrates River on a fifth bridge that was under construction. Highway 8 ran through the southern part of the city, paralleling the Euphrates River and crossed Highway 1 at its Euphrates River bridge.

All of An Nasiriyah's approaches were defended with a modest, ringed, military defense. An entire Iraqi Army brigade defended the southern section of Nasiriyah, south of the Euphrates River. There was an infantry company, supported by mortars, positioned along Highway 8 near the city's power plant in southwest Nasiriyah. In the southeast, the Iraqis had positioned a company of tanks just north of the Highway 7 railroad bridge. The tanks were supported by infantry, machine guns, mortars, and artillery.

Technicals, APCs, and tanks were hidden in the tree line west of Highway 7, north and south of the Highway 8 interchange. Farther up Highway 7, within view of the Euphrates River, the enemy had dug into fighting positions all around the Tykar military hospital. They had even positioned an old tank in the hospital's courtyard. Just opposite the hospital was a motor pool on the west side of Highway 7 that was also being used as a defensive stronghold. Another Iraqi brigade was dug in inside the city. Buildings on the northern bank of Euphrates River contained sandbagged fighting positions in windows and on all of the rooftops.

The 23rd Brigade's area of responsibility was north of the Saddam Canal and the city proper. Highway 7 traversed a marshy landscape through a spiderweb of berms, canals, and ditches north of the city. The road itself was built on a levy that rose four or five feet above the flat, soggy terrain. The Iraqis had an entrenched battalion with AK-47s, RPGs, machine guns, mortars, and artillery dug in west of Highway 7, behind a twenty-foot protective berm. Several canals lie between the Iraqi line and the road, making approach nearly impossible. Another battalion of the 23rd Brigade manned positions east of Highway 7. They, too, were protected by a large berm, which ran north-south about fifty meters east of the road. A third battalion defended both of the northern Saddam Canal bridges. The 23rd Brigade was supported by mortars and artillery located north of the canal and inside the city.

Highway 7 ran for two kilometers north across open terrain from the Saddam Canal to a "T" intersection with Highway 16. A large complex of buildings, which in years past had been the headquarters for the 23d Brigade, overlooked the intersection. American and British warplanes had devastated the complex in Desert Storm, so now the abandoned buildings provided little more than an observation post and mortar position for the Iraqis.

Highway 16 ran west for nearly four kilometers from the old 23d Brigade headquarters until it dead-ended with the road leading to Baghdad— Highway 7. Just north of this second "T" intersection was the 11th Infantry

Division headquarters. This complex was an active military command center, with a sand table in the basement and a contingent of troops defending the compound. Mortars were positioned on the roof, and a battery of artillery was dug in nearby. An Iraqi military supply compound, protected by several AAA guns, was only a few kilometers north of the intersection.

The Iraqi commanders had suspected that the Americans would drop paratroopers in the open fields northeast of Nasiriyah and attack the city across the northeastern Saddam Canal bridge. So they built a fortified line of fighting trenches and mortar and heavy machine gun positions along the southern bank of the Saddam Canal. They had also registered their mortars and artillery on the raised road, just north of the bridge.

Arms caches were located at every corner of the city. Weapons and ammunition were stashed in mosques, schools, and hospitals. The area was also crawling with Uday's personal cutthroats. They had organized into a group of fanatics called the Saddam Fedayeen. At least five hundred Fedayeen had been sent to Nasiriyah to insure that the soldiers of the 11th Infantry Division and the local Al-Quds militia remained motivated. The Fedayeen provided incentive to the locals to fight the Americans by telling the soldiers that they had a choice of fighting or dying. Anyone who pondered the decision too long was summarily shot.

The Fedayeen had infested an urban neighborhood of mud-brick buildings, just southwest of the eastern Saddam Canal bridge. Very soon, the Marines of Task Force Tarawa would label this section of town as the Martyrs' District.

Saddam's political party thugs also roamed the streets. Members of the Ba'ath party militia had the highest personal stake in fighting in Nasiriyah. Nasiriyah was their fiefdom. The Ba'aths were the people who ran and controlled the city, and they ruled through fear and violence. They took whatever they wanted and lived a luxurious life at the expense of the local Shia population. If they lost, they hoped that they were killed instead of having to answer to the people of An Nasiriyah. The Ba'ath dominated the southern, suburban neighborhoods south of the Euphrates River.

Three regular Army brigades, each totaling over fifteen hundred men, were located in and around An Nasiriyah. They were reinforced by an unknown number of Ba'ath party and Al Quds militia. Another five hundred Fedayeen augmented the force. Just as during the lead-up to Desert Storm, many everyday Iraqis who had been pressed into military service just went

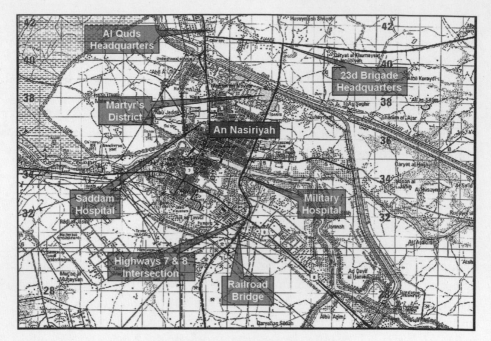

An Nasiriyah's prominent landmarks

home to their families. Even with the threats from Saddam's Fedayeen, regular soldiers deserted their positions and faded into the population.

Many more Al-Quds militiamen deserted as well. Even some of the Ba'ath Party officials decided to hole up in their walled homes and ride out the coming onslaught. At full strength, this combination of regular and irregular forces provided a military garrison in, and around, Nasiriyah of six to ten thousand men. Since it was impossible to tell how many Iraqis had already deserted, Coalition commanders hoped that most of the remaining armed defenders would lay down their arms at the first sight of the American military.

Regardless, An Nasiriyah was an armed camp, prepared to repel an attack from almost any direction. The Iraqi commanders wanted to force the enemy to dismount and enter the city on foot. Once in the city, they would cut them off at each of the bridges and rip them to shreds in an urban battle. At least that was the plan. RCT-2 had two thousand combat Marines. Fighting from the cover of an urban environment, the Iraqis had an overwhelming advantage.

THE 507TH MAINTENANCE COMPANY

During the first leg of their route, the 507th traveled off road through northern Kuwait, paralleling Task Force Tarawa's route. At 2100, they arrived at Attack Position (AP) Dawson, just south of the Iraqi border. They ate and refueled their vehicles, then attempted to get some rest. The 507th stayed at Dawson for ten hours, waiting for their turn to move into Iraq.

2D BATTALION, 8TH MARINES
AND NBC NEWS

It was an incredibly clear night. As Kerry Sanders waited to head north, he watched the Army hurl missiles into Iraq. Kerry's enthusiasm and excitement was instantly crushed by terrible news. The secretary of defense had just issued a directive—No civilian vehicles would be allowed on the battlefield. Kerry's hopes were dashed. After all of his hard work, it now seemed that "Down and Dirty 2" would have to be left behind. Mortenson assured him that he could still come along with the battalion. Sanders replied, "I don't work for the History Channel."[15] Without his satellite equipment, Kerry was out of a job.

Mortenson quickly juggled his vehicle assignments to free up a seven-ton truck, which he gave to Sanders. The Marines scrambled in the last couple of hours before their advance into Iraq. They removed all of the high-tech equipment from Kerry's Hummer and put it onto NBC's newest satellite TV vehicle, a Marine Osh-Kosh seven-ton truck. As the sun came up, Down and Dirty 2 sat completely stripped and all of Kerry's satellite equipment was now on the truck. Nothing was connected, but Kerry had his equipment. Before he knew it, America's Battalion was headed into Iraq.

---

15 Ibid. Sanders.

CHAPTER 5

Sea of Sand

This war, like all wars our nation has fought, was carried on the shoulders of the youth of America.

—COLONEL ROBERT E. MILSTEAD, USMC

27 October, 2003

MARINE AIR GROUP-29

Before dawn on the morning of March 21st, Marine artillery began pounding Safwan Hill in preparation for Colonel Thacker's return with Cox's recon Marines. The morning was clear, and this time the CH-46s had no problems landing atop the hill. Twenty-two Marines fanned out and took control of what was left of the Iraqi outpost. There was no fighting; anyone who had survived the previous night's air attack had fled during the night.

TASK FORCE TARAWA

Marines began heading into Iraq at sunrise. Several units moved through the berms simultaneously. Third Platoon, Company C, 2d Force Recon passed through the engineers at the breach in their fast-moving, heavily armed Infantry-Fast-Attack-Vehicles (IFAV) and led Task Force Tarawa to war. At first light, 3d Platoon, A Company, 2d Force Reconnaissance Battalion moved through the berms. Eddie Ray's LAR battalion followed Recon through the breach. Once inside Iraq, the reconnaissance units fanned out in their IFAVs and LAVs to screen ahead of the main body.

Then, after a night of watching the Army fire MLRS salvos into Iraq, Task Force Tarawa crossed the border and maneuvered cross-country in zone toward Phase Line (PL) Queensland. Natonski's first objective would be to secure Jalibah Airfield.

Bailey's 2d Marines led the main body with Grabowski's Team Tank, Team Mech, Alpha, and Charlie companies. The Timberwolves' log train followed closely behind Grabowski's maneuver units. Colonel Starnes' artillery battalion, 1/10, and RCT-2's headquarters were next in the order of march. Colonel Bailey wanted his big guns up front so that they could quickly support the Timberwolves if they ran into trouble. Bailey's modern-day mechanized legion was rounded out with his two motorized battalions. Mortenson's 2/8 and Dunahoe's 3/2 Marines were tucked in behind the artillery at the rear of the formation.

Task Force Tarawa's movement was slow. The Army got the road, and the Marines were forced to move cross-country on their planned two-day journey to Jalibah. The first night, they would stop at PL Outback, near the Al Luhays oil field. The Marines would then move to Jalibah after a short night's stop to rest and refuel.

Task Force Tarawa's Marines broke down the forward command post at 1113, packed up the equipment, and headed for Phase Line Queensland.

1ST BATTALION, 2D MARINES: THE TIMBERWOLVES

At 0500, 1/2 staged in AA Hawkins in two columns, in preparation for movement north through Task Force Tarawa's assigned breach lanes (Casey and Ginger). The Timberwolves advanced into Iraq with Captain Gregory Grimwald's LAR company and one of Grabowski's CAAT sections in the lead. Lieutenant Brian Letendre's CAAT 2 HMMWVs scrambled fifteen to twenty kilometers ahead of the battalion to conduct route reconnaissance and link up with Eddie Ray's LAR. Staff Sergeant Troy Schielein's CAAT 1 provided security for the main body.

The CAAT platoon was split into two eight-vehicle sections, CAAT 1 and CAAT 2. The vehicles traveled in pairs—one machine gun vehicle and

Task Force Tarawa's route paralleled the 507th's route

one anti-tank vehicle. CAAT's eight pairs provided a highly mobile punch for the Marine infantry. In addition to CAAT, the battalion's weapons company also contained eight 81mm mortar tubes in the mortar platoon. Each mortar team traveled in its own HMMWV. Wherever Grabowski went, his eight mortar teams were not far away.

As they closed on the border, Major Peeples lost his first tank to mechanical problems. Staff Sergeant Jeffrey Filipkowski was forced to stay behind with his 3d Platoon tank. "Flip," as his friends called him, immediately started looking for help to repair his tank. He had been one of only three Marines from the permanent I and I staff at Fort Knox to volunteer to go to war with the reserve tankers. Now, it seemed as if he would miss the war if he did not get his tank repaired. Sitting on his crippled tank, Filipkowski watched as the Timberwolves passed and slowly disappeared into the desert.

HML/A-269: THE GUNRUNNERS

On the morning of March 21st, the Marines got the "snakes" out. Colonel Thacker's Cobras launched from their ship and flew to Joe Foss Field. From Joe Foss, the Gunrunners fanned out along the Iraqi frontier. The Cobra pilots were not given specific missions, so they roamed the front line like cops on patrol. The first section out was led by Major Craig Streeter. Lieutenant Steve Faehr was Streeter's copilot/gunner. There were two other Cobras flying with Streeter. Captain Brian Bruggeman and Lieutenant John Parker were in one of the Snakes, and Captain Matt Schenberger and Lieutenant Travis Richie were in the other.

507TH MAINTENANCE COMPANY

At 0700 on March 21st, the 507th departed AP Dawson, which was located just south of the Iraqi border. They crossed over into Iraq around 1000 and continued across the bumpy desert. As soon as they left Kuwait, Grubb's truck started spewing oil out of its tail pipe. Knowing this couldn't be good, Grubb wondered how much longer his truck would last.

Progress was slow, moving cross-country, in what a Desert Storm Army colonel had called "no shit desert."[1] They traveled only thirty-five kilometers in four hours, arriving at AP Bull at noon. Again, Captain King's men and women tried to get some rest, knowing that they would be up all night again.

1ST BATTALION, 2D MARINES: THE TIMBERWOLVES

Lead elements of Rick Grabowski's First Battalion followed the Recon Marines into Iraq at 1230. They moved through the Kuwaiti berm, then

---

1 Richard Lowry, *The Gulf War Chronicles* (New York: iUniverse, 2003).

across the ten-kilometer-deep demilitarized zone that had been established by General Norman Schwarzkopf when Operation Desert Storm had ended. Once across the no-man's-land, the Marines passed through breaches in the Iraqi berm at 1630. Grabowski had set the order of movement. Major Peeples' Team Tank and a CAAT section led the battalion. Colonel Grabowski followed closely behind with the battalion's Alpha Command Group and his 81mm mortar platoon. Team Mech, Alpha Company, and Charlie Company comprised the main body of the formation, followed by Major Tuggle's Bravo Command Group and the Timberwolves' logistic train.

REGIMENTAL COMBAT TEAM-2

Colonel Starnes' artillerymen of the 1st Battalion, 10th Marines followed the Timberwolves out into the Iraqi wasteland in their seven-ton trucks, towing their 155mm howitzers. Starnes' Marines traveled in a battalion wedge kicking up a huge rolling dust cloud as they moved deeper into the Iraqi desert.

RCT-2's headquarters convoy was moving through the Kuwaiti berm by mid-afternoon, escorted by the remaining elements of A Company, 2d Force Recon Battalion. Colonel Bailey moved into Iraq with his regimental command group. Desert stretched out to the horizon in all directions, as they rolled through the scene of Schwarzkopf's defeat of Saddam's Republican Guard over a decade earlier. Every once in awhile, the Marines would encounter the burned-out hulk of an Iraqi tank, an occasional group of goatherders, little shacks, or a couple of kids here and there. The 2d Marine Regiment rolled north all afternoon across a seemingly never-ending sea of sand.

Colonel Dunahoe's Marines were not as heavily armed as Grabowski's 1st Battalion. They did not have any amphibious assault vehicles or M1 tanks. Dunahoe's Marines rode in seven-ton trucks crossing the Line of Departure (LD) with their CAAT section in the lead. Kilo Company and the 81mm mortar platoon followed CAAT. Lima Company, the main command post and India Company made up the Betio Bastards' main body, followed by the battalion's field trains. Finally, the remaining CAAT section took up the rear of the formation. Dunahoe's Marines rode fifteen per truck, three in the cab and a dozen in the sandbag-lined bed with, food, water, and ammo.

The sandbags had been laid in the bed to protect the Marines against land mines and small arms fire.

America's Battalion followed 3/2 in their seven-ton trucks and HMMWVs. It was a bumpy, boring ride through the Iraqi wasteland. The young Marines riding in the back of the trucks tried everything they could to relieve the boredom. They each had their turn scanning the horizon, watching for any sign of trouble, with their weapons at the ready. When they weren't on guard, some listened to CD players they had brought along or fought over who would have the next turn on the Game Boy. Others tried to sleep, but the practical joker of the group would inevitably stick a wet finger in his ear.

During the trip, Kerry Sanders filed his first live report from Iraq, using his satellite telephone. Kerry interviewed some of the young Marines of Echo Company as they bounced sixty miles across the desert in the back of their truck. Sebastian Rich was with Kerry, filming for later broadcast. Kerry moved among the Marines in the crowded bed of the truck, asking them where they were from and what they were feeling.

There was only a wisp of a breeze in the desert, and the dust cloud from the Marine convoy could be seen for kilometers. It wasn't so bad for the Marines in the front of the column, but the Marines in the rear were engulfed in a continuous gritty, tan cloud. They were hot and covered in dust, with some wearing their goggles. Outside the trucks, a flat, barren landscape stretched to the horizon. By the time they reached al Luhays, all of the Marines were hot, grimy, and exhausted. It had been a horrid trip.

The regiment reached PL Outback at dusk; they had penetrated fifty kilometers into Iraq. Bailey's Marines spent most of the night refueling, replenishing their food and water, and trying to catch a few hours of sleep in preparation for the next day's move to Jalibah.

1ST BATTALION, 2D MARINES
THE TIMBERWOLVES

Gunny Jason Doran's primary job was battalion FAC.[2] As the FAC, he needed to ride in the battalion's Bravo command AMTRAC with Lieutenant

---

2 Forward air controller.

Barnhart, the Bravo Command FiST leader. He rode most of the day in the track, but none of his radios were working. Finally, Doran asked if he could get out and ride in his HMMWV. Everyone in the cramped compartment welcomed the opportunity to have more room, so Gunny Doran was granted permission to ride in the Mystery Machine. He returned to his high-back HMMWV, which had been moving up and down the battalion column ferrying needed food, water, batteries, and gasoline to the forward units.

As the Timberwolves moved across the Iraqi wasteland, Doran, Day, and Doc Sabilla traveled more than twice the distance of the rest of the battalion. Doran didn't mind, because this gave him the opportunity to get to the front and the action, should the battalion run into somebody who wanted to fight. As the trio roamed up and down the column, they would take turns playing music. Doran played rock, Day, country, and Sabilla played Latin music.

Grabowski and the battalion staff knew that Gunny Doran would race to the action and be there with all of the additional supplies the combat troops would need. Doran, Day, and Sabilla ranged up and down the convoy all day long. They were like a mobile 7-Eleven. They would stop at each platoon and ask if the Marines needed any additional water, MREs, or fuel. Doran would find someone he knew at each stop. They would talk for a few minutes, and then Doran's supply wagon would move on.

After a couple of days, Staff Sergeant Cantu had had enough of AM-TRACs. The trip was hot and miserable, and there was virtually nothing to look at in the Iraqi desert. Every once in awhile, Cantu would see a goat-herder or a nomad roaming outside a little shack. It seemed that every ten minutes there was another MOPP alert. The worst thing was not knowing what was going on and not being aware of the big picture.

Cantu was one of the lucky Marines. The majority of Grabowski's Marines were riding in sweltering metal boxes, in the track's troop compartment. The upper hatches were closed in case of artillery barrage, or worse yet, chemical attack. There was no way to look outside, so the infantrymen rode for hours on end in the enclosed troop compartments. Their only break from the monotony were the constant MOPP alerts.

Day, Doc, and Doran spent the evening resupplying the various units in the battalion. They made a stop at Schielein's CAAT section, and then they moved on to Lieutenant Clayton's 81mm mortar platoon. While they were with the mortar guys, Doran asked Clayton, "Can I travel with you?"[3] Clayton jumped at the chance to have the Mystery Machine and all the extra supplies they carried traveling with his unit. So they decided that Doran, Doc, and Day would travel behind Clayton's dozen Humvees the next day.

HMM-162 THE GOLDEN EAGLES

On the morning of March 21st, Garcia was relieved by a second group of CH-46s from HMM-162. They were commanded by the squadron XO, Lieutenant Colonel Jose Vazquez. Once relieved, Garcia and his crews returned to the *Saipan*. Everyone on Garcia's helicopter was disappointed that they were about to miss the kickoff of the ground war, except Doc Gloria. As a veteran of Afghanistan, Gloria knew that not only would there be plenty of action to go around, he knew that there would be more action than anyone could want. Once Garcia had reported back to the ship, the squadron command decided that a seventy-two-hour rotation was too long, so they shortened the rotation to twenty-four hours. Garcia and his crew would get their chance after all.

507TH MAINTENANCE COMPANY

At 1800, the 507th departed Bull with the 3d FSB.[4] Their next stop would be at Lizard, which was about eighty kilometers to the northwest. Eighty kilometers is not far unless there are no roads. This leg of their journey would be another off-road jaunt across a ruddy, rolling wasteland. As they crossed the Iraqi desert in darkness, some of the heavier vehicles began to bog down in the soft sand, some broke down, and others had tires go flat. Some drivers became confused and disoriented in the Iraqi night. The Army convoys started to break up. Captain King was starting to fall behind schedule, so he split the company in two and ordered his 1st sergeant to stay behind with

---

3 Ibid. Doran.

4 Field support battalion.

the disabled vehicles. King pressed forward into the black night with the rest of the company.

Sergeant Dowdy stayed behind with the tow trucks and a contingent of soldiers to work at extracting the mired vehicles and to try and repair the ones that had broken down. One of the soldiers to stay behind was Sergeant Donald Walters. Walters was thirty-three, blond, and slim. Along with Shoshana Johnson, he was one of the company's cooks, but his police training and previous military service made him one of the few experienced soldiers in the company.

The small group left in the middle of the Iraqi desert was a cross section of American society. There were blacks, Hispanics, Southerners, Northerners, teenagers, parents, and an American Indian. They hailed from the inner cities, suburbia, the back hills of rural America, and the wide-open plains. Corporal Damien Luten, a stocky twenty-four-year old, was a religious man who joined the Army and had become a supply clerk. Damien was a native of Indianapolis Indiana; Sergeant Matthew Rose was Luten's boss and the company's supply sergeant. He, too, was a religious man and lived to serve others. Back at home, he spent his spare time as a volunteer fireman and paramedic. However, Rose didn't have much spare time, since over the years, he and his wife, Debbie, had been blessed with six children.

Jessica Lynch, another supply clerk, had started the journey across the Arabian Desert with Sergeant Rose. Their truck was one of the early casualties of the trek. Fortunately, the 507th had run across a ten-ton wrecker driven by Private First Class Edward Anguiano and Sergeant George Buggs. Buggs and Anguiano had become separated from their 3d Forward Support Battalion convoy. First Sergeant Dowdy convinced them to stay with his small convoy. So Buggs and Anguiano continued to help 1st Sergeant Dowdy throughout the night. Then they took Sergeant Rose's crippled truck in tow and tagged along with the 507th. Lynch was picked up by Dowdy and Lori Piestewa, and Rose hitched a ride with Corporal Carista.

Dowdy had a diverse group of soldiers working in his small group that had been left behind. Curtis Campbell, a stocky, Jamaican supply sergeant from New York City, rode in one of the flatbeds carrying Patriot missile repair parts, and his friend from Miami, Staff Sergeant Tarik Jackson, rode in one of the company's Humvees. Army Specialist (SPC) James M. Kiehl, twenty-two, was a computer specialist from Comfort, Texas, whose wife, Jill, was pregnant with their first child. Kiehl was a friendly guy who always was looking to help his fellow soldiers. Everybody liked Kiehl. Sergeant Joel

Petrik had been in infantry for most of his Army career. Petrik had planned to get out of the Army, but he wanted to learn a trade before he left. So, he had left the infantry and had become a radio repair technician. Once he finished his training, he had been reassigned and was new to the 507th. Brandon Sloan was a nineteen-year-old private from Cleveland, Ohio. He had withdrawn from high school and joined the Army to better himself.

Dowdy's men and women piled their rifles in the desert sand and worked all night extricating mired vehicles, repairing broken-down trucks and shepherding stragglers of the 10,000-vehicle Army convoy. While the others worked, Grubb and Elliot drove their fuel truck off to rendezvous with a larger fuel transport so they could refill the smaller truck. The 507th was now running low on gasoline. When Grubb finally found the larger refueler, it was stuck in the sand and he couldn't get within fifty feet of the trapped vehicle. Grubb and Elliot had to return to their comrades with a nearly empty fuel truck.

1ST BATTALION, 2D MARINES: THE TIMBERWOLVES

As soon as they stopped, Whidden and the other maintenance Marines started working on their tanks. M1 tanks give a whole new meaning to the term "high maintenance." Eight man-hours of work are required for every hour each tank is in the field. Refueling operations take up much of that time, but there is never a shortage of broken parts that need attention.

After Alpha Company of 8th Tanks parked in a coil for the night, they began the process of refueling and maintenance. Each tank had to move from its position in the defensive coil to the center of the formation where the fuel trucks were safely parked. Safety procedures require the tank commander to walk ahead of his tank when they are moving through a bivouac area at night. One of Major Peeples' tank commanders, instead of walking ahead, rode in the tank as he moved his seventy-ton vehicle to the refueling point.

In the field, all Marines must dig fighting positions when they stop for any amount of time. Lance Corporal Travis Eichelberger, one of Bravo Company's Marines, attached to Team Tank, had carved a small, comfortable, depression in the Iraqi sand and gone to sleep. He had not been asleep long when the unguided tank rolled over the top of his hole. His fighting position saved his life. He was just deep enough in the ground that the tank treads did not crush him like a coke can on the freeway.

Miraculously, he was still alive, but he was paralyzed from the chest down. Unable to move he tried dragging himself free with his hands. Eichelberger had suffered a crushed pelvis, shredded internal organs and legs that were swollen to twice their normal size. Marines ran to his aid and quickly called for a cas-evac. Lieutenant Colonel Jose Vazquez's CH-46s came to Eichelberger's rescue. They flew in and landed in the dark of night and Eichelberger was loaded into the back of the airborne ambulance and rushed to the medical attention that would save his life.

During that same night, Captain Cubas lost his second tank to mechanical problems. Third Platoon was now down to two tanks. Not wanting to leave a tank behind, Major Peeples had the broken tank taken in tow by one of his M88 tank retrievers, and Cubas continued on with Staff Sergeant Kamper as his lone wingman. Staff Sergeant Filipkowski had managed to get his tank repaired, but he was many, many hours behind the Timberwolves. But Filipkowski pressed forward. He moved across the Iraqi desert with his lone tank, trying to catch up to his unit.

Alpha, Bravo, and Charlie companies had only rested for four hours. Before sunrise, they loaded back into their cramped AAVs and prepared to continue their movement toward An Nasiriyah. At 0600 on March 22nd, the Timberwolves resumed their movement in a two-column, approach march formation with Team Tank leading the battalion west along Route 8.

These Marines had been traveling across some of the most desolate terrain on earth for nearly three days. They had moved all day, and many did not get the opportunity to sleep at night. The AAV Marines and tankers spent most nights refueling and repairing their vehicles, and commanders attended planning sessions and meetings. Some of the Marines stood security watches, while nerves kept other Marines awake.

507TH MAINTENANCE COMPANY

After moving all night, King's first group of vehicles arrived at Lizard on schedule, at about 0530 the next morning. Lizard was nothing more than a patch of sand in the middle of an ancient desert. The 507th was to move out

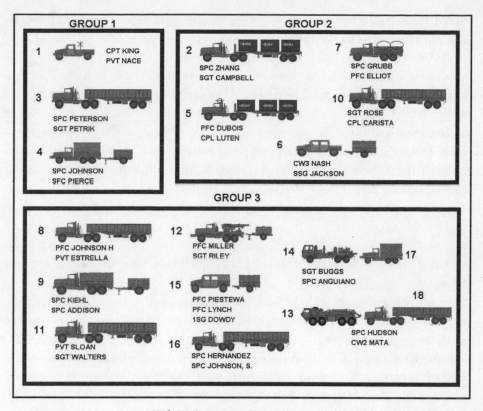

507th Maintenance Company—Serial 2

on its next leg of the journey to Rams at 1400, but Sergeant Dowdy had not yet arrived with the remaining vehicles of King's company. King sent his executive officer, 1st Lieutenant Jeff Shearin, forward with the first "serial" while he waited for Dowdy to arrive. At 1400, Shearin departed on schedule with seventeen vehicles and thirty-two soldiers.

After working all night and driving most of the day, Dowdy and the others finally arrived at Lizard at 1600. They rested for three short hours before Captain King, who had ample opportunity to rest during his fourteen hours at Lizard, ordered the remaining eighteen vehicles of the 507th, with thirty-three soldiers, forward at 1930.

This was the second night in a row that these weary soldiers would have to drive through the Iraqi desert. The men and women of the 507th spelled each other often so that each could try to get some sleep, but fatigue was starting to set in. As soon as Grubb closed his eyes, he would be asleep.

1ST BATTALION, 10TH MARINES

Colonel Starnes' artillerymen received their first fire mission on the afternoon of March 22nd. They were getting repeated hits on their counter battery radar, indicating that the enemy was shooting mortars at the brigade's lead elements. When the battalion engaged the target, the enemy shooting stopped, and forty-two Iraqi soldiers came out to surrender.

HML/A-269: THE GUNRUNNERS

Also on March 22nd, HML/A-269 Cobras roamed throughout southern Iraq. They had no particular orders other than to go out and find the fight. So they crisscrossed southern Iraq, looking for work. There was some action out to the east, near Basrah, but 1st Marine Division was encountering very little resistance in Iraq's oil fields. There were only two fiery geysers spewing smoke and flames into the blue sky. General Mattis had already started shifting his force to the west.

Some Cobras flew out across the barren desert ahead of Task Force Tarawa, but all they found were sand and camels. After a day of ranging throughout the Iraqi desert and looking for work, two HML/A-269 Cobras landed at Jalibah and the crews settled in for the night. Captains Bruggeman and Schenberger, and lieutenants Richie and Parker parked their Cobras, broke out their sleeping bags, and slept through the night as Task Force Tarawa and the 507th Maintenance Company drew closer to Nasiriyah.

TASK FORCE TARAWA

Elements of 2d LAR arrived at the cloverleaf intersection of Highway 7 and Highway 1 first and set their screen to protect the 1st Marine Division in the grassy area east and south of the intersection. Major Peeples and his tanks arrived at the cloverleaf at 1700. The team immediately established a block-ing position to augment Eddie Ray's defenses.

Iraq's Highway 1 was a brand-new, modern-day, six-lane freeway. It was so new that it was still under construction at the Euphrates river crossing. The highway crossed a dusty two-lane road that came out of the desert in the south and headed north toward An Nasiriyah. A modern cloverleaf intersection, with on- and off-ramps, connected the older Highway 7 with the newer Highway 1.

Task Force Tarawa linked up with 2d LAR on the western flank. The Barbarians held in position for several hours to allow RCT-5 and RCT-7 to pass to the west on their way to Highway 1's Euphrates River bridge. After they passed, 2d LAR moved up behind Task Force Tarawa in order to be in position to lead Colonel Dowdy's RCT-1 across Nasiriyah's eastern bridges. Colonel Dowdy was an amiable commander, well liked by his men and re-spected by his bosses. As commander of one of Mattis's regiments, he was surely on his way to the first star on his collar.

General Natonski recalled, "On the evening of the twenty-second, we were told to execute the relief-in-place (RIP), and I went up forward in my LAV, accompanied by force recon and some of the Task Force Tarawa staff riding in a seven-ton truck." Brigadier General Natonski and Task Force Tarawa's forward command element moved up Highway 1 through a glut of Army supply vehicles to Tallil Airfield. He wanted to meet face-to-face with Colonel Allen to coordinate the RIP with the 3rd Brigade combat team.

Not far from Tallil Airbase, an RPG roared across the road. It appeared that the Army was fighting a small skirmish with Iraqis who had attempted to ambush the American convoy from an overpass. Natonski ordered his ve-hicles to blow through the fight and continue north.

The general arrived at the 3rd Infantry Division's secondary Tactical Operations Center (TOC-B), co-located with the 3rd Brigade's headquar-ters, in the early evening. When Natonski met with Allen, he was informed that the Army had not bothered to move north on Highway 7, and that they had not cleared the southern end of An Nasiriyah as had been planned. In-stead, 3rd Infantry had raced up Highway 1 to the Euphrates River. In the process, they had taken Tallil Airfield. Then, the division turned left on Highway 8 and continued its charge to the west. Allen left a small com-pany/team to establish a blocking position at the Highway 1 bridge and the intersection of highways 1 and 8. The division and brigade CPs then moved into Tallil along with Army artillery batteries.

While Natonski and Allen were meeting, Task Force Tarawa fires officer, Army Lieutenant Colonel Glen Harp, met with his counterpart from the 3rd Brigade. Harp was told that there were possible enemy mortars in the city and that the Army had heard nothing about capitulation from the 11th ID. He went on to say that the Iraqis were still fighting using ambush techniques. The fire support officer closed with the statement that the 3rd Brigade combat team had no intention of going into the city, getting the eastern bridges or seizing their Objective Liberty.

Natonski and Allen coordinated the upcoming relief-in-place, which was to commence at 0430 the next morning. Then, Task Force Tarawa's commander climbed back into his personal LAV for the long drive back to his main command center at PL Queensland. As he was moving back, Natonski received new orders. In addition to relieving the Third Infantry Division at the Highway 1 bridge, Task Force Tarawa was ordered to seize both of the Highway 7 bridges on the eastern side of An Nasiriyah. They were directed to commence the operation no later than 230400Z (0700 Local) and have the bridges secured by 230700Z (1000 Local).

As the invasion unfolded, it had become evident to the MEF commanders that the 1st Marine Division could leave the southern oil fields and make their charge to Baghdad. RCT-5 and RCT-7 were ordered to proceed west on Highway 1 and to move across the Euphrates River ahead of schedule. The Marine commanders were worried about the condition of Highway 1 north of the Euphrates River and the unfinished Highway 1 bridge. So, Conway decided that he would like to develop a second route north. He reasoned that if Saddam were to order a WMD attack on the advancing Marines (or any attack for that matter), it would be much better to have the 1st Marine Division advancing along two separate corridors.

Route 7 was the logical choice for the second line of advance, and Task Force Tarawa was the right unit to secure the route. General Natonski was at the outskirts of An Nasiriyah, and his men had already planned for this operation. Everyone was convinced that the Iraqis in and around the city would capitulate, or, at the worst, shoot one or two shots and then drop their weapons. General Conway ordered Task Force Tarawa to move in and secure the eastern bridges. Colonel Dowdy was ordered to move RCT-1 up behind RCT-2 and then move north through An Nasiriyah, on Highway 7. The 1st Marine Division would then move toward Baghdad in a two-prong attack.

REGIMENTAL COMBAT TEAM-2

Colonel Bailey set up his headquarters just north of Jalibah Airfield on Highway 1, about thirty-five kilometers southeast of An Nasiriyah. Just as they were settling in for the night, Bailey received a radio message. He was ordered to come to the MEB headquarters for an orders briefing—Task Force Tarawa's orders had changed. At 1900, Colonel Bailey, his S3, Gunner, and sergeant major jumped into Bailey's Humvee and drove down to Task Force Tarawa's headquarters near Jalibah.

Bailey's operations officer, Major Andy Kennedy, was an amiable man who Bailey thought to be the best tactician in the Marine Corps. He was highly regarded by his peers and superiors and nearly worshiped by his men.

TASK FORCE TARAWA

Task Force Tarawa forward command center was up and operational at its new position near PL Queensland just as General Natonski returned from his meeting with the Army. By 2030, an orders group was convened at Task Force Tarawa to act on their new orders to secure the eastern bridges.

Natonski knew from his recent experience of fighting traffic all the way up Highway 1 that it would be very difficult for Dunahoe to move his battalion up the highway through the massive backup of Army supply vehicles, and get to the relief by 0430. Natonski ordered Reilly's recon Marines to return to the Highway 1 bridge.

Bailey and Kennedy arrived at the briefing, and they were told that the location of the RIP had changed and that the time had been set for 0430. They were also told that Reilly's recon Marines had been sent west. Knowing that there was heavy traffic on Highway 1, Bailey turned to Kennedy and said, "This could work for us."

Then they were told to seize the eastern bridges, and that movement into Nasiriyah should begin no later than 0700. Bailey had some questions. He asked the MEB staff, "What is the intel? Is there any intel?" The MEB staff had no current intelligence on the situation in An Nasiriyah. They had aerial photos that had been taken in February, but Bailey's staff already had those. They had one piece of information. Someone who had had eyes-on Nasiriyah had reported, "They are fishing from the bridges."

Bailey was perplexed. He was being asked to move directly into an "attack" on a mission that had only moments ago been a "be prepared" mission. Bailey commented later, "They were skipping a whole step in the middle."[5] RCT-2 had been driving all day, and the plan had been to consolidate the defense of Highway 1, resupply and rest on March 23rd.

"Can I get some fuel?" Bailey's vehicles needed to refuel, but the regiment had not received its entire allotment. Bailey ended his requests with, "Is there a possibility of getting the time line pushed back?" He was told there would be no delay; his Marines would have to press forward on adrenaline. At 2100, Bailey walked out of the MEB headquarters.

The MEF commanders realized that they needed to create a second route through An Nasiriyah, and that the eastern bridges needed to be secured before the Iraqis could blow them up. There was also a concern that Saddam would strike the Marines with WMD as they backed up south of the Euphrates River. There would be no pause. Bailey had to press forward.

Andy Kennedy immediately told Bailey, "We'll do a verbal order over the radio to give the battalions maximum time to prepare." Dunahoe was immediately ordered to the western bridge. Grabowski and Starnes were ordered to move forward toward An Nasiriyah and to arrive at the LD, the 20th Northing, no later than 0700. Royal Mortenson was ordered to move up behind the Timberwolves and follow in trace.

REGIMENTAL COMBAT TEAM-2

Bailey returned to his command post to set the execution of his new orders into motion. Once the verbal orders had been issued, Bailey left the details of the written order and its orchestration to the regiment's executive officer, Lieutenant Colonel John O'Rourke, and his headquarters staff. Then Bailey and Kennedy took off for the western bridge with Captain Grimwald's Charlie Company of 2d LAR. Bailey's battalion commanders were never told that the attack to seize the bridges was to commence at 0700 and that the eastern bridges were to be secured by 1000.

Bailey and Kennedy drove to the Highway 1 bridge in a convoy of thirty light armored vehicles and Humvees for the RIP. They believed that

---

5 Colonel Baileys comments taken from Reid Bonadona interview with Colonel Bailey.

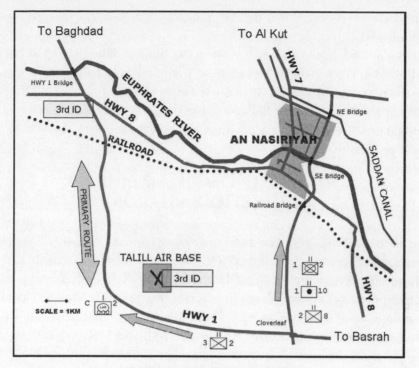

Midnight—22/23 March, 2003

there would be enough time to return to Colonel Grabowski's position along Highway 7 before the start of the secondary mission at 0700. Unfortunately, just like Natonski had done, Bailey and Kennedy ran into the massive traffic jam on Highway 1. "There were thousands and thousands of vehicles on the road." The traffic was so bad that Bailey's command element and LAR were forced to drive north against traffic in the southbound lanes.

O'Rourke was left in charge at RCT-2 headquarters. Viking 6 had already issued a verbal order to execute the BP mission. By 2200, Grabowski's Timberwolves were ordered to commence movement toward Nasiriyah and to arrive at the 20th Northing grid line no later than 0700. Without telling the battalion commanders the rationale, Bailey's staff began moving the battalions into attack position. Brent Dunahoe, Royal Mortenson, and Glenn Starnes did not get word that RCT-2 had been ordered to seize the eastern bridges in An Nasiriyah. They all still believed that their mission was to defend Highway 1. Grabowski and Sosa were also not told that the "execute" order had been issued or that the Army had decided not to send troops north on Highway 7.

As Colonel Bailey headed west to coordinate the RIP, Grabowski, Starnes, and Mortenson's Marines took their last opportunity to get a couple of hours of rest before their push north toward An Nasiriyah. There would be no rest for the Betio Bastards as they moved onto Highway 1, into the massive traffic jam, and headed for the Highway 1 river crossing.

3D BATTALION, 2D MARINES: THE BETIO BASTARDS

The Betio Bastards received their movement order at 2300. They were ordered to relieve the 3rd Infantry Division in place and establish a blocking position oriented east along Highway 8 at the western bridge. They were to prevent the enemy from interfering with the 1st Marine Division's movement up Highway 1. Once Dunahoe secured the crossing, RCT-5 would lead the charge north across the Euphrates River, followed by RCT-7.

As Dunahoe moved his battalion northwest along Highway 1 from Jalibah to the Euphrates River bridge, he encountered the same massive traffic jam as Natonski and Bailey had negotiated earlier. Army supply vehicles clogged the road. Some of the Army supply units were parked along both sides of the road; their occupants getting much-needed sleep in their darkened vehicles. Dunahoe and his men were supposed to have priority on the road. After all, they were the ones who were tasked with protecting the massive convoy at the Euphrates River crossing.

TASK FORCE TARAWA

Now that Natonski had been issued orders to clear a route through Nasiriyah, Special Forces Operational Detachment B was chopped to Task Force Tarawa. The B team was comprised of three A teams, one SEAL team, and an AC-130 Spectre gunship. The SEAL team was operating southeast of An Nasiriyah, and the three Green Beret teams had been operating in and around An Nasiriyah for several days.

One of the A teams, ODA-533, had been dropped into the area several days before the start of the ground war. One of its missions was to check out the Highway 1–Euphrates River bridge.[6] American commanders and planners had been watching the bridge for weeks through satellite surveillance. Everyone knew that the bridge was under construction. They hoped that the Iraqi work crews would progress enough with the work that the bridge would be drivable. ODA-533 was sent in to make a final check of the bridge before the Marines approached. They were also there to reconnoiter the Iraqi defenses at the crossing.

Another Army A team was temporarily attached to Colonel Reilly's recon unit. One of the soldiers, Sergeant First Class Thomas Smith, was a career soldier who had started his military service in the Marine Corps. As a young Marine, Sergeant First Class Smith had served with a young lieutenant, Richard Natonski in Vietnam. Reilly took two of his own platoons and the Army SF unit northwest to the Highway 1 bridge. He, also, fought traffic most of the way. Finally, his small unit approached the bridge around 0430, mired in a glut of Army vehicles. Lieutenant Colonel Reilly checked in on his SATCOM. After a few minutes, he managed to contact Colonel Dan Allen of the 3rd BCT. He reported to the colonel that he was on the highway near the bridge. Colonel Allen replied that he, too, was in the line of vehicles. Colonel Allen inquired, "What kind of vehicles are you in?" Reilly immediately replied over the satellite link that his men were in Marine recon IFAVs. He went on to describe his and the Army's Special Forces vehicles. "We are parked right behind you."[7] Allen announced.

Reilly climbed out of his vehicle and reported to Colonel Allen for the relief-in-place. Reilly's recon Marines spread out to begin the relief of the soldiers who were guarding the bridge and the intersection. Within minutes, Charlie Company of 2d LAR arrived at the bridge. LAR, the two recon platoons and an Army SF[8] unit relieved the soldiers defending the bridge. Bravo Company of 3-69 Armor, and 3rd Brigade continued its move west. Once the Marines had taken over, the Army trains followed in trace of the combat

---

6 Linda Robinson *Masters of Chaos* (New York: Public Affairs, 2004).

7 Personal interview with Lieutenant Colonel Reilly.

8 Special Forces.

unit west on Highway 8. The soldiers had not crossed the Euphrates. The route up Highway 1 was reserved for the Marines of the First Marine Division. Charlie Company, 2d LAR moved up and secured the Route 1 bridge, while the recon Marines probed north of the river trying to find an alternate path over to Route 7.

Until Natonski received his new orders, the Marines of Task Force Tarawa had been moving into Iraq behind the Army's 3rd Infantry Division. They did not have any battle space of their own. They were sandwiched between the 3rd ID and the 1st Marine Division. But now, the 3rd ID had moved west along the southern bank of the Euphrates River, leaving Task Force Tarawa facing the enemy in An Nasiriyah. I MEF designated Natonski's Marines as the main effort at 0600, and their mission was to secure both routes across the Euphrates River.

507TH MAINTENANCE COMPANY

Meanwhile, Captain King and his convoy were slowly moving through the blackened desert wasteland south of Highway 1, trying to get to the paved road. They struggled forward across the barren countryside. If they could find a road, they would be able to pick up the pace. They could see the lights of the convoy in the distance. They were so close to being back on track, yet still so far away. King and his soldiers continued to press forward through the night.

REGIMENTAL COMBAT TEAM-2

Bailey never contemplated that he would have to secure the western Highway 1 bridge and seize the eastern bridges simultaneously. His regiment was split. Nearly one-third of his combat strength was at the western crossing. Bailey would have to move into An Nasiriyah with his mechanized 1st Battalion supported by Colonel Mortenson's motorized infantry. Two Marine infantry battalions and twelve M1 tanks would be hard-pressed to secure ten kilometers of highway through a city of 500,000. Fortunately, little to no resistance was expected. Now, more than ever, Colonel Bailey did not want his Marines to become engaged in a street-to-street fight within the city.

3D BATTALION, 2D MARINES:
THE BETIO BASTARDS

Dunahoe's Marines continued to have their own problems traveling on Highway 1 to the western bridge. The road was still jam-packed with a wide variety of vehicles. Some of the Army vehicles were moving, but most were stopped for the night. Highway 1 had become a giant Army parking lot.

At 0300, just northwest of Tallil Airfield, and nearly three-quarters of the way to their assigned position, an MRC-138 communications Humvee, traveling with 3/2's main command post, rear-ended a darkened Army five-ton truck that had stopped along the side of the road. The collision killed Sergeant Nicholas M. Hodson instantly.

Near the rear of the long convoy, Father Brian Waite noticed a young Marine running toward his vehicle. The Marine ran up to Waite's parked vehicle. "It's bad, Chaps! It's real bad! I need you and Doc, right now!"[9] The Marine exclaimed. Waite ran forward to the site of the accident and found a barely distinguishable HMMWV.

Hodson, a career Marine, husband, and father, had become the first Task Force Tarawa fatality of the war. The other three occupants of the vehicle, 1st Lieutenant Dustin Ferrell, Lance Corporal Eshelman, and Lance Corporal Westerlink, were all seriously injured. Ferrell had been thrown from the Humvee that was crumpled like tissue paper, and he had a dislocated leg. He had also suffered a hit to the face that knocked out half of his teeth and partially blinded him in one eye.

Major Starling raced to the scene and immediately took charge. He called for a helicopter to evacuate the casualties. The Humvee was peeled apart, and the casualties and Hodson were carefully removed. Army medics and Navy corpsmen rushed to the injured Marines' aid.

It didn't take very long for the cas-evac helicopter to arrive. The Army medics stood back to let the Marines carry their injured to the waiting air ambulance. Major Starling personally helped carry two of the Marines to the waiting aircraft. Then Hodson was carried to the helicopter and all up and down the stalled line of traffic, Marines stood with heads bowed as the helicopter carried their brothers-in-arms from the battlefield.

---

9 Brain Waite *For God and Country* (HeartSpring Media, 2005).

Once the helicopter had disappeared into the Iraqi night, Major Starling got the convoy moving again. By 0700, the battalion was halted again in the massive traffic jam along Highway 1. Dunahoe's Marines had run into the tail end of the entire 3d Infantry Division. Dunahoe was standing outside his vehicle talking with a battalion commander from the 3d ID, trying to cajole his way through the traffic. "I thought I had priority movement on this road," Dunahoe said in frustration.

The Army colonel replied unsympathetically, "Yeah, I had priority movement on this road yesterday. Look where I am now."[10]

REGIMENTAL COMBAT TEAM-2

When Colonel Bailey learned of 3/2's traffic accident and that Dunahoe would be delayed getting to the bridge, he contacted Lieutenant Colonel Reilly and asked him if he would remain at the Highway 1 bridge until 3/2 arrived. Reilly had already sent some of his Marines north of the Euphrates River to look for the enemy and to try to find a passable route back east to Highway 7. Reilly's Marines did not encounter enemy resistance, nor could they find an alternate route, so they returned to the south side of the river.

Now that he had more time at the western bridge, Reilly decided he would take a small, twelve-man recon unit east on Highway 8 to reconnoiter the western approach to the city. He wanted to get a look at what Task Force Tarawa would face inside the city.

An Nasiriyah is a surreal combination of the third and the twenty-first centuries. The city itself is made up of ancient mud-brick structures and modern-day buildings. Here is where the fertile Euphrates meets the barren Arabian Desert. Downtown Nasiriyah is only a few kilometers from the ancient ruins of Ur, the birthplace of Abraham. Ancient minarets, intricately tiled mosque domes, modern street lamps, and power poles dominate the city skyline. In this eerie urban battleground, it would be impossible to detect the source of gunfire, as reports echo back and forth through the city, bouncing from wall to wall.

---

10 Personal interview with Lieutenant Colonel Brent Dunahoe, 10/27/03.

2D BATTALION, 8TH MARINES: AMERICA'S BATTALION

Now at the rear of the regiment, Colonel Mortenson's Marines were given the job of rounding up the Iraqi prisoners who were starting to come out of the woodwork. Mortenson ordered his Fox company commander, Captain Dremann, to send a platoon out with some CAAT vehicles and round up the Iraqi stragglers. Dremann sent his 1st Platoon, led by Lieutenant Wong. They were out all night, and by dawn, they had rounded up more than sixty military-age Iraqi men. They were brought to a collection point and handed over to other Marines just in time for the battalion to move forward again. Lieutenant Wong and the Marines of 1st Platoon moved toward Nasiriyah after missing their last chance for a good night's sleep.

CHAPTER 6

Ambush Alley

We are just ordinary guys with an extraordinary job.

—MAJOR CHRISTOPHER STARLING, USMC
2d Marine Regiment—2004

THE TIMBERWOLVES

At midnight, Captain Dan Wittnam woke Lieutenant Ben Reid from his short nap. "Get ready to move,"[1] he told Reid before heading off to rouse the rest of Charlie Company. Reid quickly rose and walked quietly through his weapons platoon telling his men to mount up. By 0130, the men of the weapons platoon were in their tracks, ready to go. Then they waited. They waited for more than an hour. The Marines of Alpha and Bravo companies awoke in the dead of night and filled their fighting holes, gathered their equipment, and climbed back into their AAVs. Then they, too, waited in the darkness for their advance toward An Nasiriyah. Soon, the entire battalion had come to life in the middle of the Iraqi night.

At 0300, with their engines growling, Team Tank heaved forward, leading the Timberwolves north toward An Nasiriyah. Bravo, Alpha and Charlie companies followed closely behind Major Peeples' tanks.

---

1 Telephone interview with Lieutenant James "Ben" Reid, 7/6/04.

All of Task Force Tarawa occupied the open terrain south and east of the cloverleaf intersection of highways 1 and 7. Highway 1 (Route Jackson) was a modern-day, six-lane freeway running from Basrah to Baghdad. The smaller, two-lane Highway 7 (Route Blue) crossed Highway 1 at the cloverleaf. Peeples moved his tanks toward the intersection at the head of 1st Battalion, 2d Marines.

As the battalion drove west out of the desert and approached the cloverleaf, the Marines were amazed by what they saw. The highway was backed up with bumper-to-bumper gridlock as far as the eye could see. Thousands of Army supply vehicles carrying everything from fuel and ammunition to toilet paper and Tampax clogged the highway and the intersection. The Marines couldn't believe their eyes. Silver threads of light weaved a path through the Iraqi night, out to the horizon in the east and red threads of tail lights danced along the road to the west. The Army's lights could be seen for miles in the Iraqi night. The Marines were moving into the attack with no lights on, and here was the Army driving like they were moving up U.S. I-95 on some kind of night exercise. Major Peeples reported the massive traffic jam to his battalion commander. Grabowski immediately ordered his operations officer to come forward to help get the battalion through the gridlocked mess.

Major Sosa drove forward in his Humvee, parked along the side of the road, climbed out, and walked into the middle of the intersection to take charge like a New York City traffic cop. With an exposed palm and a few choice words, he halted the vehicles that were moving toward the cloverleaf. Once he managed to clear a lane through the intersection, he waved his Marines north. Sosa remained at his post until all of his vehicles passed. Then he relinquished control of the intersection, climbed back into his Humvee, and continued north at the tail end of the armored column.

As Gunny Doran, Day, and Doc Sabilla raced north through the night, Day's exhaustion was starting to take its toll. He made it through the cloverleaf, but just as he passed the intersection, Day hit the guardrail. The vehicle jumped up on the rail, and one of the posts came through the floorboard, almost hitting Doran. Day struggled and regained control of the Humvee, but the crash punctured one of the Mystery Machine's tires. They rolled forward for about a mile before Doran decided to stop, saying, "Shit, Day! You just made us miss the war."[2] Doran immediately got on the radio and called

---

2 Ibid. Doran.

for help. Within minutes, another gunny showed up with a spare tire. They all quickly changed the flat, and soon the Mystery Machine was back on the road. Day accelerated to make up their lost time, passing vehicles like an impatient teenager on a country road. As they raced forward, Gunny Doran nodded off into a sound sleep.

Glenn Starnes began moving his artillery toward Nasiriyah at 0430. Starnes, the artillery battalion commander, moved his unit northwest on a second route that bypassed the cloverleaf to the east of Highway 7. Major Tuggle followed in trace of the 1st Battalion, 10th Marines with the Bravo command group and the Timberwolves' log train.

Once past the cloverleaf, Grabowski's Marines paused along the side of the road, waiting for the order to move north. Grabowski wanted to ensure that the entire battalion had cleared the traffic jam before he proceeded. His armored column herringboned along both sides of the two-lane road, forming a thousand-meter metal dragon. Near the head of the dragon, Colonel Grabowski waited at his HMMWV for word from Major Sosa that the entire battalion had moved north of the intersection.

507TH MAINTENANCE COMPANY

The 507th had been ordered to move across the desert and onto Highway 1 near a small airfield at Jalibah. Coming out of the blackened desert, Captain King and his convoy found Highway 1, but they could not get on the road. The weary soldiers were forced to drive east, paralleling the highway, looking for an on-ramp. The first intersection they encountered was the junction of highways 1 and 7 (routes Jackson and Blue)—the cloverleaf. By the time King arrived at the intersection, the Timberwolves were already moving north and the Army's tactical control point (TCP) had been disbanded. At the intersection, King should have moved his convoy onto the six-lane highway (Route Jackson), but contrary to his orders, he led his vehicles up Route 7 (Route Blue). Had King turned onto Route 1, he would have immediately moved back into the safety of the massive Army supply train. As it turns out, this was his first fatal mistake. The 507th pressed forward in the darkened night, moving deeper and deeper into the jaws of death.

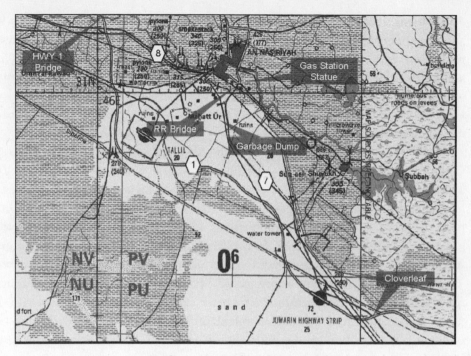

Southern Approach to An Nasiriyah

THE TIMBERWOLVES

To his amazement, Grabowski received a radio report that a small convoy was racing north on the road. Once he determined that the approaching vehicles were not his, he ordered all of his vehicles to get off the road to allow clear passage for the approaching convoy.

"Had I known who they were, I would have jumped out in the road and stopped them."[3]

The original plan had been for the Army to move a company/team north on Highway 7 to clear southern Nasiriyah and then defend in sector. Grabowski's Marines were to move north and relieve the 3rd Infantry Division's force along Highway 7. Colonel Grabowski rationalized that there must be a 3rd ID unit to his north, so the passage of these Army support vehicles did not trigger an alarm. Everything seemed to be going exactly as planned.

---

3 Telephone interview with Lieutenant Colonel Rickey Grabowski, 3/1/04.

But this was not a 3rd ID combat log train. This was Captain King and the stragglers of the 507th. King had finally reached open road, and he was pushing to catch up with the rest of his unit. The eighteen vehicles of King's serial flew past Grabowski and the Marines of the 1st Battalion. King, not stopping to speak with the Marines, pressed north. As they passed, Curtis Campbell noticed Marine tanks and tracks parked along the side of the road and casually wondered why his group was passing combat units.

Before 0600, the 1st Battalion had advanced to the 20th Northing. Grabowski was quite pleased with his men. They had been traveling for more than two days, with little or no sleep, across the Iraqi wasteland. They had moved more than a hundred miles and arrived at their objective over an hour ahead of schedule. The Timberwolves stopped and set up a defensive position awaiting their next orders. Grabowski still believed that his men were to hold a screening position at 20th Northing.

As the battalion had moved north on Highway 7, Grabowski found that his vehicles could not venture far from the hard surface road. An earlier rainstorm had made the delta marshland impassable to his heavy vehicles. Colonel Starnes rolled up the highway with his 155mm artillery pieces behind the Timberwolves. Starnes, too, could not find a suitable place along the side of the road to set up his guns, so Colonel Grabowski requested that he be allowed to move his battalion two more kilometers north to the 22nd Northing, to give Starnes' gunners some room to set up their howitzers. This would not be the last time that the 1st Battalion would have problems with the soggy Euphrates River delta.

REGIMENTAL COMBAT TEAM-2

RCT-2 headquarters moved out in the predawn hours behind the 2d Battalion, 8th Marines. They stopped south of the city, just after sunrise. RCT-2's TAC CP vehicles stopped along the side of the raised highway. It was a muddy, flood-prone terrain where tufts of brush struggled to survive on the Mars-like landscape. There they set up the regimental command post, working off the hoods of their Humvees. To the untrained eye, Colonel Bailey's command center looked like nothing more than a group of HMMWVs parked in a helter-skelter fashion along the side of the road. The multitude of whip antennae reaching into the sky indicated that these vehicles were more than just a group of lost Marines.

2D FORCE RECONNAISSANCE

Just as the sun was starting to light the early-morning sky, Reilly's small unit, traveling in five IFAVs, pushed east from the Highway 1–Euphrates River bridge with Staff sergeant Sean Disbennett's vehicle in the lead. Eleven Marines, Sergeant First Class Thomas Smith, and a single navy corpsman, Matt Stebenson, probed down Highway 8. They headed east along the southern bank of the Euphrates, toward An Nasiriyah. As they moved into the western outskirts of the city, they rolled into an industrial area. Curious Iraqi civilians watched the group move east, some even waved. The recon Marines continued forward; and, as Reilly's group neared a power plant, they noticed a building filled with Iraqis in black garb. They cautiously proceeded past the power plant, and soon they were at the edge of the city.

Something seemed not quite right. Civilians were no longer out in the open. Everything was quiet, and the building by the power plant still bothered Colonel Reilly. He stopped his advance and had just decided to go no farther, when he saw enemy soldiers running across the highway, directly in front of him.

Reilly ordered his men to turn around. As the recon Marines were turning to go back west, two shots rang out. Corporal Bobby Buckley and the other Marines opened fire and engaged the enemy with their MK19s, .50-caliber machine guns, and M-4s. A hundred Iraqis were just ahead. Reilly recalled, "There were a lot of green helmets and a lot of black pajamas off to the east."[4] The enemy had set up a classic L-shaped ambush. Fortunately, one of the Iraqis had gotten an itchy trigger finger and fired at the Americans before they had moved all the way into the "kill sack" of the ambush. Missing their ambush opportunity, the enemy now had to move west to engulf the Marines. The Iraqi soldiers started to maneuver around Reilly's flanks.

Recon Marines are not supposed to stay decisively engaged for any length of time. If they encounter an enemy force, they are trained to extricate themselves from the engagement and return to report the enemy's position and strength. That's their job, so Reilly and his men withdrew. Two Iraqi vehicles started to chase the retreating Marines, but they were quickly discouraged from following with a hail of .50-caliber machine gun rounds.

Reilly and his men sped back west past the power plant. At the same spot

---

4 Personal interview with Lieutenant Colonel James Reilly, 1/13/04.

where they had noticed the black-clad Iraqis, there were now two four-foot-high berms blocking the road, with barbed wire strung around them. As the five small vehicles approached, mortar rounds began to fall and RPGs whizzed across the road. Colonel Reilly recalled, "I was scared shitless."[5]

Reilly's Marines abandoned the road and took off across the sand. They raced around the roadblock and then back up onto Highway 8. Once past the blockade, they sped back toward the Highway 1 bridge.

THE BETIO BASTARDS

Just after daylight, the Third Battalion had weaved its way through the glut of vehicles on Highway 1 and reached the far western bridge. By 0530, they were reinforcing Bailey's LAR company. Dunahoe's Marines quickly established a defense just south and east of the bridge. They moved into blocking positions straddling Highway 8, and facing east back toward An Nasiriyah. Just as they were settling into their defense, Colonel Reilly and his dozen recon Marines approached from the east. All five of his vehicles made it through the ambush, and none of Reilly's men had been injured. Reilly reported that armed Iraqis had attacked them at dawn, six kilometers east on Highway 8. Reilly quickly reported back to Task Force Tarawa that they had encountered small arms, light machine gun, and RPG fire on the western outskirts of Nasiriyah. He went on to say, "You have an enemy that's not capitulating!"[6]

507TH MAINTENANCE COMPANY

By 0600, Captain King had led his convoy up a deserted, winding highway, across a railroad overpass, and past a yellow sign displaying WELCOME in large, black, block letters below what was obviously the same message in Arabic. He led his convoy past a company of dug-in Iraqi tanks, and then through an area filled with giant oil storage tanks.[7] Dozens of large power

---

5 Ibid. Reilly.

6 Ibid. Reilly.

7 U.S. Army "Attack on the 507th Maintenance Company 23 March 2003 An Nasiriyah, Iraq—Executive Summary," (no publication date). Unless otherwise specified, the details of the ambush of the 507th are taken from the pages of the Army official report.

lines crisscrossed the road and cluttered the sky. King continued forward into the southern portion of An Nasiriyah. He passed a garbage dump and a gas station. He then drove right through a modern intersection equipped with freeway-style traffic signs, stoplights and a small guard shack built to provide shade for a traffic cop. This major intersection was adorned with a statue commemorating the Iran-Iraq War.

At this intersection, Highway 8 went off to the west, through the southern portion of An Nasiriyah. Captain King missed the large signs, missed the traffic lights, missed the statue, and the left turn onto Highway 8. Instead of heading west toward the 3rd ID and Lieutenant Colonel Reilly's recon Marines, he led his soldiers straight into Nasiriyah on Highway 7.

He continued past a manned Iraqi Army checkpoint, and then over the Euphrates River bridge. Nowhere in his orders or on his maps was there any indication that he would be crossing the Euphrates in the middle of one of Iraq's largest cities.

Iraqi pickup trucks, loaded with armed Iraqis and machine guns mounted in their beds, began shadowing the American convoy.[8] Captain King pressed on, obviously lost. He proceeded north across the Saddam Canal bridge and through the 23rd Brigade's defenses. By now, he should have been completely sure that he was lost. Yet King drove right past the 23rd Brigade's abandoned headquarters building and turned left onto Highway 16, determined to catch up with the rest of his company. Less than a mile down Highway 16, King approached another "T" intersection with Highway 7. He led the convoy past the Al-Quds' headquarters and north for more than a mile before he finally realized that he was hopelessly lost.

So, he stopped. As the convoy ground to a halt, King decided to retrace his steps back through Nasiriyah to find the correct route. Finally, realizing that he had taken his troops deep into territory that had not yet been secured, he instructed his soldiers to "lock and load" their weapons.

King then began the cumbersome task of turning the convoy around. The larger trucks and the wreckers, with other trucks in tow, needed a very

---

8 Ever since Chad's war with its North African neighbor, Libya, Japanese pickup trucks had become a popular Third-World weapons carrier. The Chad Army mounted heavy machine guns in the bed of the pickup, providing a highly maneuverable platform for the weapon. They worked so well against the Libyans that most of the Third World adopted the technique. These commercially adapted vehicles were labeled "technicals."

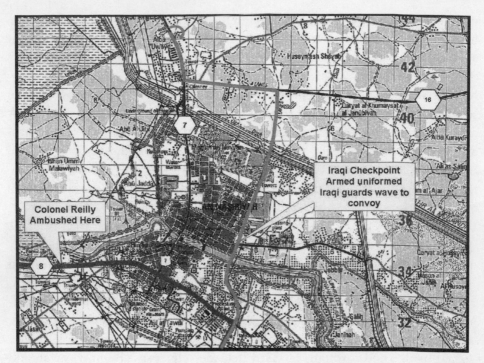

Path of the 507th Maintenance Company

large turning radius to reverse direction. This task took an inordinate amount of time. To make matters worse, Sergeant Buggs' ten-ton wrecker ran out of gas. Grubb's fuel truck was empty, so the soldiers were forced to use what gasoline was left in their five-gallon cans. Captain King's men and women nervously waited while Buggs' truck was refueled. By now, the sky was becoming light.

Unknowingly, King had stopped his soldiers and decided to turn around just in time. A large Iraqi supply area was just over the horizon. This large depot was protected by several large caliber antiaircraft guns that could have ripped King's convoy to shreds.

Finally, the 507th headed south. Grubb, exhausted from three days of no sleep, nodded off as soon as Elliot started moving. Retracing his path, Captain King turned the convoy back down Highway 16. Just as the convoy was turning (at approximately 0700), they began to receive sporadic small arms fire. Bullets whizzed overhead and hit the vehicles. A gun cracked in the distance, and a lighting bolt of pain shot from Grubb's leg to his brain, waking him instantly. The soldiers could not determine the source of the fire; the shots seemed to be coming from everywhere. The convoy immediately sped up to get away from the hot fire zone.

Near the rear of the convoy, Nash and Jackson drove into heavy enemy fire. Almost immediately, Jackson was hit, and Nash knew that they were in serious trouble. All he could see ahead were black robes. The enemy had awakened, and they were all running toward the road and shooting. Nash accelerated. Initially, he tried to swerve around the first few Iraqis, and then he just plowed through them. They were everywhere. They were in front of him, in back of him, running alongside his vehicle, and they were all shooting. Nash fumbled for his radio handset, and it fell to the floor of the Humvee.

Jackson was already down, so Nash quickly leaned over to retrieve the mic from the floor of his Humvee. More shots rang out, and his windshield exploded. Had he not bent over, he would have been killed by the burst of gunfire. Nash pushed the barrel of his M-16 through the broken windshield and fired as fast as he could while juggling the radio handset and continuing to race his vehicle east.

Captain King, leading the convoy in his HMMWV, sped forward at such a rate that the larger vehicles were unable to keep up. As the convoy raced forward, ever-increasing distances separated the beleaguered vehicles. King drove past the right-hand turn that would take his convoy back down Ambush Alley. In his panic, he continued east on Highway 16.

Not far behind, Sergeant First Class Anthony Pierce and SPC Timothy Johnson noticed that Captain King had missed the turn. Lacking a working radio, they accelerated their five-ton truck to catch up with Captain King to tell him that they knew the way back to the turn. Meanwhile, 1st Sergeant Dowdy approached the Highway 7 intersection at the tail of the fleeing convoy. Dowdy radioed ahead to tell Captain King that the convoy had missed the turn. They all needed to turn around—again.

Still under fire, the convoy continued east on Highway 16, frantically searching for a spot to turn the larger vehicles around. They continued to roll east, farther and farther from Highway 7, but there was no decent place to turn around. They pushed east for three kilometers before finally coming upon a suitable spot to turn all of the vehicles. In his small vehicle, King quickly turned around and sped west.

King briefly encountered 1st Sergeant Dowdy's Humvee as he raced back west. The two HMMWVs paused, driver to driver, and the soldiers briefly exchanged words of encouragement. "Stay straight, Nace,"[9] Dowdy said to Captain King's driver. Then, King continued his race to safety while Dowdy and the others continued east to the tail of the doomed convoy.

While attempting to make the U-turn, Sergeant Buggs' truck became stuck in soft sand. First Sergeant Dowdy raced to the disabled vehicle, and Buggs and Anguiano jumped into the back of the Humvee with Lynch. PFC Lori Piestewa sped her now-packed HMMWV away from the disabled truck, as Buggs and Anguiano returned fire with their SAW. Lynch buried her head in her knees and began to pray.

Captain King ordered Pierce to lead the convoy back to the intersection. The soldiers' situation began to rapidly deteriorate. Private Sloan and Sergeant Walters' five-ton truck was the next vehicle to break down. Still under enemy fire, PFC Miller and Sergeant Riley ground their five-ton wrecker nearly to a stop and picked up Sloan. Walters jumped from his vehicle and started laying down covering fire.

Disregarding his own safety, Walters continued to hold the Iraqis at bay as the rest of his convoy turned around and sped west. Sergeant Walters was now left alone on a dusty Iraqi highway, deep behind enemy lines. Walters fought his way south toward the Saddam Canal, killing several Iraqis before he was surrounded and captured by six Fedayeen. They were seen taking him into the Iraqi Brigade headquarters at the "T" intersection of highways 16 and 7. Sergeant Walters was definitely alive when he went into the building.

A short time later, Walters' bullet-ridden and stabbed body was carried out of the building and placed in an ambulance. The driver was ordered to take the body to the Saddam Hospital, where he was hastily buried. Some believe that intercepted Iraqi radio chatter was translated improperly and the report that went out said a blonde American fought [her] way . . .[10] This was immediately picked up and interpreted to have been Jessica Lynch's fate, since she was the only blonde female in the group. In fact, Walters was blond-haired, and he was left in a situation that could have easily turned into the Iraqi radio report. We will never really know the details of Walters' horrible ordeal. We do know that he risked his life to save his comrades and was separated from the rest of the convoy, deep in enemy territory. We

---

9 http://www.fallenheroesmemorial.com/oif/

10 Julian Coman, "The Real Hero Behind The 'Bravery' of Private Jessica," (*The Telegraph*— UK, 7/27/03). There were many reports throughout the media of Jessica's fight; this is just one.

know that he fought until he could no longer resist. Also, it is certain, Sergeant Walters was the first American lost in the Battle of An Nasiriyah. For his selfless actions, Walters was awarded the Silver Star.

The soldiers in the convoy, still under fire, reached the intersection where they needed to turn south. This time the remaining vehicles all turned to retrace their path through Nasiriyah. Captain King bolted south across the canal bridge and through the city, leaving his soldiers in the slower vehicles to fend for themselves. Lori Piestewa, 1st Sergeant Dowdy, Lynch, Buggs, and Anguiano stayed behind with the slowest vehicles.

The faster group of vehicles, led by Captain King and his driver, Private Dale Nace, sped through the city under increasing fire. Pierce and Johnson followed King south as they raced their five-ton tractor-trailer back through the city. Sergeant Joel Petrik and SPC Nicholas Peterson managed to keep their tractor-trailer going fast enough to keep up with Captain King's Humvee. The three vehicles rushed south through Ambush Alley as the Iraqis attempted to block their passage with vehicles and debris. The trucks weaved their way through the obstacles. They pressed forward over the Euphrates River bridge.

As they drove south, Petrik noticed a dump truck in the road ahead. The Iraqis had driven the truck onto the road to use as a barricade. An Iraqi officer was standing in the road, waiving for Nace and Captain King to stop. Nace accelerated, and the Iraqi dove for cover behind the barricade. Pierce and Johnson swerved around the dump truck and followed King south. By the time Petrik and Peterson had reached the roadblock, the Iraqi officer was back on his feet in the middle of the road with his pistol drawn, and he was firing at the approaching eighteen wheeler.

Petrik and Peterson returned fire with their M-16s, and the Iraqi jumped to safety again. Petrik swerved around the right side of the dump truck and momentarily off the road. Now there was an Iraqi technical directly ahead of them. Petrik jerked the wheel back to the left, and his large truck jumped back up onto the road. The gunner in the technical sprayed the passing truck with machine gun fire as Petrik raced past.

Once past the roadblock, there was a short pause in the shooting. Petrik's rearview mirror had been shot out, so he asked Peterson, "How many vehicles are in back of us?"[11]

---

11 Conversation taken from telephone interview with Sergeant Joel Petrik (USA), 5/24/05.

"None," Peterson replied.

"None?" Petrik couldn't believe it. "Look again!"

Peterson checked again. There were no vehicles in sight. Petrik was flabbergasted. Where had all the other vehicles gone? Petrik considered stopping and waiting for the rest of the company, but the enemy fire picked up again, and then he saw four Iraqi tanks. There were two tanks on either side of the road.

King's three lead vehicles sped through a hail of gunfire, past the Iraqi tanks, and over the railroad bridge. At the crest of the bridge, Petrik noticed more tanks in the distance. They were American M1 tanks. Petrik thought, "Please don't let the Abrams shoot, because they don't miss."

Army Specialist Jun Zhang and Sergeant Curtis Campbell led the second group in another five-ton tractor-trailer. PFC Marcus Dubois and Corporal Damien Luten followed in a second truck. CW3[12] Marc Nash and Staff Sergeant Tarik Jackson were towing a trailer with their HMMWV, and PFC Adam Elliot and Sergeant James Grubb followed in their empty fuel truck. Finally, Sergeant Rose and Corporal Francis Carista rounded out the second group in their five-ton tractor-trailer.

These ten soldiers raced south in their five vehicles. Corporal Luten tried to protect the group with the company's only .50-caliber machine gun, but it jammed. After frantically trying to clear the group's only powerful weapon, Damien leaned over and reached for his M-16. As he was reaching for his rifle, an Iraqi bullet ripped through his leg, shattering his knee.

Zhang, Dubois, Jackson, Elliot, and Rose swerved around obstacles and over the Euphrates River bridge. They raced south past the intersection with Highway 8, past the dug-in tanks, and back up on the railway bridge. Zhang and Campbell's truck crested the railway bridge, only to find a terrifying sight.

The Iraqis had blocked the southern end of the bridge by pushing two dilapidated buses across the road. Iraqi fighters peppered Zhang and Campbell's vehicles with small arms and RPG fire. Campbell recalled, "I have never been so scared in my life."[13] While rolling down the bridge, their vehicle was hit repeatedly by RPGs and small arms fire. The vehicle rolled forward from momentum only. Though the engine had ceased to work, Zhang

---

12 Chief Warrant Officer 3.

13 Telephone interview with Sergeant Curtis Campbell (USA), 5/11/04.

somehow managed to maneuver the truck around the roadblock of buses but their tractor-trailer soon rolled to a terrifying stop.

Zhang and Campbell immediately jumped from their disabled vehicle. Zhang jumped onto Dubois and Luten's truck as it passed, but Campbell, who had been riding "shotgun," was now left alone with the disabled truck. He tried to return fire and was shot in the thigh. Nash and Jackson screeched to a stop and picked up Campbell, even though Staff Sergeant Jackson had already been hit several times. The HMMWV kicked up dust and stones as it accelerated to continue south. But the three didn't get very far before their vehicle was hit and disabled. Dubois, Luten, and Zhang raced south past Captain King and the first group. Soon they noticed vehicles on the highway ahead—lots of vehicles.

Elliot maneuvered the empty fuel truck through the ambush while Grubb attempted to return fire with his M-16, but it kept jamming. Grubb frantically pounded his rifle on the dashboard to clear each jam. As they raced south, Grubb was hit in the arm. He continued to fight the Iraqis with his malfunctioning rifle and one good arm. Then he was hit in the other arm.

Grubb watched as an Iraqi pitched a hand grenade at the cab of his truck. Fortunately, the grenade missed its mark but hit the truck. In all the noise and confusion, all Grubb could hear was the grenade clanking as it hit the truck, bounced down into the open chassis, and rattled to the ground like a pachinko ball. It had to be impossible, but all Grubb could hear was clank, clank, clank. Then the grenade exploded beneath the truck, momentarily lifting the rear wheels off the ground with a loud "whump."

Sergeant Rose followed Elliot and Grubb through, around, and over the obstacles in the road while also under fire. Rose's passenger, Corporal Carista, was hit by a piece of flying shrapnel. Rose and Elliot ground their vehicles to a stop next to the disabled HMMWV.

The beleaguered soldiers were starting to run out of ammunition. Then Campbell remembered that there was some ammo stored in the cab of his truck. He returned to his truck dragging his wounded leg. He climbed up into the cab, retrieved the ammunition, and returned to the stranded group who were now settled in a trench.

The small group formed a defensive perimeter. Rose dressed the others' wounds as they waited for the Iraqis to overrun their position. Each of the soldiers had resigned himself to the fact that the situation was hopeless

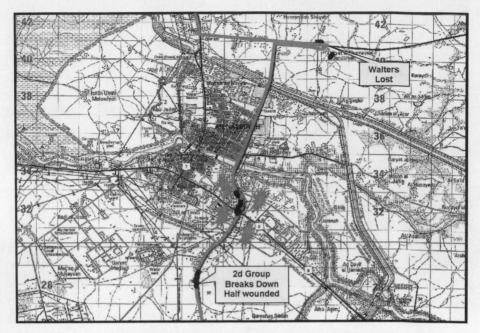

Ambush of the 507th Maintenance Company

and that he would probably die soon. They all decided to hold out as long as they could. They agreed that they would go down fighting and not be captured. One said, "I am going to take fifteen or twenty of them with me."[14]

The slowest group of vehicles was comprised of a five-ton tractor-trailer driven by PFC Howard Johnson with Private Ruben Estrella-Soto riding in the passenger seat. SPC Jamaal Addison and SPC James Kiehl rode in a truck towing a trailer. SPC Joseph Hudson and CW2 Johnny Mata were in a HEMTT[15] wrecker towing a tractor-trailer. Another five-ton tractor-trailer followed with SPC Edgar Hernandez and SPC Shoshana Johnson. Then came 1st Sergeant Dowdy's HMMWV. Finally, PFC Patrick Miller, Sergeant James Riley, and Private Brandon Sloan were riding in a wrecker. These larger vehicles had taken the longest to turn around and were several hundred meters behind the other two groups.

---

14 Ibid. Campbell.

15 Heavy expanded mobility tactical truck.

Hudson and Mata managed to reach the railroad bridge at approximately 0720, a short time after Campbell and the others had just barely made it across. Hudson was not able to make it through the obstacles. His HEMTT wrecker was hit and burst into flames not far from the southern base of the bridge. Hudson was captured, and Mata was killed.

Addison and Kiehl never made it to the railroad bridge. Kiehl was already wounded and was having difficulty controlling his vehicle. By now, the Iraqis had moved a tank into the intersection of highways 7 and 8. As Addison and Kiehl swerved to avoid the tank, their five-ton truck, which had been towing a trailer, careened through the intersection, jumped the curb, and rolled onto its top, killing both soldiers.

Howard Johnson and Ruben Estrella-Soto were right behind Addison and Kiehl. As they approached the tank in the intersection, the Iraqi gunner inside was furiously trying to rotate the turret into position to shoot down the road at the remaining vehicles. PFC Johnson swerved to avoid the tank, but the traversing main gun hit his vehicle squarely in the windshield. The gunmetal barrel smashed the windshield and completely obliterated the truck's cab. The impact probably killed both soldiers immediately, but the large tractor-trailer continued forward. It, too, jumped the curb coming to rest within feet of Addison and Kiehl's overturned vehicle.

Edgar Hernandez and Specialist Shoshana Johnson rode their five-ton tractor-trailer through the ambush. They made it past the statue at the intersection of highways 7 and 8 but they didn't make it to the railroad crossing. In a hail of gunfire and rockets, Hernandez lost control of the vehicle. The tractor and flatbed trailer jackknifed and skidded to a stop along the side of the road. Racing directly behind Johnson and Hernandez, Piestewa could not react fast enough, and she crashed into the rear of Hernandez' flatbed. Shaken, but not injured, Johnson and Hernandez jumped out of their disabled vehicle and took cover. Piestewa, Dowdy, Anguiano, Buggs, and Lynch did not fair as well. They were all trapped in the wreckage, dead, dying, or severely wounded.

Miller, Riley, and Sloan's five-ton wrecker was taking up the rear. Miller ducked his head below the dashboard and floored the accelerator. He popped his head up just often enough to keep the large truck on the road. The last vehicle in the convoy was taking a lot of incoming fire, as Iraqis attacked from every direction. At one point, an Iraqi jumped in the road, and Miller ran him over. Bullets bounced off the hood and whizzed through the cab. Then, silently, Brandon Sloan slumped over in the seat. A bullet had pierced his forehead, killing him instantly.

Just as Miller and Riley were approaching Lynch and Piestewa's crash scene, more bullets slammed into Miller's vehicle. Finally taking their toll, his truck, too, sputtered to a stop. Miller and Riley jumped out and ran nearly a kilometer toward Dowdy's HMMWV. Miller quickly looked inside to find a mass of tangled bodies. Believing that everyone in the HMMWV was dead, Miller and Riley turned their attention to Shoshana Johnson and Edgar Hernandez who had taken shelter beneath their vehicle at the front of the horrific crash scene.

Keeping his cool, Private Miller surveyed the situation. Everyone in the HMMWV appeared to be dead, Sloan was dead, Johnson and Hernandez were safe for the moment, and he and Riley were still able to fight. Miller saw the Iraqi dump truck parked about fifty meters ahead on the road. He decided to run for the truck, hoping that he could start it and use it to get his friends to safety.

Miller broke into a run, bullets hitting at his feet. Shoshana Johnson, fearing that the next Iraqi bullet would hit its mark, began screaming at Miller to take cover. He continued to sprint toward the truck. As Miller ran, a bullet sped beneath Shoshana's truck and pierced both of her ankles. She went down instantly, screaming in pain. As he neared the vehicle, Miller saw a group of Iraqis setting up a mortar. He immediately zigged, changed his course, and dove behind a berm across the road from the dump truck and mortar team.

Miller was hidden less than twenty-five meters from the seven-man mortar team. When he first peeked over the berm, he saw an Iraqi moving to drop a mortar round down the tube. He fired a single shot, and the Iraqi fell. Then Miller's M-16 jammed. He pounded his hand on the slide, and the next round slid home. He peeked over the berm again. Another Iraqi was preparing to launch a deadly projectile toward Johnson, Hernandez, and Riley. Another single shot from Miller felled the second Iraqi.

Miller's rifle jammed a second time, and he pounded the round home—again. He waited, peeked, and shot the third Iraqi dead. Miller got into a rhythm. Peek, shoot, slam the next round home, then wait. Seven times he repeated the sequence, until no other Iraqis appeared in his sights.

Soon, the Iraqis had surrounded the four stranded soldiers. Sorely outnumbered and with failing weapons, Johnson, Hernandez, Riley, and Miller surrendered. They were whisked away before the Iraqis pulled Lynch and Piestewa from the wreckage of their HMMWV.

Iraqi soldiers immediately surrounded First Sergeant Dowdy's crumpled Humvee. As they glared into the wreckage, they found a twisted mess of human bodies. First Sergeant Dowdy had been killed instantly when his passenger side wedged under the back of Johnson's flatbed. The three occupants in the rear had been tossed around like rag dolls. Buggs and Anguiano were dead. Then, to their surprise, the Iraqis found that Lori Piestewa and Jessica Lynch were still alive. Piestewa was pulled from the driver's seat, and Lynch's shattered body was removed from the back of the wreckage.

Buggs' and Anguiano's bodies were pulled from the vehicle and loaded into the back of a pickup truck. Fedayeen whisked the bodies away. They drove the two American soldiers through the streets, firing their weapons into the air, in a frenzied celebration of their victory over the Americans. They drove up and down the streets to insure the people of Nasiriyah would know what would happen to anyone who tried to stand up to Saddam's regime.

Lynch and Piestewa were quickly moved away from the scene of the ambush and taken a short distance north to a school near the Euphrates River. Eventually, they ended up in the Tykar Military Hospital, just south of the Euphrates River bridge. Hudson, Johnson, Hernandez, Riley, and Miller were whisked away into the Ba'ath party district in southwest Nasiriyah.

By now, the Iraqi commanders thought that the Americans had started their attack on the city. Word spread throughout Nasiriyah that the defenders had defeated the first American attack. For a moment, the Iraqis thought that they might actually be able to repel the American invasion. Civic leaders and the populace feared a repeat of their 1991 uprising against Saddam. If there was any chance that Saddam's forces would be victorious, all the locals had to help resist the American onslaught.

Iraqi soldiers and militiamen quickly started returning to their posts. As the sun rose, Iraqis hurried to man the city's defenses. Any hope of capitulation was now gone. The enemy was now ready for a fight. Little did they know that they had just celebrated their last victory and that a U.S. Marine regimental combat team was moving into attack position.

THE TIMBERWOLVES

Just as Captain King's soldiers were coming under fire north of the canal, Team Tank was moving to take the lead at the head of the battalion. Staff Sergeant Schielein's CAAT Humvees were interspersed with Peeples' tanks as the CAAT Platoon pushed north from the 20th Northing. Schielein's eight heavily armed HMMWVs bounded forward by two. Every few hundred meters they stopped to scan the horizon with the high-powered optical sights on their TOW launchers. While the TOW gunners scanned, Schielein searched from side to side with his binoculars. The Marines were looking for any sign of trouble. They had only proceeded about a kilometer when Schielein heard *fump, fump, fump, fump*. He immediately thought, "Damn, those are mortars!"[16]

Schielein got on the radio, but other Marines were clogging the network with the everyday business of moving the battalion forward. Schielein interrupted with, "Break! Break! Stand by! I believe I just heard mortars fire."[17]

Major Peeples responded with, "Keep pushing."[18] Just as he finished his transmission, the first mortar round exploded only two hundred meters in front of the CAAT section and about a hundred meters east of Captain Dyer's tank. The explosion left a huge smoke ring that lingered just off the ground. Dyer's first thought was that they were being gassed, and he only had a second to wonder about the gas.

His attention was quickly shifted to an Iraqi machine gun as it opened fire from a building on the right side of the road. The bullets whizzed over Dyer's head and began slapping the desert floor in front of Schielein's men, landing closer with each impact. Dyer and Peeples dropped down in their hatches to button up but quickly found that they could not see what was going on. Within a few minutes, they were both back up out of their hatches in what they called "name tape defilade."[19] They were exposed from the chest up.

A second machine gun opened up on the Marines. Schielein's CAAT Marines began searching for the enemy guns using their TOW missile sights. One of the Marines found the source of the mortar fire on the top of a nearby building. Schielein could see black-clad Iraqis running around on the roof, so he quickly called in a fire mission.

---

16 Ibid. Schielein.

17 Ibid. Schielein.

18 Ibid. Schielein.

19 E-mail from Captain Scott Dyer. The men's bodies were exposed from the name tag above their breast pocket.

CAAT machine gunners raked the first enemy machine gun position with fire while Captain Thompson moved to the right and destroyed it with a well-placed main gun round. The second Iraqi machine gun continued firing from a more secure position inside a building. The CAAT Marines shifted their attention to the second gun as a technical vehicle raced up in back of the building.

Schielein was standing in front of his HMMWV when a third machine gun attacked his unit from the west side of the road. The gunner was close, hiding in a building only about a hundred meters away. Bullets started peppering the ground only a few meters in front of Schielein. Schielein turned and yelled to his machine gunner, "Shoot that son-of-a-bitch!"[20]

Corporal Sullivan swung his .50-caliber around and fired a burst right through the window where the enemy had been firing. Now only one machine gun continued to fire at the Marines from the building on the east side of the road. The CAAT machine gunners were having a hard time getting a clear shot at the last bunker. More black-clad Iraqis were running into the same building carrying AK-47s. Schielein called out to one of his TOW gunners, "Shoot that motherfucker!"[21] Corporal McCall let loose his missile, and it screamed across the battlefield and slammed into the building.

As the first battle continued to rage, King, Nace, Johnson, Pierce, Petrik, and Peterson raced south toward the Marines on Highway 7. Not far behind the first group, Dubois, Luten, and Zhang thought the vehicles on the southern horizon were more Iraqis, so they quickly turned their truck around and returned to their stranded friends just south of the railroad bridge. Then, around 0730, King's Humvee, a small truck, and a semi barreled south past Peeples' lead tanks and screeched to a stop. Sitting atop his M1 tank near the 22nd Northing, Major Peeples watched the beleaguered vehicles approach. Captain King jumped out, pistol drawn, and took cover behind the passenger side door.

Under fire, Major Peeples climbed down from his tank and briskly walked over to King. "What in the hell is going on?"[22]

"I got more people up there!" King replied, motioning north. King was almost hysterical.

---

20 Ibid. Schielein.

21 Ibid. Schielein.

22 Telephone interview with Major Bill Peeples, 1/29/04.

"What is the situation up there?" Peeples tried to get a picture of what he was up against. "Where were you receiving fire?"

King was frazzled. He couldn't provide any useful information.

Peeples tried once again. "How many soldiers are left up there?"

"I . . . I just need . . . I need you to go get some people. I got people up there." King babbled.

"Okay, fine!" Peeples left King standing in the road and returned to his tank. Major Peeples got on the radio and reported his bizarre find to Grabowski—then ordered his tanks forward. Captain Dyer pulled back on the road and followed his commander north. As they rolled forward, Major Scott "Hawk" Hawkins started calling Cobras. He told them to start searching for more of the 507th soldiers with their high-powered scopes. As Team Tank charged forward to rescue King's soldiers, other Marines escorted King south to the relative safety of Grabowski's battalion command post.

Major Peeples' tanks advanced by bounds up the road, but the platoons were not able to provide covering fire to one another. The narrow road was slightly raised above a muddy delta. There was very little room for the tankers to maneuver. On his second bound, Captain Thompson radioed Peeples. "Hey, I see them,"[23] he reported. Thompson abandoned the bounding overwatch and just kept moving forward four kilometers toward the embattled soldiers of the 507th.

As the first contact ended, Troy Schielein remembered that his daughter's birthday was March 22nd. Then he thought that, with the time difference, it was still the twenty-second back home in the United States. He turned to his machine gunner and said, "I am ready to die for a good cause . . . but please don't let it be today, not on my little girl's birthday. She'll never forget it."[24]

Until now, Task Force Tarawa had no air support. All of the air assets had been assigned elsewhere. But now that Task Force Tarawa had reported "Marines in contact," commanders began pushing attack aircraft toward An Nasiriyah.

Two Cobra crews from HML/A 269 had camped out for the night at Jalibah. Captain Matt Schenberger, Captain Brian Bruggeman, Lieutenant Travis Richie, and Lieutenant John Parker got up around sunrise after an uncomfort-

---

23 Ibid. Peeples.

24 Ibid. Schielein.

able night's sleep lying on the desert floor next to their refueling trucks. With their choppers parked and dormant, they had no communication with the outside world. They took their time eating breakfast and preparing their helicopters for the day. They finally climbed into their aircraft, cranked the engines, and lifted into the morning sky. As soon as they were airborne, they heard the reports that Task Force Tarawa was in contact. They turned north and raced toward An Nasiriyah to help their fellow North Carolina Marines.

RUNNING low on ammunition and with five wounded, the ten stranded soldiers had already resigned themselves to the fact that they would not survive the day. They all resolved that they would go down fighting. They had been lying in the trench for nearly an hour waiting for the Iraqis to close in on their position. Suddenly, Staff Sergeant Tarik Jackson, the most seriously wounded, cocked his head, "Listen!" he exclaimed. "Do you hear that? It sounds like our tanks!"[25]

Someone peeked up out of the trench and saw Captain Thompson's tanks approaching. Team Tank rolled up and straddled the trench at the "Garbage Dump," just south of the railroad overpass. Thompson's tankers began picking targets and methodically destroying the enemy with main gun rounds. Hawkins called for Cobra support, and the helicopters swooped in and attacked the enemy from above.

After spending forty-five minutes of sheer hell, believing that they were going to die that day and not knowing that any American forces were nearby, the sound of M1 tanks and Cobra helicopters immediately rallied the despondent soldiers. They would survive. The Marines had saved the day.

Cobras and Hueys swooped in overhead and braved antiaircraft fire to protect the soldiers on the ground. The pilots reported large numbers of fighters moving toward the trapped soldiers. They flew in low and fast, engaging enemy troops and weapons systems. Every now and then, antiaircraft artillery fire would climb up after them.

Shortly after the tanks arrived, the enemy fire was so intense, Dyer began to fear the fuel pod strapped to his tank might catch fire and kill his crew. He jumped up on top of the turret to kick it off. After thirty seconds of standing on top of the turret and stomping the pod with no success, Dyer

---

25 Ibid. Campbell.

felt Hawkins punch his leg. He frantically motioned for Dyer to get down. He pointed to the dirt kicking up around the tank from enemy bullets. Dyer jumped back into his hole, as Hawkins chewed him out.

Enemy mortar fire continued to creep toward the tanks and soldiers. Dyer radioed over to Lieutenant Carter, the company's forward observer, "What the hell are you doing about shutting down the enemy mortars?"[26]

"I can't get anyone at 1/2 on the net." Carter proclaimed.

"Well, fucking call Regiment or Nightmare,[27] and get us some counter-battery fire." Dyer ordered.

Carter came back, "What the hell do you think I was doing? I am talking to Nightmare right now!" Dyer said "roger" and let him get back to work. Despite the stress and lack of contact with Battalion, Carter was doing his job, and doing it well.

Working as a combined arms team, Peeples' tankers, the aircraft overhead, and the artillery were able to destroy several platoon-sized enemy formations, two ZSU 23-4[28] antiaircraft weapons, several mortar and artillery positions, as well as engaging two T-55 tanks spotted moving toward the ambushed soldiers.

As soon as Dyer had seen Campbell and his comrades huddled in the ditch, he called for a cas-evac. Alpha Company sent two AAVs with Gunny Justin LeHew and 1st Sergeant James Thompson's casualty collection team forward to assist the wounded soldiers. The Iraqis were still firing as Thompson rolled up in his AMTRAC, A312.[29] Peeples' tankers continued to lay down covering fire as 1st Sergeant Thompson and his corpsmen ran to the aid of the wounded soldiers.

When Thompson saw the five casualties, he was astonished. All five had already had their wounds bandaged. As they loaded the casualties onto their track, Thompson noticed some commotion near the soldiers who were not wounded. An Army warrant officer, CW3 Nash, was refusing to get into the AMTRAC.

---

26 Personal account provided by Captain Scott Dyer via e-mail on 6/13/05.

27 "Nightmare" was the call sign of 1st Battalion, 10th Marines—Starnes' artillery.

28 Russian-built antiaircraft gun.

29 Each company in the 1st Battalion had twelve tracks. They were numbered by company, AAV platoon and vehicle. Alpha Company had A301 through A312; Bravo had B201 to B212; and Charlie had C201 through C212.

"I can't leave my men behind, First Sergeant,"[30] he protested to Thompson. "I got men all over the place. They ambushed us bad."

Thompson tried to calm the Army warrant officer. "Hey, sir, the Marines have landed. You gotta leave them. You can't stay here." Thompson didn't wait for a response: he just dragged Nash into the track. "We will do everything we can to find them." Thompson's tracks raced south with the wounded and drove them back to the battalion aid station. After the soldiers had been safely removed, Major Peeples continued to fight until most of the enemy had been silenced. Then, he withdrew south, back down the road to his original position at the 22nd Northing.

Some of Peeples' tanks were now in need of fuel. He reported to Grabowski that his tanks were indicating red fuel levels (less than half a tank of fuel remaining). Grabowski ordered Peeples to move his tanks to the rapid-refuel point at the tail end of the battalion column to refuel. While the tanks were gone, Grabowski would consolidate his position and clear the nearby buildings from which his men had been receiving fire. As ordered, he would make sure that the enemy could not move south to disrupt traffic on Highway 1.

As Hawk's Cobras circled overhead like giant metallic birds of prey, Bravo Company rolled up to the Garbage Dump, and 3d Platoon dismounted from their tracks. The infantrymen fanned out and moved to clear the cluster of buildings on the west side of the road. Alpha Company was ordered to clear the small village on the east side of the road.

Around 0900, Major Hawkins handed over control of the air battle to Captain Dennis "Mouth" Santare in Bravo Company. Once the CAS handover was complete, Team Tank withdrew. Santare controlled the fixed wing and rotary wing assets overhead of Charlie and Bravo Company as they moved up abreast of one another.

General Natonski, a former commander of the 1st Battalion, 2d Marines, recalled later, "I'm back in the COC in Queensland,[31] and I'm wondering why are they taking so long."[32] The previous night's FRAGO (fragmentary order) had ordered the attack on the bridges to begin at 0700

---

30 Telephone interview with 1st Sergeant James Thompson, Jr., 8/1/04.

31 Phase Line Queensland, east of the cloverleaf, was Task Force Tarawa's limit of advance on March 22nd.

32 Personal interview with Brigadier General Richard Natonski, 10/27/03.

and the operation to be complete by 1000. Natonski jumped in a Huey and flew up to the front.

Colonel Bailey had just returned to his main CP after an all-night journey to the far western bridge when he received the report of Grabowski's encounter with the 507th. Instead of stopping at his CP, he continued north on the highway to his lead unit at the oil towers. Just as he approached Grabowski's position, Bailey noticed a Huey headed up the road from the south. Then he saw a group of soldiers standing along the side of the road. Bailey pulled up next to Captain King, who had been brought back to the battalion headquarters. King immediately pleaded, "Aren't you gonna help us? Aren't you gonna help us?"[33] Bailey talked with King for a moment trying to calm him and get more information about the Army unit. Then, he moved north to speak with his battalion commander.

General Natonski landed on the road just south of 1/2's tactical command operations center, which was nothing more than Grabowski's command AM-TRAC, its chase vehicle, and a handful HMMWVs. Natonski jumped from the chopper before the blades had stopped whirling. The first thing that caught his eye was the sight of several wounded soldiers lying on the ground at the battalion aid station.

Natonski walked over to the wounded and asked them who they were. They told him that they were with the 507th Maintenance Company. Natonski wanted to offer up his Huey for their evacuation, but when he saw that there were five wounded and none of them had a life-threatening injury, he decided that it would be better to wait for a cas-evac Phrog.

After his short visit with the soldiers, the general looked around to take in the surroundings. Iraqi snipers were still taking potshots at the Marines, and Grabowski's infantry was working on both sides of the road to clear the area. First Battalion's armored column was halted along the side of the road, so Natonski got on the road and started forward.

As Natonski walked forward, he came upon another group of soldiers huddled around a tan HMMWV. The soldiers were trying to repair their shot-up vehicle. "Who are you guys?"[34] Natonski inquired.

"We are the 507th," one of the men replied.

---

33 Ibid. Bailey.

34 The following conversation taken from personal interview with Brigadier General Richard Natonski.

"Who's in charge here?"

"Oh, I am, Captain King."

Natonski offered, "I just talked with some of your wounded. Is this all of you?"

King replied, "No, we got ambushed in the city, and there's more behind us."

While Grabowski was on the radio, Colonel Bailey showed up. Then, just as he got off the radio with Peeples, General Natonski appeared. Bailey walked up to Grabowski and asked, "Rickey, what's going on here?"[35]

Colonel Grabowski replied, "We're clearing buildings here that we had taken fire from. We're holding."

General Natonski asked, "Why are you holding?" Not waiting for an answer, he added, "I have an entire RCT behind you. We need to get them through today. I need you to get up there and seize the bridges as quickly as you can." Natonski was worried that at any moment the Iraqis would blow the bridges, leaving only Highway 1 open.

Until this moment, Grabowski thought that his mission was to defend in sector. Colonel Bailey, having been on the road all night, assumed that the previous night's FRAGO had been passed down to his battalions. However, for some reason, RCT-2's staff had not passed on the order to seize the eastern bridges. Regardless, General Natonski had the 1st Marine Division breathing down his neck. They were chomping at the bit to attack toward Baghdad, and the bridges needed to be secured before the Iraqis had a chance to destroy them. Task Force Tarawa was behind schedule.

Grabowski immediately walked over to coordinate the attack with his operations officer. When Grabowski walked up, Sosa was just completing a conversation on the radio. "The battalion aid station has reported that there are still more soldiers, but they don't know where they are." Sosa reported.

General Natonski looked at Colonel Grabowski, lowered his head, and said, "Rickey, see what you can do to find the rest of them. They would do it for us. We need to do it for them."

"Roger!" Grabowski replied.

General Natonski, Bailey, and Grabowski were all concerned that the

---

35 The following conversations were taken from interviews with Brigadier General Richard Natonski on 3/25/04, Colonel Ron Bailey on 3/25/04, and Lieutenant Colonel Rickey Grabowski on 3/1/04.

Iraqis would destroy the bridges before they could be secured. Their concerns were redoubled now that reports of armed resistance were coming in. To further complicate the situation, there was an unknown number of American soldiers trapped behind enemy lines.

Colonel Bailey pulled Grabowski aside and asked, "What do you need?"

Grabowski confidently stated, "We will take those bridges, sir."

Bailey responded like a supportive father, "I know you will."

Bailey and Natonski's visit lasted about a half hour. By the time Colonel Bailey had driven away and General Natonski's Huey had lifted off to return to his command operations center at Queensland, Major Peeples had moved all of his tanks to the rear, and he had started to refuel.

Gunny Doran had Day drive north as soon as they heard about the action. When they arrived at the Timberwolves' command center, they found several soldiers standing around their shot-up vehicles. Day pulled the Mystery Machine up next to the soldiers. Doran leaned out and asked, "Can I take your gas?"[36]

Task Force Tarawa was already low on fuel. They had not received their complete allotment the night before. Doran wanted every additional drop of gas he could get his hands on, So he and Day jumped out of the Mystery Machine, went to the back, grabbed some empty gas cans, went out in the road, and began to drain fuel from the Army vehicles.

When Major Peoples arrived at the rapid-refueling point, he found that they only had 1,400 gallons of fuel remaining. There was also only one fuel pump that was still operational. It would take more than ten minutes to refuel each of his tanks. With only one pump, it could be hours before he finished the job. Peoples ordered his four Team Mech tanks to refuel first. Only moments after they started refueling, the last remaining fuel pump broke down. So, the tankers were forced to gravity feed the tanks. This process was painstakingly slow, and each tank needed more than a half hour to be fueled.

While they were refueling, Captain Dyer walked over to the soldiers of the 507th. He asked a staff sergeant what had happened. The staff sergeant told Dyer about their trip north and how they had to turn around twice. He went on to tell of their harrowing flight back through the city. Dyer told him that he might have to go up there and asked for a report.

"That's not good tank country up there, sir. There are canals and berms

---

36 Ibid. Doran.

all over the place—it's really muddy. You won't be able to get off the road. If you do, you'll get stuck, and there is a shitload of Iraqis up there."[37] The staff sergeant provided Dyer with the best intelligence report he had received since he got on the ship in North Carolina. Wounded, shocked, and deeply sad over his fellow soldiers' fate, he had the presence of mind to describe in detail what had occurred, enemy positions, and fortifications as well as the terrain. He provided Dyer invaluable battlefield intelligence.

AMERICA'S BATTALION

Lieutenant Colonel Mortenson's Marines had risen before sunrise, climbed back into their seven-ton trucks and HMMWVs and had pushed off early in the morning. They rolled north in the dawn's early light and moved up behind Starnes' artillery battalion. By the time they reached the cloverleaf, most of the Army traffic on Highway 1 had subsided and Highway 7 was clogged with Marine logistics vehicles.

They were still twenty kilometers south of the city, and America's Battalion had stopped in a barren area. The open field on the left side of the road was littered with trash; flies were everywhere. Mortenson's Marines stayed in their trucks, sweltering in the heat. Innumerable flies seemed to invade each truck. Everyone struggled to keep them out of their mouth and away from their face, but it was futile.

Mortenson knew that something was happening because of all of the radio traffic, but there was very little regimental radio traffic. In an effort to find out what was going on, Major Fulford and Lieutenant Colonel Mortenson jumped in a Humvee and drove forward past Starnes' artillery to find the regimental headquarters. Colonel Bailey was just returning from his meeting with Natonski and Grabowski as Fulford and Mortenson arrived.

REGIMENTAL COMBAT TEAM-2

There was a flurry of activity at the regimental command post. As the 2d Marines were frantically preparing to go on the attack, Lieutenant Colonel

---

37 Ibid. Dyer.

Eddie Ray appeared. Ray was the only one in the group that had seen combat, and everybody was a little bit shocked that morning when he showed up. They were in the first fight of their lives, from Colonel Bailey on down. Furthermore, Ray's 2d LAR Battalion wasn't even attached to Task Force Tarawa.

Yet, there was Eddie Ray, a decorated Gulf War veteran. He strolled up with no MOPP suit top, exposed suspenders, and T-shirt. To complete the picture, a well-chewed cigar hung from the corner of his mouth. Mortenson and Ray were old friends, and Colonel Bailey also knew him.

"What do we have, sir?"[38] Ray inquired. Then he added. "I am here to help. I have my whole battalion here to help you."[39]

Bailey told Ray that he was concerned that they were going to encounter a lot more problems moving through An Nasiriyah than had been originally expected. He had already seen the results of the 507th's attempt to travel through the town, and his lead elements had just passed through a few hundred meters of enemy positions. They hadn't even reached the Euphrates River, and Bailey had even taken fire on his return from the meeting with Grabowski.

Lieutenant Colonel Ray, a Desert Storm hero and winner of the Navy Cross, offered up one of his LAV companies to support the assault on the city. With the regiment's LAR company committed at the far western bridge, Bailey welcomed the offer. He wanted to get another force in the fight. He wanted more firepower.

The Light Armored Recon Battalion's job is to lead a Marine division into battle. They are equipped with highly mobile, heavily armed, eight-wheeled light armored vehicles. These LAVs are designed, and their crews are trained, to lead the attack. While not as heavily protected as the M1 tank, they offer slightly more protection than an AMTRAC. These high-tech vehicles also carry the eyes and ears of the division. They have advanced day/night-vision systems. Their optical systems are so sophisticated that their operators can see people through windows—hiding in the shadows of darkened rooms, hundreds of yards in the distance. The LAR unit also carries

---

38 Telephone interview with Lieutenant Colonel Eddie Ray, 2/17/04.

39 Ibid. Ray.

advanced signal intelligence (SIGINT) equipment, which enables them to monitor enemy radio traffic. And, if they encounter the enemy, they carry 25-mm bushmaster guns, TOW missiles, and a 25-mm air-defense Gatling gun that can be used in a direct-fire mode. Lieutenant Colonel Ray characterized his new antiaircraft weapon as "the kind of gun that will send everyone home."[40]

The LAV is designed to be out in front, and Colonel Bailey knew that Ray's LAVs could dramatically improve his regiment's fighting ability. All Marine Corps officers knew the capabilities of the LAV, and each of the 1st Marine Division's regimental combat teams had an attached LAR battalion. RCT-5 had 1st LAR attached, RCT-7 had Okinawa's 3d LAR attached, and RCT-1 had all but one of Ray's Camp Lejeune–based 2d LAR companies. Task Force Tarawa's LAVs had been ordered to the Highway 1-Euphrates River bridge to provide security at the Euphrates River crossing site west of the city. Now that General Natonski had received orders to execute the "Be Prepared To" mission of securing the eastern Nasiriyah bridges, RCT-2 was the only regiment lacking LAR support, so when Ray offered his assistance, Bailey gladly accepted.

Bailey had word passed to Grabowski informing him that he was sending LAR up to help. Grabowski wanted to take the bridges, and the Timberwolves had been planning this operation for weeks. He knew that the right course of action was to proceed with the plan. It would not be wise to give the mission to another unit that, no matter how capable, was not prepared. Bailey had not taken the mission away from Grabowski's battalion. To the contrary, he was just trying to give him more fighting punch.

As ordered, Colonel Grabowski pressed the attack. He got on his battalion net at approximately 1100 and told his Marines, "If we don't take those bridges now, Regiment will give our mission to LAR . . . it will be a cold day in hell before I allow Regiment to send an LAR company to assume our mission especially when Apache-6[41] has had no time to plan or prep for this task like we have! Now press hard for those damn bridges . . .

---

40 Ibid. Ray.

41 "Apache-6" was Captain Ivan Monclova's call sign. He was the A Company commander of 2d LAR Battalion.

Timberwolf-6. Out!"[42] But his tanks were still refueling. What else could possibly go wrong?

When Fred Pokorney heard Grabowski's order come over the battalion net, he turned to his friend, Ben Reid, and said, "This is not good. We are going to get killed today."[43]

42 Lieutenant Colonel Rickey Grabowski e-mail to author, 1/5/05

43 Ibid. Reid.

CHAPTER 7

Bloody Sunday

Being ready is not what matters. What matters is winning after you get there.

—LIEUTENANT GENERAL VICTOR H. KRULAK, USMC

HMM-162: THE GOLDEN EAGLES

At 0500, Garcia, Schroeder, Hetterscheidt, Lewis, Morton, and Griggs got an early-morning wake-up call, rousing them from their clean sheets and soft mattresses on the USS *Saipan*. Eric Garcia opted for a few extra minutes of sleep instead of getting up for breakfast. Captains Garcia and Morton had drawn the assignment for the next cas-evac rotation, and Garcia would lead the two-ship mission. Soon, he and Morton would move into Iraq in their CH-46 helicopters. They would replace the two Sea Knights that had relieved them the day before. Garcia and his crew would not miss the action, after all.

For this mission, Captain Eric Garcia's call sign would be Parole-Two-Five. Lieutenant Tod Schroeder was Eric's copilot, Gunny Hetterscheidt was the crew chief, and Corporal Lewis was the aircraft's door gunner. Because they were set up for casualty evacuations, Eric also carried two Navy corpsmen, Doc Mark Kirkland, a Search Air Rescue corpsman, and Doc Moses Gloria, a veteran of Afghanistan. This was the best overall crew in the entire squadron. Garcia was undoubtedly the best pilot in the squadron; Gunny Hetterscheidt the best crew chief in the Corps; and Gloria was a war-hardened veteran of Afghanistan. They jokingly called themselves the "A-Team."

Captain Billie Morton flew the Dash Two aircraft. His call sign was Parole-Two-Six, and he flew in the squadron's 03 aircraft. Captain Eric Griggs was his copilot. Corporals Ryan and Allen, plus Doc Scott Reid and Doc Peyton rode in the back of Dash Two. Griggs explained, "As the second helicopter in the section, it was our job to keep up and shut up."[1]

The crews of Parole-Two-Five and Parole-Two-Six each moved through their morning routine in preparation for the mission. Garcia, Schroeder, Morton, and Griggs attended briefings while Hetterscheidt and the other crewmembers checked their aircraft. Doc Gloria nervously smoked cigarette after cigarette on the smoking deck.

Gloria had learned in Afghanistan to never smoke his own cigarettes before a mission. He never knew how long he would be ashore, so Gloria stuffed his pockets with his own cigarettes and bummed a new cigarette from every sailor and Marine who appeared that morning. Everyone knew that Gloria was headed inland and that he was one of the few veterans aboard, so Gloria "paid" for each newly lighted cigarette with a war story. His storytelling had become legendary aboard ship to the point that his friends would kid him every time he started a new story. Gunny H was the worst. Whenever Gloria started, he would interject, "Yeah, one time, in Afghanistan," parodying the phrase from *American Pie*. Gloria passed the time smoking and joking until it was time to board the aircraft.

Finally, everything was ready, and the two helicopters launched at 0830 on a warm, clear Sunday morning. Garcia's two Phrogs flew west in formation. Soon the azure Persian Gulf waters gave way to the khaki-colored Kuwaiti desert floor. Garcia made a quick stop at Camp Ryan to drop off a bag of mail then lifted off across the Arabian Desert. An hour and a half after leaving the metal flight deck of *Saipan,* they arrived at Task Force Tarawa's headquarters at Queensland, between Jalibah and the intersection of highways 1 and 7.

The Navy-gray CH-46 Phrogs, actually designated as Sea Knights, have been the Marine Corps' flying workhorse for over twenty-five years. Most of the aircraft are older than the Marines they carry. The Sea Knight is a scaled-down version of the Army's CH-47 Chinook. Its smaller size is more suited to the Marines' mission aboard amphibious carriers. They are a little over forty-five feet long when their rotor blades are folded for storage. The

---

1 Taken from personal written narrative of Captain Eric Griggs.

Phrogs can carry twenty-two combat loaded Marines and can be armed with two .50-caliber machine guns, one on each side of the aircraft.

These helicopters, nearly the oldest in the Corps' inventory, are held in high esteem by veteran Marine aviators. Colonel Milstead described them like they were a living entity, "I call them the old war horse. They flare their nostrils. They can smell the cordite. They hear the sound of cannons."[2] When they are not being used for combat assault, the Sea Knights provide support to the Marines ashore by ferrying mail and supplies and standing ready for rapid casualty evacuations.

Now there were four CH-46s at Queensland: Garcia's section and the CH-46 section that he would relieve. Lieutenant Colonel Vazquez and his cas-evac crews had been up most of the night running missions. Garcia and Morton's crews went over to one of the other CH-46s for a short briefing and handover so that the exhausted crews could return to the ship for some much needed rest.

General Natonski's Huey also sat ready at Queensland. Hueys are the most widely used helicopter in the world, and the Marines have been using them since Vietnam. If the Sea Knights are the airborne buses of the Corps, then the Huey is its airborne taxi. The smaller-capacity aircraft is used for many utility functions. Unit commanders use the Huey as an airborne command center, and it can also be used as an ambulance or fitted out for special operations missions. The general's Huey was armed with 2.75 inch Zuni rockets and a 7.62mm mini-gun.

A Huey pilot who had been flying all night with the CH-46s was also at the turnover. The Marines sat down inside the CH-46 and began their handover. The Huey pilot said, "It's starting! They're shooting at us."[3]

"Oh, yeah?" Gunny Hetterscheidt cynically inquired.

"Yeah!" The Huey pilot excitedly replied. "It sounds like . . . It sounds like—you can hear it. It sounds like it does when you go to the rifle range and you are pulling butts.[4] You can hear it!"

Gunny Hetterscheidt thought to himself, "Yeah, right!" Then he brushed off the pilot's description saying, "Yeah. Okay. Whatever."

---

2 Ibid. Milstead.

3 Telephone interview with Gunnery Sergeant William Hetterscheidt, 2/9/04.

4 On Marine Corps rifle ranges, targets are raised and lowered manually using a chain pulley. Marines working in the trench, below the targets are said to be "pulling butts."

While they were talking, a Marine came running out of the main command post and said that they had a need for an immediate cas-evac. Garcia interrupted with, "We will take it." The briefing, which hadn't even started, was concluded, and Garcia and Morton's crews raced to their planes, fired up, took off, and headed north. No sooner had Parole-Two-Five and Parole-Two-Six taken to the air, than the mission was cancelled. Garcia peeled off and decided to fly to Jalibah to top off his fuel.

Garcia and Morton landed on a dusty smudge of blacktop in the middle of the Iraqi desert. Jalibah Airfield, code-named Viper, was in a dry riverbed. It would become the first of several forward operating bases (FOBs), which would allow the aircraft of MAG-29 to leapfrog deep into Iraq. That day, it was nothing more than a couple of fuel trucks, several Marines, and a sand-swept road.

Garcia refueled both of his aircraft, and then Parole-Two-Five and Parole-Two-Six lifted back into the clear morning sky to return to Task Force Tarawa's command post at Queensland. The dust cloud from their landing hadn't even settled when Garcia was given another mission.

REGIMENTAL COMBAT TEAM-2

While Eddie Ray was speaking with Colonel Bailey, Colonel Joe Dowdy appeared. Colonel Dowdy was one of the chosen few. He was the commander of Regimental Combat Team-1. He had all the right connections and was respected by his peers and his men. Joe Dowdy was on the fast track to general. Dowdy immediately went to Ray, his LAR commander, and a short but heated discussion ensued. Then Ray was dismissed with a curt, "I will handle it from here."

Dowdy turned to Bailey. "You don't have authority to take LAR!"[5]

"Hold it." Bailey countered. "He offered—I'm taking."[6]

After a short discussion, Bailey relented and turned to his XO and said, "John, call Rick and tell him we don't have them. Let's just push on."[7]

This was one of those moments in life when a person's career can

---

5 Personal Interview with Colonel Bailey.

6 Ibid. Bailey.

7 Ibid Bailey.

change in a heartbeat. Joe Dowdy's life changed in that conversation. Dowdy left RCT-2's headquarters and returned to his unit unaware of the eventual repercussions of his encounter with Bailey. Ray had already returned to his vehicle, put on his headset, and nodded off to sleep—waiting for the call to lead RCT-1 through An Nasiriyah.

Bailey realized that Grabowski might have taken the offer of LAVs as an indication of a lack of confidence. Bailey knew Grabowski well enough to realize that he would perceive his offer of LAV support as more than just an offer to give him more firepower, so he immediately called for his HMMWV and a security detail. Bailey wanted to reaffirm his confidence in his battalion commander, face-to-face.

Bailey put his "Three" and his "Two"[8] in his vehicle and went up to get a firsthand look. They made it to the rear of Grabowski's battalion at the railroad bridge where Bailey's small entourage came under intense enemy fire. Realizing that he could not command his regiment from a HMMWV that was taking fire, he turned around and returned to his headquarters. Bailey never got the chance to explain his decision to Grabowski.

TASK FORCE TARAWA

By now, RCT-1 was backed up along Highway 7. They were waiting to pass RCT-2 and move through Nasiriyah toward Baghdad, but the route was not yet cleared. I MEF staff began to contact Task Force Tarawa's headquarters to inquire why the schedule was delayed. Everyone at MEF headquarters still believed that the operation to seize the bridges would be little more than a security mission.

Little incidents were starting to delay the advance to Baghdad. The Timberwolves had run across a small Army supply convoy that had wandered into Nasiriyah and had been shot up. The Highway 1 bridge was in terrible condition, and Colonel Reilly's recon Marines had come under fire along Highway 8. Everyone's high hopes for capitulation in Nasiriyah were starting to dissipate. General Natonski decided to get back into his Huey and fly north again to personally assess the situation.

No sooner had Bailey returned to his headquarters than Natonski had

---

8 Referring to the regimental S-3 (Operations) and S-2 (Intelligence) officers.

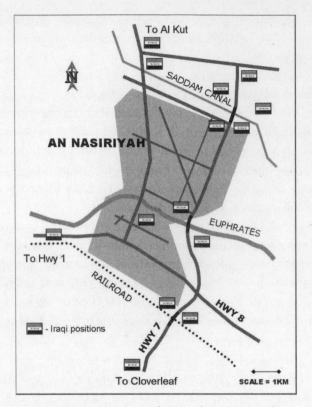

Iraqi Disposition In, and Around, An Nasiriyah

returned to check on the progress of the attack on the bridges. General Natonski reiterated, "We are holding up the entire MEF."[9] Bailey assured General Natonski that his regiment would not fail. Bailey, already irritated by
Dowdy's lack of cooperation, replied, "We will take those bridges,"[10] and
the short meeting was over. General Natonski, satisfied that Bailey's Marines
were doing everything in their power to move forward and secure the bridges,
climbed back in his helicopter and returned to Queensland.

Bailey had every confidence in Grabowski, and he knew that his battalion commander would not let him down. After a slow start, Bailey's
staff was swinging into action. Starnes was ordered to prepare his artillery,

---

9 Ibid. Natonski.

10 Ibid. Bailey.

and Mortenson's battalion was told to be ready to move north behind Grabowski.

THE BETIO BASTARDS

Meanwhile, Dunahoe's Marines had set into defensive positions at the western crossing—facing east, to protect Highway 1. They pushed far enough east to protect the bridge and the Highway 8 intersection from mortar attack. In the late morning, a small caravan of white Toyota pickup trucks, bristling with strange weapons, equipment, and bearded men wearing ball caps, blue jeans, and bandoliers appeared at Dunahoe's command post. An Army Special Forces master sergeant of ODA 553[11], wearing a Boston Red Sox hat and Oakley sunglasses, walked up to Dunahoe and asked how far his Marines were going to move east into Nasiriyah.

Dunahoe asked the group, "Who's in charge here?"

One of the strangely clad figures responded, "I think Bob is. Joe is the captain, but Bob is in charge."

The soldiers wanted to do some sort of linkup at a safe house somewhere just west of the city. Dunahoe told the master sergeant that his Marines were digging in and that they would be staying in this position for the time being. He never really asked, but the sergeant hoped that Dunahoe would provide an escort into the western suburbs. Finally, he asked, "Hey, can we just spend the night with you guys?" The soldiers had been shot at for days since their insertion, and they all welcomed the opportunity to get some much-needed rest. They parked their pickup trucks in a small circle close to Dunahoe's command post and set up camp.

THE TIMBERWOLVES

By 1100, Grabowski's Marines had begun to move forward with Charlie Company on the left side and Alpha Company on the right side of the road. For the time being, the Timberwolves would proceed north without their tanks. Grabowski ordered Bravo Company to take the lead on the road, so

---

11 Robinson. 278.

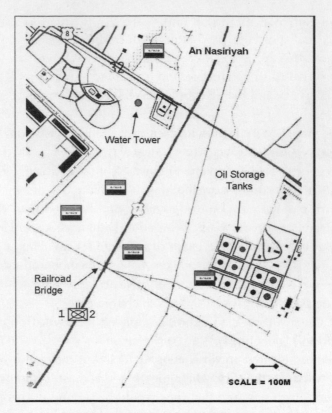

The Iraqi's First Line of Defense

Lieutenant Letendre split his CAAT 2 section. He left one squad of four vehicles with the battalion log trains while he took his 2d Squad forward to provide security for Grabowski's 81mm mortars.

At the southern side of the railroad bridge, Bravo Company paused. Hudson and Mata's Army tow truck and the flatbed it had been towing were engulfed in flames in the center of the road, billowing two columns of black smoke into the clear blue sky. To the Marines' surprise, there was a substantial bridge running over the railroad tracks.

After a short pause, Captain Newland ordered his AMTRACs forward again. Second Lieutenant Troy Garlock, Bravo Company's lead platoon commander rolled through the black smoke in B201 and moved up onto the railroad bridge. As he crested the bridge, B201 jerked to a stop and then quickly backed down from the apex. Garlock's gunner opened fire with his gun.

The company net crackled, "Tanks!"

Garlock had spotted a T-55 tank north of the bridge. Other tanks were rolling—some dug in. Some were traversing their turrets while others sat dormant. Just north of the bridge, the Iraqis had set up a tank company in hidden defensive positions. The tanks were supported by mortars, machine guns, and infantry, and they were waiting to ambush the next American vehicles. They were not expecting a Marine mechanized infantry battalion.

Captain Newland immediately called Troy Schielein's CAAT section forward. As they moved forward to their first contact, the CAAT platoon came alive with Schielein's now familiar, "Net clear, net clear," followed by Johnson's rendition of the Lord's Prayer. It didn't take long for Schielein's armored Hummers to show up. When they pulled up, Schielein could see Captain Newland standing on top of his track.

When Newland saw Schielein's team, he pointed north and screamed, "Schielein—CAAT—CAAT! We got tanks!"[12] Schielein's machine gun vehicles raced up on the bridge and began laying down suppressive fire with their .50-calibers while the TOW vehicles set up, scanned for targets, locked on, and fired their deadly missiles at the Iraqi tanks. The TOW teams worked in a round-robin, one firing while another was moving up on the bridge and the others were reloading. In short order, the CAAT section destroyed eight Iraqi tanks.

While CAAT was working over the enemy, a Bravo Company Javelin gunner set up on top of Garlock's AMTRAC. He let loose his missile, which shot out of the launch tube and traveled less than a hundred feet, when it seemed to stall. It dropped like an F-14 jet when it is catapulted from the flight deck of a carrier. Then the Javelin's rocket motor ignited, and the missile shot almost straight up. Soon, the white trail arched back to earth, and the Javelin came screaming down out of the sky. The deadly missile slammed into the top of the enemy tank and exploded in a massive fireball. When the smoke cleared, the charred remains of the chassis lay? destroyed? on the battlefield.

The Marines were taking enemy fire from a tree line on the west and some oil storage tanks on the east. Captain Santare immediately sent a section of Cobras over to the western tree line.

Mouth was riding in Bravo Company's command track, B204, with Captain Newland, the weapons platoon leader, the AAV platoon leader, a

---

12 Ibid. Schielein.

team of forward observers, and a group of radio operators. Santare rode with the track hatches open, standing on the bench of the crowded troop compartment so that he could have a clear view of the battlefield. He could not communicate with the battalion air officer in the Alpha command AM-TRAC, so he was forced to organize the entire air battle. He worked the air flow and the battle simultaneously. He used Huey helicopters overhead as his eyes on the battlefield. The Huey pilots provided Santare with a bird's-eye view of the road ahead. By now, Santare was involved in a continuous conversation with the pilots. He diligently worked to keep track of the aircraft as they came and went. Never faltering, he attacked with ferocity, sending wave after wave of Cobra helicopters at the enemy.

Soon fixed-wing aircraft checked in, and Santare sent them deep. He ordered them to attack targets north of An Nasiriyah. By now, several Cobra helicopters were swarming like bees over the battlefield, and one of the Cobras took out another Iraqi tank that was hiding in the tree line off to the west of the road.

AMERICA'S BATTALION

As soon as the high-level meeting broke up at RCT-2, Colonel Mortenson called his XO forward. Mortenson knew that Grabowski had already encountered resistance, but he didn't know how much. Reports of missing soldiers and ambushes cluttered the net. The fog of war was starting to roll in. Major Alford, Mortenson's XO, stopped at each of the companies and picked up his company commanders. Captain Dremann knew that he would soon be in the fight. He had been listening to his radio and knew that 1/2 had already engaged the enemy. He could see Cobra's making gun runs in the north, and there were several black columns of smoke rising in the distance. The scene at RCT-2 was chaotic. Humvees were scattered on both sides of the road, mixed in with 1/2 and 1/10 log train vehicles. Eddie Ray's LAR was strung out along the road, ready to move into the battle.

Major Alford briefed his officers from the hood of Mortenson's HMMWV. He spread out a map and told them what he knew, that 1/2 was in a heavy fight and that they had been engaging tanks. The Timberwolves had not yet reached the southern bridge. Grabowski's Marines were fighting their way to the Euphrates River, and America's Battalion had been ordered up to clear behind them. Echo Company would clear the west side of Highway 7, and Rich Dremann's Fox Company would clear the east side of the road. Golf Company would follow on the road as the battalion reserve. America's Battalion would clear the route from the intersection of highways 7 and 8 to the Euphrates River where they were to link up with 1/2 about one hundred meters south of the bridge. Dremann's Marines were already moving forward, and as the briefing ended, Fox Company passed the command group. Captain Dremann waved down his own vehicle, hopped in, and began issuing orders to his platoon commanders over the company net.

THE BETIO BASTARDS

By now, the Betio Bastards were running dangerously low on gasoline. They had left most of their logistic support back with the regiment on Highway 7, so Major Starling filled his pockets with 3/2 coins[13] and took his empty re-fuelers and several trucks in search of supplies. They drove the short distance south to Tallil, where the Army was setting up a giant logistics site.

Major Starling first went to one of the site's commanders, an Army lieutenant colonel, who told him emphatically that he could not have anything, and that these supplies were reserved for the Army. Undaunted, Major Starling went in search of someone more willing to help. He found a young supply lieutenant who was much more amiable. It probably didn't hurt that he was junior to Major Starling.

Black clouds of smoke were billowing into the sky from Nasiriyah, and American jets were circling high overhead. Starling told the lieutenant that his regiment was in a fight and they sorely needed fuel, food, and water. The young lieutenant agreed to help the Marines. Major Starling pulled a single Betio Bastards coin out of his pocket, placed it in the palm of his right hand, and shook the Army officer's hand—leaving the brass coin with the lieutenant. Even soldiers know the value of Betio Bastard coins. They are valuable collector's items, and the lieutenant was thrilled with the gift.

In exchange, he gave the Marines 1,800 gallons of gasoline, three days worth of chow for the entire battalion, and all the bottled water they could cram into their trucks. Starling had his men quickly load up their treasure

---

13 Military unit "challenge coins" have been around since the 60s. A Betio Bastard coin is one of the highest valued, because of the battalion's heroic history.

and get out of Tallil before the lieutenant colonel discovered what his young, generous lieutenant had done against his wishes.

HML/A-269: THE GUNRUNNERS

Lieutenant Colonel Jeffrey M. "Huey" Hewlett was the commanding officer of MAG-29s' attack helicopter squadron, HML/A-269. With the invasion underway, Hewlett had flown ashore from *Saipan* earlier that morning looking for Streeter and Schenberger, but they were already approaching Nasiriyah. Hewlett could see billowing smoke in the distance, so he headed for the action. When he arrived on station, he checked in with Streeter and Schenberger and the FAC on the ground. By the time Hewlett caught up with his pilots, there were already F/A-18s and four Cobras on station, working over the enemy.

Since there were so many aircraft, Hewlett ordered his sections to land to conserve fuel and wait their turn to enter the battle. When the other Cobras started pulling off station, Streeter's section took to the air, pushed up, and started engaging targets south of the bridge. They attacked and destroyed two BMPs[14] and a technical that were dug in within a stand of palm trees.

While they were working over the tree line, Santare yelled into his microphone, "SAM[15] in the air! SAM in the air!" Instantly, all of the Cobras scattered, spewing flares to avoid the deadly missile. Fortunately, all of the helicopters managed to avoid the poorly aimed RPG. Bruggeman and Parker took a moment to collect themselves, and then they returned to the battle, hovering directly over the Timberwolves' shoulder until they expended all of their ammunition. Then, they turned to make a mad dash back to Jalibah to refuel and rearm. As Bruggeman, Schenberger, Parker, and Hewlett moved off station, more waiting Cobras lifted into the air and moved in to support their fellow Marines on the ground. As they were leaving, Lieutenant Colonel Hewlett radioed, "Mouth, I'm going to Jalibah, and I'll be right back."[16]

Every available Cobra was pushed forward. As they arrived, they joined

---

14 Soviet-built, armored personnel carrier.

15 Surface-to-air missile.

16 William Hodgkins, "Investigation of Suspected Friendly Fire Incident Near An Nasiriyah, Iraq, 23 March 03" (MacDill Air force Base, United States Central Command, Mar 06 2004). p H-30.

the tag-team. Soon there was a continuous stream helicopters attacking the enemy, returning to Jalibah, refueling and rearming, flying back to Nasiriyah, and waiting on the ground for their next turn at the action.

THE TIMBERWOLVES

While Bravo and CAAT were fighting at the railway bridge, Grabowski pulled his Alpha Command Group off onto the side of the road into a protected culvert. He could see Captain Newland's track up on the bridge. Grabowski said to his gunner and sergeant major, "We're not going any farther until we get some tanks up here."[17] He then got on the radio and called Major Tuggle and ordered him to get back to the refueling area to find out what was taking the tanks so long. Next, Grabowski called Newland on the radio and said, "As soon as you guys get the tanks, press and press hard, we need to get to the next bridge."[18]

Newland was parked only meters away from Grabowski on the bridge, in the shade of a large palm tree. It was hard for him to tell the source of the enemy fire until he heard a *dat dat dat dat dat* and the ball of the palm tree over his head exploded. A few moments later, another machine gun burst hit the same spot, dropping more palm fronds onto Newland's track and splintering the tree. Captain Newland thought that the source of the fire was from the east side of the road. Some Iraqi was probably hiding in a hole, and every few seconds, he was reaching up and pulling the trigger, not bothering to aim his fire. Several Marines started shooting to the east, and a Cobra swooped in to attack the Iraqis near the large oil storage tanks about five hundred meters from the road. A round hit one of the petroleum tanks and blew a gaping hole in its side. Flames shot from the tank creating another giant column of oily, black smoke that rose into the clear blue sky.

While they were stopped, Santare sprinted back to the Alpha command track to brief the air officer and the S3, and then he ran back to his own vehicle. "We had two or three FACs and the aircraft on the TAD net, and no control from battalion."[19] Santare continued to direct the air attack. Once

17 Telephone interview with Lieutenant Colonel Rickey Grabowski, 3/1/04.

18 Ibid. Grabowski.

19 FFIR—Santare's testimony.

all of the visible tanks had been taken out, he turned the airborne gunners' attention toward machine gun bunkers and, finally, to dismounted Iraqis carrying AK-47s and RPGs.

Sergeant Major Arrick spent his time at the railroad bridge searching for the occupants of the burning Army vehicles. He got as close to the vehicles as he dared only to find bullet holes and smears of blood. It didn't look good for the occupants of the tow truck. Arrick began a methodical search along the sides of the road, hoping to find the soldiers, but they were nowhere to be found.

The battalion's 81mm mortar fire capped at a garbage dump, two kilometers south of the railroad bridge. Gunny Doran had picked the spot. Tactically, it was perfect for the battalion mortars, but the place was nasty; it was just rancid. The stench alone would have kept the enemy away, and the area was swarming with flies—more flies than anyone could possibly imagine. While they were there, several Marines walked over to Luten's truck and salvaged his .50-caliber machine gun and ammo. Gunny Doran decided that this would be a perfect time to return to the log trains and replenish his supplies.

Lieutenant Colonel Grabowski anxiously waited at the southern base of the railway bridge for his tanks to return. Finally, around 1130, Major Peeples decided to abandon the refueling operation and send Gunny Howard's four Team Mech tanks forward with only forty additional gallons. Grabowski saw the first tank rumble through the black cloud of smoke billowing from the 507th's truck, which, by now, was fully engulfed in flames. No sooner had the first tank rolled into view, than a second tank broke through the smoke. Then came the third and, finally, the forth tank of Team Mech appeared.

Grabowski wasted no time in ordering the battalion forward. With Team Mech's tank platoon (Diablo), and Sergeant Schielein's CAAT section in the lead, the 1st Battalion, 2d Marines raced over the railroad bridge and into Nasiriyah's suburbs toward their first objective, the Euphrates River bridge. Bravo's twelve AAVs followed closely behind.

Still standing on the troop compartment bench, Captain Santare sent Cobras up the road to lead the push to the Euphrates River. As Bravo Company's tracks lurched forward, Santare was busier than ever. He was holding a large map of An Nasiriyah and two radio handsets, and all the while, he was jotting down notes and trying to maintain situational awareness.

At this point, if an Iraqi appeared with a weapon or looked hostile, he was dead. Whatever the Iraqi plan had been, it was now moot. They were now committed to mortal combat with Tarawa's Marines. The Iraqis could hide in buildings or they could fight, but they couldn't run. The Cobras roamed the skies and swooped down like birds of prey upon anything that looked like it was a threat. Elation started to turn to concern in the local Iraqi command centers. Their southernmost defensive position had just been decimated in a little over thirty minutes.

CORPORAL Matthew Walsh jerked to the side in his seat as his Bravo Company AAV began to move forward into the city. Members of his squad had opened the overhead hatches of the vehicle, and Marines with heavier weapons were standing to provide additional firepower on either side. Corporal Walsh was sitting at the feet of the track's gunner. While inside the track, his job was to prepare the .50-caliber ammunition for the up-gun. Team Mech hadn't been moving for long when the Marines started receiving enemy small arms fire, more potshots than anything else. Walsh rode helplessly along in the belly of his track while his friends began to open fire with their SAWs and 240G machine guns.

Walsh moved blindly forward into battle. He could hear the fight, but he could not see what was going on outside. He wanted to stand and get a look at what was happening, but he would have blocked the other Marines' line of fire. So he sat nervously waiting. With all the shooting going on, Walsh thought that anyone out there would surely be destroyed before he got close.

Lance Corporal Hyler, who was standing, continued to provide the Marines riding blind in the track with a blow-by-blow description of the unfolding events. His first announcement to the Marines below was that there were burned-up trucks and HMMWVs all around. Then he announced they were entering the city, followed by, "It looks like Jacksonville, only shittier."[20]

Grabowski's Alpha Command group, in their HMMWVs and two command tracks, followed directly behind Bravo's tracks. A column of a dozen more soft-skinned Humvees fell in behind the command tracks. Captain Blanchard, the AAV company commander, rode at the end of the column.

---

20 Corporal Walsh sent me a personal letter from Afghanistan, detailing his participation in the Battle of An Nasiriyah. This quote was taken from his letter.

Blanchard had chosen to ride in a Humvee for a couple of reasons. First, his battalion commander was in a Humvee. More important, the smaller, more agile vehicle afforded Blanchard a better opportunity to maintain radio contact with all of his AAV platoon and section leaders. He was free to move forward or fall back to keep track of all of his vehicles.

Gradually, the battalion began to move up the road. Captain Brooks's Alpha Company fell in behind Grabowski's command group. Then Charlie Company moved back onto the road and followed in trace. The battalion's mortar platoon remained fire capped at the 29 Northing to cover the advance to the Euphrates River. Major Tuggle stayed with the Bravo Command Group and the main command post at the southern end of the formation.

During the previous night, Major Peeples had been ordered to move his combat train to the rear of the formation with the rest of the log trains. Gunny Wright's combat train normally traveled on the heels of the tank platoons in four Humvees and the two M88 tank retrievers, but now they were with the battalion log trains.

As Alpha Company approached the railroad bridge, they began taking sporadic small arms fire. Alpha's Marines shot back. The Timberwolves were headed into battle, and each Marine had his own personal inner struggle. Staff Sergeant Jason Cantu wasn't scared, he was anxious. Others wondered if they would do the right thing when faced with real combat. How would they react to battle? How would they deal with the first contact with the enemy? Would they perform as the heroic Marines throughout history, or would they falter? For others, their thoughts were of friends and family, life and death. Fear and anticipation rode in every track, along with excitement and dread. Words cannot describe the raw emotions of men going into battle. One thing is certain: the fatigue caused by three days of travel across the desert was gone.

AMERICA'S BATTALION

The plan was for Grabowski's armor and mech forces to make a penetration to the bridges and for Mortenson's infantry to move in to clear and secure. America's Battalion moved north behind the Timberwolves, and Echo, Fox, and Golf companies rolled north in their seven-ton trucks. They had been ordered to move to the intersection of highways 7 and 8, dismount, and clear both sides of the road from Highway 8 to the southern bridge. Fox and Echo companies were in the lead, followed by Golf. From their position south of the garbage dump, the Marines could see the clouds of black smoke and Cobras returning from the front with their rails clear. There was clearly a fight up ahead.

As the radio chatter increased, some of Mortenson's Marines began to get nervous. Others were anxious to press forward and get into the fight. Once the Timberwolves secured the eastern bridges, Echo Company would drive into the city and secure the route between the two bridges. Now, with a battle raging, some of the Marines began to wonder about the sensibility of moving into Ambush Alley in lightly armed trucks.

HML/A-269: THE GUNRUNNERS; JALABAH

Bruggeman and Parker returned to a much different scene at the Marine airfield than what they had awakened to earlier in the day. Helicopters had been ferrying in supplies and Marines all morning. Jalibah had become a busy airfield. The morning calm had changed into hustle and bustle, as Cobras, Hueys, Black Hawks, and Phrogs were all jockeying for positions at the refueling stations and rearming points. Helicopters were constantly landing and taking off. It was organized mayhem.

The Marines on the ground had formed human chains to help replenish the ordinance on the waiting Cobras and Hueys. Every available pair of hands was carrying 20mm rounds and rockets to the helicopters. They all knew that Task Force Tarawa was in a fight, so the MAG-29 Marines worked as fast as they could to help get their choppers back into the fight.

507TH MAINTENANCE COMPANY

Miller, Riley, Hudson, Hernandez, and Johnson were all thrown into the back of a pickup truck and quickly whisked away into southern Nasiriyah by their captors. They were taken on a terrifying journey through the streets of the city to what appeared to be an Iraqi headquarters. They were stripped of all their equipment and then filmed. As soon as the filming was completed, they were hustled into a Toyota 4-Runner and driven north to Baghdad.

Lynch and Piestewa, both badly injured, were separated from the group. They were taken to a schoolhouse along Highway 7, just south of the Euphrates River. It is not known how long they stayed at the schoolhouse or even why they were taken there. It is not known why they were not taken directly to the hospital. Nearly three hours passed before armed Fedayeen brought the two young female soldiers to the Tykar Military Hospital on the southern bank of the Euphrates River.[21] Doctors moved the badly injured women into the hospital and began to administer IV fluids. Lynch appeared to be in much worse condition. Piestewa had suffered a serious head wound, and Lynch, unconscious, had several broken bones and had lost a massive amount of blood from severe internal injuries. Some of her injuries were not consistent with an automobile accident. It is highly likely that she was abused by her captors during those lost three hours.

Soon after the IVs were started, Lori Piestewa stopped breathing. The doctors worked to revive her to no avail, but she was gone. Lynch, nearly lifeless and now alone, barely clung to life.

THE TIMBERWOLVES

The Timberwolves had been moving across the Iraqi wasteland for the last two days and nights. Most were running on adrenaline. They were all exhausted, having only been able to sleep in small, two-hour catnaps. Most had driven all day and worked into the night. Colonel Grabowski had planned to set in his blocking defense just south of Nasiriyah and give his men some much-needed rest after their long, hot, bumpy journey across the Iraqi desert. Instead, the Timberwolves had been ordered immediately into battle.

The men of the 1st Battalion, 2d Marine Regiment rose to the occasion. While weary, they did not complain, they did not falter, instead they pressed forward with the attack. They drove north past Campbell, Jackson, and the other wounded soldiers. Will Bachmann saw the wounded soldiers of the 507th as he passed the battalion aid station. He had a detached feeling— like when driving past an accident on the freeway. This glimpse of the first few casualties was little more than a curiosity to the young Marines. They

---

21 Rick Bragg *I Am a Soldier, Too,* (New York: Knopf 2003) 79–80, 95–96.

all craned their necks trying to get a glimpse of the commotion along the side of the road.

Bachmann gazed north at the half dozen columns of billowing black smoke on the horizon. He and his friends had come halfway around the world and had spent the last two days crossing the Iraqi desert in their cramped armored vehicles. They were on an adventure of a lifetime, and no one in the track stopped to think that they were approaching the gates of hell. They were invincible. They were trained. They were tough. First Battalion possessed an enormous amount of resources. They had tanks, AAVs, artillery, and they had air support. The young Marines of 1st Battalion moved forward, confident of victory and with the innocence of young warriors who have never before been exposed to the horrors of combat.

CHAPTER 8

The Euphrates River

Keep moving.

—2D MARINE REGIMENT MOTTO

THE TIMBERWOLVES

Schielein's CAAT section and Gunny Howard's Team Mech tanks crested the Euphrates River bridge first. From his position farther back in the column, Grabowski watched as the tanks and HMMWVs disappeared from view. He thought out loud, "there's no turning back now, we're committed!"[1]

As soon as Schielein's CAAT vehicles moved to the dusty streets on the north side of the bridge, all hell broke loose. Schielein's field of view was filled with Iraqis running in all directions. He saw muzzle flashes for one-hundred-eighty degrees in front of him. Bullets cracked all around his vehicle. Schielein immediately ordered, "There will be no TOW shots."[2] In a confined urban environment, the TOWs can be more dangerous to the Marines than the enemy. Backwash from its rocket can instantly melt the skin off a person, so the Marines in the TOW vehicles reached for their SAWs.

Schielein's CAAT section came rushing down off the bridge with guns

1 Telephone Interview with Lieutenant Colonel Grabowski, 4/1/04.

2 Ibid. Schielein.

blazing. They were firing every SAW, every .50-caliber, and every MK19 they had. Drivers and loaders were firing their personal M-16s. Schielein's Marines threw everything they had at the enemy. The MK19 grenadiers hurled grenades as fast as they could, leveling everything in sight.

At the base of the bridge, Schielein jumped from his Humvee into the middle of the street and began to lay down M-16 fire. As the rest of his section moved across the bridge, Schielein noticed an Iraqi technical in the corner of his eye. The Iraqi gunner in the back of the pickup was swinging his heavy 12.7mm machine gun in Schielein's direction. Gunny Howard's *Lucille2*[3] came clanking up and stopped between the Iraqi and Schielein. Howard's turret was moving before the large tank ground to a stop. The turret completed its traverse and, *boom!* Schielein was knocked back from the concussion, ears ringing and stars twirling in his eyes.

"Holy crap!"[4] Schielein shouted in surprise. Howard's main gun had taken out the Iraqi technical, saving his life.

Grabowski was still following behind Tim Newland and Dennis Santare, who were riding in Bravo Company's command AMTRAC. Dave Sosa followed his boss in another HMMWV. The battalion's Alpha command track trailed Sosa.

As Newland and Santare approached the Euphrates River bridge, Santare could see a group of Saddam Fedayeen off to his right. The group was milling about a mortar on the southern bank of the river. Santare quickly relayed his discovery to Cobra pilots overhead. As the Cobras swooped in, the enemy scattered. From the air, the mortar appeared unmanned, so the Marines held their fire. Bravo Company continued forward up onto the bridge, leaving the enemy mortar undamaged. "The problem with being in the air is that you don't understand the gravity of the situation on the ground."[5]

The Iraqis were hiding nearby. As soon as the overhead threat was gone, they returned to their gun and resumed dropping mortar rounds into the city. Iraqis all over the battlefield were using this "shoot and scoot" tactic to avoid the Marines' withering fire.

---

3 Gunny Howard had served in a Marine M-60 tank battalion during Desert Storm. He was the loader in a tank that his commander had named *Lucille*. In remembrance of *Lucille*, he named his M1 tank *Lucille2*.

4 Ibid. Schielein.

5 Personal interview with First Lieutenant John Parker, 1/12/04.

B204 crossed the bridge and moved into downtown Nasiriyah. They turned right, as enemy rounds continued to crackle overhead. Two RPGs narrowly missed Newland's command track, and Santare could see more black-clad fighters. They were hiding behind women and children and forcing families out into the streets to block the Marines line of fire. More gunmen were popping out of doorways and windows, and they would unleash a few shots at the Marines and then disappear.

The Timberwolves continued to pour into the city. They rolled in so fast that the enemy couldn't have broken contact if they wanted to. Cobras were buzzing overhead, as vehicle after vehicle rolled up onto the Euphrates River bridge. Santare directed his Cobra's out away from the urban area and sent them east of the city to spearhead Grabowski's thrust onto the salt flats.

Bravo Company moved into Ambush Alley, and Grabowski drove up on the bridge around 1300. He expected it to blow at any second, but the bridge remained intact. As soon as Grabowski reached the north bank of the Euphrates River, he realized that the first objective was now in his control. Elated, he immediately radioed Bailey, "We got RCT Objective 1! It's ours now!"[6]

As soon as they came down off the northern side of the Euphrates River bridge, the Timberwolves were greeted with a flurry of RPGs. Fortunately, they were not well aimed, or the grenadiers had neglected to remove the arming pins. Had the Iraqis been trained, dozens of RPGs would have landed home and many tracks would have been damaged. RPGs bounced off the tanks and tracks, and others skidded across the ground or snaked wildly through the air. Team Mech's tanks, then Bravo and the battalion forward command element took a hard right turn into the narrow streets that led east between the mud block buildings of Eastern Nasiriyah.

The plan was to avoid a hazardous drive through the city streets. Bailey and Grabowski wanted to skirt the edge of An Nasiriyah and approach the Saddam Canal bridge from the open terrain of the eastern salt flats. Under this hail of rockets and gunfire, Grabowski was now convinced that they had made the right decision to skirt the main thoroughfare. The tanks moved east for less than a kilometer, through narrow alleyways that were barely wide enough for the armored vehicles. The alleys opened into a large garbage-strewn field. As the tankers exited the confines of the alleys, they fanned out in the open space. Just as they reached the field, they noticed

---

6 Ibid. Grabowski.

a handful of Iraqi soldiers—Regular Army. Gunny Howard quickly cut them down with a burst of machine gun fire. Most of Bravo Company's tracks turned left onto other roads leading north of the open area, and some moved out into the field.

BRAVO COMPANY

Team Mech's tanks lumbered into a quagmire. Almost immediately, the lead tank became stuck in the mud, and the second tank was forced to stop. When the third tank stopped, it, too, became stuck. To make matters worse, Iraqis were firing on the American column from every direction. The ground had looked passable. On the surface, there was a six- or seven-inch layer of hard, crusted mud. Beneath the sun-baked surface was two or three feet of muck—a mixture of thousand-year-old Euphrates River silt and Nasiriyah's putrid sewage. The tanks sank all the way up to their chassis.

Sergeant Mark Sarmiento had been popping his head up out of the top of the track every once in awhile to see what was going on. He took a few seconds to look around as his track negotiated the narrow streets, and then he dropped back down to give his SAW gunner more room. Sarmiento was the assault team leader for 1st Squad of Lieutenant David Beere's 3d Platoon. Beere and Sarmiento were traveling close to the front of Team Mech's tracks.

Suddenly, Beere's track appeared to struggle, then just stopped moving altogether. Sarmiento popped up again to find that his track was stuck in the mud in the middle of an open field. Beere ordered his infantrymen to stay in their tracks. Sarmiento tried to open the back door, but the track had sunk so deep that it was blocked. The assault team climbed out the top, jumped down into nearly waist-deep muck and struggled to set up security around the mired track.

First Platoon's 1st Squad track managed to avoid the muddy mess. It pulled onto a piece of dry ground, and the crew chief announced, "Ramp's coming down!" Corporal Jose Gomez, 1st Squad's leader, jumped from the track along with the rest of his squad and took cover. Gomez ran to 1st Sergeant Parker to get his orders.

The driver of Grabowski's Alpha Command track tried to avoid the muck. He pulled his track up next to a building onto what looked like dry ground. Just as it stopped, the surface broke like ice on a Wisconsin lake in early spring and the command track sank. Water, muck, and mud began to ooze up around the vehicle as the trackers tried to extricate themselves from the gooey mess. The driver had made a critical mistake in pulling up next to the building. Sewage was everywhere. People had pipes coming out of their houses, and the open pipes drained into open ditches next to each house. The chase vehicle moved up to pull the C7 out of the mud, and it got stuck, too.

One of Schielein's CAAT HMMWVs bogged down next, right in front of Grabowski's Humvee. Another Humvee bounced into the disabled HMMWV, ramming it several times until it was freed from the muck. Most of the Humvee column was stopped nose to tail in the narrow alleyway, caught in the traffic jam.

Some of the CAAT Humvees cautiously moved up with the tanks and attacked a house from which the Iraqis were firing on the rear of the mired vehicles. As they moved to a supporting fire position, one of the trucks got stuck again.

Grabowski jumped from his vehicle and ran across the muddy field to the back of his command track. A Marine told him that eight tracks and three tanks had driven into the mess and had become stuck. His command track was trapped in a narrow path between two two-story buildings, and they were having problems establishing communications. Grabowski looked into the track and asked the air officer, Captain Greene, "got any comm[7] with any aircraft?"[8] Greene gave Grabowski a slashing sign across his throat and said, "None, sir!" Greene had no working radios, effectively removing him from the battle. Grabowski turned to the artillery liaison officer (LNO), who offered, "I had comm before we got in the city, but I haven't talked with any of the forward observers."

Major Sosa added that he had no communications with Regiment. Grabowski ordered, "keep working comm," and then raced back across the muddy, open terrain to his vehicle. He feared that Captain Wittnam would try to follow Bravo Company, since that was the original plan. Grabowski tried several times to raise Wittnam on the battalion net to warn him not to turn east, but Wittnam never answered his call.

Gunner Dunfee and Sergeant Major Arrick had jumped from Grabowski's Humvee, rifles at the ready. Their first order of business was to

---

7 Communications.

8 Ibid. Grabowski.

protect their battalion commander while he tried to use his radio. Rounds were hitting around them and curious civilians filled the area—mostly children and old women. Dunfee thought to himself, "Okay, they're going to use these buildings,"[9] so he started scanning the rooftops. Just overhead, he saw a black head of hair. "Aha!" he mumbled under his breath as he zeroed in on his target. The head came closer to the edge, and a set of shoulders appeared.

The Iraqi was wearing a bright white shirt. The young man peered over the edge and saw that Dunfee had him directly in his sights. The figure quickly scurried away, and Dunfee continued to scan the rooftops. As quickly as he had disappeared, the young man had returned, and Dunfee noticed his head again. He looked over the edge into the street below again, and Dunfee pointed his weapon at him a second time.

The figure quickly disappeared like one of the pop-up targets at an old-fashioned shooting gallery. Dunfee was positive that this Iraqi was up to something. He thought to himself, "the third time he comes out, I'm going to whack him."[10] Fortunately for the young man, he never reappeared.

Radio communications were nearly impossible. Everyone with a radio was trying to talk at the same time. Most of Grabowski's Marines were in combat for the first time, and the adrenaline rush had caused everyone to forget radio discipline. Grabowski remembered, "It was like being in a basketball pregame warm-up. Everybody was shooting at the same basket. One ball was going to go through the hoop, but all the others were going to bounce off and not get through."[11]

Following behind the tanks and the lead tracks in Newland's command track, Captain Santare continued to talk with the aircraft overhead. He immediately called in a section of Cobras to provide cover for the mired vehicles. "We got some tanks stuck. You're going to have to cover these guys until they can get out of there."[12] Bruggeman and Schenberger's Cobras swooped in close overhead and began taking out Iraqis who were firing from the rooftops. Only feet above the Marines on the ground, the Cobra's

---

9 Personal interview with Gunner David Dunfee, 3/25/04.

10 Ibid. Dunfee.

11 Ibid. Grabowski.

12 Friendly Fire Incident Report, Santare testimony.

shell casings showered down on the open field as they poured from their rapid-fire guns.

Soon, Bruggeman and Parker saw a mass exodus. The local inhabitants were fleeing east, leaving the city. They hurried along, carrying their small children through short trees, shrubs, and then across small canals that interlaced the landscape. The civilians were trying to get away from the battle.[13]

The Cobras stayed on station for as long as they could, but within an hour, they were either out of ammunition or fuel. Prior to leaving, they checked out with Santare and then peeled off for the thirty-minute flight back to Jalibah. They spent another thirty to forty minutes refueling and rearming, and then they returned to the fight. A constant round-robin continued. Some Cobras were on the ground at Jalibah, others en route to Nasiriyah, and still more were parked just south of the battle. More Cobras were supporting the Timberwolves while the last wave was on its way back to Jalibah to start the cycle all over again.

Captain Blanchard finally got out of the narrow alley to find utter chaos. Two tanks, both command tracks, and a couple of HMMWVs were stuck in this suburban quicksand. Blanchard leapt from his Humvee into the muddy field and sank up to his knees. He plodded out of the mud and got his men working to retrieve their vehicles. He would move a track up to pull one out of the quicksand, and it, too, would get stuck. The trackers worked for hours freeing tracks, and then sticking others. It seemed nearly futile.

Under Captain Newland's direction, Marines poured out of their vehicles and began to set up a defensive zone around the colonel's HMMWV. They battered down doors and cleared nearby buildings in an effort to develop a safe perimeter around the bogged-down vehicles. Then, Newland ran over to talk with his boss. Grabowski told Newland, "Take what you can and continue north and get up there and take that bridge."[14] Then Grabowski turned to Sosa, "You're coming with me. We're going north." Then he got on the radio to Tuggle. He wanted to know where the rest of his tanks were and what was taking them so long. He sent Tuggle to personally insure that they were coming forward—immediately.

---

13 Ibid. Parker.

14 Telephone interview with Captain Tim Newland, 2/13/04.

ALPHA COMPANY, 8TH TANKS

Tuggle raced up to the RRP[15] in his Humvee and slid sideways to a halt. He jumped out of his vehicle and ordered Peeples to get the rest of his tanks forward. "The entire battalion is in contact, and we need to commit the battalion reserve, *now*!" Tuggle looked frustrated. Obviously, the battle in the north was not going well. Captain Cubas and Gunny Kamper had nearly topped off their fuel and were waiting alongside the road for Team Tank to finish refueling.

When Cubas saw Tuggle screech to a halt, he tried to get Major Peeples on the net, but Peeples was out of his tank. Cubas radioed Kamper. "Let's just go," he told his wingman. Third Platoon's two tanks drove back up on the road and headed north toward the battle.

When Peeples heard Tuggle's order, he immediately told Team Tank to push forward and assist Bravo Company. Within minutes, Jim Thompson had abandoned his efforts to refuel his remaining tanks. Peeples moved forward with his last five tanks, Captain Thompson's three remaining tanks of Red Platoon, and his two command tanks.

Cubas and Kamper were in the lead, racing to Gunny Howard's aid. Peeples, Carter, Dyer, Hawk, Thompson, and the company's remaining tanks were not far behind. Now that all of Alpha Company's tanks were moving again, the maintenance Marines in the company's combat train prepared their own rescue mission. No order was necessary.

Gunny Wright, Staff Sergeant Cooke, two corpsmen, and several other Marines donned their helmets and jumped in their soft-skinned Humvees and the company's two M88 tank retrievers. Randy Whidden had been standing security for the refueling operation, and when he saw all the commotion around the combat train vehicles, he raced over to Staff Sergeant Cooke and asked him what was going on. Cooke replied, "Our tanks are stuck up there. We gotta get them out."[16]

Whidden jumped in the back of the maintenance chief's Humvee with his SAW. The four Humvees and two tank retrievers rolled north, but they had not traveled far when they ran into a group of Marines stopped along the road just south of the railroad bridge. The tankers stopped at the tail end

---

15 Rapid resupply point.

16 Telephone interview with Corporal Randy Whidden, 1/19/05.

of the small traffic jam. Gunny Wright jumped from the lead vehicle and ran back to talk with his men.

Cooke and Whidden had stopped right next to one of the 507th's bullet-ridden trucks. Whidden could almost reach out and touch the truck, and he could see a half dozen bullet holes in the driver's door. Blood was everywhere. There was so much blood that Whidden thought the driver probably hadn't survived.

Gunny Wright told his Marines, "We have no comm. We have no orders to go in here. Anybody that doesn't want to go, let me know." No one answered, so Wright continued, "As far as I can tell, our mission is to take care of our tanks . . . therefore, we are going in."[17]

"Let's do it." Whidden replied. "Whatever we do, we ain't sitting here."

Peeples' combat train rolled north over the rail overpass, and they started taking fire from the tree line. They stopped again at the intersection of highways 7 and 8. The enemy fire had increased, so the tankers got out of their vehicles and took cover. As Whidden ran for the side of the highway, he looked south and saw Iraqis running all over, attempting to close off the road behind the Marines.

ALPHA COMPANY

Alpha Company's AAVs had come down off the Euphrates River bridge behind Grabowski's command group into the seemingly endless volley of RPGs. The tracks swerved and pirouetted to avoid the rockets while Captain Brooks's Marines fired at dismounted Iraqis from the open hatches.

Staff Sergeant Cantu was in the second-to-last track to cross the bridge behind Lieutenant Martin, Alpha's XO. They ground to a stop. Cantu pleaded, "We gotta get out!"[18] But the tracks stayed buttoned up, waiting for Brooks's orders to deploy. As they waited, an Iraqi ambulance appeared in the distance, off to right side of the road. Six or seven Iraqis jumped from the ambulance and began firing at the Marines.

Before Cantu and his men could react, the Iraqis jumped back in the ambulance, and it raced behind a nearby berm. Once they thought they had

17 Ibid. Whidden.

18 Ibid. Cantu.

found cover, they jumped from the vehicle again and continued the fight. Cantu's up-gunner rotated his turret and tore the group up with several bursts of his .50-caliber machine gun and a couple of well-placed grenades.

Cantu was still looking east and shooting his M-16 in that general direction when his driver started yelling, "Staff Sergeant! Staff Sergeant!"[19] Cantu turned to see that they were also getting shot at from the west. Enemy rounds were plinking off the track. "Oh, shit!" he exclaimed. Cantu, a firearms instructor, hadn't really been aiming until now. He started talking to himself, "Aim—Squeeze—Aim—Squeeze." With each squeeze, another Iraqi fell.

First Sergeant Thompson came up onto the bridge in the company's last track. As Thompson crested the bridge, a taxi cab drove up behind him. Thompson and his men waived frantically, trying to keep the taxi occupants out of harm's way. "Go back," they motioned.

The vehicle continued to race north toward Alpha Company. Then, to the Marines' surprise, armed men jumped from the taxi and began firing at Thompson and his men. The Marines quickly returned fire, killing them all. A312 clanged down off the bridge and positioned itself to defend against further attacks from the south and within minutes, a second white taxi, adorned with orange fenders, sped over the bridge. The Marines immediately destroyed this one.

Captain Brooks called for support from the battalion's 81mm mortars, but they were still more than a kilometer south of the railroad bridge and hopelessly out of range. Brooks ordered his 60mm mortar section to set up their tubes in a shallow drainage ditch across the highway. There wasn't much cover in that ditch, but Alpha's mortar teams quickly fire capped and started raining mortar rounds down on the advancing enemy. Their fire stopped surge after surge of armed Iraqis who were racing into the battle from inside the city.

Finally, the order came to dismount. By 1315, the Euphrates River bridge was solidly in Task Force Tarawa's hands. Alpha Company's Marines scrambled out of their tracks and fanned out into a horseshoe perimeter, north of the Euphrates River. Brooks sent First Platoon to cover the north, and he ordered Second Platoon to the east side of the road to defend to the east and southeast. He then positioned his Third Platoon along the wall on the west side of the main road to defend to the west and south.

---

19 Ibid. Cantu.

First Sergeant Thompson kept his track in the middle of the road, shooting at anything that tried to cross the bridge.

Brooks moved his command track northwest to the corner of a long wall that paralleled the main supply route. "I could see all the way into the city, along a wide mall area."[20] The area was quiet for the first ten minutes or so. Then the enemy fire slowly began to escalate like someone was slowly turning up a dimmer switch.

Upon hearing Brooks's call for fire, the 81mm mortar platoon commander, Lieutenant Clayton, decided to move up so that he would be in range to support the battalion. He ordered his men to load up the mortars into their eight HMMWVs and move north. While they were repositioning, Clayton received orders to move across the Euphrates River and to link up with Alpha Company.

When Day, Doc, and Doran finally got back to the trash heap, Lieutenant Clayton and his mortar platoon were gone. Doran told Day to just floor it, and they raced north. Soon, they had caught up with Clayton's 81s[21] as they were being escorted by Letendre's CAAT vehicles.

BRAVO COMPANY

After about a twenty-minute delay, Grabowski continued his attack through the narrow streets and alleyways of Nasiriyah. Bravo Company and the Alpha Command Element split in two. Five of Newland's tracks, all three of 1st Platoons vehicles, the FiST track, and one of 3rd Platoon's tracks avoided the quagmire and were now staged north of the open area. Grabowski moved north with about a dozen Humvees, on a track parallel with Newland to the east. James Johnson's CAAT machine gun Humvee and McCall's TOW vehicle provided rolling security to the colonel's vehicle, while Newland's mortar section provided dismounted security for the entire Humvee column.

Newland ordered the rest of Bravo Company to stay behind. Gunny Howard's tanks, all of 2d Platoon, and the rest of 3rd Platoon stayed behind to provide security for the trapped vehicles. Two of Lieutenant Beere's tracks remained hopelessly stuck in the mud, so he finally ordered his men to dismount and set up a perimeter.

---

20 Personal interview with Captain Michael Brooks, 10/27/03.

21 81mm battalion mortars.

Walsh's 3d Platoon track stopped, and three SAW gunners jumped out to provide security for the stuck tracks. Then the track moved carefully forward looking for a dry patch of ground to safely stop. The track pulled up on a street, and the rest of Walsh's squad was ordered to dismount. After spending hours riding inside the armored vehicle and only being able to hear the raging battle, Walsh took the order to dismount with mixed emotions. He was terrified at what might await outside, yet he was relieved that now he would finally be able to see what was going on.

Walsh's squad was ordered to stay with the mired tracks along with H&S Company, while the rest of Bravo Company moved forward. Walsh's men poured out of the small door in the back of the track and stacked one in back of the other along a courtyard wall which was a couple feet to the left of their vehicle. Walsh and Lance Corporal Walden were ordered to the east side of the street. They crossed the street, sinking to their knees in the gooey mud. In the center of the street, Walsh got hung up. He pulled himself free and charted a drier course. Eventually, he made it to the far side of the street only to find that he and Walden were in the open, with little protective cover. Walsh saw a stack of cinder blocks just to the north of a small alley, and the two Marines raced for the cover of the stacked block wall.

The shooting had stopped. It was as if they had entered the eye of a hurricane. People started coming out of their houses and roaming around. Women, children, and old men appeared. Fighting-age men with short hair and devious grins walked the streets. A small group of civilians rushed a bleeding Iraqi to one of the corpsmen at the back of one of the tracks. In the blink of an eye, the shooting resumed, causing the streets to empty again. Rounds started buzzing by Walsh and Walden, and then they noticed Iraqis on the rooftops.

CHARLIE COMPANY

The plan had been for Charlie Company to follow Bravo Company across the Euphrates River. As a result of the order in which the companies had moved north, Alpha was ahead of Charlie, so they had moved to take the Euphrates River bridge first. Charlie Company moved to cross over the Euphrates River as the last company. Captain Dan Wittnam ordered 3d Platoon into the lead. The 3d Platoon's leader, Lieutenant Mike Seely, was Captain Wittnam's most experienced officer. He was a Desert Storm hero and former recon Marine. As a sergeant, he had won the Bronze Star and a Purple Heart in the first war with Iraq.

Lieutenant Seely led 3d Platoon up onto the road in C209. The rest of his platoon followed in C210 and C211. Just as they began to move forward, they started taking fire. Seely pressed forward, but as he approached the railroad bridge, his track broke down. Seely's Marines had repeatedly trained for this occurrence in their "bump" drills in Camp Shoup. Moving like a well-oiled machine, the 3d Platoon Marines abandoned the disabled track.

Lieutenant Seely jumped from the track and took Sergeant Pompos's place in C211. Sergeant Pompos moved to take his planned position in C210, but Lieutenant Meador, Charlie Company's XO, refused to give up his comm, so Pompos begrudgingly found a spot to sit on top of the crowded track. C209's track commander and the platoon's AAV section leader, Sergeant Beavers, followed Seely and relieved C211's track commander, Sergeant Michael Bitz. Bitz took over as the track driver. The Marines of 1st Squad, who had been traveling in C209, split up, too. One fire team was ordered to stay with the broken-down vehicle, and the remaining Marines boarded C210 and C211. Seven more Marines scrambled onto the top of C211.

Sergeant Jack Maloney, 1st Squad's leader, found a prime position in C211. He rode standing in the front of the track's troop compartment, on the left side. Will Bachmann stood next to Maloney. Three other Marines stood on the left side of the track. Standing back-to-back with Bachmann and the others, Lance Corporal Quirk, Cline, and Coroporal Mead faced outward on the right side. Cline and Bachmann were together and were watching each other's backs as they moved on.

The troop compartment below was packed from front to back with Marines and their gear. Seely's 3d Squad leader was a twenty-year-old Marine from Pennsylvania, Corporal Randy Glass. Randy made sure he kept his seat in the right rear of the track so that he could be first out when they were ordered to deploy.

Down to eleven tracks, Charlie Company did not hesitate when C209 broke down. Lieutenant Swantner took the lead with his 1st Platoon in C201, C202, and C203; followed by Captain Wittnam's track, C204, and Reid and Pokorney's mortar track, C208. Second Platoon moved up behind the mortar track in the second section of AAVs—C205, C206, and C207—commanded by Staff Sergeant Lefebevre.

Third Platoon completed their Chinese fire drill and quickly caught up with the rest of the company in C211 and C210. First Sergeant Henao brought up the rear of the AMTRAC column in the company's med-evac track—C212. Three company HMMWVs followed close behind C212 with extra ammo and combat supplies.

Now, with 1st Platoon in the lead, Lieutenant Swantner and Sergeant Schaefer, First Platoon's AAV section leader, led Charlie Company toward the Euphrates River in C201. Corporal Edward Castleberry, twenty-one, had joined the Marine Corps the day after 9/11, in Seattle, Washington. A year and a half later, he was halfway around the world driving a 28-ton AMTRAC filled with Marines into the first major battle of Operation Iraqi Freedom.

As they moved forward, Sergeant Schaefer's seat broke. In the lowest position, the gunner can stand on the seat with his head outside the turret. A spring-loaded mechanism allows the user to easily raise and lower the heavy metal seat into several different positions so that the gunner can sit inside the turret and fight with the hatch open or closed. With his seat broken, Schaefer could not easily raise and lower his seat, so he decided to raise the seat to its highest position and latch it in place. Schaefer had to drop down into the turret, get under the seat, and push it up into position. Once he latched it in place, he knew that he would have to spend the rest of the day in this position. Schaefer cursed his bad luck. He knew that he would not be able to get his seat fixed until nightfall. If he needed to button up, he would be extremely uncomfortable scrunched down in the turret.

Castleberry, Schaefer, and Swantner led Charlie Company across the Euphrates River. As soon as C201 reached the northern bank, Iraqis started firing on Schaefer's vehicle from all directions. Schaefer stopped behind Alpha Company, awaiting orders. As he waited, he fired at the enemy with his .50-caliber machine gun. At the crest of the bridge, Captain Dan Wittnam scanned the city ahead, looking for Bravo Company. By this time, they had turned northeast and out of view from Wittnam's position. Wittnam tried to raise his commander on the radio, but it was a futile task. All of the radio nets were still filled with excited chatter. He quickly decided that Bravo must have pushed directly north through the city. He immediately ordered Sergeant Schaefer to drive straight through Ambush Alley.

In his short stop, Schaefer had fired four hundred rounds as the Iraqis had continued to increase their fire. Schaefer verified his order to attack, then commanded Castleberry to move forward. Schaefer announced his movement over the company net. "Eight Ball, Oscar Mike."[22] As the lead track in the lead section of the lead company, they were now the point of the spear. One of Schaefer's primary duties was to provide situational reports to Wittnam. He was the eyes and ears of Charlie Company, or in his own words, he was "the dumb-ass up front who takes all the fire."[23]

Several Iraqis ran to the middle of the road, stopped, and began shooting RPGs at Schaefer's vehicle. Two rockets whizzed by, scraping the side of C201 as they flew past. Other RPGs were duds and bounced off the armored vehicle. Castleberry watched in amazement as another Iraqi jumped into the road and leveled an AK-47 at the lead track. He rummaged around in the driver's compartment trying to keep the 28-ton vehicle driving down the road, while he struggled to bring his M-16 rifle up through his hatch. Unable to free his rifle, he steered straight for the enemy soldier, who was spraying the front of the track with bullets. Castleberry accelerated, crushing the Iraqi under his treads. Finally, he managed to free his weapon. Now he was driving forward and shooting his rifle at the same time.

Schaefer looked over and asked Castleberry, "What in the hell are you doing?"

"It makes me feel better." Castleberry replied.

Schaefer didn't share the helpless feeling that had surged through Castleberry. He was shooting back from his up-gun. His loader could barely keep up with the firing, so he began to string all the links together into a continuous chain. Schaefer continued to fire 40mm grenades and .50-caliber rounds at the Iraqis, who were firing from almost every doorway, alley, and rooftop. "There were thousands of them."[24] The Iraqis charged the vehicle and were trying to grab on and climb aboard.

Separated by fifty to two hundred meters, Charlie Company's vehicles moved deeper into the urban corridor behind Sergeant Schaefer's track. Most of the Marines' fire was focused on the west side. Schaefer encouraged the company over the radio, "Keep it tight." Iraqis were swarming out of nearly every door and alleyway, and seemingly one out of every four was armed with an RPG. Schaefer would see another trail of smoke, and he

---

22 Sergeant Schaefer's radio call sign was "Eight Ball," and "Oscar Mike" was radio slang for "On the move."

23 Personal interview with Staff Sergeant William Schaefer, 6/15/04.

24 Telephone interview with Staff Sergeant William Schaefer, 3/10/04.

would key his radio, "RPG!" Everything was happening in slow motion. As the adrenaline pumped through his bloodstream, Schaefer felt as if he were in *The Matrix*, able to see the bullets flying.

At the tail of the armored column, First Sergeant Jose Henao, Gunny Myers, and Doc Luis Fonseca came down off the bridge and into Ambush Alley. They hadn't traveled three blocks when Henao saw a large mosque on the left side of the road. There was a large, sandbagged bunker sitting atop the mosque, and a single Iraqi stood in the bunker, just watching the Americans drive into town. Before C212 had traveled another block, all hell broke loose, so Henao dropped down into the track and buttoned up.

Not quite halfway to the canal bridge, the Iraqis drove a bus onto the road, and more soldiers in black garb rushed out into the street. Schaefer mowed them all down with his .50-caliber machine gun, and another bus appeared on the road. Castleberry was forced to stop momentarily, causing all of Charlie Company to grind to a halt in the center of the city. Schaefer immediately lobbed a 40mm grenade into the bus.

By now, all of Charlie Company's tracks were engaged with the enemy in Ambush Alley. Guns blazing, the Marines in the back of each track fired a steady stream of SAW, Golf, and M-16 rounds at rooftops, windows, and alleyways as the armored column plowed forward. Up-gunners sprayed .50-caliber rounds toward the enemy and repeatedly lobbed 40mm grenades into enemy positions. Charlie Company cut a path through the enemy, hurling metal and explosives in all directions.

C201 ground forward again, turning and maneuvering to work its way around the two buses. All of Charlie Company began to move again. Finally, Schaefer could see the canal bridge in the distance. Two soldiers were on the bridge. He immediately dispatched the guards and raced across the Saddam Canal.

The Iraqis were surprised by this very different response. Earlier, the soldiers of the 507th Maintenance Company were nothing more than targets as they raced through Ambush Alley. They had wildly returned fire with a few M-16s and a single SAW. Now, the Marines were inflicting heavy casualties. Curtis Campbell had been terrified when he saw Iraqi soldiers and vehicles blocking his path. Castleberry and Schaefer couldn't shoot fast enough. The Iraqis learned quickly that a mechanized Marine infantry battalion was much different than an Army maintenance company. They had originally ambushed a lamb, and now they were fighting a lion.

As Wittnam moved through the city, he found a bizarre scene. On the right

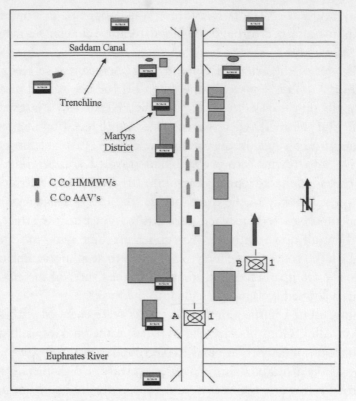

Charlie Company moved through Ambush Alley

side of the road, civilians were walking around with kids, and others were hanging their laundry out to dry. They were acting like they would on any spring Sunday morning. Small arms and RPG fire was coming from almost every building on the west side of the road. Wittnam thought to himself, "Who in their right mind would be out in the streets when this thing was going on?"[25]

CAPTAIN Romeo Cubas reached the Euphrates River with only two of his platoon's tanks, just as Charlie Company was crossing. As they approached the bridge, his tanks began taking machine gun fire from the tree line on the west side of the road. He worried about how much weight the structure

---

25 Personal interview with Captain Dan Wittnam, 3/24/04.

could handle. Up until now, everything he had seen in Iraq had been shab-bily built. Nearly all of Dan Wittnam's tracks were on the bridge, and Cubas did not want to chance taking his seventy-ton tanks up on the span before most of Charlie Company was safely across. So Cubas and Kamper were forced to stop while the Iraqi machine gun continued to fire.

Bullets bouncing off his turret, Captain Cubas anxiously watched as Charlie's AMTRACs drove down off the bridge. Finally, Cubas ordered his two tanks forward and slowly moved up onto the bridge. As soon as they were across, Cubas and Kamper peeled off to the right and headed for their comrades in 2d Platoon. Gunny Howard talked them in over the radio.

Under Howard's direction, Cubas led Kamper through eastern Nasiriyah's narrow alleyways. The buildings were so close together that the seventy-ton tanks were knocking over telephone poles and crushing donkey carts. At the narrowest points, Cubas knocked over walls of buildings to clear the path. They hadn't gotten far into the maze of mud-block buildings when Staff Sergeant Kamper's driver said, "Hey, its getting a little smoky in here."[26]

NOT far behind Schaefer, Fred Pokorney and Ben Reid were trying to keep out of the line of fire in C208. In the midst of their journey through the gaunt-let, an Iraqi bullet whizzed into the troop compartment, ricocheted, and hit Pokorney in the arm. The bullet hit with such force that it knocked him off his feet. Fred immediately got up and grabbed the intercom, "It hurts like hell, but I am alright." Other Marines in the crowded vehicle returned fire.

Lieutenant Seely ended up near the rear of the armored column. C211 was extremely crowded. The vehicle was carrying more than two dozen Marines. Corporal Will Bachmann was standing on other Marines in the back of C211, his upper body exposed on top of the track. A half dozen Marines hunkered down atop the overcrowded track.

As soon as C211 crossed over the Euphrates River and moved through Alpha Company's position, they, too, entered the torrent of enemy fire. It was coming from every conceivable hiding place on both sides of the road. Bachmann and others in his squad fired at every succeeding target as they raced through Ambush Alley. The farther north they traveled, the more intense the battle became.

---

26 Telephone interview with Gunny Sergeant Alan Kamper, 12/3/04.

Nearly halfway through the gauntlet, Seely started noticing RPGs skipping across the road. Seely glanced to his left and saw an Iraqi move into an alley and kneel to a firing position. A plume of smoke erupted around the Iraqi, and another RPG came screaming out toward Charlie Company. Distracted by the grenadier, Seely did not see the RPG fired from the opposite side of the road. He only felt the earthshaking explosion, and his radios went dead immediately.

Shrapnel spewed into the troop compartment nearly slicing Corporal Randy Glass's leg off, and wounding several other Marines. Sergeant Jose Torres, who had been seated next to Glass, was temporarily blinded. Corporal Mead and Private Keough both had severe shrapnel wounds in their legs. The explosion set the right side of the vehicle aflame.

Seely began hitting Mike Bitz' helmet, "Go! Go! Go!"[27] He shouted. Then he turned to find Mead writhing in pain atop the track. "How many casualties do we have?" Seely screamed at Maloney and Bachmann.

Bitz accelerated to move out of the hot zone. Fighting the steering of the doomed AMTRAC, he started going over, around, and through everything in his path. C211 raced past most of 2nd Platoon, as rounds continued to ping off the track. Bitz kept pushing until he finally made it across the Saddam Canal bridge.

Schaefer, Castleberry, and Swantner had crossed the northern bridge first in C201. On the north side, Schaefer brought his three tracks on line about three hundred meters north of the canal. He wanted to leave room for the rest of the company to establish positions on the north bank.

As soon as Bitz got across the bridge, his burning armored vehicle shuddered to a stop, two hundred meters north of the river. They were right in the middle of the elevated road. Lieutenant Seely hit Bitz on the helmet again. "Drop the ramp!" he commanded, and then he leapt from the troop commander's hatch and moved across the top of the track, commanding his men to get out of the vehicle. Bitz tried, but the ramp would not drop. So, the Marines began climbing out the top and tried to lift the wounded to safety.

Nearby, Schaefer saw the smoking track grind to a stop. He jumped from his vehicle and ran to C211. As soon as Schaefer jumped from the vehicle, Castleberry drove C201 down off the elevated road and up against

---

27 Lieutenant Michael Seely's interview with Reed Bonnadonna, 5/4/03.

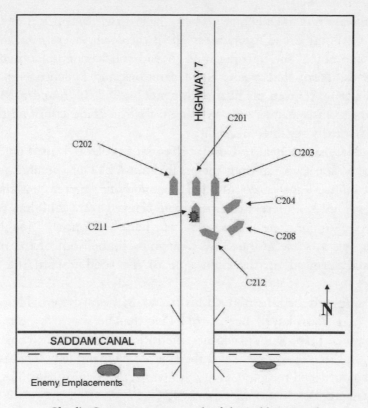

Charlie Company moves north of the Saddam Canal

a small berm, just off to the right. When Schaefer reached the back of the burning track, he opened the back door.

Smoke and flames poured out of the blackened interior, followed immediately by Marines as they piled out of their AMTRAC. They scurried out of the smoke-filled troop compartment, then lifted the wounded to safety. Randy Glass was carefully, but quickly, passed out through the door by a dozen hands, like he was crowd surfing at a Courtney Love concert.

Schaefer had never seen anyone so badly mangled. Glass's leg dangled by a thin strip of skin, and he was bleeding profusely. Schaefer thought, "What the fuck am I supposed to do here?"[28] The shock of seeing Glass so badly wounded quickly faded as Schaefer helped his wounded comrade to the side of the road.

---

28 Ibid. Schaefer.

Bachmann remained behind to help the last two Marines, Sergeant Torres and Corporal Mead. Only after all of the others were safe, did Bachmann climb out of the burning hulk. Mead and Keough also had serious leg wounds. Torres had burns and lacerations and had been temporarily blinded, but he refused medical treatment. Instead, he found a Marine to guide him to his machine gun section so that he could continue the fight. Torres eventually regained his sight.

First Sergeant Henao, Gunny Myers, and Doc Luis Fonseca had rolled to a stop two hundred meters behind C211 at the end of the armored column. Fonseca could hear the enemy fire increase as they came to a stop. C212's intercom came alive, "Hey, Doc, C211 has been hit. You need to go out there. They need your help."[29] Fonseca thought, "Oh, shit, here we go" He grabbed his gear and climbed out of the med-evac track, and sprinted up the right side of the road toward the burning vehicle.

As he approached, he noticed his friend, Sergeant Bevers. He ran up to Bevers, "Are you okay?" Bevers told Doc that he was okay but that the grunts needed help. Doc turned his attention to the wounded that had already been brought to the side of the road. Bachmann left Mead with Doc Fonseca and rushed to help Glass, who was screaming in pain. He grabbed Randy's hand, "You're gonna be okay."[30]

Bachmann stayed with Randy as the corpsman rushed to adjust the tourniquet on his leg. Doc used anything he could find for a splint—ramp jack and pick handles. He carefully wrapped bandages around the wounded Marine's leg to hold the splints in place and to keep it from flopping around. Doc Fonseca bandaged the wounds as best he could. Then he shifted his attention back to the other wounded.

By now, C212 had pulled up closer to C211. As he worked, Fonseca could feel the heat of the burning track on his face. Sergeant Bevers came up and said, "We got to get these Marines out of here 'cause we are about to have secondary explosions."[31] As soon as Doc had the wounded stabilized, he had them moved into the med-evac track. Bachmann helped carry Glass to C212, and Cline helped move Keough.

---

29 Telephone interview with Head Nurse Luis Fonseca, USN, 6/4/04.

30 Telephone interview with Corporal Will Bachmann, 5/25/04.

31 Ibid. Fonseca.

The light-green interior of C212 was set up to handle six litter-borne patients. Fonseca quickly gave Glass, Mead, and Keough each a shot of morphine to ease their pain. The casualties were made as comfortable as possible, and Doc started monitoring his patients.

NOT far behind C211, Pompos and Meador pushed C210 over the north bridge into an artillery barrage. They drove around the burning track and C212. They pushed north for another six hundred meters, then they pulled off the west side of the road, well ahead of the 1st Platoon tracks.

Schaefer got back in C201, and 1st Platoon pushed nearly a kilometer north of the main canal to the 396 Northing. They pulled off onto the west side of the road into a three-vehicle herringbone. Two of Swantner's tracks faced northeast, and the last track pulled up and faced northwest. Before the Marines had a chance to dismount, an artillery round exploded in the road five hundred meters north of their position and smaller mortar rounds began hitting on the east side of the road. Small arms fire erupted on both sides of the tracks. They were under heavy fire.

A fire team jumped out of C201 and moved to the west to provide security. Soon the rest of 1st Platoon dismounted to join the fire team west of the road, and Corporal John Wentzel jumped down to join his men. Wentzel, a smart young Marine, was one of Swantner's squad leaders, a position normally held by a staff NCO. Wentzel stayed with his squad watching Swantner for his next order.

Pompos moved his Marines into the trench west of the parked tractor, and then returned to the troop commander's hatch atop the vehicle. Pompos asked Meador what was going on. Meador told him that C211 had been hit and that Seely had casualties. Pompos quickly turned and looked back down the road. He could see smoke and flames spewing from C211. "That was my track!"[32] He thought to himself. He didn't know where his lieutenant was, or if he were even still alive. He didn't know where most of his men were, but he couldn't worry about that now. He had to get back to work.

Pompos jumped from the track and returned to the ditch. All of the infantry Marines had pushed forward into an open field. A lone Javelin team remained behind. All of a sudden, another artillery round exploded overhead,

---

32 Reed Bonadonna's interview with Staff Sergeant Anthony Pompos, 5/4/03.

causing a power line to come snaking earthward. The two Marines jumped from the trench just in time, and the severed cable landed right on top of the Javelin launcher, in a hail of sparks.

Six hundred meters south of Pompos, Mike Seely remained calm under ever-increasing fire. He was a model of Marine Corps leadership. He continued to evaluate the chaotic situation as he glanced back at his track, which was now spewing smoke. His men's rucksacks, which they had strapped along the sides of their vehicle, were now fully engulfed in flames. Seely knew that it would not be long before all of the ammunition and fuel inside would start to cook off. He ordered his Marines to move the wounded to a safer spot, and then he ordered one of Sergeant Torres' three-man machine gun teams to the west side of the road. He also told Sergeant Maloney to take his remaining Marines to the berm, fifty yards to their east.

At the berm, Bachmann found his best friend, Cline. They quickly checked each other for wounds that might have gone undetected in the rush of adrenaline. Now that Cline and Bachmann were together, everything would be fine. They were both positive that they could protect each other from whatever the enemy could throw at them. Bachmann said, "Stay with me,"[33] and they both moved south along the berm.

Gunny Meyers pulled his med-evac track up with 1st Sergeant Henao. He drove down off the right side of the raised highway, pivoted, and brought C212 to rest, facing west, right next to Seely's makeshift casualty collection point. Mead and Keough were quickly loaded into the back. Once his wounded were in the hands of the med-evac team, Seely ordered everyone who had been helping load casualties to move to the west side of the road to bolster his defensive position.

More and more Iraqi fire was sweeping across the raised road. Seely braved the road first. One by one, ten of Seely's Marines ran up the shallow embankment, out into the line of fire, across the road, and back down to the relative safety of the western side. Fribley, Martin, Woznicki, Carl, Emrath . . . they all dove into a small ditch as the Iraqis on the west side of the road started firing.

Then in a continuing chorus of cracks, pings, pops, and explosions, 3d Squad's ammunition began to cook off, sending deadly rounds out in every direction from the burning track. Will Bachmann dove for cover as he

---

33 Ibid. Will Bachmann.

watched his vehicle self-destruct. As he dropped to the ground, he saw, in what seemed like slow motion, a .50-caliber round head straight for him. He had just enough time to think to himself, "Oh fuck!"[34] The round hit the dirt a couple feet in front of him, glanced off the desert floor, and whizzed over his head. Had he been standing, the errant round would have hit him squarely in the chest.

Captain Wittnam was in the fourth track across, C204, following 1st Platoon. He had his driver pull off to the right side of the road and ordered the rest of the company to pull up into its familiar herringbone formation. Soon after stopping, Wittnam watched as C211 ground past his position, trailing black billowing smoke, and continued to watch as the crippled vehicle shuddered to a stop. Wittnam checked his GPS and then immediately got on his radio to report to his battalion commander. Wittnam came in broken on Grabowski's radio, "Timberwolf Six, this is Palehorse Six, we are at the three-nine-two Northing, we are on the bridge, and I have got a track that's been hit. I have an undetermined number of casualties."[35]

BRAVO COMPANY

Captain Rohr, in the C7, came up on the radio and said, "Sir, he reported that he seized the second bridge. He has seized the second bridge."[36] Grabowski responded and asked Wittnam if he needed a med-evac helicopter up there. "No!" Wittnam replied. "There's no way we are going to be able to get a helicopter in here!"[37]

When Grabowski heard Wittnam's report that he had taken the northern bridge, he slammed his fist on the hood of his HMMWV and immediately got on the regimental TAC net[38]. He reported to Colonel Bailey that they had captured the second bridge. Tragically, neither Newland nor Santare heard Wittnam's declaration on the net. By now, Greene and Rohr,

---

34 Taken from Bachmann's personal written account, which was sent to the author while Will was serving in Afghanistan.

35 Telephone interview with Captain Dan Wittnam, 2/18/04.

36 Ibid. Grabowski.

37 Ibid. Wittnam.

38 Tactical (radio) network.

Grabowski, and Santare were in three separate locations. Santare was moving forward with Tim Newland and the column of Bravo Company AM-TRACS. Grabowski was several blocks to the east, moving north with the Humvee column. Rohr and Greene were still with the mired Alpha Command track, surrounded by a Marine perimeter that Newland had left behind for security.

Hiding behind the cinder blocks to the north of the muddy square, Walsh could see Iraqis on two different rooftops. They were in civilian clothes, and they did not appear to have any weapons, so he held his fire. Walsh and Walden waited behind the block pile as rounds snapped around them. An H&S Company Marine appeared at the cinder-block wall. He looked like he had just stepped out of Hue City. He had no MOPP suit top or helmet, and he was pale as a ghost. Walsh and Walden finally realized that they were in the middle of a major urban fight.

When the Iraqi snipers began taking potshots at Bravo's stalled vehicles, Santare dropped down into his track, and his radio operator took his place to return fire with his M-16. Santare managed to contact Greene for an instant. The AO said, "Mouth, I need you to get on guard and get any air support you can get!"[39] Santare knew that this had to be serious, because the "guard" frequency was normally only used in peacetime emergencies.

As soon as Santare received the battalion air officer's request, he began to take over, again. He pulled his radio operator back down into the track, jumped back up on the bench, grabbed the radio handset, and announced on a open channel, "On guard! On guard! On guard! This is Mouth in the vicinity of An Nasiriyah! We have troops in contact and need immediate air support!"[40] Almost immediately, every fixed-wing aircraft within earshot began checking in. Santare started stacking the planes, hoping that a Navy or Marine jet with an airborne FAC would answer his call. None did.

Two Air Force A-10s from the Pennsylvania Air National Guard, Gyrate-73 and Gyrate-74, showed up on the "guard" frequency. They began tracing a high-altitude giant circle north and northeast of Nasiriyah while they tried to get a feel for what was happening on the ground. They circled for more than fifteen minutes, talking with Santare and taking turns scanning the ground with their binoculars. From high above, people were

---

39 Friendly Fire Incident Report, H-31.

40 Ibid. FFIR, Santare.

not visible, and vehicles appeared as small specks on the road. Gyrate-73 and Gyrate-74 spent several minutes trying to determine Santare's position on the ground.

After several passes, Gyrate-73 and Gyrate-74 had fixed Captain Santare's position in eastern Nasiriyah, north of the Euphrates. Unaware of Charlie Company's charge north, Santare believed that Bravo Company was the forward unit. He reported that to the pilots, and they all agreed that anything north of the Saddam Canal was fair game.

So Gyrate-73 and Gyrate-74 focused their attention north of the city. There was a black column of smoke rising from the road, north of the canal. They couldn't see what was burning, but they could see a dozen vehicles nearby, which were all military green.

Gyrate-73 and Gyrate-74 reported that a vehicle was burning in the middle of the road, just north of the Saddam Canal. Santare could see the billowing cloud of black smoke rolling into the sky to his north, but the nearby mud-block houses obstructed his view of the source of the gray-black column of smoke. Santare and the pilots all used the smoke from Seely's burning track as a common point of reference, but none stopped to wonder what it was that was burning.

ALPHA COMPANY, 8TH TANKS

Alan Kamper's driver was having problems following Cubas's tank through the tight streets. "Hey, Staff Sergeant, I can't see." The driver reported over the intercom.

"Don't worry about it. You're doing great." Kamper responded. It had not yet sunk in that the driver had a real problem. Kamper thought that dust from the crumbling buildings and the city streets had made his driver's view a little hazy.

Captain Cubas finally broke out of the confined alleys into the northwest corner of the large square where the other Timberwolves were stuck. He drove out onto what seemed to be solid ground, and he sank, too. Kamper ordered his driver to stop. They avoided the muddy mess, but there was another problem in Kamper's tank. "Staff Sergeant, I can't breathe!"

Kamper finally looked down into the tank, and his turret was completely filled with thick, black smoke. Kamper rotated the turret off of center. "Get out of the tank! Get out of the tank!" Kamper ordered. Kamper's crew all scrambled out of the tank, and they found that two large NBC filters had become clogged and the overheated air had ignited the charcoal inside the filters. Kamper shut down the tank and beat back the fire with a couple fire extinguishers while the crew took cover atop the tank.

The tankers were in an open area that wasn't quite a square. There were three houses running east to west on the north side. There was a building off to the east, and another building that looked like a house in the southeast corner of the square. A line of buildings ran east to west along the southern side of the square, and there was another line of buildings in back of them, to the west.

Gunny Howard's platoon was stuck in the southeast corner of the field. The AMTRACs were south of Kamper's tank, stuck in a west-to-east line. At first glance, the ground looked hard. Patches of standing water dotted the field, but the dry areas looked solid. It wasn't until Kamper jumped off his tank and sank to his knees that he realized what he was in. The open area was a sewage pit, filled with a bunch of strips of fabric and little bits of trash. It smelled like an outhouse at a rock concert.

Captain Cubas's tank was hopelessly stuck in the mud. He had tried everything to get free. He had ripped the thermal "don't shoot me" panels off the side of his turret and thrown them under the treads for traction. They slid deeper into the mucky mess, and the tank didn't budge. Cubas feared that when the enemy got word that they were stuck, they would swarm down on the Marines. Finally, he went on the regimental net. "This is Panzer! I need air! We're stuck!"[41]

The regimental net crackled, "You realize you are on Regiment?"

"Roger, but I need air, and I need it now!" Cubas responded. Within ten minutes, Cobras were buzzing overhead. They were flying so close that Cubas's Marines could hit them with a rock.

ONCE Gunny Wright realized that the Marines at the intersection were not planning on moving anytime soon, he ordered his men back into their vehicles, and they raced north. They drove through 2/8's lines. They drove past Dowdy's HMMWV accordioned into the back of Shoshana Johnson's jackknifed flatbed. Then they drove across the Euphrates River bridge into

---

41 Telephone interview with Captain Romeo Cubas, 1/14/05.

Alpha Company's gunfight. Once on the north bank, they came under heavy fire. Wright and his men pulled off to the right side of the road, jumped out of their vehicles, and joined in the battle. Soon, Wright realized that Alpha Company was locked in a battle and would not be moving forward. When a lull came in the shooting, Wright's men remounted and headed toward their companions who were still stuck in the mud. They drove right past the Iraqi ambulance that Cantu and his men had just shot up, and into the narrow alleyways on the east side of town.

BRAVO COMPANY

Back in the city, Colonel Grabowski had ordered Bravo Company's XO to bring up the trailing platoon and protect the trapped vehicles while he took the rest of Bravo Company north toward their objective. Bravo Company's move north became a street-to-street advance. In a scene strangely reminiscent of the fighting in *Black Hawk Down*, they fought their way through each intersection of the narrow, filthy streets running between mud-brick houses.

Bravo Company's 1st Sergeant Parker ordered 1st Platoon to find a clear route for the tracks to move north. As Corporal Gomez and his squad moved north, they became involved in a house-to-house battle. The Iraqis were firing at the Bravo Company Marines as they bounded forward through the dusty streets. Every corner brought a new fight. Every Iraqi house brought a new hazard. Iraqis clad in civilian clothes would run through a courtyard, past the open gate to the street, and spray AK-47 rounds at the advancing Marines.

Each Marine would have less than three seconds to get out of the line of fire and then aim and fire at the running men. First Platoon's First Squad pressed forward past each courtyard and intersection. Gomez continued to encourage his men forward as they methodically advanced. "Watch the rooftops!" he yelled, then, "Take cover!"

As they slowly moved through the neighborhood, the Marines' 240G and SAW gunners would lay down suppressive fire on the corner of each building as the infantry moved another block north.

After fighting their way forward for many blocks, 1st Sergeant Parker rushed over to Sergeant Gomez and ordered, "Call command and tell them where we are."

"Where the hell are we?" Gomez asked.

"Ask the trackers—they know."

Gomez returned to his track, which had been following close behind his infantrymen. They didn't know where they were, either. Bravo Company's 1st Squad was lost in the tangled mess of alleyways, power lines, mud houses, and Iraqis: They were somewhere in the middle of the eastern side of Nasiriyah.

Grabowski's small group fought their way north through the city for three kilometers. They then stopped and consolidated their position. Gunner Dunfee sent Sergeant Johnson and Corporal McCall in their two CAAT vehicles out to the east to protect the unit's right flank. They found an Iraqi platoon trying to move toward the canal bridge to cut off Bravo's movement north. The Iraqi commander was trying to trap Grabowski's men in the city, so Johnson quickly opened up with his 40mm grenade launcher, killing several Iraqis, and scattering the rest to the winds.

Meanwhile, Newland's tracks fought their way north while Santare talked with Gyrate-73. The pilot told Santare that he had targets north of the Saddam Canal. Santare asked Gyrate-73 to stand by while he checked on the forward trace.[42] Santare tried again to contact his air officer and the battalion staff. The comms were still terrible. Captain Wittnam had only had a moment to speak with his boss, and now his radios were completely out. Santare didn't know that Charlie Company was north of the canal, let alone that the black, billowing smoke was coming from a destroyed AMTRAC. Everyone in Bravo Company's command track continued to believe that Bravo Company was still leading the battalion. Santare cleared Gyrate-73 and Gyrate-74 hot, north of the Saddam Canal. The two A-10 pilots began to position themselves to attack the nine or ten vehicles they saw along the side of the road.

Captain Newland's small group of AMTRACs were slowly moving north through the eastern side of the city, but they had a house-to-house fight on their hands.[43] Through the fight, Santare was directing Cobras out to the east and trying to keep track of all the aircraft that were checking in to help. He was trying to do his job as the Bravo Company FAC and the job

---

42 Friendly Fire Incident Report, H-32. When a FAC clears a zone "hot" the pilots overhead have permission to attack that zone with their weapons.

43 Ibid. Hawkins.

of the battalion air officer. He was juggling radios and maps, trying to fight the air battle overhead while his track rolled north through scattered fighting in An Nasiriyah's narrow streets and alleyways. In all of the confusion, only Grabowski and Rohr knew that Charlie Company was north of the bridge. No one got word to Bravo Company's command track. Newland and Santare both thought that they were still lead trace.

While moving north, Santare noticed two TF-2 HMMWVs up ahead of his track. Bravo Company was supposed to be the lead trace. How could these vehicles be ahead of his? *"Abort!"* he radioed to Gyrate-73. He checked with Newland again and was told "We are the forward trace,"[44] so Santare again cleared the A-10s hot north of the canal.

---

44 Friendly Fire Incident Report, H-33.

CHAPTER 9

North of the Canal

I have no one on my left, and only a few on my right. I will hold.
—1ST LIEUTENANT CLIFTON B. CATES, USMC
Belleau Wood, 19 July 1918

CHARLIE COMPANY

After his short radio conversation with his boss, Captain Wittnam jumped out of his track and began to lead his company. He would not be able to raise Grabowski on the radio again for the remainder of the battle. He was on his own. Wittnam had no forward air controller to call in air support, and he could not contact his boss. The Marines of Charlie Company would have to do their best as a mechanized infantry company. They still had the mortars and machine guns of their weapons platoon. They still had ten AM-TRACS, each carrying a .50-caliber machine gun and a 40mm grenade launcher. They still had an enormous amount of firepower.

A torrent of hostile fire greeted Charlie Company. The Iraqis were throwing everything they had at Wittnam's Marines. Heavy machine gun and small arms fire raked the road. RPGs whizzed through the air, and all sorts of artillery shells exploded around the Marines. They initially had problems identifying the source of the fire. It seemed to be coming from nowhere—and everywhere. All of Wittnam's tracks were firing their .50-caliber machine guns and 40mm grenade launchers, yet the Marines were receiving more enemy fire than they were managing to send out.

Inside C204's gun turret, Lieutenant Tracy couldn't see where the enemy fire was coming from until he started seeing Iraqis jumping out from behind some nearby buildings to the east. They would rattle off a burst of gunfire and jump back to cover. Tracy started raking the adobe buildings with machine gun fire.

C208 ground to a stop near Captain Wittnam's track. C208 was Charlie Company's mortar carrier, loaded to provide indirect fire support. Instead of carrying infantry within its protective box, it housed a mortar, its crew, and a large amount of high-explosive ammunition. Lieutenant Reid threw his Kevlar helmet and maps to the ground, removed his track helmet, and jumped down from the track. He scooped up his maps, donned his Kevlar, and ran to the back of the track to link up with Lieutenant Pokorney. The back ramp dropped, and Pokorney and a mortar team rushed out into the bright sunlight. Reid ordered his men to take cover.

Next, Reid ran the short distance to C204 to get the rest of his mortar men. He ordered one team to start shooting at a large white building about two kilometers north of their position. He ordered his other two teams to set up and begin firing on enemy positions south of the Saddam Canal. The heaviest enemy fire seemed to be coming from a group of buildings just south of the canal and west of the road. Lieutenant Ben Reid's Marines quickly set up three 60mm mortars and began to return fire.

Reid moved up on the elevated road where he had a better view of the battlefield. From the road, he could easily spot targets for his men. He watched for a few moments, and once he was confident that his three mortar teams were hitting their targets, he moved down off the road in search of Lieutenant Pokorney, who could reach neither Timberwolf nor his artillery battalion on his radio. He had no idea where the battalion 81mm mortars were located or even if they were in range. Pokorney and the 81's FO worked frantically, trying to call in fire missions either at 1/10 Artillery or to the battalion mortars. All the while, Reid's mortar teams were dropping rounds on enemy positions as fast as they could.

Reid left Pokorney and went back up on the road to find more targets for his 60s, which were starting to turn the tide of the battle. Captain Wittnam met Reid on the road and pointed at some enemy vehicles in the distance. "If you can get fire on those vehicles, we are winning." Almost as quickly as he had appeared, Captain Wittnam ran off to lead the fight from another position.

Sergeant Lefebevre brought his section of tracks, carrying Lieutenant

Lapinsky's 2d Platoon, through the city and over the bridge. They moved into defensive positions in a herringbone fashion. Sergeant Lefebevre was responsible for C205, C206, and C207. Initially, the infantrymen of 2d Platoon remained in their tracks, and C206 turned south to battle Iraqis on the southwest side of the bridge. The Martyrs' District was infested with enemy fighters firing heavy machine guns, recoilless rifles, mortars, and RPGs across the river at Charlie Company. C206's up-gunner, Corporal Velazquez, fired continuously trying to silence the enemy. With the exception of C206 and C212, all of Charlie Company's ten remaining AAVs were now parked in a herringbone formation along the road.

Meanwhile, the men of 1st Platoon had jumped from their defensive positions and began to advance toward the enemy in the west. Mike Seely looked up from the relative safety of his ditch and saw other Marines moving west on his right and left, so he ordered his men forward. As they advanced, mortar and artillery rounds began falling nearby, and more and more Iraqi rounds whizzed and cracked through the air. Seely's men could hear the thud, and then there would be an explosion fifty meters in front of them. Another thud would yield an explosion fifty meters behind them. They were being bracketed. A shower of mortar rounds began to fall on the Marines. Fortunately, the soggy ground swallowed much of the force of the exploding shells.

It wasn't difficult for the Iraqis to zero in with a burning track on the road. Soon, mortar rounds were raining down on the road. Each mortar round impacted closer and closer to the parked AAVs. Seely quickly moved his men to another ditch, and they hunkered down to avoid the artillery. They remained in the ditch for quite a while. Then seemingly out of nowhere, Sergeant Bitz appeared, carrying an M-16 and still wearing his track commander's helmet. He dove into the ditch, head-to-head with Seely. Bitz glanced at the burning hulk of C211, then turned back to Seely, "I guess I'm a grunt now."

A little farther north, Pompos and his men were moving west. They had crossed a ditch fifteen meters from the road and worked their way through a spiderweb of smaller canals and ditches. They pressed forward with enemy machine gun rounds whizzing overhead and mortar and artillery fire exploding all around them. The Iraqis were lobbing RPGs at Charlie Company. They were taking small arms fire, too, from the southwest and northwest. They could not see muzzle flashes, yet they continued to methodically advance toward the unseen enemy.

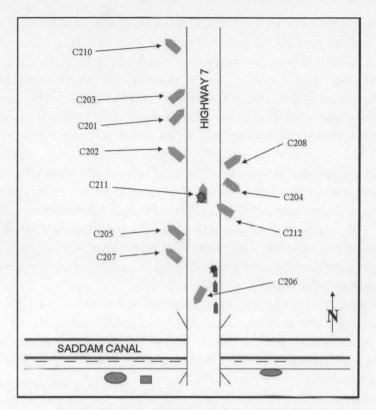

Charlie Company moves north of the Saddam Canal

Staff Sergeant Phillip Jordan ran up and told Reid, "Torres has been hit."[1] Reid told Jordan to focus the machine gunners back into the city and fight the close fight. Reid would use the mortars to attack the targets that were more than two kilometers out. Next, Lieutenant Swantner called Reid on the radio and asked for support. "We are taking enemy mortar fire."

Reid moved back up on the road to try to find targets for his mortars. He was standing there, searching for the source of the enemy fire, completely oblivious to the battle raging around him, when Lieutenant Pokorney ran up and tackled him. "Get the fuck down!" Pokorney screamed. Lying on his back in the middle of the road, Reid noticed a "crap load" of rounds

---

1 The following quotes taken from telephone interview with Lieutenant James Rein, 2/8/05.

whizzing through the air for the first time. Reid had been so busy fighting that he had not noticed the intensity of the enemy fire.

Reid and Pokorney moved down off the road. "We need to disperse our mortars," Reid told Jordan. Then he ordered Espinoza to take his place spotting while he took Corporal Garibay's mortar south. Then, Lieutenant Reid led his men south on the east side of the road. He wanted to get one of his mortars firing back into the city at the Iraqis who were in a gun battle with C206.

Artillery and mortar rounds continued to rain down on Charlie Company. One round landed close to C206, knocking out the radio and wounding Corporal Velazquez. Inside C212, Doc Fonseca got another cry for help. Gunny Myers came over the intercom and told him that C206 had been hit. "They need your help out there again."[2] Enemy fire was increasing, and the mortar and artillery impacts were growing closer. Fonseca was certain that he was not going to survive the day.

Somehow, this realization calmed him. Positive that he would soon die, he turned his attention to his work. As he jumped from the relative safety of the med-evac track a second time, he thought, "I'm just gonna try to get as many of these boys as I can back home alive." Buoyed by his faith, he never thought of himself for the rest of the battle.

Fonseca could not find C206, so he decided to run up and down the side of the road to check for other casualties. As he ran north, he ran into Captain Wittnam, who was moving south. "Keep up the good work." Wittnam told Fonseca. "We are starting to win." Unable to find C206 or any other wounded Marines, Fonseca returned to C212.

Just as Fonseca climbed back in, there were three consecutive explosions. One enemy round landed to the right of his track, the second and third exploded right on top of the vehicle. Then, an RPG slammed into the side of the armored ambulance. He knew that if they stayed in the track any longer, they would all be dead. Fonseca started quickly moving casualties outside.

He helped Glass and Mead off the track, and they took cover in a trench alongside the road. Then, astonishingly, C212 began to move. It drove off to get out of the kill zone, leaving Fonseca with the wounded Marines. Mortar rounds continued to land nearby. Fonseca threw his body over his two

---

2 Ibid. Fonseca.

casualties with each explosion. By now, all the tracks in the south were moving about, trying to avoid the incoming mortar and artillery rounds.

Meanwhile, Reid's men had quickly set up one of their mortars, and Reid dropped a round into the tube to set the base plate. An enemy round screamed over their heads and landed in a distant field. Reid tried to estimate his next shot. He continued to fire. A second enemy projectile landed on the opposite side of the road as the mortar team tried to zero in on their own target. Reid and the Iraqis were locked in a deadly mortar duel. A third round screamed over their head and landed much closer this time. "I wasn't smart enough at the time to realize that they were bracketing us."[3]

Pokorney told Reid that he had finally gotten through and had managed to pass a fire mission over the battalion TAC NET. He had talked with the Artillery LNO in the Alpha Command track.

A fourth round whistled in, and Reid was thrown to the ground by a thunderous explosion. A lighting bolt of pain shot from his arm into his brain. Dazed, his first thought was that his arm had been blown off. As the dust and smoke cleared, he found that his arm was intact but had been peppered with shrapnel.

Through the ringing in his ears he heard Garibay shout, "Buesing is dead!" Reid turned to a grisly site. Lance Corporal Brian Buesing's face had been blown away, and he was surely beyond help. Staff Sergeant Jordan lay face down next to Buesing. Reid rolled his friend over, only to find that he, too, was dead. Jordan had been standing between the Lieutenant and the point of impact, and his body had shielded all but Reid's arm. Through his death, Jordan had saved his lieutenant's life. A short distance from Jordan, Reid saw Fred Pokorney laying there motionless. The sight was just too much for Reid to bear. He turned away, not checking to see if his friend was dead. He swiveled his head to the left and saw his mortar team had been decimated. Garibay, Gonzales, Nixon, and Burkett were all seriously wounded, but Gonzales was in the worst shape.

The Iraqis had zeroed in and were dropping mortar rounds onto Reid's mortars and C208. Without warning, another round hit right next to the mortar track. Corporal Nicholas Elliot, C208's track commander, had just stuck his head out of the turret to check on his Marines on the ground. The explosion spewed deadly shrapnel out in all directions, killing Corporal

---

3 Ibid. Reid.

Kemaphoom Chanawongse as he was helping to get mortar rounds to the mortar teams. Chanawongse, a native of Thailand, had come to America when he was a young boy, and he loved being a Marine. Elliot was hit in the neck by small piece of the red-hot shrapnel from the same explosion.

Elliot was on his radio immediately to his friend, Schaefer, "I'm hit!"[4] He exclaimed. The explosion had damaged his radio. Elliot could transmit but not receive. Schaefer answered his friend, "I'm coming to you," but got no response. Elliot continued to try to contact Schaefer, "Eight Ball, I'm hit." Each time Elliot repeated his call for help, Schaefer became more worried about his friend.

Meanwhile, Lieutenant Reid had pulled himself to his feet and was racing toward C208 to get help for his decimated mortar team. Reid hadn't run twenty yards when another horrendous explosion erupted ten feet in front of him, knocking him through the air. When he landed, face down, he saw a mass of blood in the sand. His face had been badly mangled by the second explosion.

Reid struggled back onto his feet and continued on to the mortar track. He ran directly to the gunnery sergeant and asked him if his right eye was still in his head. The Gunny quickly, but carefully inspected Reid's face and said, "You're good to go, sir."[5] Reid ordered the mortar track back to the site of the wounded Marines.

Reid told the remaining members of the mortar team, "If I don't come back, no matter how much it hurts, get these guys loaded on the track and get them south to the battalion aid station."[6]

An AAV approached Bachmann, Cline, and the other stranded Marines. The AMTRAC stopped, and the infantrymen began climbing on board. Bachmann and Cline remained outside the armored vehicle, covering the other men as they dove to the relative safety inside the giant metal box. Finally, Bachmann climbed into the track, but Cline did not follow. Standing at the ramp of C204, Cline watched in horror as the mortar platoon took a direct hit. Instead of seeking shelter with Bachmann and the others, he sprinted through artillery, mortars, and heavy machine gun fire to see if he could help. As the heavy metal door of the vehicle was pulled shut, Bachmann shouted

---

4 Personal interview with Corporal Nick Elliot and Staff Sergeant William Schaefer.

5 Telephone interview with Reid.

6 Ibid. Reid.

out. "Cline! Where is Cline?"[7] That was the last Bachmann ever saw of his good friend.

Cline, Williams, and Nixon were still out in the open, loading the mortar team's casualties onto C208. Patrick Nixon who had grown up wanting to teach history was now making history. Only after all the wounded were safely aboard, did Cline, Nixon and Williams climb in.

As Cline and others were loading wounded into C208, Sergeant Schaefer was frantically trying to raise his commanders on the radio. The radio nets were still overloaded—platoon leaders, AAV section leaders, company commanders, battalion staff, and almost everyone who had a radio were all trying to get their reports and requests for support out over the radio.

Lieutenant Reid looked back north, and his other two mortar teams were gone. He ran to the west side of the road looking for the rest of his weapons platoon. Again, in the middle of the road, he was knocked off his feet. Reid got back up and ran toward the Marines fighting on the west side of the road.

No one will ever really know what happened to Fred Pokorney. Ben Reid never saw his friend again, after leaving him at the site of the deadly explosion. Reid thought that Pokorney had been one of the Marines killed in the explosion, but Fred's body was later found up on the road. Some think that Pokorney, dazed and wounded, continued on just like his friend Ben Reid and that an RPG hit him in the chest as he, too, tried to cross the road. Others believe that he was hit in one of the A-10 strafing runs. Regardless, Lieutenant Pokorney died that afternoon on a battlefield while fighting a tenacious enemy. The tragedy does not lie in how he died but in the fact that his loving wife, Chelle, was now a widow and his darling daughter, Tyler, would never see her father again.

Fonseca, still huddled over Mead and Glass, looked up and saw a track headed south. He jumped out of the ditch and waved it down. Staff Sergeant Lefebevre and Corporal Washburn stopped C205 and helped load Glass and Mead into the nearly empty troop compartment. Then, Lefebevre charged back across the Saddam Canal and through Ambush Alley, carrying Glass, Mead, and Fonseca.

When Captain Wittnam saw Lefebevre heading south, he thought to himself. "Where in the hell is he going?"[8] He was not so much upset with

---

7 Personal letter from Will Bachmann.

8 Ibid. Wittnam.

Lefebevre as he was with himself for not having the control he should over his company. He was now down to nine operational tracks, and the enemy attack was intensifying.

Lefebevre ran the gauntlet south through the city, past Alpha Company's position at the Euphrates River, over the southeast bridge, to 2/8's battalion aid station. Doctors quickly began working on Glass and Mead. They determined that the two young Marines needed more medical attention—they needed to be in a hospital. Mortenson's doctors called for a cas-evac, and Glass and Mead were flown to the rear. After Lefebevre dropped off the wounded Marines, he quickly returned to Alpha Company's position.

Wittnam took his two radio operators, the mortar FO, and one of the remaining mortar teams, to the west side of the road. With all the artillery falling, Wittnam and his small team dove into a fifteen-foot-wide irrigation ditch. They thought they would be able to cross, but once they got down in the water and mud they found that it was more than six feet deep. Wittnam was positive that someone would have drowned if they tried to cross, carrying all the equipment they had with them, So he ordered his team to hunker down until the enemy artillery let up a bit. The muddy water soaked into Wittnam's radios, making them useless.

Then Joe Raedle showed up. "Hey, Joe, you need to get your ass in the water down here."[9] Wittnam commanded. "I can't! I've got my camera."[10] Raedle replied. Wittnam couldn't believe his ears. He almost grabbed Raedle and pulled him in, but he stopped and thought that photography was Raedle's life and the only thing that mattered to him was trying to capture this event for history. Wittnam's respect for Raedle skyrocketed. They were two men on a battlefield, both doing their job. It was highly likely that both would die trying.

Two hundred meters to the north of Wittnam and Raedle, Sergeant Schaefer was still directing his section's up-gunners. He could see Iraqis moving all along a large berm, a kilometer to the west. Schaefer and the other track gunners laid down a massive amount of fire along the berm as their infantrymen pushed west.

Pompos and his men had advanced to the point where only a large open

---

9 Ibid. Wittnam.

10 Telephone interview with Joe Raedle, 11/8/04.

area lie between them and the enemy who were hiding behind the twenty-foot berm. The sergeant decided that even under Schaefer's covering fire, it would be suicide to attempt to dash across the open area, so he ordered his men to take cover.

From their protected position, Pompos took a moment to analyze the situation. He was surveying the enemy berm in the distance when he first saw the A-10. It was directly over the berm, flying north to south. Pompos yelled out to his Marines, "Hey, there's an A-Ten, an A-Ten! You better take cover!"[11] He remembered Staff Sergeant Jordan's constant warnings, "Don't trust those A-Tens." Jordan had learned from the first Gulf War that an A-10 can be just as deadly to Marines on the ground as it is to the enemy. He, too, had experienced friendly fire in Desert Storm. Pompos lost sight of the aircraft, but soon he heard the buzz of its gun.

It didn't take long for Swantner to realize that moving forward was not the smartest thing to do. Not able to easily ford a small canal, Swantner decided to withdraw back to the tracks. When Pompos saw Swantner's Marines pulling back, he, too, said "Okay, let's go" and Pompos's men worked their way back to C210. Just as Seely began to move forward again, he noticed that the platoons on his right and left were almost back to the tracks. He had no radio—no way to communicate with the rest of the company, so he pulled his men back to the road.

As Seely and his small squad neared the road, he could see Marines in the track hatches excitedly waving their arms, gesturing him to come to them. The infantrymen were quickly disappearing into the rear of their vehicles. It appeared as if the Marines were preparing to move to another location.

When Seely reached the first track, he yelled up to the driver, "What's going on?" Stating the obvious, the driver replied, "We're loading up." Seely ordered his men into the tracks. Seely's men moved toward the back ramp, and just as they were ready to climb aboard, an A-10 swooped overhead from west to east, Gatling gun whining. As if the enemy's indirect fire wasn't bad enough, the A-10s were strafing the road.

Corporal Wentzel watched in horror as the impacts of the Warthog's cannon walked down the road toward C201. The strafe came right across the back of his vehicle. Lance Corporal David Fribley was running toward the back of the track as the 30mm rounds kicked up dirt in the distance.

---

11 Ibid. Pompos.

Fribley and the deadly string of fire were on a collision course. When the two paths crossed, David Fribley was cut down instantly with a 30mm round to the chest. Without pause, the deadly impacts continued down the road as Fribley was slammed to the ground. Wentzel, Bitz, Carl, Woznicki, Seegert, Martin, and Seely were all hit with pieces of flying shrapnel. Most had minor injuries, but Corporal James Carl was out of the action, and Lance Corporal Brad Seegert had suffered a hit to his triceps, shredding it. Within seconds, the Marines on the ground shot two red pop-ups into the air to warn the aircraft that there were friendlies below—but they kept coming.

On the next A-10 pass, a 30mm round slammed into Schaefer's AM-TRAC. The round easily penetrated the aluminum alloy skin and whizzed below Schaefer's feet. Had his seat not been broken, Schaefer would have been sitting low enough that the round would probably have taken off his leg. Instead, the projectile penetrated the engine compartment and lodged in the transmission cooler. Unknown to Schaefer, his track was irreversibly damaged. Vital hydraulic fluid began to flow out of the cooler.

Seely, Swantner, and Bitz began to load the casualties into C201. Bitz worked to help his fellow Marines, with his own blood streaming from his face and back. Sergeant William Schaefer recalled after the battle, "He was acting like nothing was wrong."[12] Fribley's body was laid on the floor of the troop compartment, and Martin, and Seegert were helped into the track. Carl, unconscious, was carefully carried into the track. Then the rest of Wentzel's Marines piled back inside. Wentzel believed that his Marines and the casualties would be taken north to a casualty collection point, but they headed south, back toward Ambush Alley.

When Pompos returned to C210, he climbed up to the TC hatch looking for the XO. "Where in the hell are we going? What are we doing?" he demanded. Meador told Pompos that they were going to link up with the rest of Charlie Company. Pompos climbed down and got in the darkened troop compartment, and C210 began to move.

Meanwhile, there was a large explosion directly over Schaefer's 1st Platoon tracks. In C203, the explosion instantly killed Lance Corporal Thomas Slocum and seriously damaged the vehicle. The track's suspension was

---

12 Connell and Lopez "A Deadly Day for Charlie Company" (the *Los Angeles Times*, 26 August 2003).

destroyed, making it unusable for anything more than a pillbox. Shrapnel from the explosion spewed into C201's troop compartment, wounding Wentzel. "Once I realized I had movement in my shoulder, I pretty much blew it off."[13]

Back in C203, Lance Corporal Randal Rosacker quickly jumped up to close the troop compartment overhead hatches. Then, the next A-10 swept in overhead, and 30mm rounds slammed into C203, instantly killing Rosacker. The Marines quickly abandoned the doomed track and climbed into C201 and C202.

On the last strafe, Gyrate-74 swooped down the road, guns blazing. Captain Wittnam was lying on the east side of the road within arms reach of Sergeant Jose Torres, when he heard the burp of the Gatling gun. Torres, who had narrowly missed serious injury in C211, was back on the line at his company commander's side. Wittnam thought to himself, "Thank God. A-Tens are here, and they're going to take out that entire Martyrs' block . . . we're finally going to get some good suppression in there."[14]

Then Wittnam's world went black. The plane's 30mm rounds impacted all around him, kicking up the dirt with such violence that Captain Wittnam literally could not see his hand in front of his face. The line of impacts passed within inches of the captain. He quickly checked himself, not believing he was still alive. Then he turned and saw that Torres had been hit. Torres was still alive, but half of his butt had been blown away by a depleted uranium 30mm antitank round.

The Timberwolves had been very concerned about the old military complex at the northern "T." Prior to Desert Storm it had been the 23d Brigade's headquarters. The Marines had intelligence reports that if the Iraqi 11th Infantry Division resisted, the 23d Brigade would attack the Marines once they were north of the canal.

Santare sent Gyrate-73 and Gyrate-74 north to check the abandoned 23d Brigade headquarters complex. As the two A-10s peeled off to check out the old buildings, Charlie Company was granted a brief respite from the friendly fire.

---

13 Toler "Wounded had to wait on battle" (*Jacksonville Daily News*, August 19, 2003).

14 Friendly Fire Incident Report, J-159.

SCHAEFER had been trying for quite some time to contact his platoon leader, Lieutenant Tracy, on the net. He wanted guidance on how he should move the mounting number of his wounded comrades to safety. Tracy never answered. Schaefer thought Tracy was probably dead, so he took charge.

Schaefer made a command decision he regrets to this day. He ordered C210 to follow him. Once the casualties had been loaded, Schaefer pulled C201 back onto the elevated highway, and Corporal Brown, Meador, and Pompos followed in C210. Schaefer turned south looking for C208 and his friend Corporal Elliot, who had been calling for help.

Before heading south, Sergeant Schaefer broke out an American flag he had been carrying and mounted it on his vehicle, right behind his up-gun. "I wanted to use the flag to rally the tracks that were heading back with the casualties. It was a stupid thing to do. Every Iraqi within sight started shooting at the flag. It actually got shot off before we got far into the city."[15] Second Platoon's lead track had already ventured south, leaving C206 and C207 with no section leader. The artillery barrage had left them with no comm, so as Schaefer headed south with his flag unfurled, the trackers in C206 and C207 decided to join Schaefer. C207 fell in behind C210.

As it turns out, Elliot, a young newlywed who had recently married his high school sweetheart, had not been seriously wounded. But his track was loaded with dead and wounded Marines. He knew that if Schaefer was heading south, he, too, had to try to get the wounded back to the battalion aid station, so Elliot commanded his driver to move out. C208 drove up onto the highway in front of Schaefer, and C206 did the same. This left Charlie Company with two good tracks. Captain Wittnam's track remained on the east side of the road, and C202 was parked opposite Wittnam's track on the west side of the road.

C206 was the first to move up onto the canal bridge. Corporal Elliot was close behind in C208. Sergeant Schaefer pulled up behind Elliot, followed by Corporal Brown in C210. C207 was the last track in the column.

When Schaefer left with 3d Platoon's remaining track, Lieutenant Seely and Lance Corporal Emrath were left standing in the Iraqi wasteland— alone. Seely looked north and saw a ten-foot whip. He could see the A-10s

---

15 Ibid. Schaefer.

continue to make runs farther south. Seely and Emrath turned north and ran up to 2d Platoon. Seely grabbed the radio operator and said, "Put that damn thing on battalion TAC! *Now!*"[16] Then he started barking out orders to 2d Platoon's Marines to push out north and west. Seely was concerned that the Iraqis would take advantage of the chaos and attack. So Seely set 2d Platoon into a defensive perimeter, waiting, and expecting the worst.

Then Seely saw something that made his heart sink. Tracks were moving back south over the canal bridge. He began to think that he and his small group of Marines were the only ones left north of the canal. Captain Wittnam watched his tracks head south, too.

Gyrate-73 and Gyrate-74 returned and saw the tracks moving south. Both pilots wanted to stop the vehicles from getting into the city, so Gyrate-73 rolled in first, spraying 30mm rounds. The aircraft were so high that their cannon fire had no effect. The vehicles continued toward the canal bridge.

507TH MAINTENANCE COMPANY

As the battle raged, Jessica Lynch's broken body was loaded into an ambulance in the Tykar Hospital compound, just southeast of the Euphrates River bridge. The ambulance drove out of the north gate, turned left, and darted down a dusty dirt road for five hundred meters. It drove up over the paved highway, at the base of the Euphrates River bridge and continued west along the dirt road. Any other day it would have been quicker to cross the Euphrates on the southeastern bridge, but Captain Brooks and Alpha Company were involved in a fight on the northern bank of the river.

The driver therefore weaved his way through the date palms of the suburbs along the southern bank of the Euphrates River, until he reached the southwest bridge. He raced across the Euphrates and to Nasiriyah's largest hospital. At Saddam Hospital, armed Iraqis delivered Lynch, who was unconscious and near death, to Dr. Harith Al Houssona. She was admitted and given the only orthopedic bed in the hospital. Blood transfusions were started immediately.

---

16 Ibid. Seely.

The Saddam Hospital was rapidly filling with wounded from the battle to the east. The staff was stretched past its capabilities by the throng of casualties, yet they took good care of Lynch. Two of the bottles of blood she was given that day were donated by members of the hospital staff. Had it not been for their care, Lynch would have surely died.

NBC NEWS

By now, America's Battalion was methodically moving north astride Highway 7. Fox and Echo companies were clearing buildings on both sides of the road that the Timberwolves had bypassed earlier. Colonel Mortenson held his log trains and CP in the rear until he knew that it was safe to move them forward. The main CP and ALOC would be halted for a while. With his soft southern drawl, Major Julian Alford told Kerry to take cover. There was a battle ahead.

So Kerry and Sebastian climbed down out of the NBC seven-ton truck, moved off to the side of the road, and laid down, using the elevated road for cover. Sebastian set up his camera, and he and Kerry went live with the first broadcast from the battle of An Nasiriyah. Shots could be heard in the background, and, off in the distance, there was an ominous black column of smoke snaking its way into the sky.

Details were few. Kerry didn't even have the correct name of the city ahead, but it was apparent that they were near the action. Kerry Sanders, adorned in a civilian blue flak jacket and helmet, was lying as flat as he possibly could. So were the Marines around him. Live on MSNBC, Kerry crawled forward a few feet to talk with a Marine who was watching over the news team. The Marine was diligently scanning the horizon through his M-16 sights.

"Rodriquez, what are you sighting?" Kerry asked as he shifted his microphone to the Marine.

"I'm keeping an eye on that building." The Marine answered, not looking away from his work.

"Do you see any movement?"

"Not at the moment." Kerry back crawled away from the Marine. Once Kerry was certain that he had returned to safe cover, he continued his live report from the battlefield. He drew two parallel lines in the sand, then drew a single perpendicular line, explaining as he drew that there were two rivers running from west to east. The southern was the Euphrates River, and the northern was the Saddam Canal. The perpendicular line was Highway 7. The Marines were fighting to secure the two bridges.

ALPHA COMPANY

The situation at the Euphrates River bridge was getting worse by the moment. Captain Brooks positioned his track on a corner, which enabled him to see west down this wide-open strip, which he called "the mall." He could see several kilometers down the mall into the heart of An Nasiriyah. Iraqis all along the mall were moving south and east toward his position. To make matters worse, many of the approaching Iraqis were clearly noncombatants, and virtually all were dressed in civilian clothes.

Alpha Company's Marines tried to maintain their fire discipline and follow the rules of engagement. Each Marine had to make split-second decisions of life and death—not once, but over and over again. Was the person in their sights a threat? Did he have a weapon? Was he or she just trying to get a better view of all the commotion? Each time a Marine paused to evaluate the situation, he placed himself in peril for an instant. But these young men tried to make sure they were only firing on enemy combatants. As they considered every shot, the enemy fire kept increasing.

After checking with each platoon, Lieutenant Martin returned to Cantu's position. The situation continued to worsen. Realizing that Alpha Company wasn't going anywhere soon and that they could start taking casualties at any time, Martin told Cantu, "We need to clear a casualty collection point if we are going to stay here much longer."

Martin grabbed a couple of corpsmen, and they went with Cantu to clear a nearby building. The small group searched the building on the west side of the road, only to find it abandoned. The corpsmen stayed inside and started setting up a casualty collection point. Cantu rushed back outside just as C206 was rolling up.

The noise level continued to increase as more and more Iraqis entered the fight. Captain Brooks started getting concerned that if the enemy continued to fire at his Marines at this rate, Alpha Company would soon be taking casualties. Brooks continued to try to raise Colonel Grabowski on the battalion net, and the Iraqis just kept attacking.

ALPHA COMPANY, 8TH TANKS

As he approached the railroad bridge, Major Peeples' command tank broke down. Peeples was forced to abandon "Wild Bill" and switch to one of the company's functioning tanks. It was the fastest "jump tank" in history. He grabbed all of his gear, his maps, his list of authorized radio frequencies and his data terminal, and a couple spare batteries, when he reached his new tank, he blew the mine plow and left it along the side of the road.

Peeples started forward, working to set up the radios in his newly acquired tank. The rest of Peeples' tanks, Dyer, Thompson, and Staff Sergeant Swain continued to motor forward, crawling along at five kilometers per hour to give the major time to get squared away. As soon as Peeples caught up, all four tanks moved to cross the railroad bridge, but the tankers were surprised by the Iraqi tanks north of the bridge. They quickly began firing at the tanks that Schielein's CAAT section had disabled earlier.

Hawkins was now sitting atop the railroad bridge, calling in air support when an Iraqi tank rolled out from under the bridge. Hawk handed a division of Cobras over to Santare, and then he dropped down into the turret to load a round into the main gun. He had to kick the round home in the breech. Once Hawk had loaded the main gun, Dyer shot and destroyed the last Iraqi tank at the bridge.

Peeples' tankers had been issued old multi-purpose antitank (MPAT) rounds for their tank main guns. These rounds had been sitting around in storage for years, and some of the casings were swollen. At the railroad bridge, the loaders found it nearly impossible to load the swollen rounds into the main gun. The rounds got stuck around an inch or two out of the breech, and the loaders would have to kick the rounds home that last inch or two.

After firing at one of the tanks, Staff Sergeant Swain's loader stuck an MPAT round in the breech. It wasn't an inch or two, it was stuck halfway into the breech, and he couldn't get it in or out. Swain's main gun was useless until he got that round out of the breech. The four tanks were forced to stop just north of the bridge. Dyer, Thompson, and Peeples surrounded Swain's tank, and Swain depressed his main gun, jumped out of the tank, and rammed the stuck round out from the muzzle with a bore plunger. Swain threw the swollen round out onto the side of the road and pressed forward to the Euphrates River.

As they moved forward, Hawkins checked in with all of the company's tank crews. He had clear communications with everyone. He could even talk with the tanks that were mired on the east side of the city. There was a lull in helicopter activity, so Hawkins spent the time trying to gain a situational awareness of what lie ahead. By now, Hawkins had enough information to know that there were severe problems ahead. He knew that nearly a third of the battalion was stuck out on the east side of the city and that they were having problems with the rooftops. Soon, another division of Cobras showed up, and Hawkins immediately sent them to help the mired tanks and Bravo Company. Hawkins told the helicopter pilots overhead that they were cleared hot. "Do what it takes to protect the tanks and the Marines on the ground."[17]

Finally, the tank maintenance Marines reached their bogged-down tanks on the east side of town. Whidden jumped out in an alley, just south of the open area, and set his SAW up to provide security for his fellow Marines while they worked to free the vehicles. Initially, he set up in a position that provided little cover. Whidden noticed a pile of cinder blocks, and he and another Marine moved over to the block pile and set to work building a small semicircular fighting position with the concrete blocks. Soon, they were protected by a large wall at their back and their newly fashioned block bunker.

The crews of the M88 tank retrievers set to work to pull the armored vehicles from the muddy mess. One of the M88s tried to extricate Sergeant Sarmiento's 3d Platoon track, and, in the process, the tank retriever became stuck. The second M88 finally managed to pull Beere's track free.

The 8th Tanks corpsmen stopped near Sarmiento's squad and started giving aid to the injured Iraqis. They set up a mini-aid station in the middle of the street, and Sarmiento's squad set up to provide them with security. The corpsmen started taking in civilian casualties, doing everything they could to help. They bandaged wounds and gave out medicine. Soon a small crowd gathered. All of the sailors and Marines worked like this was just another day of training. Everybody was calm, and everybody was doing their job.

BRAVO COMPANY

North of the square, Corporal Matthew Walsh and Lance Corporal Walden were still manning their position behind their own cinder-block pile when

---

17 Ibid. Major Scott Hawkins.

the enemy fire increased. Bullets were flying down the street between Walsh and the rest of his squad. For the moment, he and Walden were cut off. Walsh was starting to get anxious when he saw Sergeant Hamilton coming down the narrow alley. Hamilton stopped in a doorway close to their cinder-block bunker.

Walsh and Hamilton had a quick conversation, shouting back and forth to each other. Walsh told Hamilton that there was too much fire to try to move forward or back across the street to the rest of his squad. Hamilton shouted over the gunfire, "Don't worry Walsh. H and S will save you. We have secured the next block over."[18] Hamilton told Walsh and Walden that they could all backtrack down the alley and go around the back of the building to safety.

Walden and Walsh abandoned the cinder-block pile and darted across the small alley to the doorway. Just then, a mortar round came sailing over the building across the street and landed among the three Marines and the cinder blocks. It landed with a dull thud—failing to explode.

Walden, Walsh, and Hamilton raced back down the alley, not waiting for another round to land. AK-47 rounds followed them down the alley, and then another Iraqi let loose an RPG in the group's direction. It wobbled through the air, with a huge trail of smoke. It sounded like a jet airplane as it sailed past the Marines and exploded in a junk pile, not twenty feet in front of them. A blast of heat swept over the men, and the shock wave knocked them into a wall. None of the three was hurt, but the ringing in their ears lasted for hours. They quickly continued their journey back to the large, open space where the tanks and tracks were stuck.

CHARLIE COMPANY

Ever since Lefebevre had raced south in C205 with Glass and Mead, the Iraqis had been waiting for Charlie Company to retreat back through the city. Fedayeen fighters in the Martyrs' District opened fire with rockets, mortars, and machine guns as soon as they saw C206 crest the Saddam Canal bridge.

As if the Iraqi fire wasn't bad enough, just as C206 rolled into Ambush Alley, Gyrate-74 rolled in and unleashed a Maverick missile. The missile

---

18 Personal letter from Walsh to the author.

narrowly missed the AMTRAC, exploding in the road just behind C206. The explosion, however, severely damaged the rear of the track. The back ramp dropped, and Sergeant Brendon Reiss, twenty-three, the son of a decorated Vietnam veteran, was blown out into the street. The center heavy metal rail that ran from front to rear along the top of the troop compartment fell into the track.

C208 came down off the bridge, not far behind C206. Gyrate-73 swept in, locked on, and fired another Maverick missile. Schaefer was crossing the bridge as the Maverick screamed toward its target. Just feet behind C208, Schaefer saw the horrendous explosion in front of his track. Body parts flew out of the destroyed track, and to Schaefer's amazement, he was looking at the bottom of Elliot's 28-ton AMTRAC. The explosion was so powerful that it threw the vehicle fifteen feet into the air as if it were a child's plastic toy. Miraculously, C208's track commander, Corporal Nick Elliot, and its driver, Lance Corporal Noel Trevino, lived through the catastrophe.

C208 came to rest in the center of the road, right in front of the Martyrs' District. Elliot climbed out and found that Trevino was also still alive but he could barely see. Both Elliot and Trevino had been shielded from the massive explosion in the troop compartment by the AMTRAC's engine. Elliot had a baseball-size chunk missing from his right lower calf as if an angry pit bull had taken a bite out of his leg. He had inhaled a fireball at the instant of the explosion. His lungs and face were badly burned. Trevino had also suffered flash burns, and the flash had temporarily blinded him. He was shaken and in shock. Together, they still made one good Marine. Trevino took Elliot's arm and supported his mangled leg. Elliot led the way, looking like they were in a three-leg race in Hell.

Everyone else was dead. Burkett, Cline, Garibay, Gifford, Gonzalez, Hutchings, Nixon, and Williams were all gone, torn apart by the tumultuous explosion. Cline and Williams epitomized the Marine ethos. They had sacrificed their lives while helping their fellow wounded Marines.

C201 raced down past the shattered remains of C208 into the city, through a hail of gunfire. Then Schaefer's vehicle finally had lost enough hydraulic fluid that Castleberry lost his steering. Castleberry struggled to keep his track driving south, but the armored vehicle started to veer to the left. About four hundred meters into the city, Castleberry shouted, "Hold on!" No sooner had he uttered his warning than the vehicle crashed into a large telephone pole. Just as the track crashed to a stop, Gyrate-74 returned and let

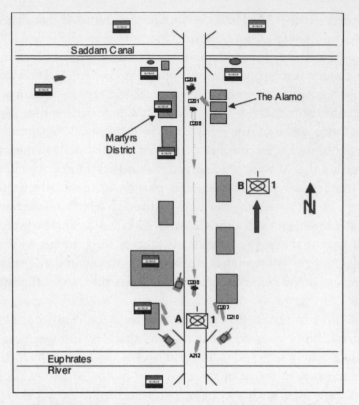

Charlie Company Tracks Attempt to Med-Evac Casualties

loose a third Maverick.[19] It screamed down and hit C208 again, completely obliterating the already doomed track. The explosion lifted C201's rear end completely off the ground, and as soon as the tractor landed, Castleberry quickly dropped the back ramp. Wentzel looked out and thought, "Oh my God! What in the hell are we doing in the middle of the city?"[20]

Lieutenant Swantner and Sergeant Schaefer jumped from their hatches in the front of the track and ran into the center of the road. Swantner went around the front of the track. He assumed that everyone, except Schaefer, was dead because he didn't see any other Marines. Swantner didn't see his Marines because they had exited the rear, carrying their wounded, and quickly moved to the left to the closest cover they could find. Fribley's body

---

19 Friendly Fire Incident Report.

20 Personal interview with Corporal Wentzel, 6/16/04.

had to be left in the track. There was no time to move bodies. The Marines were under fire and in enemy territory.

Sergeant Schaefer and Lieutenant Swantner were now alone in the center of Ambush Alley. Schaefer took a knee and began to fire at Iraqis who were charging out of the Martyrs' District. There were Iraqis all around his crippled track. Schaefer fired his weapon as fast as he could. He recalled later, "Corporal Brown saved my life."[21]

Brown turned his track around and returned to pick up his friend. As Brown brought C210 to a stop, Sergeant Pompos heard a knocking on the back door. He opened the door, and Swantner jumped in, followed by Schaefer. Schaefer only had five M-16 rounds left. Swantner was sandwiched into the blackened compartment atop Marines, who were stacked like cordwood. It was so crowded that Swantner's head was touching the top of the track. Schaefer dove in next to Swantner, on top of a Marine who was lying on top of another Marine. C206 continued to plod south, dragging its rear ramp through the city in a trail of dust and sparks behind C207. Pompos closed the rear door, and C210 raced south, too.

"THE ALAMO"

Elliot and Trevino ran through a hail of bullets toward C201, a few hundred meters south. They moved solely by force of will. Elliot should not have been able to walk, let alone run. As they hobbled south, the rest of C201's Marines moved into a small courtyard between two buildings, east of their disabled track. Then they noticed that the other tracks were gone and a group of Iraqis was already converging on their crippled track. Wentzel's men lobbed a few grenades in the direction of the Iraqis, causing them to disperse. Corporal John Wentzel's squad took shelter in two small houses, and Wentzel followed his squad into the dwellings. Once their hasty defense had been set in the courtyard, four of the Marines raced back out to their track to get Carl, who had been left for dead in the confusion.

As they were getting Carl, Wentzel's Marines saw Elliot and Trevino. They had almost reached C201 by the time they were noticed. Wentzel's men provided covering fire as Elliot and Trevino staggered closer and closer.

---

21 Personal interview with Sergeant Schaefer.

After what seemed an eternity, Elliot and Trevino made it to safety. Wentzel's squad cleared both buildings just as they had been trained to do. They methodically checked and cleared each room on the first floor, then carefully moved up a stairway to the second floor, and repeated the clearing operation in the upstairs rooms.

Once they were certain that the building was secure, they moved Trevino, Elliot, Carl, and Seegert to a casualty collection point (CCP) where they could be treated and protected. Lance Corporal Smith rushed to attend to the wounded. Smith was a certified EMT, and he bandaged Elliot's leg and tried to stop the bleeding.

Marine gunners and grenadiers manned critical observation points at the corners of the second floor as the Iraqis charged the buildings and the disabled AAVs from the Martyrs' District across Ambush Alley. Wentzel and his sixteen Marines fought off attack after attack, isolated in the center of the enemy's stronghold. They would only be able to hold on until their ammunition ran out, so Wentzel ordered his men to make every shot count.

The Iraqi attacks became subversive. An unarmed Iraqi would casually stroll around a corner out into the open. He would soon be followed by a second Iraqi, wildly spraying bullets from an AK-47. A third man would quickly pop from cover and unleash an RPG toward the Marine fortress. The Iraqis continued this tactic, at times switching their roles. Soon the embattled Marines adjusted and were able to kill the teams as soon as they appeared. They were stranded and would have to hold in their Alamo-like fortress for two and a half hours.

ALPHA COMPANY, 8TH TANKS

Peeples and his four tanks zipped through the Highway 8 intersection. Just as they crossed over Highway 8, Hawkins noticed an Iraqi man standing out in a wooded area. He was standing there with his kids behind him, and he was cheering. Hawkins got on the intercom and said to Dyer, "I wonder if he is happy. Is he waving us in to liberate them, or is he trying to wave us to our death?"[22]

---

22 Ibid. Hawkins.

Hawkins continued to develop the situation. He knew what was happening with Bravo and their tanks. By now, Captain Brooks, Alpha Company was fully engaged. As Dyer and Hawkins ground north toward the Euphrates River, Hawkins thought to himself, "Oh, God! How are we going to get out of this one?"[23] Dyer's tank had only a third of a tank of gas, and Hawkins fully expected that they would run out in the middle of the fight.

CHARLIE COMPANY

Back north of the canal, Captain Wittnam was now left with only two operational AMTRACS and a little over a platoon's worth of infantrymen. His FO was dead, he had no FAC, his FiST team leader was severely wounded, and one of his mortar tubes destroyed. The Iraqis continued to pound Charlie Company, and Wittnam's infantry was isolated and separated into two units. Lieutenant Seely was north and west of the Highway with 2d Platoon, and Wittnam was still on the east side of the road with what was left of 3d Platoon. Wittnam's radios had all been taken out of commission when he and his men dove for cover in the irrigation ditch, but his radio operators continued to try to get them working again.

The A-10 pilots above decided that they should not pursue the vehicles farther into the city, so they moved back north. Gyrate-73 still had a Maverick missile left, and there was a lone vehicle sitting on the east side of the road that appeared to be undamaged—C204. Gyrate-73 lined up on Captain Wittnam's AMTRAC and started his run in to release his last missile.

By now, Lieutenant Seely was on the battalion TAC, "Cease fire! Cease fire! Cease fire!"[24] Grabowski came up on the radio and asked "What do you got?"

Seely reported, "We're having friendly air strafing our pos—A-10s. Check fire!" Then Seely said, "Cease everything!" Seely turned to the radio operator, "Get me on tank's freq, quick!"[25] Seely finally got in touch with

---

23 Ibid. Hawkins.

24 Friendly Fire Incident Report interview with Lieutenant Seely.

25 Reed Bonadonna's interview with Lieutenant Seely.

the tanks. "You need to push north of the north bridge. We are fifteen hundred meters north of the north bridge."

When Santare finally realized that Charlie Company was north of the Saddam Canal, he called off the A-10s with, "Check fire! Check fire!"[26] Gyrate-74 was about to unleash his last Maverick when Santare called, "Abort! Abort! Abort!"

The A-10 pilots aborted their attack and returned to their high-altitude circular orbit. "What's going on?" they asked Santare.

"We think we may have friendlies north of the canal. Stand by while I sort things out." Santare still believed that he was in the lead and that someone had confused the Euphrates River with the Saddam Canal. So he called the battalion again. He was told to cease the air operations north of the canal, so he relayed the order to the A-10 pilots. Not really sure what had happened, the pilots asked Santare for his call sign, and then they quickly left the area. No one wanted to believe that the A-10s had been firing on Charlie Company.

ALPHA COMPANY, 8TH TANKS

At 1405, Major Peeples arrived at Alpha Company's position, just north of the Euphrates River bridge. All of the Iraqi fighters immediately focused on the tanks. RPGs slammed into the tanks. Peeples could see tracks parked on both sides of the road. While the tankers had no problems talking with each other on their company net, the battalion net was still a mess. Peeples scanned the tracks until he found the one with a white diamond painted on its side.[27] Captain Brooks's track was parked at the head of the tracks on the left. Major Peeples drove toward Brooks and ordered Captain Thompson and Sergeant Swain up the road. Peeples tank came to a stop, and the major climbed out of his hatch.

Dyer's driver, Lance Corporal Michael Shirley, followed Peeples and drove straight toward the wall where most of Alpha Company was taking

---

26 Friendly Fire Incident Report.

27 The Marines had come up with a simple visual identification system. All of 1st Platoon's tracks had a white ^ painted on each side; 2d Platoon had a >; and 3d Platoon had a ᵥ. The company commander's track had a white diamond.

cover from the enemy, west in the city. As soon as Dyer's tank rolled up, the young grunts got "tank muscles."[28] They smiled and gave Captain Dyer a thumbs-up. As they pulled up, Hawkins could see the Marines get pumped full of energy. They started jumping out in the open to fire down the side streets and alleyways while Dyer started pumping main gun rounds into a number of houses, reducing the buildings to rubble. Enemy sniper rounds continued to whiz dangerously close to Dyer.

Black-clad fighters continued to attack Alpha Company. They charged Dyer's tank, only to be mowed down by his gunner, Corporal Charles Bell. They fired RPGs and AK-47s. Another single round snapped overhead. This time Dyer saw the muzzle flash. He dropped down in the turret and directed his turret toward the sniper's hideout. Dyer took one last look through his sights to confirm that he had targeted the right building, and then ordered, "Fire!" Bell let lose the main gun, and the building in the distance collapsed.

When Brooks saw the tanks, he knew his problems were over. He was determined to not let them go by his position. Brooks ran out into the road. By the time Peeples had climbed down off the back of his tank, Brooks was in the middle of the road. Peeples ran over to Brooks and asked, "What do you need?"[29]

Brooks pulled out his map. "I got a platoon here and I got a platoon here and a platoon here," pointing to their locations on the map. "I need you to take two tanks up to the north and reinforce this platoon." Then he told Peeples that he was having a lot of problems with buildings to the west. Dyer and Hawkins were already taking care of the buildings to the west, and Thompson and Swain had already pushed north, so Peeples climbed back onto his tank, drove over the center guardrail and moved to the east side of the road.

Infantrymen kept telling him, "Shoot the building with the blue door." There were three blue doors, so he put a tank main gun round in each. The tank main guns crumbled buildings while the tank machine guns swept the battlefield. The tide of the battle quickly turned, and the Iraqi fire became manageable.

Hawkins now had three jobs. He continued to load the main gun, kicking rounds home. As Dyer shot, Hawkins was down loading, then he was

---

28 "Tank muscles" is a false confidence acquired by having friendly tanks nearby.

29 Ibid. Peeples.

back up in the hatch firing his 240G machine gun. Then, he would turn around and search for the helicopters overhead. There was so much air traffic coming in that he couldn't keep all the call signs straight. Loader—gunner—FAC—loader—gunner—FAC. Eventually, his machine gun jammed. Hawkins was relieved that now he only had two jobs, not stopping to think that he had lost his own personal protection when his machine gun went down.

Throughout their whole time in the city, the tankers worked hard not to kill any civilians. They only shot into enemy positions that were threatening the Marines. The enemy, on the other hand, was doing everything they could to cause civilian casualties. They were using women and children as shields and pushing them out into the street.

ALPHA COMPANY

C210 carried Charlie Company's XO, the 3d Platoon sergeant, Pompos, and twenty-one Marines back through Ambush Alley to safety. When they arrived back at the Euphrates River bridge, Brown dropped the back ramp. Swantner, Schaefer, Pompos, and the others poured out of the track.

Staff Sergeant Pompos emerged into the crowded city. There were tanks and tracks all around. He didn't have a clue where he was, so he ordered his men to lay down against the embankment on the eastern side of the road until he could get his bearings. There was gunfire all around, but it was nothing like what Pompos and the others had experienced north of the canal.

Lieutenant Meador ordered Pompos to take his men southeast, but as he was running south, Pompos noticed a bunch of Marines hunkered down against a wall, on the west side of the road. Pompos quickly switched directions and led his men across the road. As soon as he reached the other Marines, he realized that he was at Alpha Company's position.

Sergeant Schaefer raced around the area trying to find someone to report to about the dire situation north of the bridge. Schaefer finally found Major Tuggle in the Bravo command track. He stuck his head inside the back of the track and pleaded with Tuggle to send Marines north to help Charlie Company.

Major Tuggle told Schaefer that there was nothing he could do. Schaefer spewed a few choice phrases into the Bravo command track, then left to try to find someone who would listen to his pleas to help Charlie Company.

CRIPPLED and dragging its back ramp, C206 came screaming into Alpha Company's position with a loud roar. Before they were safe, the Marines in C206 would have to travel through Alpha Company's firefight with the enemy. As C206 moved through the final intersection, an RPG slammed into the side of the track, rocking the mammoth vehicle. In the blink of an eye, a second RPG flew in the open back and detonated, killing Sergeant Michael Bitz. Several Marines and sailors sprinted across the fire-swept street to help the Marines in the smoldering track. Gunnery Sergeant Justin LeHew was the first Marine to arrive.

As he reached the back of the destroyed track, he found a gruesome scene of tangled metal and body parts. Knowing that no one left inside could have survived this catastrophe, LeHew climbed inside to collect weapons and zero the radios. First Sergeant Thompson showed up next with his medical team. LeHew turned, "First Sergeant, it's a mess in here."[30] He returned to the task of getting to the radios, when he heard a groan beneath the twisted metal and torn bodies on the floor of the track.

LeHew called out to Thompson, "Hey, I got a live one down here."[31] Corporal Matthew Juska, 6'2", two hundred twenty pounds, had miraculously survived the explosion, but he was severely wounded and trapped. The Marines began to quickly, yet gently, sift through the bloody debris to free Juska, who was pinned at the head by the large metal bar that had held the top hatches in place. When the track had been hit as it crossed the Saddam Canal bridge, the ramp fell and the metal roof came crashing down onto Juska. The heavy piece of metal nearly killed him. But minutes later, it saved his life when it shielded him from the RPG blast at the Euphrates River.

Two other Marines, Velazquez and McGinitie, were wounded but still able to walk. Michael Bitz' body was removed, and everyone continued the delicate work of freeing Juska from the wreckage. Captain Brooks's radio began to crackle with reports of, "Casualties at our pos," from one of his platoon leaders, 2d Lieutenant Campbell Kane. It was impossible for Brooks

---

30 Gunnery Sergeant LeHew's personal, written account.

31 Ibid. Lehew.

to sort out who was hurt. Were his men reporting the casualties in C206, or were his own men starting to fall to enemy fire? He couldn't tell from the radio reports. All that he could do was to get some help for whoever was wounded. But his men were already in action.

Alpha Company's FAC, Captain Jim "Kool Aide" Jones, was on his radio in an instant, "Any aircraft, any aircraft! This is Kool Aide on TAD, over."[32]

Jones repeated the call several times and was almost ready to switch to the guard frequency when a Huey pilot overhead responded, "Kool-Aide, this is [Huey pilot], go ahead."

"[Huey pilot], this is Kool-Aide requesting an emergency med-evac in Nasiriyah."

The Huey pilot replied, "Kool-Aide, you are barely readable. Say again."

Jones repeated, "[Huey pilot], this is Kool-Aide requesting an emergency med-evac in Nasiriyah."

"Kool-Aide, understand you are requesting an emergency med-evac?"

"That's affirmative. We have injured personnel that need immediate med-evac!"

"Roger, Kool-Aide, stand by."

Captain Jones waited for several anxious moments. Then, the now-familiar Huey pilot's voice crackled over the radio, "Kool-Aide, we're checking off station, you have med-evac inbound."

While Jones called for the med-evac, Captain Brooks took off on foot to check his company and try to learn the extent of the casualties. Brooks first ran into Sergeant Cantu, Lieutenant Kane's platoon sergeant. Brooks talked with Cantu about the casualties, then he told Cantu to stay tough. Cantu, whose men were holding the most critical part of the line, replied, "We will, sir."[33] Brooks moved on in search of the casualties. Next, he ran in to Gunnery Sergeant Merriman, who led him to a HMMWV that already had Sergeant Bitz's body loaded in the cargo bed. Marines were still struggling to free Juska from the tangled wreckage.

When Cantu reached the crippled track, they were pulling Juska out of the wreckage. The top of his helmet was cracked open, and he was bleeding

---

32 The following radio conversation was provided by Captain Jones in a e-mail to the author. Jones could not remember the Huey pilot's call sign.

33 Ibid. Cantu.

profusely. Thompson came over and asked Cantu if he had any smoke to mark an LZ. He gave him the only color he had left—violet. One of the other wounded survivors was obviously in shock. He kept saying 'My track! My track!' Velazquez, McGinitie, and the walking wounded were helped to the casualty collection point in the building that Martin and Cantu had just cleared. "Stay here." They were told. "You will be safe in here."

BRAVO COMPANY

As if there wasn't enough going wrong, the Cobras that had been protecting the stranded vehicles reported to Hawkins that they were "Winchester."[34] Hawkins got on the radio immediately and asked them if they would stay and just keep the sound of their rotor blades on top of the tanks. By now, the Iraqis were terrified by the presence of the deadly Cobras. Hawkins hoped that the sound alone would keep the Iraqis at bay.

"Roger that," was their only reply, and the Marine aviators selflessly continued to make low-level, high-speed passes over the mired vehicles, with no means to defend themselves.

As Newland's tracks fought their way north, Grabowski's HMMWVs had stopped, about three-quarters of the way through the city. The Marines could see Ambush Alley off in the distance, toward the setting sun. They set up a mini-defensive position in a drainage ditch area off the highway. Grabowski decided that they would wait there for the rest of Bravo Company to retrieve the mired vehicles and come forward.

Grabowski sent Dunfee to check the road. Dunfee moved over to Ambush Alley with two CAAT vehicles and took cover next to a house on the east side of the road. They were only eight hundred meters from the canal bridge. They could see C201 with the naked eye. When Corporal McCall used his TOW sight, he could see Iraqis roaming the street. "They got weapons!" he exclaimed. Then he reported, "They are in uniform."

Sergeant James Johnson's finger was twitching on his MK19 trigger. "Hold on a second." Dunfee ordered, thinking there still could be Marines in the track. They continued to watch as a blue Chevy Suburban drove to the track, was loaded, and then sped off. Still taking sporadic fire, Dunfee

---

34 "Winchester" is the universal call sign for being out of ammunition.

ordered his men to stay put, and he went back on foot to bring the rest of Bravo Company and Colonel Grabowski up to the road.

As he was walking back, an Iraqi machine gun opened fire on Grabowski and his Marines. Lost in the moment, Grabowski didn't even notice. Sergeant Major Arrick ran to Grabowski. "Get down! Get down!" Arrick shouted as he motioned for his boss to hit the deck.

Dunfee watched all of the Marines gathered around Grabowski's Humvee hit the deck. The years of being around firing weapons had severely damaged Dunfee's hearing. He couldn't hear the rattling report of the gun, so he walked up to Grabowski's vehicle and casually asked, "What's going on?"

Grabowski was lying next to his HMMWV, holding his radio headset, with the cord stretched to its limit, trying to talk with his men. He turned to Dunfee and yelled, "A heavy machine gun is shooting at us! I'm too old for this shit"

"Oh, shit!" Dunfee replied as he quickly took cover, too.

Once they silenced the machine gun, Bravo Company and what was left of Alpha Command headed west toward the main road that they had chosen to avoid earlier. They moved west about four hundred meters into an open area next to the road, just south of the Saddam Canal.

THE TIMBERWOLVES

By now, the battalion staff had abandoned the C7. The battle had deteriorated into a handful of separate struggles. Colonel Grabowski had pulled together Bravo Company and his command group and was starting to regain communications with his other companies. But Bravo and Charlie Companys were scattered all over the battlefield. There were still vehicles stuck in southeast Nasiriyah, and Corporal Wentzel was hanging on at the "Alamo" with sixteen Marines. Alpha Company was Grabowski's only unit still intact.

Gunny Doran, Lieutenant Letendre, and the 81mm mortars finally arrived at the Euphrates River bridge. Letendre's four CAAT vehicles rolled across the bridge first. While under heavy enemy machine gun fire, Letendre jumped out of his vehicle and directed his two machine gun vehicles to return fire on the enemy's heavy guns located in buildings off to the west. He then ordered his two TOW vehicles to the east side of the road to support Alpha Company with their SAWs. Iraqis started firing a heavy machine gun

USS *Kearsarge* departs with the 2d Marine Expeditionary Brigade.
US Navy Photo

USS *Kearsarge* was General Natonski's Flag Ship.
US Navy Photo

USS *Saipan* was the second "Big Deck" in the Magnificent Seven.
US Navy Photo

Inside the USS *Ponce*
Gunner David Dunfee USMC

Ships of Magnificent
Seven line up to enter the
Suez Canal.
Gunner David Dunfee USMC

Re-supply at sea
Gunner David Dunfee USMC

One of many signposts
in Camp Shoup
Sgt. Joe Muccia USMC

Alpha Company M1 Abrams tank in Camp Shoup
Sgt. Joe Muccia USMC

L to R: SSgt Lonnie
Parker, SSgt Phillip
Jordan, and 1st Lt.
James Reid in Camp
Shoup
1st Lt. James Reid USMC

HMMWVs parked in
front of 1st Battalion,
2d Marines' Head-
quarters tent in Camp
Shoup
*Gunner David Dunfee
USMC*

Colonel Ron Bailey
at Camp Shoup
USMC Photo

1st Battalion, 2d Marines staging for war at Camp Shoup
Gunner David Dunfee USMC

HMM-162 Sea Knight Helicopters at Jalibah
Anon

Crew of Parole-Two-Five.
L to R: GySgt. William
Hetterscheidt, Captain
Eric Garcia, Corporal
Lewis and 1st Lt. Tod
Schroeder
Captain Eric Griggs USMC

SPC Hernandez's and
SPC S. Johnson's flatbed
truck jackknifed along the
side of Highway 7.
HMMWV carrying
Piestewa, Dowdy, Lynch,
Buggs and Anguiano can
be seen crashed into the
rear of the flatbed.
Sgt. Joe Muccia USMC

Photo taken from C211
as Charlie Company drove
north on Highway 7
toward An Nasiriyah.
Smoke in the distance is
from burning 507th Main-
tenance Company vehicles
Cpl. Will Bachmann USMC

Hudson's and Mata's burning HEMTT wrecker, just south of the Railroad
GySgt. Alan Kamper USMCR

Destroyed Iraqi tank at the
Railroad Bridge
Gunner David Dunfee USMC

Parole-Two-Five flying
up Highway 1 toward
An Nasiriyah
Captain Eric Griggs USMC

Eastern Euphrates River
Bridge
Gunner David Dunfee USMC

Bravo Company tracks
moving through Eastern
An Nasiriyah
Gunner David Dunfee USMC

Tanks stuck in Eastern
An Nasiriyah

Gunner David Dunfee USMC

Captain Cubas' tank in the middle of the open field, east of An Nasiriyah
GySgt Alan Kamper USMCR

An Nasiriyah
Gunner David Dunfee USMC

Narrow alleys in Eastern
Nasiriyah
Gunner David Dunfee USMC

SgtMaj. Charles Arrick and
LtCol. Rickey Grabowski in
the command HMMWV
Gunner David Dunfee USMC

Major Bill Peeples' tank in Ambush Alley
Anon

Shattered remains of C208
Gunner David Dunfee USMC

Loading Casualties into Captain Garcia's helicopter, north of the Saddam Canal on 23 March. The Iraqi 23rd Brigade Headquarters can be seen in the distance.
Captain Eric Griggs USMC

Iraqi Artillery piece that was located at Western "T"
Gunner David Dunfee USMC

The Alamo
Gunner David Dunfee USMC

Fox Company at the Euphrates River Bridge on the morning of 24 March
SSgt. Kevin Ellicott USMCR

Lima Company prepares to go out on patrol on 26 March
Captain Harold "Duck" Qualkinbush USMC

LtCol. Dunahoe and Scout Sniper team atop The Citadel
Captain Harold "Duck" Qualkinbush USMC

Captain Harold "Duck" Qualkinbush and an Iraqi Family
Captain Harold "Duck" Qualkinbush USMC

Iraqi artist's depiction of the 9/11 attack painted on the wall of a military command center in An Nassiriyah.
Anon

Standing at the base of the Saddam Canal Bridge with Ambush Alley behind them. L to R: LtCol Glenn Starnes, Capt Billy Moore, Capt Tim Newland, Col Ron Bailey, LtCol Rickey Grabowski, Captain Mike Brooks, Captain Dan Wittnam and Capt Karl Rohr.
Gunner David Dunfee USMC

at Letendre's men from a tree line on the southern bank of the river. CAAT's machine guns quickly returned the fire and silenced the heavy gun.

As the Mystery Machine moved up over the crest of the bridge, the first thing Doran saw was the smoking remains of C206, stalled in the middle of the road. In disbelief, Day exclaimed, "What's that?"

"It's an AMTRAC," Doran answered, in shock.

ALPHA COMPANY

On the north side of the river, Gunny Doran jumped from his Humvee and started yelling. "Get the fuck out of the vehicles!"[35] Sabilla and Doran were both shooting. All of a sudden, Sabilla shouted, "RP—," and Doran turned to see the grenade glance off the back tarp of his vehicle, hit a telephone pole, and explode. A hot blast of air hit Doran in the face. In an instant, Doran was firing his shotgun again. He emptied it in the direction of the Iraqi grenadier. Other Marines turned their weapons on the same Iraqi, who quickly fell dead on the ground.

Doran paused to reload his shotgun, and then enemy rounds started kicking up dirt on the right side of his Humvee. Doran turned again and saw that Iraqis had moved up on the bridge behind them, just as they had done earlier with 1st Sergeant Thompson. Doran thought to himself, "We're surrounded."[36]

The battle had turned into a porous urban fight. There was no front. There was no safe rear area. Many Iraqi fighters had been bypassed along Highway 7 as the Timberwolves charged forward to secure the bridges. Now, Grabowski's companies were spread throughout An Nasiriyah, each fighting its own 360-degree battle.

Lieutenant Clayton deployed his mortars several hundred meters north of the river on the right side of the road. They were in a good position to support Captain Brooks, but they were in a wide-open field. There was so much enemy fire that Clayton's men had to lay flat on the ground or jump into a nearby drainage ditch after firing every shot. Iraqis were seemingly everywhere.

---

35 Ibid. Doran.

36 Ibid. Doran.

WHEN Pompos reached the wall on the west side of the road, the Marines were still receiving sporadic gunfire. Cantu was aghast when he saw Pompos. "His eyes looked liked he'd been to Hell—like he'd seen a ghost."[37] Pompos kept saying, "We gotta get back up there."[38]

There were a few tracks parked facing west, along with several Humvees. Pompos ran to Gunny Merryman, who told him of the gruesome scene at C206. It didn't sink in that the Gunnery Sergeant was talking about the casualties in C206. All Pompos could think about was getting back north to his company. He reached into Merryman's Humvee and grabbed the radio handset. "Timberwolf 6, this is Staff Sergeant Pompos." Someone snapped back that he should not use his name over the net. Pompos angrily continued, "This is Pale Horse-Three-Three. I've got fifteen bodies. We are co-located with Alpha Company. I am looking for a vehicle. We need to get back up there."[39]

In the middle of his report, Captain Brooks came up to Pompos. Pompos put down the handset, turned to Brooks, and repeated that he had fifteen Marines and that his company was getting hammered in the north. "I need a vehicle. I need to get back there." Brooks looked Pompos squarely in the eye and told him. "I need your Marines here." Then he sent Pompos and his men to fill in the defenses at a break in the wall. He told Pompos to provide covering fire for the approaching cas-evac helicopter.

AMERICA'S BATTALION

As soon as Colonel Bailey heard that Brooks was requesting relief, he called Colonel Mortenson and said, "We need you to get to the bridge—now!"[40]

Mortenson replied, "We are already moving forward." All three of Mortenson's companies were pushing north in their trucks.

Bailey reiterated, "I need you to get up to the southern bridge."

---

37 Ibid. Cantu.

38 Ibid. Pompos.

39 Ibid. Pompos.

40 Personal interview with Lieutenant Colonel Royal Mortenson, 6/15/04.

"Roger!"

Mortenson and Major Fulford quickly issued a FRAGO from the hood of their HMMWV. They changed the battalion's positioning and sent Dremann's Fox Company and two CAAT sections straight to the bridge. Then Mortenson shifted Golf Company up to assist Echo in the clearing operation. Echo Company would continue to clear on the west side of Highway 7, and Golf Company was moved up to clear east.

Major Fulford was quickly up on the net issuing the new orders. "We're moving north." He told Dremann. "Clear from Phase Line Jackie to the southern bridge and link up with 1/2."[41]

Phase Line Jackie was a small road that crossed Highway 7 about a kilometer south of the Euphrates River. Dremann immediately ordered his men to mount up. Fox Company's sergeants passed the word down to their Marines, "1/2 is getting fucked up. We're going in!" The Marines quickly remounted and sped north with two CAAT sections. The lead CAAT vehicles raced ahead and quickly arrived at the southern base of the Euphrates River bridge. Fox Company's Marines blew right through the intersection with Phase Line Jackie and continued rolling north in their seven-ton trucks. Fox Company was only four hundred meters from the bridge when the lead CAAT section leader reported back to Dremann that he was at the planned link-up grid and that there were no friendly units in sight. He ended his report with, "I'm taking heavy machine gun fire from the west."[42]

Meanwhile, Golf and Echo companies came to a stop at Highway 8. Golf moved through the intersection and herringboned its trucks two to three hundred meters to the north. Golf's Marines dismounted and moved to the right of the road. As Echo Company rolled up behind Golf, Captain Yeo had this strange feeling that something wasn't right. He began yelling on the radio to his Marines, "Dismount!"[43]

Yeo's trucks hadn't finished rolling when the Iraqis opened fire with AK-47s and machine guns. The enemy fire punctured the company's Water Bull and shredded four or five truck tires. All the trucks received minor damage, but, luckily, the sandbagged truck beds protected Yeo's Marines, and none

---

41 Personal interview with Major Rich Dremann, 6/17/04.

42 Ibid. Dremann.

43 Telephone interview with Captain Kevin Yeo, 5/4/04.

were injured. The Marines returned fire as they pushed out toward the enemy. Then the Iraqis started dropping mortar rounds on Echo Company. There were only three or four explosions before the Iraqi mortar was silenced by Starnes' artillery.

Echo Company pushed out to a handful of buildings sitting back from the road. They moved methodically to clear each one. Yeo ordered his men to clear back at least four hundred meters from the road. His platoons fanned out in the four-hundred-meter corridor and cleared as they moved north toward the Euphrates River.

The Iraqis, who had been firing from the scattered buildings, wanted nothing to do with Yeo's Marines and fled west as the Marines approached. Captain Ross's Golf Company got held up on the east. They were being fired on from a considerable force in a tree line, so they dug in.

America's Battalion was now fully engaged in the battle. Mortenson's battalion had its hands full clearing a little more than a two-kilometer-stretch between Highway 8 and the Euphrates River.

NBC NEWS

Fifteen kilometers to the south, Sanders was feeling more at ease. He sat upright for his second report from the battlefield. Black smoke continued to reach into the sky in the background, but now Marines could be seen standing in the distance. "The Marines have run into resistance," Kerry reported.

He drew his map in the sand again. This time he added a circle between the two parallel lines. He went on to report that Fox Company was moving to secure the Euphrates River bridge and Alpha Company was fighting here (inside the circle) to get to the second bridge. The details of the battle were still sketchy. He told his American viewers that artillery shelling had been going on for three or four hours and that infantrymen of the 1st Battalion, 10th Marines had suffered casualties. This mistake was understandable, in retrospect. Glenn Starnes' artillerymen were nearby, and Kerry knew little of Grabowski's Timberwolves, who were actually in the fight.

Glass and Mead had been evacuated to 2/8's battalion aid station, which was very close to Sanders' current position. These were the first two casualties that the NBC news crew knew of, and the first casualties of the battle to be reported to the American public. In his second live report, he said, "Most of the fighting is the heavy fighting inside the city."[44]

In the middle of his live report, Kerry Sanders told the viewers that he saw a Marine Sea Stallion flying over the city. "These are the large Marine helicopters with two rotors," he went on to explain. What Kerry Sanders actually saw was a CH-46, Sea Knight, helicopter headed north toward An Nasiriyah.

1ST BATTALION, 10TH MARINES

Colonel Starnes' artillery batteries continued to bound forward to cover Charlie Company. Two batteries would continue their supporting fires while the trailing battery broke down and moved ahead of the other two. While Bravo Battery's Marines were breaking down for their next move, they started receiving mortar fire. They quickly packed up and drove north to their new position, but nowhere along Highway 7 was secure. The Iraqis had free reign of the territory once they were out of eyesight from the road. Bailey simply did not have the manpower to clear the entire route. He was stretched way too thin.

REGIMENTAL COMBAT TEAM-2

The regimental headquarters was abuzz with activity. Colonel Bailey and his staff had done pretty much all they could. They had called in air, and they had pushed 2/8 north to clear behind the Timberwolves. Now, all they could do was monitor the radio nets and wait. The radio traffic was frightening. Marines listened intently, trying to tally the casualty reports. With all of the chaos on the radios, casualties were being double and triple counted. At one point, Bailey thought that there were fifty dead and one hundred wounded. From Bailey's position, the situation looked grim.

Members of Bailey's staff would not believe the numbers. They tried and tried to validate the number of casualties, but communications were so

---

44 NBC News live report from An Nasiriyah; March 23, 2003.

bad and the situation so confusing that no one on the battlefield really knew how many casualties the Timberwolves had taken.

In fact, the situation was much bleaker for the enemy. The Timberwolves had taken the Iraqis completely by surprise. After a slow start, they had decimated the Iraqi tank company at the railroad bridge, raced to the Euphrates River, and taken the bridge. Then Grabowski had unexpectedly moved a force out to the east of town. This move completely dumbfounded the Iraqi command.

As the Iraqis had fought to trap Alpha and Bravo in the city, Charlie Company had made a mad dash through the city and had taken the northern bridge. Now, a seemingly unending stream of Marines was moving up Highway 7 to solidify their foothold at the bridges. Then there was the artillery. The Iraqis were slowly losing their mortars and artillery to counter-battery fire. If all this wasn't enough, they were constantly being attacked from the air. The situation may have been chaotic at Bailey's regimental headquarters, but a disaster was unfolding in the Iraqi headquarters. And the Marines kept coming.

THE BARBARIANS

Lieutenant Colonel Eddie Ray woke from his fitful nap in a start. "Why haven't we been called to move forward?"[45] He wondered to himself. Ray climbed down out of his vehicle and headed for the RCT-2 command center. He hadn't made it far when he ran into an officer from Colonel Bailey's staff. The officer told him that 1/2 was heavily engaged with the enemy in Nasiriyah and that Charlie Company had taken more than one hundred casualties.

Lieutenant Colonel Ray's heart sank. Immediately he wondered if his LAVs could have made a difference. To this day, Ray believes that he should have acted differently at the earlier meeting with his CO. He should have sent some of his unit forward with the Timberwolves.

Ray did not have long to contemplate what could have been. His self-recriminations were interrupted when Colonel Dowdy appeared and asked him for an update. Ray relayed the terrible news.

---

45 Telephone interview with Lieutenant Colonel Eddie Ray, 1/22/04.

The news hit Dowdy like a ton of bricks. Instantly, it was apparent to those around him that Dowdy knew that he had let down the Corps that he so dearly loved and that he was responsible for lost Marine lives. In shock, Dowdy responded with, "What do you propose we do?"

Ray snapped back, "Give them everything they need."[46]

---

46 Ibid. Ray.

CHAPTER 10

The Gauntlet

Casualties many; percentage of dead not known; combat efficiency, we are winning.

—COLONEL DAVID M. SHOUP, USMC
Tarawa, 1943

REGIMENTAL COMBAT TEAM-2

All of Bailey's mechanized battalion was now fighting in Nasiriyah. The reports coming back to Regiment were scattered and infrequent. It appeared that Charlie Company's Marines were in a fight for their lives and that they were taking heavy casualties. Bravo Company was bogged down on the east side of town along with Grabowski and his command group. Captain Brooks had just called for a med-evac and reinforcements so that he could race to Charlie Company's aid.

Bailey had just committed America's Battalion to the battle. He feared that he was going to get his whole regiment sucked up into An Nasiriyah. Bailey called back to the MEB, "I need all of the air you can give me as fast as possible and keep it coming."[1]

---

1 Colonel Bailey interview with Reed Bonadonna, 5/8/03.

ALPHA COMPANY

Cantu punched out a fire team to his south to deal with an Iraqi machine gun that was firing on the Marines from an elevated position on the west side of the road. He sent his Marines to the corner of a nearby building with a SMAW rocket launcher. They tried to knock the machine gun out but were unsuccessful. Cantu told his squad leader to stay at the corner and try to, at least, cover the Iraqi machine gunners and make them keep their heads down.

Across the road, Gunny Doran noticed the machine gun raking Alpha Company's positions, so he asked Lieutenant Clayton if he could take one of his mortar teams to fire on the Iraqi machine gun. Clayton ordered Sergeant Griffin to go with Doran.

Before Doran left, he turned to Clayton, "Hey, sir. I'm going to go across the street and pull those Marines off that corner. When you see me fire two shots, you will know it's safe to open fire."[2] Griffin moved his team out into an open field, and they started setting up while Doran raced across the street.

Cantu had been going in and out of the building to check on the wounded at the makeshift casualty collection point. He came out and saw his fire team running toward him from the corner of the building. "Who pulled you off that corner?" Cantu asked. "Some gunny,"[3] was their answer.

Cantu was headed for the corner of the building when he recognized Gunny Doran walking around with his shotgun. The Iraqi machine gun erupted again, tearing away giant pieces of the building's corner. Had the two Marines still been at their post, they would have surely been wounded, if not killed.

Fortunately, all the Iraqis had succeeded in doing was annoying Doran. Irritated that they had the audacity to shoot at his Marines, Doran jumped from cover and leveled two shotgun blasts in their direction. The shots were more of a statement than anything else. Had Doran stopped to think, he

2 Ibid. Doran.

3 Ibid. Cantu.

would have realized that the machine gun was well outside of his effective range. Cantu watched Doran run out in the alley, shoot, and then walk back to cover. Across the street, Griffin saw Doran fire, too. He immediately started lobbing mortar rounds onto the building. Griffin pointed his tube nearly straight up and fired his rounds with no extra propellant to hit the close-in target.

Only one of Griffin's rounds went astray. It landed on the building that housed the casualty collection point, blowing out all of its windows. One of Cantu's Marines blurted out, "Holy shit! What in the hell was that?" Then, one of the wounded Marines came hobbling out the door as fast as he could move. "I thought you guys said I would be safe in there."[4]

When Griffin's team opened fire, every Iraqi in view started firing on the mortar team. Riflemen atop a nearby mosque opened fire, and the machine gun started raking the field. The Marines hit the deck.

By this time, Doran was moving back to the east side of the road. Someone shouted out that Griffin was hit. Doran ran to the mortar team and flopped on top of Griffin. Doran shouted to the other team members "Get the fuck out of here!"[5] No one moved. Doran repeated his order, and one by one they rose to their feet and ran to safety.

Doran kicked over Griffin's mortar tube, hoping that if the mortar was down, the Iraqis would shift their attention to other threats and the shooting would subside. Some of the shooting stopped. Doran quickly checked Griffin. "You're just hurt. You're not wounded," he told Griffin. "We need to get the fuck out of here."[6] Just as they were starting to move to cover, one of Peeples' tanks showed up.

As soon as the tank came into view, all the Iraqis shifted their fire to the armored vehicle. A flurry of RPGs exploded as they hit the tank. Flames and smoke momentarily blocked the entire tank from Doran's view. When the dust and smoke cleared, the M1 tank stood there unscathed. Its turret began to rotate and a main gun round slammed into a nearby building. The tank continued firing, and once again, buildings began to crumble to the ground.

---

4 Ibid. Cantu.

5 Ibid. Doran.

6 Ibid. Doran.

Griffin and Doran rose and quickly moved to cover. Griffin had been holding his mortar tube when it was hit by gunfire. The reverberation of the impact had wrenched his arm. Griffin and the others had thought that he had been hit. Luckily, he was just badly shaken.

Meanwhile, Clayton had started firing on the mosque across the street. The mosque, with its large blue dome, was an enemy strong point. Armed Iraqis were running in and out of the structure, and they were using the high roof to snipe at the Marines on the ground. Under fire, Clayton's mortar men dropped over one hundred rounds on the mosque in just a couple minutes.

SCHAEFER kept looking for someone to help him get back to Charlie Company. He finally found a radio and heard Lieutenant Seely report that he had less than a platoon of Marines left. Schaefer thought that that was all that remained of Charlie Company, and he feared they would be overrun at any moment. Major Peeples had heard Seely's report, too.

Sergeant Schaefer crossed back to Corporal Brown's track. Marines were yelling at Schaefer to take cover, but after what he had just been through, the enemy fire at Alpha's position seemed light. A constant cacophony of gunfire deadens one's senses. For Schaefer, the heavy gun battle at the Euphrates River was nothing more than an irritation.

Around 1500, Major Peeples went to Captain Brooks and told him he had to take his tanks north. Brooks shifted immediately from a feeling of security back to desperation. "Can you at least leave me a couple tanks?"[7] Brooks urged. Peeples relented and ordered Captain Thompson, Swain, and Team Tank's infantry platoon to stay with Alpha Company while he and Captain Dyer took their tanks through Ambush Alley to assist Captain Wittnam and Charlie Company.

While Peeples and Brooks were planning their next move, Sergeant Schaefer was trying to rally enough Marines to return to Charlie Company with Sergeant Brown in C210. A short discussion ensued. The infantrymen and trackers all agreed that they would probably never make it back to Charlie Company, but they had to try.

---

7 Ibid. Brooks.

THE GOLDEN EAGLES

As Captain Jones waited, the Huey pilot relayed the med-evac request to RCT-2's forward command post. Eric Garcia received the call for assistance, and within minutes he launched from Queensland. Gunny Hetterscheidt heard the radio crackle with the call for help, "We got an urgent cas-evac mission. You will be going into a hot zone."[8] Garcia flew north until he found RCT-2's command post set up along the side of the road. He brought his two Phrogs in and landed but kept his "rotors" rotating. Garcia jumped out of the helicopter and went in search of an escort.

Hetterscheidt and Lewis began going through the motions that they had practiced so many times in training. First they checked the helicopter. Then they checked their .50-caliber machine guns and staged their ammo. Docs Gloria and Kirkland nervously watched Hetterscheidt and Lewis prepare for war.

After what seemed like an eternity, Hetterscheidt saw Garcia returning to the aircraft. "Okay. It's game time now,"[9] Hetterscheidt thought. Then he turned to Lewis and shouted into his helmet, "Here we go! If anything happens to me, I want you to find my kids, and you tell them what happened and let them know I love them."

Garcia had found an escort, two West Coast Hueys. Garcia and Morton lifted off and headed toward Ambush Alley.

Soon, Captain Garcia and his Dash-2 arrived over the southern suburbs of An Nasiriyah. Garcia's escorts requested that he hold south of the city while they moved to clear the route. Garcia's Huey escorts led the cas-evac mission into Nasiriyah, circling in a wagon wheel to provide cover. Garcia and Morton waited over a cluster of palm trees southeast of the city. As they waited for the escort to call them in, Garcia checked in, "Kool-Aide, Kool-Aide, this is Parole-Two-Five, checking in on TAD."[10]

"Parole-Two-Five, this is Kool-Aide, say type of aircraft."

"Kool-Aide, we are CH-46s with a Huey escort."

After some conversation back and forth about what type of aircraft

---

8 Ibid. Hetterscheidt.

9 Ibid. Hetterscheidt.

10 Entire radio conversation documented by Captain Jones in e-mail sent to the author.

were coming to Alpha Company's aid, Captain Jones continued, ". . . we need an immediate med-evac for wounded personnel . . . break . . . we are located just north of the Euphrates River on the east side of town . . . break . . . let me know when you can see the Euphrates River."

"Roger, Kool-Aide, we're just south of the river now."

"Parole-Two-Five, you will see our tracks oriented into the city for roughly a quarter mile north of the bridge."

"I see the bridge, Kool Aide, but I can't see any tracks."

The skies over Nasiriyah were filled with Cobra and Huey gunships, which continued to fire into the city. Garcia's radios crackled with ground controller requests for artillery and air support. Dash-2's copilot, Griggs, saw at least eight gunships working over the city.

Once the Huey escorts had settled in their wagon-wheel pattern, they called in Parole-Two-Five and -Two-Six. Garcia headed straight in, as he searched below for the LZ[11]. Alpha Company was dispersed north of the Euphrates in an urban area that was cluttered with buildings, power lines, and street lamps. There was very little room to land anywhere near Mike Brooks's Marines. It was certain that two CH-46s would never be able to set down north of the Euphrates River bridge. Garcia informed Dash-2 that he would land alone and ordered Dash-2 to remain airborne.

"Kool-Aide, we have your tracks in sight."

"Kool-Aide copies, be advised there are multiple sets of large power lines on the east side of the road—by the trees . . . break . . . and we are still taking fire from multiple positions on the west side of the road."

"Copy, understand that the LZ is secure?"

"Parole-Two-Five, *negative,* the area is as secure as we can make it right now, but we are still taking fire from the west."

Garcia acknowledged with a simple, "Roger," and continued his approach, heading for the billowing purple smoke.

As Garcia approached, red smoke bloomed on a nearby rooftop of an Iraqi stronghold. Cantu's purple smoke was billowing from a site near C206's destruction, and green smoke was rising from the proposed LZ on an east/west alley. Alpha Company's Marines were firing into the three-story, salmon-colored building that had the red smoke streaming from its rooftop.

---

11 Landing zone.

Garcia had flown right into the heat of the raging ground battle. Orbiting in the wagon wheel, Captain Griggs saw the lead Huey fire into the city as his radio crackled with continuous chatter.

Garcia landed on an east-to-west heading, right on top of the purple smoke. As Cantu watched the helicopter come in, he thought to himself, "That damn thing is going to get shot down."[12]

Captain Brooks got a sick feeling in stomach when he saw Garcia's Sea Knight land right in his heaviest fire zone. Before Brooks could react, Captain Jones told Garcia to move out of the hot zone. Garcia deftly manipulated the controls and quickly lifted his helicopter up through a swirl of dust streaked with green and purple smoke, over some power lines, and then he expertly sandwiched his helicopter into a small alley on the west side of the road. "I don't know how he got in there. There was no clearance, and the LZ was ringed with power lines."[13] Captain Tod Schroeder, Garcia's copilot, would recall later.

Manning the starboard .50-caliber, Gunny Hetterscheidt was staring at the side of a building, only feet away. He dropped the rear ramp and waited to receive the casualties. Lewis, manning the other .50-caliber, trained his machine gun down a small alley, which headed back south toward the river.

Marines on the ground, and in the air, rushed to provide security for Garcia's helicopter. Staff Sergeant Cantu could not believe his eyes. Even after Garcia's move into the alley, he believed that the Iraqis would soon zero in on the helicopter. Parole-Two-Five was still not safe. Cantu's men instinctively pushed forward to cover Garcia's helicopter. They all quickly directed their fire at the buildings and alleyways around Garcia's aircraft. Lieutenant Letendre moved his CAAT section to further protect the landing zone.

As Garcia settled his helicopter snugly into the alley, Morton and Griggs began to receive enemy fire from the pink building, and then a large explosion buffeted their aircraft. One of Major Peeples' M1 tanks had pounded the building with a main gun round, causing the upper floor to crumble to the ground. Morton did not wait to figure out where the sound had come from. He cartwheeled his aircraft and headed south out of the hot zone.

---

12 Ibid. Cantu.

13 Personal interview with Captain Tod Schroeder, 1/12/04.

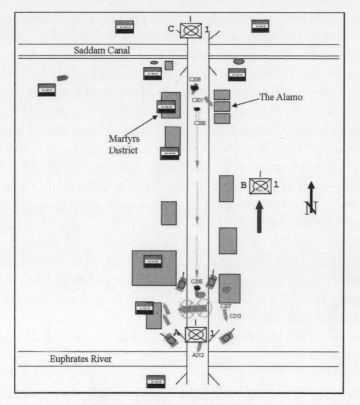

Saddam Canal
C208
C201
The Alamo
C206
Martyrs
District
B
C206
C207
C210
A
A212
Euphrates River
N

Garcia lands to pickup Casualties

Meanwhile, back in the alley, Schroeder wished he were Garcia's size as his 6'4" frame sat exposed in the cockpit. He tried to shrink down into his copilot seat, but Tod and Eric could not avoid being exposed to enemy fire.

"We were there about fifteen minutes, waiting for the wounded Marines to be brought to us."[14] Trying to do something to protect himself, Tod pulled out his 9mm service pistol and pointed it out his window. Eric glanced over and began to laugh. "You look like you are some kind of drive-by gangsta."[15]

Gunny Hetterscheidt could see a small open area to the front of the aircraft, from about the one-o'clock to two-o'clock position. There was a corner

---

14 Ibid. Schroeder.

15 Telephone interview with Captain Eric Garcia, 11/10/03.

of a building off in that direction, so that's where he aimed his machine gun. All of a sudden, he started hearing that noise that the Huey pilot had described earlier in the day—a popping sound. The gunny thought, "Holy shit! He was right!" They were taking fire. Then he noticed a rifle barrel at the corner of the building. He could see puffs of smoke coming out of the rifle. Almost immediately, a number of rounds hit the corner of the building. Cantu's men had seen the puffs, too. Hetterscheidt held his fire and watched as the Marine infantry shot up the building.

As Eric Garcia waited helplessly in the cockpit, he noticed a dog lazily roaming the street in front of the helicopter. The dog did not seem to have a care in the world, even though a major gunfight was raging all around it. Garcia keyed the mike on his intercom and said to his crew, "Hey, look at that dog."[16]

In an effort to calm his crew, he rationalized, "The dog is not bothered by all this, everything is going to be fine." Just as he finished his sentence, one of the circling Hueys raced low overhead and spooked the dog. The dog broke into a run and headed straight for Parole-Two-Five. Without breaking stride, the dog ran under the helicopter and down the length of the fuselage, then out of sight.

"Well, so much for being safe," Garcia apologized. Schroeder, Hetterscheidt, Lewis, Gloria, and Kirkland all sat nervously waiting for the casualties as the minutes dragged by.

Finally, Matthew Juska was brought to Garcia's helicopter. One of Cantu's Marines ran up the ramp to the crew chief, "It's hot! It's a hot LZ!"[17] He shouted above all the noise, telling Gunny Hetterscheidt what he already knew.

"Hurry up!" Hetterscheidt ordered, as the Marines were having a hard time getting Juska's large frame into a litter in the aircraft.

"No, we're done! Put him on the ramp! We're getting out of here!"[18] the crew chief shouted. The Marines obeyed and gently laid Juska on the deck of the helicopter, then stepped back from the aircraft. Before the

---

16 Ibid. Garcia.

17 Ibid. Cantu.

18 Ibid. Hetterscheidt.

plane had left the ground, Gloria and Kirkland were attending to Juska. He was in bad shape, bleeding from the ears and several cuts on his head. Blood was everywhere. Gloria quickly established an IV and pushed some morphine and antibiotics. Then Gloria tried to stop the bleeding from Juska's head.

Hetterscheidt closed the ramp, and Garcia gunned the engine to full power and picked up right over buildings filled with Iraqi fighters. He pulled to the right, crossed back over Ambush Alley, and got out of the city as quickly as possible. Within thirty seconds, Parole-Two-Five was safely back over desert sand, heading toward a field hospital. Gloria continued to check Juska, repeating his mantra, "Head to toe. Head to toe. Head to toe."[19] Gloria did not want to miss anything.

Captain Brooks watched Garcia lift his gray Sea Knight helicopter into the blue, afternoon sky. After seeing Juska's crushed helmet and severe head injury, Brooks was certain that he would soon be dead. But Corporal Matthew Juska would survive, only because of the efforts of many Marines on the ground and the selfless actions of Garcia, Schroeder, Hetterscheidt, Lewis, Kirkland, and Gloria on Parole-Two-Five.

AMERICA'S BATTALION

Dremann stopped his convoy less than a half kilometer from the river and ordered his men to dismount. As soon as his men started pouring from their trucks, they began taking fire from the west. Dremann ordered 1st and 3d platoons to the west side of the road and 2d Platoon to the east.

Lieutenant Southwick dismounted his men and began to press the final one hundred meters to the bridge. As they moved toward the bridge, they continued to take sporadic small arms and machine gun fire from the west side of the road. The east side was quiet.

Fox Company fanned out on both sides of the road and began to methodically clear buildings as they pushed north. First Platoon pushed out a couple hundred meters to the west and cleared four or five buildings. Second Platoon had a large complex of buildings on its right, set back four or five

---

19 Telephone interview with HN3 Moses Gloria (USN), 11/17/04.

hundred meters from the road. There were a handful of buildings sprinkled between the complex and the highway, but everything was quiet to the east. Second Platoon moved north at 1st and 3d platoons' pace.

First Platoon had found nearly fifty terrified civilians huddled in the buildings to the west. Dremann immediately got on the net to ask Major Fulford what to do. Dremann told Fulford that he had "a shit pot full of civilians"[20] and that clearing the remaining buildings would probably take a while. Then he asked, "Do you want me to get to the bridge, or do you want me to clear all the way to the bridge?"[21]

Fulford ordered, "Get to the bridge."

Dremann immediately pulled his men out of the buildings. As they left, they told the frightened civilians to stay inside. Dremann's remaining CAAT section moved up on the road, and the infantry platoons moved in loose columns along both sides of the highway. They then pushed north the remaining hundred meters.

Second Platoon reached the bridge first. Southwick moved his platoon up onto the crest with a CAAT section while 1st Platoon moved to the southern bank of the Euphrates River and secured the west side of the bridge. Dremann shifted 3d Platoon back across the road, and they moved to secure the southeast side of the bridge.

Just as Southwick's 2d Platoon moved up onto the Euphrates River bridge, a large-caliber machine gun opened fire on a CH-46 helicopter flying high overhead. Southwick looked down onto the southern bank of the river to find an Iraqi technical firing. He immediately called for one of his CAAT TOW vehicles. They moved over to the rail of the bridge and fired one of their deadly antitank missiles. It was a clear shot, and the technical was completely destroyed.

STAFF Sergeant Filipkowski finally caught up with Task Force Tarawa, but he was stopped at 2/8's position along Highway 7. When Filipkowski protested that he had to get north to his unit, someone from Regiment told him that he wasn't going anywhere. He was needed to help escort a convoy

---

20 Ibid. Dremann.

21 Ibid. Dremann.

north. As a result, he was forced to sit along the side of the road, listening on his radio to the entire battle.

ALPHA COMPANY, 8TH TANKS

By now, Peeples was back on his tank and moving slowly forward with Carter, Captain Dyer, and Hawkins. Realizing that he must travel straight up Ambush Alley, Peeples told his driver that once he got past the Alpha Company Marines, he wanted him to go through as fast as he could. Peeples dropped down and buttoned up his hatch, and his driver gunned the engine. The M1 accelerated to over thirty miles per hour and raced up Ambush Alley, kicking up a trail of dust. Shirley accelerated and followed his company commander. By the time Schaefer got his track moving, Peeples and Dyer were already gone, leaving the lone track to run the gauntlet on its own, not far behind the speeding tanks.

The tanks hadn't moved far when Peeples realized that he could hardly see anything through the vision blocks in his turret, so he opened his hatch to the protected position. This enabled him to peek out onto the streets below. He kept hitting his head, so he finally just opened his hatch and rode through the rest of the city exposed from the chest up.

Another flurry of RPGs and bursts of machine gun fire greeted the tankers in Ambush Alley. One of the RPGs flew over the back deck of Peeples' tank. Peeples continued to direct Lieutenant Carter's fire toward threatening windows and doorways as they raced through the city. Down in Dyer's turret, Bell kept acquiring and destroying targets. With booming guns and rattling machine guns, the tankers pressed north through streets teeming with Iraqis in black and tan uniforms.

Within a few minutes, Peeples could see the Saddam Canal bridge in the distance. He raced over the bridge to find a grisly scene of blown tracks and wounded Marines. Peeples started looking for the familiar white diamond on the side of Captain Wittnam's command track. It didn't take Peeples long: there were only a few tracks in sight. Wittnam's lone track was parked on the right side of the road. Peeples stopped and jumped down from his tank, asking, "What do you need?"[22]

---

22 Ibid. Peeples.

CHARLIE COMPANY

Charlie Company had been battling the enemy north of the canal for over two hours by the time Peeples and Dyer showed up. When Captain Wittnam saw the tanks coming over the bridge, his heart skipped. Finally, relief was on the way. Wittnam ran up on the highway and greeted Peeples.

Seely saw the tanks crest the canal bridge, too. "Push forward. Push forward."[23] He commanded into the radio handset. He was still worried that his lone platoon would come under ground attack at any moment. Seely was talking to Panzer 5 (Captain Dyer). Dyer stopped momentarily at the north bridge, and Seely's heart sank again. Mortar rounds were still raining down on the highway ahead. The air was black with dirt from the impacts.

Wittnam told Peeples that he needed him to silence the enemy fire coming from the southern bank of the Saddam Canal and that Lieutenant Seely was farther north. Peeples sent Dyer forward to find Seely and to reinforce his position, while Peeples turned back south and started putting tank main gun and machine gun fire into buildings across the canal. Captain Wittnam climbed up onto Peeples' tank, and lying atop the turret, he continued to direct Peeples' fire. "I need you to put a salvo on this house, this house, and this house."[24] Peeples immediately started pounding the buildings that had been hiding the enemy's heavy machine guns. He shot five main gun rounds in rapid succession, and the shooting stopped. The Iraqis did not want anything to do with the M1 tank.

Meanwhile, Hawkins and Dyer slowly rolled north up the middle of Highway 7 to Seely's position near 395 North. Lance Corporal Emrath ran up on the road and popped a smoke. Dyer, Hawk, Bell, and Shirley came creeping up in their tank, stopped, and sat right in the middle of the road. Seely was never so happy to see a tank.

No sooner had Dyer and Hawkins pulled up, than an artillery round exploded seventy meters in front of them. Hawkins' first thought was,

---

23 Ibid. Seely.

24 Telephone interview with Captain Dan Wittnam, 3/11/04.

"Damn it, Sprout,[25] you are shooting at us."[26] Hawkins had no idea where the enemy artillery was coming from, so he contacted two A-10s that had just come on the scene. Just as they began to search, another round exploded in the exact same spot. Then there was a third explosion. "Shit, it's them." Hawkins thought. They weren't adjusting the fire. The A-10 pilots saw the cannon flashes over by the western "T." They swooped in and laid down a line of cluster bombs on the enemy positions. The explosions in the road in front of Dyer and Hawk abruptly stopped.

Dyer could see a lot of Iraqis running in the 23d Brigade headquarters complex at the northern "T." He began firing on the enemy with his machine guns and tank main gun while Hawkins worked the air support. There still were mortar and artillery rounds landing nearby, and small arms fire intermittently whizzed overhead. Dyer and Hawkins continued to pound the enemy and, slowly, the enemy fire decreased.

Then more Cobras arrived. Hawkins brought in flight after flight. The pilots found a line of ten to fifteen mortars set up in a trench, just south of the canal which had been pounding Charlie Company all afternoon. Hawkins immediately directed the pilots to take out the Iraqis in the trench line. The Cobras swooped in, firing rockets into the trench. In Major Peeples' tank, Lieutenant Carter, the FO, helped Hawkins by calling in Marine counterbattery artillery fire. The battle was rapidly turning. Peeples, Carter, Dyer, and Hawkins started bringing order back to the battlefield as they led a combined-arms counterattack on the enemy.

One by one, the Iraqi artillery and mortars were silenced. Heavy machine gun and tank main gun rounds took out the enemy's heavy guns, and the enemy fire along the highway subsided. The three things the Iraqis did not want to mess with were the M1s, LAVs, and Cobras. Once the Marines were able to effectively bring in air, artillery, and M1 tank ground fire, the Iraqis packed up their bags and got the hell out of Dodge.

---

25 The artillery forward observer was riding with Major Peeples. Lieutenant Jim Carter's call sign was "Sprout."

26 Ibid. Hawkins.

ALPHA COMPANY

As soon as Garcia lifted his helicopter to safety, Captain Brooks ordered, "Mount 'em Up! Mount up the infantry." Cantu gathered up the casualties from the casualty collection point and loaded them into his tracks. Then he ran across the road to Lieutenant Clayton's mortar men. Some of Clayton's men were already in the process of breaking down their guns and loading them into their vehicles, but others were still firing on the nearby mosque.

Cantu told Clayton that the company was heading north. Clayton acknowledged that he already knew. "Yeah, I got one more mission," he told Cantu. Then Clayton turned to Doran. "Hey, Gunny, do you want to go with us?"

"I ain't staying fucking here,"[27] Doran replied.

Clayton's men shot several more rounds into the mosque, broke their weapons down, climbed into their trucks, and headed north with the company. Cantu returned to his track, made one final check to make sure that he had everyone, and then started to close his ramp.

Meanwhile, Sergeant Pompos had been looking for tracks for his Marines. As he moved along the wall, tracks were buttoning up, backing out, and then heading north. As Pompos and his Marines moved along the line, four Marines would jump in one track, four in the next. Before leaving, Cantu took as many of Pompos's Marines as he could, but one track commander waved Pompos away, "No! We're full,"[28] he told Pompos.

When Pompos reached the last track, he still had seven Marines on the ground. Pompos looked up into the TC hatch and, to his surprise, the crew chief was Corporal Goodman. Goodman had been one of Pompos's recruits when he was a drill instructor at Parris Island. Pompos shouted, "Corporal Goodman!"

Goodman turned toward the shout and immediately smiled. "Staff Sergeant, oh, my God!"

"I got to get my Marines in your track."

"Get 'em in," Goodman replied, and the back door swung open. Pompos and the last seven Marines on the ground scurried into the last AMTRAC.

---

27 Ibid. Doran.

28 Ibid. Pompos.

Goodman backed out and took up position at the tail end of Alpha Company.

All of Alpha Company pushed through Ambush Alley at top speed. They moved forward with Captain Thompson's two-tank platoon, Alpha Company's tracks, Team Tank's infantry platoon, and Charlie Company's remaining track—C207. Brooks's Humvees, the battalion's 81mm mortars, Gunny Doran's Humvee, and Letendre's CAAT section all moved in the shadow of the armored column.

As they raced through Ambush Alley, Lieutenant Letendre's four CAAT vehicles kept up constant fire along the route. Letendre's Marines purposely placed themselves between the enemy and the thin-skinned vehicles of the 81mm mortar platoon and other units, utilizing what armor protection and firepower they had to shield their fellow Marines.

BRAVO COMPANY

After two hours of fighting their way through eastern Nasiriyah, Gomez' men in 1st Squad, of the 1st Platoon, were at the point of exhaustion. They were so tired, they could not even raise their weapons. They climbed back into their track and drove forward until they reached an open area. The field was about two-thirds of the way to the Saddam Canal bridge, and the Marines could see Ambush Alley off to the west, across the open space.

The rest of Bravo Company was on the right side of Ambush Alley, about fifteen hundred to two thousand meters from the canal bridge. They set up a defensive perimeter, waiting for the remaining vehicles to be freed from the mud. From their new position, they watched Alpha Company cruise by at 45–60 kilometers per hour.

As Captain Blanchard watched Alpha Company race north through Ambush Alley, he noticed that one of his tracks, C207, was having a hard time keeping up—it was barely limping along. Something was obviously wrong. Its engine had been knocked off its mounts in one of the many catastrophic explosions that had erupted near it earlier. Blanchard waived C207 over to a stop, fearing that a single straggling track would never survive the journey past the Martyrs' District.

From Bravo Company's new position, the Marines could clearly see C208 and C201 in the distance. They had intermittent radio contact with Corporal Wentzel, who was stranded with his squad in the "Alamo."

Wentzel only had a small portable squad radio, and the battery was quickly dying. Captain Blanchard would ask Wentzel a question, and Wentzel would key once for "yes" and twice for a "no" answer. Blanchard and Wentzel hoped that they could conserve enough battery power to last until Wentzel's squad could be picked up. For now, all the Marines at Bravo Company's position could do was to wait for orders to move.

Gomez was upset that his company was not moving forward, but Grabowski was trying to reestablish his situational awareness, wait for the rest of his vehicles to be retrieved, and to regain control of the battalion. The first order of business was to silence the enemy fire coming from the Martyrs' District. First Lieutenant Fanning, Bravo Company's FiST leader, was calling for artillery fire. "One round, just give me one fucking round!"[29] He screamed into the radio.

"THE ALAMO"

As they raced past in the Mystery Machine, Doc Sabilla saw Marines waving from the second-story windows of an Iraqi house on their right. "Stop! Stop!" Sabilla screamed at Day. "Turn around! Turn around!"[30]

Corporal Wentzel ran out in the street displaying a purple "don't shoot me" panel. Gunny Doran's HMMWV pulled up, and he shouted to Wentzel, "What do you need?" Wentzel replied that they were out of water, and they needed batteries for their radio.

Day pulled the Mystery Machine up right behind C201. It was evident that there had been a fight here. There were dead bodies everywhere. Day jumped out of the driver's seat and ran to the back of his trailer. He began rummaging through the boxes, looking for batteries. All the while, he was thinking to himself, "I am going to get myself killed looking for batteries!" Finally, he found a radio battery. He grabbed it and threw it in Wentzel's direction, then raced back to the driver's seat.

Doran tossed Wentzel a canteen, told him he would be back to get them, and drove off. Wentzel ran back inside the building, only to find that the canteen was nearly empty and that Day had given him the wrong size batteries.

---

29 Personal written narrative of Corporal Jose Gomez.

30 Ibid. Doran.

FOX COMPANY

For the first time all day, the southeast Euphrates River bridge was blocked to enemy traffic, but without the rest of the battalion, Fox Company was just another lone company, isolated on a porous battlefield.

Second Platoon moved to the crest of the bridge to find only the shattered remains of C206 ahead at the northern base of the bridge. By now, all of the Marines of 1/2 were gone and a pretty large crowd had gathered around the destroyed AMTRAC. Fox Company was still taking heavy machine gun fire from the west, and the Iraqis were shooting from both the north and south sides of the river. Dremann ordered his men forward to clear the two buildings that were closest to the road, just north of the bridge.

Just as his men reached the north bank, Dremann was told that all of the 1st Battalion had moved north of the Saddam Canal. Everything along Ambush Alley, north of the Euphrates River, had become a free-fire zone. Mortenson ordered Dremann to pull everyone back to the bridge for the night. As ordered, Dremann pulled his men back to the crest of the Euphrates River bridge and consolidated his defenses. Lieutenant Southwick had his Marines stretch concertina wire across the road on the bridge to stop any Iraqis from approaching his position during the night.

The enemy continued to fire heavy machine guns at the Marines on the bridge from a stand of trees to the southwest. First Sergeant Howard Gatewood moved to a position atop the Euphrates River bridge. Gatewood scanned the tree line below, looking for the muzzle flashes of the machine gun. Within a few minutes, he had pinpointed the enemy's position. Gatewood called in the gun's coordinates, and Marine artillery fire came down on the Iraqi gunners, silencing the gun.

Fox consolidated its position at the bridge, and Echo Company moved up behind Fox to take up positions west of Euphrates River bridge. Golf Company defended to the east, along Highway 7.

"THE ALAMO"

Captain Wittnam was still lying on Peeples' turret, directing his fire when word came over the radio that there were Marines stuck in the city. Peeples turned to Wittnam, "You better get off. I'm going to go back in there and see if I can help these guys."[31] Wittnam jumped down, and Peeples headed back across the Saddam Canal in search of the trapped Marines.

As soon as he crossed the bridge, he saw a squad of Marines in some buildings on his left. Shots started ringing out from the Martyrs' District on the west side of the road. Peeples drove his tank up next to the buildings and ordered Lieutenant Carter to return fire. Then Major Peeples jumped to the ground and went inside the building to find out what was going on.

Wentzel had four wounded: Elliot, Trevino, Carl, and Seegert. Peeples asked Wentzel if his men could foot march out with the protection of his tank. Wentzel replied that they would be fine in the building. "We just need you to get the wounded out."

Peeples raced back out to tell Carter to rotate the turret to expose the back deck. Then he raced back in the building to help with the casualties. Under constant enemy fire, Peeples led Trevino, who still couldn't see; Elliot, hobbling and eyes swollen shut from the burns to his face; and Seegert, with a serious shoulder wound, out to his tank. He helped them up onto the back deck. Then, four Marines carried Carl, who by now was unconscious, out to the tank.

Peeples helped pull Carl up onto the tank. Then he jumped in his hatch and slowly drove the four wounded Marines out of the city to the casualty collection point north of the canal. Several corpsmen gently lifted the wounded down off the tank deck and began tending to their wounds. Two corpsmen took Elliot and gave him morphine. Peeples left his gunner in charge of his tank and walked over to check on Thompson and Swain. They had both shut off their engines and were nearly out of gas.

CHARLIE COMPANY

By late afternoon, Alpha Company was rolling across the Saddam Canal. When Pompos arrived, he ordered the Marines in his track to dismount and take positions against the eastern berm, about three hundred meters north of Captain Wittnam. As each of Brooks's tracks pulled up, its Marines rushed out to fill in more of the line. Soon, there was an impenetrable defense on both sides of the road. Brooks went in search of Wittnam, and

---

31 Ibid. Peeples.

when he found him he couldn't believe his eyes. Wittnam was covered in mud and blood and looked like he had just returned from hell.

First Sergeant Thompson and Gunny LeHew were in the last Alpha Company track to cross over the canal. When they pulled up to Charlie Company's position, the scene was chaotic and shocking. Body parts were strewn all over, and several tracks were still smoking. Thompson turned to Lehew, "Gunny, tell me this ain't our Marines." LeHew solemnly replied, "It's our Marines, First Sergeant."[32]

Nearly at the tail end of Alpha Company's convoy, Day accelerated and raced for the canal bridge. As he drove across, the shots faded behind him, only to be replaced by reports to his north. It was instantly clear that the men of Charlie Company had been in a fight for their lives. Everything was in disarray. Gunny Doran jumped from his Humvee and walked toward Gunny Blackwell in the distance, to see if he could help.

As he approached, Blackwell and a small group were collecting the dead Marines. Doran couldn't bring himself to go over there, so he turned away. Then he saw Sergeant Pompos. Pompos ran over and shook Gunny Doran's hand. Doran was shaking his head, thinking, "This is screwed up."

"What's the matter, brother?"[33] Doran inquired.

"I can't find my platoon," Pompos confided.

"Well, I just saw some Marines in the city." Doran replied.

"I don't know if they are mine. I'm missing everybody."

"Holy shit!" Doran exclaimed. Then he yelled for Day and Doc Sabilla. He told some eighty-one guys to disconnect his trailer, and he turned to a nearby group of Marines. "I need two SAW gunners to go back into town." At first, the group stood frozen. One Marine started to step forward, and then they all did. Doran picked two and put them in the back of the Mystery Machine.

Then he went to Lieutenant Letendre and told him of the stranded Marines. "Can I go with you?" Letendre asked.

"Yes, sir."

"What's the plan?" Letendre inquired.

"Drive fast—kill everybody—and get our boys out of there," Doran responded.

---

32 Telephone interview with 1st Sergeant James Thompson Jr., 8/1/04.

33 The following is a composite of a conversation, taken from a telephone interview with Jason Doran and Reed Bonadonna's interview with Anthony Pompos.

Letendre looked Doran in the eyes, smiled, and said, "That sounds like it might work." Then he went over to his men, "You are either going to love me or hate me—we are going back in."[34] Without question or comment, the CAAT Marines mounted up in their four armored Humvees. Letendre asked Doran if he wanted the armored Hummers to lead. "No," Doran replied, "I know where we are going."

Doran bummed a cigarette from Lieutenant Clayton and stuck it, unlit, in his mouth. Then Day drove up on the road, heading south toward the canal bridge. Letendre's four CAAT vehicles fell in behind the Mystery Machine. Doc Sabilla sat quietly in the back, praying in Spanish. Doran repeated his prayers, and Day just sat there quietly driving his Humvee toward near-certain death.

As they drove up on the bridge, it was quiet. Doran could hear the tires humming on the pavement. As soon as the Iraqis in the city noticed Doran's Humvee convoy, they opened up with everything they had. Two large guns in the Martyrs' District fired on the Marines first. Then a third machine gun on the east opened fire. Fortunately, the Iraqis were horrible shots, and they were unable to hit the speeding vehicles. Doran could hear the rattling of Letendre's .50-caliber machine guns behind him as they raced down off the bridge.

The Iraqis continued to fire on the small convoy, but now they were out of the line of fire of the big guns. AK-47 rounds continued to whiz by as the Humvees skidded to a stop at C201. Doran looked at the Marines in the rescue team. A few moments earlier, they had been full of Marine bravado. Now that they had been through the maelstrom atop the bridge, they were starting to get scared.

Doran was concerned that some Marines might lose it. He took the cigarette from his mouth, bummed a light, and stood in the middle of the road smoking. He wanted his men to realize that things were not as bad as it seemed. He stood out in the open for what seemed like a long time, smoking his cigarette. Then he tossed the cigarette to the dirt, screwed it into the ground with his boot, and looked up and said, "This fucking place sucks."[35]

---

34 Ibid. Doran.

35 Ibid. Doran.

Doran moved in the open gate of the "Alamo," gathered Wentzel's remaining Marines, ran upstairs to make sure that no one was left behind, and then returned to the courtyard. As he ran out in the street, the Mystery Machine had already pulled away. Doran jumped on the hood of another HMMWV and hung on for dear life. Miraculously, all five loaded vehicles made it safely back across the canal bridge.

Once Doran had left for the rescue mission, Pompos took Corporal Willis, his squad leader, and one other Marine, and they walked all the way down to Charlie Company. When Captain Wittnam saw Pompos, he walked up and hugged him. Pompos asked, "Do you know where Lieutenant Seely is?"

"Yes." Wittnam replied. "I have comm with him. He's right across the road."

First Sergeant Henao and Gunny Blackwell were busy with the casualties, so Captain Wittnam said to Pompos, "You got the company."[36] Pompos sent Willis back north to retrieve his squad, and Pompos went to work trying to regroup the company. It wasn't long before Pompos looked up and saw Lieutenant Seely walking across the road. Seely and Emrath had left 2d Platoon in the north, and they had walked south looking for the Marines of 3d Platoon. They continued back to where they had originally crossed to the west side and crossed back over to the casualty collection point.

After hours of fighting, all of a sudden, everything went quiet. There were still sporadic reports echoing through the city but north of the canal, it was over.

AS soon as Cantu had gotten out of his track, a Marine came up to him and said, "Hey, Jose is hit." Torres and Cantu were good friends. Shocked at the news, Cantu spent some time making sure his Marines were set in their position, and as soon as things had quieted down, he went out to find Torres. As he came up to the casualty collection point, he overheard Staff Sergeant Parker say, "Fucking A-10s."[37] Then he saw that there were more

---

36 Ibid. Pompos.

37 Ibid. Cantu.

than a couple dozen Marines on the ground. It was clear that they had been separated into two groups. The first group had Marines standing and crouching around bandaged bodies that were being tended by teams of corpsmen. The Marines in the second group were all motionless and covered.

Cantu rushed to the group of casualties, hoping that Torres was not in the second group. As he walked up, he saw a Marine lying on his stomach. Another Marine was sitting on his rear end. Cantu quickly realized that the Marine on the ground was Torres. The second Marine was trying to apply pressure to Torres' butt to slow the bleeding.

Morphine had reduced Torres' pain to a manageable level. He was lying there, awake, smoking a cigarette. Cantu thought that the worst thing Torres could be doing now was to be smoking a cigarette, so he took it from him. After seeing Torres reaction, Cantu quickly returned the cigarette to his friend. He looked in Torres' eyes, "I hope you make it."[38] Then Cantu returned to his men.

By now, Ben Reid was lying on the east side of the road with Torres and the others, getting medical attention. The corpsman inserted an IV and told Reid that he was going to take his flak vest off to make him more comfortable. Several Marines were hovering over Reid and the other casualties. As the corpsman opened Reid's vest, he exposed a bloody red shirt. "Holy shit!" the corpsman exclaimed. Reid's friends' eyes got real big, and they all started telling him, "You're gonna be okay."

Scenes from war movies flashed through Reid's mind. "They always tell the wounded guy he is going to be okay when they think he is going to die," he thought. "I knew I was going to be okay because I had been moving around for the past couple hours. But this worried me a little." Then Lieutenant Seely walked up, looked at Reid, slapped him on the leg, and laughed at him like: How did you manage to mess yourself up so badly? This actually made Reid feel that he really was going to be okay.

THE GOLDEN EAGLES

After safely delivering Juska to the rear, Garcia and Morton returned, at 1554, to Nasiriyah. They landed on the road north of the canal, right next

---

38 Ibid. Cantu.

to the casualty collection point. Doc Kirkland and Gloria unhooked their intercom cables and hurried down the ramp into a mass casualty scene. They immediately started triaging the wounded. Kirkland and Gloria would take the litter patients. Reid, Carl, Elliot, Espinoza, Keough, and Torres were quickly loaded onto Garcia's plane.

Gloria sent some of the lesser wounded Marines back to the Dash-2 aircraft. The Marines on the ground had already started loading the bodies of the dead Marines into the back of Dash-2 from a nearby Hummer. Corporal Will Bachmann was one of the Marines shanghaied into loading the poncho-draped bodies. The whirling helicopter blades had blown the poncho off of one of the bodies. Blood was everywhere. When Bachmann lifted the body into the helicopter, blood streamed down the front of his uniform.

The walking wounded had to be turned away from Dash-2. They returned to the casualty collection point to wait for the next cas-evac. Meanwhile, Gloria and Kirkland filled all six of the aircraft's litters and then brought another half dozen wounded Marines aboard. They sat them in the troop seats and turned their attention to the most critically wounded. Torres, with half of his butt missing was one of the first Marines Gloria turned to. As Garcia's flying ambulance pulled itself into the sky, Torres said to Gloria, "I'm okay. Take care of my buddy."[39]

Morton and Griggs took six Marines who had been killed onto Dash-2. Among the dead were Fred Pokorney, Phil Jordan, Brian Buesing, and Jorge Gonzales. Most of the bodies were badly mangled. While Chief Reid was working to load the dead, a sniper shot rang out. Reid thought nothing of it until he got home months later and a flattened bullet fell out of his flak jacket. Gunny Blackwell came to the back of Dash-2 just before it lifted off and said, with a tear in his eye and a crack in his voice, "They were all good men."[40]

Garcia flew his load of casualties to an Army field hospital, where Elliot remembers being loaded into a Humvee and taken into a tent. Army doctors, medics, and nurses swarmed around the Marine casualties like they were in a scene from M.A.S.H. Reid was stripped naked, and Elliot passed out on the table.

---

39 Ibid. Gloria.

40 Ibid. Gloria.

BRAVO COMPANY

Colonel Grabowski had delayed for as long as he could. If there were still vehicles stuck in the south, they would have to be abandoned. Soon it would be dark, and the last thing Grabowski wanted to do was to leave his Marines in the city overnight. Equipment can be replaced, and his Marines' lives were much more important. So, he ordered the vehicles stripped of their weapons and essential equipment. Once the vehicles had been cleared, they were ordered to come forward and move across the canal bridge.

When the Marines in the muddy field got word to move, they stripped the vehicles. Lieutenant Daniels, Bravo Company's XO, told his men to help get everything of value off the immobile vehicles. They grabbed maps, packs, ammo, radios, and weapons, and loaded them into the vehicles that could still move. Schielein emptied two CAAT trucks that were hopelessly stuck. He took his radios and weapons, and then tossed a white phosphorous grenade in each truck.

The sun was starting to go down, and the Iraqis were starting to shoot at the Marines again. Hueys and Cobras circled the isolated Marines like buzzards looking for carrion. As the sky darkened, Walsh could see tracer fire headed into the sky. The Iraqis tried their best to shoot down the helicopters, but they were quickly losing their battle with the Skids overhead.

It wasn't long before Walsh got word that they were leaving. He made his way back to his squad and their track. The tracks made a mad dash through the city, taking small arms fire and an occasional RPG along the way.

BY now, the maintenance guys had freed Captain Cubas's tank from the putrid quicksand and they had restarted Kamper's tank. Cubas radioed Howard and told him that they were ready to head north. Howard told Cubas that his tanks were also free of the bog and that they would be okay, so Cubas ordered Kamper to head north.

Kamper led the way back through the narrow, tangled alleyways toward Ambush Alley. After spending several hours in the city, Kamper had noticed that during the lulls in the fighting, the local inhabitants would pour out into the streets. As soon as there was any hint that the shooting would start again, they would all disappear.

He was relieved to see the narrow streets crowded with people. When the Iraqis saw the Marine tanks, they moved aside but stayed to watch the giant armored vehicles roll through their neighborhood. At one point, an Iraqi raced into the street, climbed into his car, and drove it out of the street, just before it would have been crushed under Kamper's treads. As Cubas' two tanks approached Ambush Alley, the crowds disappeared. Kamper knew that this sudden change meant that there was a fight ahead.

Kamper and Cubas rolled their tanks up onto the divided highway and moved north, abreast and separated by the median. They were greeted by another flurry of RPGs and wild AK-47 bursts. They just kept rolling until they reached Bravo Company's position. Grabowski's HMMWVs and Newland's AMTRACs were waiting for Cubas and Kamper to lead them north over the bridge.

Cubas fell in behind Kamper's tank, and they both traversed their turrets to the left, toward the Martyrs' District and stopped on the highway at Grabowski's position. Then, Colonel Starnes' artillery opened up on the Martyrs' District. After a short but deadly barrage, the tanks drove slowly forward, and Newland's tracks fell in behind Cubas to provide an iron curtain for Grabowski's soft-skinned Humvees. Leading the way, Kamper was riding in the turret with his hatch open. As he passed C208, Kamper saw bodies of Marines around the destroyed track. "Sir, I need to stop,"[41] he radioed to Cubas.

"Negative, you're not stopping." Cubas couldn't risk losing more Marines to pick up the bodies, Kamper obeyed and continued to roll north. But Newland ordered one of his tracks to stop at C201. Gomez' track stopped, and some of his Marines jumped out and retrieved Lance Corporal Fribley's body from Schaefer's track, zeroed out the radios, and then they quickly returned to the armored convoy. The two columns of armored vehicles and Humvees continued to move slowly north through Ambush Alley. They finally moved up over the canal bridge, and nearly all of the Timberwolves were now consolidated in the north of the city.

When Gomez arrived north of the canal, he found that his friend Corporal Jose Garibay was one of the Marines who had been killed. Then he heard that his roommate and longtime friend "Gonzo," Corporal Jorge Gonzalez, was also dead. Gonzalez and Gomez had entered the Marine Corps

---

41 Ibid. Kamper.

together and had both attended the School of Infantry with Cline. A wave of sadness swept over Gomez when he heard the news.

During the long struggle to free the vehicles, Gunny Wright had lost one of his M88s. It was hopelessly embedded in the Iraqi silt and sewage along with two of Schielein's vehicles and both of Grabowski's command AM-TRACs. It was nearly dark when Wright, Cooke, Whidden, and the rest of Peeples' combat train left the muddy square. They drove back through the narrow alleyways, and then pulled back into Ambush Alley. The last group of Marines in the city raced over the eastern canal bridge. As they reached the north bank of the canal, Whidden could smell C211 burning.

Captain Dennis Santare found a Charlie Company platoon leader who told him that he thought some of the casualties had been from the A-10s firing overhead. Santare was devastated. He had cleared those aircraft. How could this have happened? Why didn't someone tell him that Charlie Company had moved north of the canal? Why had his air officer's radio broken down? Why didn't the pilots recognize the Marine AAVs? Why hadn't he been more careful? What could he have done differently? Santare will probably continue to ask himself these questions for the rest of his life.

He had tried so hard to keep his Cobras out to the east, away from the civilians and his Marines. It was only logical to send the fixed-wing aircraft north of the Saddam Canal. All of the intelligence reports had warned of enemy forces occupying that area. Charlie Company was supposed to be behind Santare and Bravo Company, but no one in his track ever knew that Captain Wittnam had raced north. Sometimes the fog of war works in your favor, other times it does not. This time it led to tragedy. Everyone on, and above, the battlefield was working toward the same end. Santare, the A-10 pilots, Greene, Grabowski, and Wittnam were all trying to defeat a determined enemy and preserve all of the lives of the Marines on the ground. Sadly, events in war are uncontrollable.

THE GOLDEN EAGLES

As soon as Reid, Torres, Elliot, and the others had been dropped at the field hospital, Captain Garcia headed back to retrieve the casualties he had left behind on his last visit to the Timberwolves. The sun was setting as Garcia landed his Phrog on the road. The remaining casualties were loaded onto the helicopters, but there was still one more body to be removed. Lance Corporal David Fribley had been lying in an isolated spot up against the berm since he had been brought north by Gomez' men. Someone had covered him with an American flag. A group of Marines went over to the flag-draped corpse, slowly lifted their comrade, and carried him to the waiting aircraft. A hush fell over the nearby Marines, as Charlie Company's fallen warrior was moved to the waiting CH-46.

Once Fribley was aboard Dash-2, Garcia and Morton lifted off into a rapidly darkening sky. Just as they got airborne, an A-10 came screaming in front of Garcia, inbound on a strafing run. Garcia jerked his stick, and his aircraft rolled right. As they flew south, along the canal, the Iraqis opened fire on Garcia and Morton, spewing a stream of tracers into the sky.

Piloting a helicopter at night with night-vision goggles (NVGs) is difficult. Even the most experienced pilots hate to be flying during twilight and having to transition to NVGs in mid-flight. Nevertheless, after flying all day, Garcia and Schroeder overcame one more obstacle and safely shifted to their NVGs.

REGIMENTAL COMBAT TEAM-2

By now, Bailey was convinced that he had lost nearly all of his 1st Battalion. He knew that Grabowski was north of the canal but confusion prevailed. No one south of the city really knew the extent of the Timberwolves' casualties. It would be days before Grabowski had an accurate accounting of the dead and wounded.

Bailey would just have to wait for Grabowski's update. In the meantime, he put his staff to work to ready a quick-reaction force. Bailey wanted a plan for sending aid to Grabowski if he were to come under attack again. Colonel Ray was the first to step up with an offer to help. He immediately offered Bailey one of his LAR companies.

Bailey gladly accepted. An LAR Company was a perfect unit to supply relief to 1/2. It was fast and powerful, and it could race through Ambush Alley and provide Grabowski with the punch to repel almost any attack. LAR could help Mortenson at the southern bridge, too. Bailey immediately chopped Captain Ivan Monclova's Apache Company to Royal Mortenson's battalion. Mortenson accepted the additional firepower and quickly sent Monclova and one his platoons north to the Euphrates River bridge to support Fox Company. He held the rest of Monclova's company in reserve as the core of the QRF.[42]

NBC NEWS

Kerry Sanders made his last report of the day as the sun was setting on Nasiriyah. He stood with the familiar background of smoke rising from the embattled city. "Right now it is a pitched battle."[43] Kerry used one of Colonel Mortenson's many colorful statements: "It's like a knife fight in a phone booth."

After several minutes of rehashing what he had told us in earlier reports; he added a fresh piece of news. Kerry reported a strange story of Iraqis feigning surrender, only to open fire on some U.S. soldiers. He reported that some of the soldiers had been wounded but that he had few other details. Kerry graciously gave credit for this scoop to his colleague from NBC's Dallas affiliate, Ken Kalthoff, who was embedded in 1/10. At the time, neither Kerry nor Ken knew that they had just heard the first report of the ambush of the 507th Maintenance Company. No one ever feigned surrender, but the Iraqis had used the tactic of pretending to be unarmed, then firing on the Americans throughout the battle.

THE TIMBERWOLVES

Kerry also didn't know that Lieutenant Mike Seely and Captain Dan Wittnam had held their position, north of the Saddam Canal, against insurmountable odds. At the end of this long, bloody day, Grabowski consolidated all of his battalion north of the canal bridge. He positioned most of Peeples' tanks, which were now almost entirely out of fuel, just north of the canal bridge to defend to the south. Captain Brooks was ordered to move north and then west along Highway 16 to a defensive position that was about halfway to the western "T" intersection. The rest of the battalion set a 360-degree, hasty defense along Highway 7, about halfway

---

42 Quick-reaction force.

43 NBC News live report from the battlefield, March 23, 2003.

between the canal bridge and the northern "T" intersection. The battalion log trains remained south of Nasiriyah, parked along the road, near the regimental headquarters.

Pompos and Seely still had one Marine missing. Cline was nowhere to be found. They decided that they would make one last sweep west of the road before the light completely faded. They crossed over and started moving north. After walking north a good distance, Seely stopped. "This is the ditch where I was. This is the last position where I was when I was fighting off the A-10s. [sic]"[44]

"No" Pompos countered, "This is where I was when the power line fell on us." Seely's pyrotechnics and Pompos's Javelin missile were still lying in the ditch. After Pompos had left with the tracks, Seely had ended up in the same spot as his platoon sergeant. Never really seeing each other the entire battle, they had occupied the same Iraqi ditch only minutes apart.

Pompos and Seely ended their search for Cline as the last light of the day disappeared. They hoped that he had traveled south with casualties and was somewhere south of the Euphrates River with other units. They prayed that he was still alive. Hopefully, a new day would bring good news of Cline's whereabouts.

AMERICA'S BATTALION

Fox Company had set a firm foothold at the Euphrates River bridge. Dremann had set his sniper team at the crest of the bridge and had dispersed his CAAT vehicles on and under the bridge in supporting fire positions. He had a platoon defending either side of the bridge and one at the bridge itself. Ivan Monclova had arrived and placed two LAVs on the southern slope of the bridge and one on either side of the bridge on the southern bank of the river. Dremann had moved his seven-ton trucks forward to the base of the bridge and tucked them in between his infantry platoon's line. The eastern Euphrates River bridge was now extremely well defended.

By now, Captain Yeo had consolidated his position just south and west of the bridge. Echo Company had moved into a date palm grove, which afforded excellent concealment from the enemy. Yeo placed one of

---

44 Entire conversation taken from Pompos's interview with Reed Bonadonna.

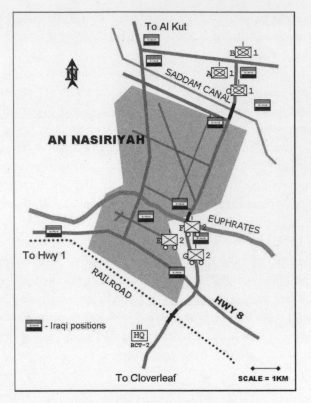

RCT-2s consolidation on the 23rd

his platoons facing north toward the river, another platoon dug in facing west, and his third platoon defended to the southwest and south. Echo Company was set in a half circle, with the bridge and Fox Company on their right and Highway 7 on their left. The Marines dug fighting positions deep in the tree line and settled in for the night.

Golf Company dug in between the hospital and the intersection of highways 7 and 8, in almost a 360-degree defense on the east side of the highway. Ross's infantry was dug in off to the side of the road. Their backs were covered, in the west, by their trucks that were parked along the road. While Mortenson's orders were to secure the bridge and all of Highway 7, his Marines were hard pressed to secure the bridge and a short narrow strip along the highway just south of the river.

Just before darkness fell, two British commando vehicles showed up at Dremann's command post, on the southern end of the Euphrates River bridge. They had been hanging around the regimental command post all day, and now that the sun was going down, they had decided to head north. A British lieutenant walked up to Captain Dremann and told him that they wanted to go through the city. Dremann asked him if they would check the destroyed track as they passed.

The British lieutenant was hesitant. He told Dremann that he had to consult with his sergeant. Dremann left the British soldiers alone to discuss what they would be doing, and when Dremann looked back toward the bridge, the British soldiers were gone. After speaking with Captain Dremann, they had climbed in their vehicles without any discussion and proceeded up through Ambush Alley.

THE TIMBERWOLVES

Gunner Dunfee could not believe his eyes. Two military Land Rovers were racing north through the city. They darted through Ambush Alley and up over the canal bridge. The British commandos stopped at the Timberwolves' headquarters and told Grabowski that their job was to proceed north to Qalat Sikar. Grabowski explained that nothing was secure north of his position. The British soldiers were not to be deterred. They climbed back in their vehicles and headed west toward the continuation of Highway 7.

When the Brits reached the western "T," the sky lit up. They turned north onto Highway 7, just as Captain King and the 507th had done so many hours earlier. Once on Highway 7, the enemy fire increased. Too dangerous, even for a British recon team, the lieutenant decided to return to the Timberwolves position at the northern "T." The British forces had been planning to drop a parachute regiment in Qalat Sikar, but not able to recon the LZ, they decided to abort the paratrooper drop.

Just after sunset, Lieutenant Colonel Grabowski called for his company commanders. Brooks, Newland, Peeples, Blanchard, Rohr, Sosa, Tuggle, and Wittnam all came together at the makeshift battalion command post along the side of the road for which they had fought so hard, earlier in the day. Grabowski asked each to report on their casualties. Brooks had no killed or missing. Newland and Peeples reported that they had not suffered any fatalities and that all their men were accounted for.

"I've got nine killed, I've got nine missing, and twelve wounded,"[45] Wittnam solemnly reported.

The Timberwolves had seen the elephant. They had been robbed of their inner peace and sense of well being, leaving a vast nothingness, a loneliness, a guilt, and a feeling of mortality. They were now all combat-tested veterans.

Grabowski radioed Bailey with the bad news. He read the names of the known wounded and killed, and then he followed with a list of the nine missing Marines.

AMERICA'S BATTALION

Colonel Mortenson sat silently listening to the somber radio report. He decided that the gloves were going to come off. From this point forward, Iraqis would surrender or die. Now with LAR support and Fox, Golf, and Echo companies dug in around the Euphrates River bridge, orders were given to shoot anyone carrying a weapon.

Monclova's LAVs proved invaluable that night. With their night-vision systems and heavy guns, they sent a powerful message to the enemy lurking in the city. "Your day is done. You're either going to go away or you're gonna die."[46] The thermal sights in the LAVs turned night into day for their gunners. Whenever an armed Iraqi appeared in a window or on a rooftop, they would be taken out with 25mm cannon fire.

During the night, it was like a shooting gallery for Echo Company. The Iraqis could not see the Marines hidden in the trees on the southern bank of the river, but the Marines could easily see the enemy moving around in the city on the northern bank of the Euphrates. One of Yeo's snipers shot and killed thirty combatants that night. One of his victims was an Iraqi man who was standing on a balcony with a woman and was holding a child, a map, and a cell phone. The Iraqi would look out toward the Marines' position, consult his map, and then talk into his cell phone. Soon, an Iraqi mortar round would whistle toward the Marines. After the second round hit, the Marine sniper shot the man dead without hurting either the child or woman.

---

45 Ibid. Grabowski.

46 Telephone interview with Major Rob Fulford, 4/28/04.

FOX COMPANY

During the evening, an Iraqi approached Fox Company from north of the bridge carrying a Marine dog tag. He said that it was from a body that was in C206. It turned out that this was a dog tag dropped by a Marine who was not even injured. But there was still a Marine missing from C206. By now, the crowd around C206 had dispersed, but Captain Dremann ordered his sniper team to keep an eye on the track throughout the night.

Dremann's men started taking fire from a footbridge that was one hundred meters west of the main bridge. They could see Iraqis passing back and forth across the bridge most of the night. They could also see sandbagged fighting positions atop the buildings in a complex that was southeast of the bridge. The east side of the road remained quiet all night, but the Marines would occasionally receive fire from both the north and south side of the river, on the west. Every time Dremann's snipers saw an Iraqi attempting to cross the footbridge with a weapon, a single shot would ring out and the Iraqi would fall dead in his tracks.

ALPHA COMPANY, 8TH TANKS

Dyer and Hawkins rolled north and stopped on the edge of the road in the middle of a field containing the military compound. Hawkins ran thirty-five missions with A-10s, F/A-18s, Cobras, F-14s, UH1s, and Harriers. Hawkins thought the A-10s and Cobras were the best among them.

As nightfall approached, Hawkins had already run two sections of A-10s, and Colonel Hewlett had returned for his last Cobra run of the day. Before Hewlett left, Hawkins told him, "You have to provide us with perimeter security tonight."[47] The Marine aviators did just that. They kept Cobras available to the Timberwolves all night long.

THE BETIO BASTARDS

Dunahoe and his commanders had been glued to their radios all day, trying to figure out what was happening. Sitting in their command post, things did

---

47 Ibid. Hawkins.

not sound good. They heard people on the regimental TAC talking about 1/2 getting to the bridges. They heard that the Marines were taking fire from all sides. Then they heard the reports of tanks stuck and A-10's firing on Marines. They heard Seely's calls of "Abort! Abort!" Then they heard Regiment order 2/8 into the fight. It was as if they were sitting at home in North Carolina, listening to the war on NPR.[48]

Colonel Dunahoe and Major Canfield knew that they would soon be called back to the east, so they started making plans to attack along Highway 8. They would push forward ten kilometers to the intersection of highways 7 and 8 and link back up with RCT-2, just south of the eastern Euphrates River bridge. Dunahoe and Canfield reasoned that this would be the quickest course of action to relieve pressure on 1/2 and 2/8. From the radio transmissions they had been listening to all day, it looked like the rest of the regiment would be needing reinforcements, and they would need them soon.

While Dunahoe and Canfield worked on plans to get into the fight, Gunner Nick Vitale set the lines for that night's defense. He called the company's FiST leaders and XOs together to lay out the plan. India Company would dig in, its left flank anchored on the Euphrates River. Kilo Company defended to the east, straddling Highway 8, and Lima Company's line stretched south out into the Iraqi desert. Vitale ordered a small outpost set up out in front of Kilo Company on the road. In the middle of the briefing, one of the battalion's younger lieutenants asked, "Is this a checkpoint?"[49]

"No. No. It's not a checkpoint. We are in combat. I want you to shoot," Vitale excitedly answered. Vitale, a veteran of Panama and Desert Storm, knew that if Iraqis approached their lines during the night, it could get very ugly. He was a professional soldier, a veteran of the Battle of OP4 in Operation Desert Storm and a well-read military historian. Vitale fully expected a fight that night.

Just after sunset, the Marines manning the outpost on the road noticed a pickup truck driving west on Highway 8, coming out of An Nasiriyah. When the driver saw the Marines, he ran from the vehicle screaming, "Take

---

48 National Public Radio.

49 Telephone interview with Gunner Nick Vitale, 6/30/04.

the car, I did not want to do it anyway!"[50] Marines moved out to the abandoned vehicle and found an AK-47, gas mask, maps, and other documents.
They quickly surmised that this lone Iraqi was probably a scout. Twenty
minutes later, two more vehicles rolled west, in the distance. A Marine
sniper engaged one of the vehicles with his .50-caliber M82A3 sniper's rifle,
hitting the vehicle in the driver's door. Then, Lima Company Marines fired
a Javelin missile at the second truck. The Javelin was a direct hit in the radi-
ator, demolishing the front end of the vehicle.

Dunahoe's Marines, all along the line, watched the missile scream
through the night sky, ending in a flash of light and a loud explosion. The
Iraqis probably never knew what hit them. The survivors poured from the
trucks and took cover. As the missile struck, a resounding cheer erupted all
along the battalion's lines, like the home team had just scored a winning
touchdown.

The small group of surviving Iraqis scrambled away from their vehicles
and started firing mortars and small arms in the Marines' direction. As the
fighting started, Colonel Dunahoe went over to where the Special Forces
guys had laid out and were resting for the night. Most were sleeping soundly
in their sleeping bags. Dunahoe told them that it looked like their position
was going to get hit in a minute.

"Hey, go get 'em," one soldier replied. Another chimed in, "Give 'em
hell!"[51] Then they both rolled over and went back to sleep.

The Iraqis began walking mortars in on 3/2's position. Captain "Duck"
Qualkinbush called for Cobra support. As soon as the Iraqi mortar men
heard the sound of the Cobra's rotor blades, they scattered. By the time the
Cobras swooped in, they only found the glowing hot mortar tubes in their
IR sensors. Just the sound of the helicopters had broken the enemy and
ended the firefight. They shot up the mortars and flew off into the darkness.

These were Iraqis that had been in the center of the city all day, fighting
the Timberwolves. They had decided to move east under the cover of darkness, to flee the Marine onslaught and had run right into the Betio Bastards.
Believing that they were probably surrounded, they fled back toward the city.

---

50 Officer in Charge, HUMINT Exploitation Team 16, "Input for Command Chronology," 24
May 03.

51 Ibid. Dunahoe.

Dunahoe's men captured nearly 150 weapons from those vehicles and had fired their first shots in anger. The Betio Bastards had had their first taste of battle, albeit a small taste. Not long after their small skirmish, Grunwald's LAVs opened fire from atop the Highway 1 bridge. Two uniformed Iraqi soldiers had been caught in one of Grunwald's gunner's night-vision sights. The Iraqis thought that they were moving under the cover of darkness, when in fact, they could be seen as clearly as if they were walking in the open in the light of day. They were both killed with a quick burst of 25mm cannon fire.

REGIMENTAL COMBAT TEAM-2

By the end of the long day, Colonel Bailey had his three infantry battalions scattered across the battlefield. His 3d Battalion and his LAR company were far west guarding the Highway 1 bridge. They were so far away that Bailey could not provide them with supporting artillery. First Battalion was in artillery range north of the Saddam Canal, but they were reeling from their fight for the eastern bridges and badly needed re-supply. The 2d Battalion, 8th Marines were holding defensive positions south of the Euphrates River at the eastern bridge. None of Bailey's battalions were in a position to easily support each other during the night.

Fortunately, Eddie Ray had sent his Apache Company to Bailey's aid. Bailey had quickly assigned the Apaches to Mortenson's infantry so that he could put together a quick-reaction force to move north to assist Grabowski if he were attacked during the night. Bailey's worst-case scenario had come true. Two-thirds of his regiment had been pulled into an urban fight in An Nasiriyah. Bailey called the MEB and said, "I need to get my LAR off the western bridge." He wanted to have the force to "kick somebody's butt"[52] if things got tight.

Bailey knew he had to consolidate his forces. If the Iraqis launched a concerted counterattack, he would be hard pressed to support Grabowski north of the canal, even with Monclova's LAVs. So, late on March 23rd, Bailey ordered Dunahoe to retrace his path on Highway 1 and to bring the 3d Battalion up Highway 7 to support the regiment. Bailey left his LAR

---

52 Bailey interview with Reed Bonadonna, 5/8/03.

company and Reilly's recon Marines at the Highway 1 bridge. Natonski wanted more forces at the bridge, so Bailey scraped together more Marines to send west. The heart of his new force would be his 2d Force Recon Battalion.

Once Dunahoe returned, Bailey would have his regiment in a position to fight as a single unit. Ray's LAVs were critical to holding the eastern bridge during the night. Now, with Dunahoe returning, the next order of business was to get fuel, ammunition, and supplies up to Colonel Grabowski. Marines worked through the night to prepare to send a light and mobile combat train north in the morning of March 24th to provide needed fuel and ammo to the beleaguered Timberwolves.

THE TIMBERWOLVES

Bill Peeples settled in for the night guarding the canal bridge. His tanks and his men, seemed to be running on fumes. They were physically and emotionally drained. All of the men of Alpha Company, 8th Tanks had performed as heroes, but Bill Peeples had performed with extraordinary valor. He had started the day as a tank company commander who rescued ten soldiers from certain death. He moved forward as a tank platoon leader to turn the tide at Alpha Company's position. Then, he commanded a section of tanks as he and his XO braved Ambush Alley to relieve Dan Wittnam's embattled Marines north of the Saddam Canal. Next, he drove back into the city as a tank commander to rescue fellow Marines who had become stranded inside Ambush Alley. And, finally, he jumped from the safety of his tank, as an individual Marine, to help load his wounded comrades for evacuation. Major Bill Peeples would be awarded the Bronze Star with "V," for valor in combat for his actions on that clear, sunny day. No accolade could adequately reward Major Peeples for his selfless contribution.

AROUND 2200, Grabowski noticed a bright blue oscillating light out in the east. After three days with virtually no sleep, Colonel Grabowski thought his eyes were playing tricks on him. He wasn't sure what he saw. Were the Iraqis attacking? This was the first civilian vehicle they had seen since they moved north of the canal. He radioed Newland to try to identify the source of the pulsating blue light. Newland told Grabowski that it was an Iraqi ambulance. Tired and hesitant to shoot at an ambulance, New-land's men had let the ambulance pass.

The driver raced past Alpha Company's position at the 23rd Brigade headquarters and made a sharp left-hand turn. Lights flashing, the ambu-lance drove right past Grabowski at nearly sixty miles per hour and headed south for the eastern canal bridge. Grabowski got back on the radio and told Peeples, "Don't let that vehicle on the bridge."[53]

Peeples' tankers blocked the road, forcing the vehicle to stop. They or-dered everyone out, then they carefully searched the ambulance. First, they found a carefully wrapped Iraqi Army colonel's uniform and a pistol in the glove compartment. After some time, the Marines discovered that one of the commanders of the Iraqi 23d Brigade was in the ambulance. He was mas-querading as a paramedic. One of his aides was driving, and they had a se-verely burned soldier in the back.

Corporal Randy Whidden was ordered to guard the newly acquired pris-oners until they could be picked up. Peeples' corpsmen left the injured Iraqi in the back of the ambulance and tended his wounds. Whidden herded the five Iraqis over to the M88 and lined them up. He stepped back several paces and stood guard with his SAW.

THE GOLDEN EAGLES

For a third time, Garcia dropped off casualties at a field hospital. He was now low on fuel, so he flew to Jalibah. When he arrived, he found a bustling Marine airfield. The Marines had been setting up tents and bringing in equipment and supplies all day. Jalibah was like a madhouse. Garcia and Morton refueled and flew back to RCT-2's headquarters at the Garbage Dump. They touched down at 2230, after a long day of flying, dodging gun-fire, and saving lives.

At 2300, the Timberwolves called for a cas-evac for the burned Iraqi. It had been fifteen hours since Garcia and his men had left the flight deck of *Saipan*. They had been flying all day and they needed to rest, but Garcia went off to the command post to see if he could arrange for an armed es-cort for one last evacuation. There were no rotary wing escorts, and Garcia

---

53 Telephone interview with Lieutenant Colonel Grabowski.

thought it wise to not venture back into the battle zone without an armed airborne escort, so he ordered his crews to stand down.

Parole-Two-Five and Parole-Two-Six became minibarracks. Each crewmember picked a stretcher and lay down for the night in the back of their planes. Griggs had a hard time falling asleep, remembering that only hours earlier his bed had been holding the body of a dead Marine.

THE TIMBERWOLVES

Exhausted from lack of sleep, some of the Timberwolves collapsed. Major Peeples was at his very limit. He was more tired than he had ever been, and he had been going pretty much nonstop since he had left Camp Shoup. He decided to make one last check of each of his tanks before he rested. He climbed up on the back deck to check one of his tanks. Instead, he fell asleep.

Captain Dyer wasn't much better off; he was babbling completely unintelligible phrases. Thompson told Dyer that he needed to lie down and get some sleep. Dyer took his friend's advice, and he, too, laid down. He was asleep almost before his head touched the ground.

Other Marines couldn't sleep, still affected by the day-long adrenaline rush of combat. Some were still in shock. They gathered in small groups at the berm, in trenches, and in their fighting positions and talked until they could no longer stay awake. The spirits of Jordan, Bitz, Burkett, Gonzalez, Cline, and the others moved from group to group, still alive in the fond remembrances of their friends and fellow Marines.

Many Marines needed to stay alert; there was still work to be done. Security posts needed to be manned all night. Randy Whidden was stuck guarding the Iraqis all night long. With no cas-evac coming until morning, he had a long night ahead of him.

Every now and then, a corpsman would climb into the ambulance and turn on the interior light to check on the badly burned soldier. Whidden was cold and exhausted. He stayed awake talking to his prisoners. Whidden had no idea if any of his charges spoke English, but that didn't stop him.

One of his prisoners, the one on the end of the line, kept looking around the front of the tank retriever. He kept glancing out into the dark Iraqi night. There was nothing but sage brush and desert on the other side of the vehicle, and it was obvious to Whidden that this Iraqi was contemplating an escape.

"Just go ahead,"[54] Whidden said to the Iraqi on the end, as he motioned with the barrel of his SAW. "Go ahead and run. You run, and I'm shooting you." Whidden didn't care if anyone understood him. "Why don't you all rush me? Then I can shoot all of you. Then I can go to sleep, and you all can see your virgins and whatever else you gotta do. Then we'll all be happy."[55] No one moved and Whidden was forced to stay awake guarding them until the sun came up.

AMBUSH ALLEY

For the residents of Ambush Alley, this had been a day that they would never forget. Most awoke to gunshots at dawn, as the 507th had tried to race south to safety. That was followed by the jubilant celebration of Saddam's followers and a hurried preparation to beat back the next wave of American invaders. Then came the horror of the Timberwolves' battle as they fought their way through the city. By day's end, many Iraqis, both combatants and civilians, lay dead on the city's eastern thoroughfare.

Once the shooting had stopped, the residents quickly moved to collect and bury their dead. They found Brendon Reiss's body in Ambush Alley and transported him to the Saddam Hospital, where he was buried with the victims of the 507th Maintenance Company's ambush. Other Iraqis searched C201 and C208 near the Saddam Canal. They, too, found the gruesome remains of several Marines. These charred and broken bodies were all but indistinguishable, but the civilians respectfully gathered them up and buried them within a few feet of the destroyed vehicles.

---

54 Telephone interview with Randy Whidden.

55 Ibid. Whidden.

CHAPTER 11

America's Battalion

Retreat, hell! We just got here.

—CAPTAIN LLOYD S. WILLIAMS, USMC

Commanding Officer of the 51st Company 2/5 at Belleau Wood, World War I

THE TIMBERWOLVES

Sometime between midnight and early morning, Santare came to Grabowski to tell him about the friendly fire incident. He told Grabowski that he had cleared the A-10 pilots to attack north of the Saddam Canal, and that the responsibility for the incident was his. Grabowski told Santare that there would surely be an investigation but to return to his duties for the time being. Then, Grabowski called Bailey and told him that he needed to speak with him—face-to-face.

Major Tuggle also came to Grabowski in the predawn morning. He told his boss that he had to go get food, fuel, and ammo. "We are almost out of ammo." [1]

Grabowski responded, "You can't go back through there!"

"Sir, I have to." Tuggle pleaded.

Grabowski knew full well that his men needed supplies—he just did not want his XO to risk another trip through Ambush Alley. Finally, the battalion

---

1 Ibid. Grabowksi.

commander begrudgingly gave in to Tuggle's plea. Before dawn, Major Tuggle raced back south with a couple AMTRACs while most of the remaining enemy was still asleep.

THE BETIO BASTARDS

The Betio Bastards started breaking down their defensive line and moving back to their trucks at 0430. Within a half hour, the Third Battalion was rolling back south on Highway 1 through the darkness. This time, the highway was packed with 1st Marine Division vehicles, all moving to cross the Route 1 bridge.

The Marines joked that they looked like the Beverly Hillbillies going off to war. By now, they were all haggard and dirty, and their dusty vehicles were crammed full of supplies, equipment, and ammunition. The Marines had no room inside for their rucksacks, so they were lashed to the outside of the trucks.

AMERICA'S BATTALION

Yeo and Dremann had been awake all night. Just before sunrise, Captain Dremann thought he would get some rest. As he laid down, one of Monclova's LAVs opened up with a burst from its bushmaster cannon. A half dozen armed Iraqis had tried to cross the footbridge. The Marine gunner could easily see the Iraqis through his LAV's night-vision system. His quick burst of 25mm cannon fire killed all six of the Iraqis and ended Dremann's short nap.

As the Iraqi night gave way to daylight, civilians started walking up on the bridge from the northern bank of the river. They told the Marine interpreters that American POWs were being held in the area. The stories all had a common thread: two American females were being held at the hospital.

Soon, Colonel Mortenson and Major Fulford appeared at the Euphrates River bridge to meet with Dremann and the battalion's other company commanders. As his first order of business, Mortenson walked to the crest of the bridge with Dremann to survey the situation. The crest of the bridge was the highest point for miles and the best possible vantage point for the colonel to get a view of his battalion's deployment.

Mortenson first looked north into the city. C206 could be clearly seen in the distance—a grim reminder of the previous day's battle. Iraqis were roaming the streets in the city, and some even ventured up on the bridge. Mortenson could look down on both banks of the river. On the north bank, just to the right of the bridge was a small two-story building shaped just like a grounded ship. It looked just like the USS *Recruit* at San Diego's defunct Navy Recruit Training Center. There was a large painting of Saddam Hussein at the front of the building. There was no suspicious activity in, or around, the "boat house," but the building itself looked foreboding. As Mortenson turned south, he first noticed a portion of Fox Company along the south bank of the Euphrates. Then he saw the Tykar Military Hospital complex only a few hundred meters to the southeast.

The hospital complex occupied a few acres. There were a half dozen buildings in the compound: two large buildings dominated the surrounding terrain, with a handful of smaller outlying buildings sprinkled throughout the area. Mortenson could clearly see sandbagged fighting positions on the roof of the larger buildings. The hospital was flying the familiar Red Crescent flag, indicating that it was a place of refuge and aid.

Next, Dremann pointed out where Golf Company was positioned, south of the hospital. Then, they turned their attention to the southwest. Echo Company was dug in along the southern bank of the river and in a lush stand of date palms. As Mortenson continued his 360-degree survey, he noticed the small pontoon footbridge. "What is that?"[2] He asked. The Iraqis were still using the footbridge to move back and forth across the river. "Drop it." Mortenson ordered, and then the group walked back down off the bridge.

Mortenson told his officers that he was going to push the human intelligence exploitation team (HET) and civil affairs team up to the bridge to make an announcement with their loudspeakers. He knew that Grabowski's supply column would soon be headed north through Ambush Alley, and that they would be followed by the entire 1st Marine Regiment. He also knew that each movement through the city would be preceded by an artillery barrage. The civil affairs team would make an announcement for the citizens of An Nasiriyah to disperse and clear the road.

---

2 Ibid. Mortenson.

THE TIMBERWOLVES

After the previous day's mayhem, Grabowski's Marines were now consolidated in open terrain and angry. Today, the Iraqis would experience the complete futility of fighting U.S. Marines on an open battlefield.

Throughout the day, the battalion was attacked from all sides by a mix of Fedayeen militia and uniformed soldiers using AK-47s, RPGs, mortars, and artillery. The Timberwolves engaged enemy mechanized vehicles, technicals, and Iraqi infantry north of the Saddam Canal over and over again, always with the same result. Every time the enemy would give away their position, American artillery or Cobras would rain death and destruction down on them.

Grabowski's men fought a deep battle with long-range weapons. The battalion's 81s fired thirty missions at targets in all four directions, silencing enemy mortars and disrupting enemy counterattacks. Not a single Iraqi ever got close enough to fire an effective shot at a Marine, nor did the Marine Infantry ever need to engage the enemy with small arms. Cobras, artillery, company and battalion mortars, heavy machine guns, and sniper teams were used exclusively. The Iraqis tried to dislodge the Timberwolves' foothold north of the city. They trucked in reinforcements from the north and east, but were never able to get close to the Marines.

Just after sunrise, one of Peeples' tankers yelled "Incoming!" Alan Kamper heard the first explosion, but it didn't occur to him that it was enemy fire until a round landed 150 meters in front of his tank. The mortar barrage didn't last very long. Starnes' counterbattery radar picked up the "red rain," and the artillerymen fired up the enemy mortar position.

Then the tankers started taking sniper fire, but the Marines quickly found the source. They could see muzzle flashes coming from the building in the distance. Three of Alpha Company's tanks immediately opened fire on a small building. They raked the area with machine gun fire and main gun rounds, destroying the structure.

By 0600, 1/2 had silenced the halfhearted enemy counterattacks, but now they were nearly out of ammunition. Major Tuggle had not yet returned with the combat trains to resupply the battalion. He was still south of the Euphrates collecting all of the battalion's refuelers and ammo trucks. While he was putting the relief column together, he came across Major Peeples' abandoned tank. The maintenance Marines had worked through the night to repair the vehicle. He also ran into Filipkowski in Captain

Cubas' Third Platoon tank. Tuggle gladly added the two tanks to his convoy. Once everything was organized, Tuggle drove north with the resupply vehicles to 2/8's command post and added a few of Mortenson's LAVs to his convoy. Tuggle proceeded to the Euphrates River bridge with truckloads of fuel, ammunition, food, and water. The small convoy would be escorted by Peeples' tanks, a few tracks, and a platoon of Eddie Ray's LAVs. When they reached the bridge, they paused and waited for the order to proceed through Ambush Alley.

THE GOLDEN EAGLES

Garcia's first mission of the day was to head back north of the Saddam Canal and pick up the Iraqi who had been badly burned. He had survived the night under the watchful eyes of Alpha Company's corpsmen. Garcia and Morton made the short flight from RCT-2 headquarters to Grabowski's position and touched back down on the road. The burned Iraqi was wheeled on the ambulance's gurney to Garcia's helicopter and placed in the care of Doc Gloria and Doc Kirkland. Five Iraqi prisoners were also hustled onto the aircraft.

Garcia and Morton lifted off and headed south to the field hospital. While en route, one of the prisoners, an older Iraqi, complained of chest pains. He didn't look well at all. Garcia had been called back to *Saipan*. He barely had enough fuel for the trip back to the ship, so their casualty drop at the field hospital needed to be quick. When Garcia landed, Hetterscheidt and Lewis shuffled the prisoners off the helicopter while Gloria and Kirkland carefully moved the burned Iraqi.

Just as they all got off the aircraft, the older Iraqi collapsed. Gloria told the corpsman on the ground that he thought the guy was having a heart attack, and then he rushed back to Parole-Two-Five. Garcia lifted his plane into the air and turned for the Persian Gulf. In a little over twenty-four hours, Garcia and his crews had flown four cas-evac missions. It is an absolute certainty that they had saved Corporal Matthew Juska's life. Two or three more Marines could have died had they not been quickly taken off the battlefield in the second lift. Two Iraqis owed their lives to Garcia, and more than a dozen other Marines had been brought to safety. Garcia and his crews had been in the air more than seventeen hours since they left the flight deck of *Saipan* the day before.

THE GUNRUNNERS

Hewlett's Cobra pilots started their second day at Jalibah. They lifted off and flew directly toward the continuing action in An Nasiriyah. When Bergan and Parker arrived, they found that 1/2 was taking fire from under the canal bridge. Bergan and Parker ducked their Cobra down low and found a dump truck under the bridge with a mortar team in the back. They took out the mortar with their guns. "It blew big and burned for a long time."[3] Taxicabs were ferrying enemy fighters all over the battlefield, so the Cobra pilots were ordered to take out the white cabs with orange fenders. Parker shot a TOW missile under one of the taxis, and the explosion flipped it off the road. To Parker's surprise, four armed men scrambled out of the demolished vehicle. "They must have been wearing Kevlar underwear," Parker recalled later.

AMERICA'S BATTALION

Mortenson and Fulford had returned to the battalion command post, located just south of the railroad bridge, to make preparations to take their TAC command post to the eastern Euphrates River bridge. While they were gone, Kevin Ellicot and the civil affairs team drove to the bridge in their Humvee. Mounted on the roof were loudspeakers handed down from the Army. They pulled their mobile PA system up onto the bridge. They parked near the crest, and their interpreter made the announcement in Arabic, per Mortenson's orders. He told the crowd to disperse—to clear the roads and return to their homes. "You have one hour."[4] Ellicot's PA system was nothing more than a bullet magnet. Few Iraqis in the crowd heeded the warning. While the civil affairs group was getting shot at, Dremann sent a team to destroy the footbridge. They set charges under the watchful protection of an LAV. Then they moved back to the southern side of the river, took cover, and blew up the bridge.

The mood during the planning sessions in Kuwait was much different than it was today. During the planning, the higher commands were preaching

---

3 Ibid. Parker.

4 Telephone interview with Captain Dremann, 6/5/04.

capitulation. As an excellent infantry commander, Yeo wanted to plan for the worst-case scenario, so he had set to work to develop an artillery preparation scheme. Yeo had been working on his strategy since early February.

He submitted his plan for artillery preparation of the road between the two bridges. It had potential Iraqi strongholds preregistered and called for a barrage of high-explosive (HE) rounds. His artillery plan was quickly returned to him, and he was told that he could not plan for an artillery barrage inside a civilian area. Yeo made a single change and resubmitted the plan as an illumination barrage. Yeo had only changed the HE rounds to flares, but kept all of the same target registrations.

1ST BATTALION, 10TH MARINES

On this day an artillery preparation was not only authorized, it was welcomed. Colonel Starnes had used Yeo's targets to put together an artillery group to clear the way through Ambush Alley. The barrage was named "Code Red." The Code Red artillery barrage was perfectly timed to precede friendly movement up the road. The idea was that as the artillery started to fall, the enemy would dig in or move away from the road. Directly on the heels of the artillery shells, the Marine convoy would race north at fifty miles per hour, as artillery impacted only three hundred meters ahead of the Marine vehicles.

Around noon, exactly one hour after the civil affairs loudspeaker announcement, Iraqis in Ambush Alley started hearing the distant sound of big guns firing in the south. Within seconds, artillery rounds came screaming down on the road inside the city. Explosions erupted from south to north along Highway 7. The rolling barrage moved north and seemed to stall at the Martyrs' District. As round after round exploded in the Iraqi stronghold, Tuggle's streamlined emergency log train moved north into Ambush Alley behind the Code Red shelling.

THE TIMBERWOLVES

Peeples' M1 tanks and a platoon of LAVs from 2d LAR's Black Knights led the way behind the rolling barrage. The tanks and LAVs were followed by Tuggle's fast-moving convoy. As quickly as it started, the shelling ended, and Tuggle's vehicles disappeared from view.

The Code Red accomplished its intended task. None of the supply vehicles were hit by enemy fire and no Marines were hurt. Peeples' tankers were elated when they saw Filipkowski crest the canal bridge. When they had left him at the Kuwaiti border, they thought that he would probably miss the entire war, but Filipkowski wouldn't miss the action after all. Once the tanks, LAVs, and Grabowski's supply vehicles had reached 1st Battalion, the Black Knights turned around and moved back through Ambush Alley to return to their battalion.

FOX COMPANY

Just as Tuggle's resupply convoy was passing through, an Iraqi doctor in civilian clothes approached the Marines near the hospital with a letter written in English. He told Dremann that the letter was from the director of Tykar Hospital. The letter said that they were very thankful for the Americans. It went on to explain that the buildings in the distance were all part of a civilian hospital filled with civilian patients. The letter ended with a plea to, "Please protect us and leave us alone." Dremann sent the letter up the chain of command. Then he assembled a small patrol to move east along the southern bank of the river, in preparation for the expansion of his lines toward the hospital.

Just after Tuggle went through, Lieutenant Southwick put together a squad of Marines. They planned to move to C206 to see if there were any bodies to retrieve or sensitive equipment to remove. Southwick took two LAVs with him for covering fire and to carry anything that they might need to bring back over the bridge.

Southwick's men pushed down off the bridge and surrounded the destroyed track. The LAVs raced in, and some of their Marines searched the AMTRAC. They quickly realized that there was nothing in the track worth saving and there were certainly no bodies to retrieve. The LAV pulled back up onto the bridge, and Southwick's men broke down their security cordon and withdrew. The entire operation took less than a half hour.

REGIMENTAL COMBAT TEAM-2

General Natonski still thought that Task Force Tarawa needed a larger contingent at the western crossing, but Bailey needed all of the combat power he could muster on the east side of the city. So Bailey got creative. He pulled together Task Force Triton, using Marines snatched from throughout the regiment. The unit was made up of Marines from A Company of his 2d Force Recon Battalion, 81s, artillery, and A Company of his 2d Combat Engineering Battalion.

Task Force Triton was sent out west to the Highway 1 bridge to relieve Charlie Company, 2d LAR by 1500. Once relieved, Bailey's LAR Company would race back to the east side of the city.

Task Force Triton set up vehicle checkpoints and began controlling all vehicle and foot traffic near the crossing site. They also started daily mobile patrols of nearby villages and the surrounding area. Suspicious Iraqis were rounded up, and several enemy weapons caches were seized.

THE TIMBERWOLVES

Ever since the Timberwolves had first rolled across the canal bridge, the buildings at the northern "T" had been a source of enemy fire. Colonel Grabowski had finally had enough. He ordered Dan Wittnam to secure the 23rd Brigade headquarters. As they moved in, Charlie Company found that the Iraqis had quickly abandoned the buildings. After securing the compound, Charlie Company was held in reserve for the rest of the day. They were entitled to a much-needed pause in the action, especially after the previous day's fight. They spent their day setting up checkpoints, stringing concertina wire, and putting up Arabic signs reading, GO BACK! and DO NOT COME THIS WAY!

AMERICA'S BATTALION

Everyone was concerned about the reports of American POWs in Tykar Hospital and the letter Dremann had received. It was supposedly from the director of the hospital and had only served to add to the uncertainty of what was happening in that facility. So Colonel Mortenson ordered his Golf company commander, Captain Brian Ross, to send a patrol over to the hospital to check it out.

Captain Ross led the small squad-sized patrol personally. Ross and his men walked north along the road to Dremann's position first. He told

Dremann that he had gotten word that there were possibly American POWs in the hospital and that they were going in to investigate. Then Ross moved his small patrol east to the edge of the hospital complex. The facility consisted of a half dozen buildings, scattered over several acres. When Ross realized the enormity of the facility, he returned to Fox Company's lines and told Dremann, "I'm not going in there with just a squad."[5]

Captain Ross returned to his company in the south, and Dremann decided to relinquish the defense of the west side of the road to Captain Yeo and Echo Company. He ordered his 1st Platoon to move to the east side of the bridge.

THE BETIO BASTARDS

Dunahoe's Marines arrived at the cloverleaf before noon and continued north on Highway 7. They slowly weaved their way through the hundreds of parked supply vehicles that were waiting to move north through Ambush Alley. Staff Sergeant Fowler wrote in his journal, "The whole Marine Corps is here."[6] As they neared their destination, they started passing combat vehicles—tanks, AMTRACs, and CAAT teams. Finally, after many hours of movement, they pulled into an assembly area near RCT-2's headquarters at the Garbage Dump.

As his Marines were setting into their familiar hedgehog defensive perimeter, Dunahoe drove a short distance north to Colonel Bailey's headquarters. By now, Colonel Dowdy was vacillating and trying to decide whether he should proceed through Ambush Alley. He contended that the route had not been completely secured. Bailey had already sent Grabowski's supply convoy through Ambush Alley, and he knew that while he could not say that the streets of Nasiriyah were clear, a mechanized regimental combat team should have little trouble moving through no more than four kilometers of contested road.

But, it was Task Force Tarawa's job to secure the route, so Bailey and Kennedy had come up with a plan. The Betio Bastards would drive north through Ambush Alley to the north side of the Saddam Canal, dismount,

---

5 Ibid. Dremann.

6 Telephone interview with Staff Sergeant Fowler.

and then attack back into the city to secure the Saddam Canal bridge and Ambush Alley.

Dunahoe returned to his own command post to work out the details with his staff. The more analysis they did, they started thinking, "This isn't good!"[7] They were being asked to move through Ambush Alley in soft-skinned Humvees, seven-ton trucks, fuel trucks, and ammo trucks. They were supposed to park their vehicles in an open area that was already proven to be susceptible to enemy artillery and indirect fire, and then to turn and attack back into the city with dismounted infantry. "It didn't pass the bullshit test."[8]

✯

AS Dunahoe's staff mulled over the plan, patrols were sent out. The Marines could see a large ruin of a pyramidlike building, about two miles to their west. They did not know it at the time, but they had bivouacked in the shadow of the four-thousand-year-old ziggurat[9] of the ancient city-state of Ur. Lying between the ancient historical site and the Marines' camp was a small mud-brick village. Staff Sergeant Fowler took a small patrol to the village to make sure there were no hostiles hiding within sniper range of his battalion.

Fowler, who had spent many tours in the Middle East, was shocked when he saw the conditions in the village. The people were the poorest he had ever seen and were not a threat. They were just struggling to survive. The people were frightened and quiet as the Marines moved from house to house and room to room, looking for enemy fighters.

It must have been terrifying for the civilians to see large men dressed in bulky uniforms and bristling with large weapons roaming through their homes, almost as if they had been invaded by aliens. Soon the people realized that these fearsome creatures were not there to hurt them. These were Americans, and since they certainly looked impressive and could seemingly do nearly anything, a young mother reasoned that they could save her baby. She walked up to the Marines, cradling a young child in her arms. She had a look on her face that transcends language. Her eyes pleaded, "save my baby," as she held the infant out toward the Marines.

---

7 Personal interview with Lieutenant Colonel Brent Dunahoe.

8 Ibid. Dunahoe.

9 Holy Estate.

Doc Johnson was the corpsman who had come out with the patrol. He took a quick look at the three-month-old baby and realized that the child had been extremely ill from birth. Back in the United States, the infant would have been rushed into a neonatal unit moments after birth and may have had a chance at survival. But here, in these conditions, death was almost certain. Doc Johnson turned to Fowler, "There is no way to get this kid out of here."[10] Doc Johnson handed the child back to his mother and turned to help those he could, patching up cuts and handing out medicine. After their short stay, the small patrol moved back to the battalion with the image of that village and baby forever emblazoned in their memories.

ALPHA COMPANY

Captain Brooks's movement west was a classic Marine attack. No longer restricted by a built-up city and a concern of inflicting casualties on the citizens of An Nasiriyah, Alpha Company kicked off around noon and executed a textbook movement to contact in open terrain. Captain Brooks used Cobras and 1/10's artillery to pound the Iraqis from the air. Then with the support of CAAT, tanks, and his AMTRAC's up-guns, he moved his infantry methodically west on the ground.

After clearing buildings to the battalion's immediate west, Brooks received orders to proceed and secure the main supply route leading into the western part of Nasiriyah. The ragtag Iraqi paramilitary fighters had little stomach for standing up against a combined-arms, mechanized Marine infantry assault. Some provided token resistance, but most fled, leaving their uniforms, weapons, and countless rounds of ammunition behind.

Brooks' Marines moved to seize the western "T" and capture the Al-Quds' headquarters on the northeast corner of the intersection. Then, they established a 360-degree blocking position at the "T," in preparation for the forward passage of the 1st Marine Division. Once the area was secure, they, too, started erecting roadblocks and signs warning the Iraqis to stay clear.

---

10 Telephone interview with Staff Sergeant Fowler, 6/2/04.

TASK FORCE TARAWA

There was a bit of a lull after Major Tuggle went north with his supply convoy. Then, Eddie Ray moved his 2d LAR Battalion up the road toward the Euphrates River and began to prepare to push north. Lieutenant Colonel Lou Craparotta moved his mechanized infantry battalion up behind Ray's LAR Battalion. Ray would lead Dowdy's regimental combat team through An Nasiriyah, and Craparotta would follow with only his armored vehicles. The 3d Battalion, 1st Marines would string two companies out along the route, between the bridges, in a picket line. They would stand guard while the rest of Dowdy's mechanized regiment moved through. Then they would pull up stakes and follow RCT-1 out of An Nasiriyah.

Dowdy was still very concerned. He ordered the majority of his 1,500 vehicles out to the far western bridge. He did not want to move his log trains through the city. He planned to send them across the Highway 1 bridge and then have them cross back over to Highway 7, north of the Euphrates River. Dowdy still did not realize that there wasn't a passable route back to Highway 7.

GENERALS Conway, Natonski, and Kelly and Colonel Ron Johnson met Colonel Bailey at the southern bridge. The high-level commanders wanted to be present when Ray took 2d LAR through the city. They all wanted to be part of this historical event when Ray led the 1st Marine Regiment's charge to Baghdad. Colonel Dowdy, still planning his movement through An Nasiriyah, was noticeably absent.

With all of the high-level commanders congregating, Bailey wanted Mortenson present. After all, it was his Marines who were holding the bridge. Bailey radioed 2/8's TAC command post and ordered Mortenson forward. Mortenson, his S2, Captain John Dupree, the battalion's sergeant major, Miles Thorne, and his driver hopped in a Humvee and drove to the Euphrates River bridge, along with two CAAT machine gun vehicles for support.

Mortenson's three Humvees drove north past a long line of LAVs parked along the road. Eddie Ray's Barbarians were preparing to move north through Ambush Alley and lead RCT-1 up Highway 7.

Just before Ray kicked off, Bailey approached Ray and asked,

"Can you leave me some LAVs?"[11] Ray left four of his light armored vehicles from Lieutenant Nunley's 3d platoon of Alpha Company with Colonel Bailey. Colonel Bailey immediately chopped Nunley's platoon to Colonel Mortenson to maintain his defense of the Highway 7 bridge. It would be nearly a month before 3d Platoon would be reunited with the Barbarians.

Around 1445, the entourage of Marine officers walked up onto the bridge, and Glenn Starnes' artillery opened up. The barrage started with rumbling reports in the south, followed by artillery shells whistling overhead. Then tremendous explosions filled Ambush Alley with smoke and debris. More cannon fire followed, more whistling shells flew overhead, and another salvo hit the road farther to the north. Ray's heavily armed LAV column started rolling across the bridge into a smoke-filled Ambush Alley, and another salvo screamed overhead. Starnes kept walking his Code Red barrage up the road, ahead of Ray's Barbarians. General Natonski, Colonel Bailey, and Mortenson all watched as the Barbarians disappeared into the smoky city. Not a shot was fired at the Barbarians. The Iraqis were too busy fleeing from the artillery barrage.

Once the artillery had subsided and 2d LAR had moved through the city, generals Conway, Kelly, and Natonski walked down off the bridge toward their vehicles. They paused momentarily to discuss 1st Marines' movement north, and they all agreed that Colonel Dowdy should move up and follow Eddie Ray.

AMERICA'S BATTALION

Fox Company was repositioning while LAR was moving into Ambush Alley. Dremann's 1st Platoon extended its positions along the southern bank of the Euphrates River. Third Platoon moved to defend to the east in a tree line along Highway 7, and Lieutenant Southwick's 2d Platoon remained in its position defending the bridge.

By now, Captain Ross had returned to his company and rallied his Marines. He was moving northeast toward Tykar Hospital with his entire company. As they stepped off, they came under intense fire from the hospital

---

11 Personal interview with Colonel Ron Bailey, 3/25/04.

grounds, and then all hell broke loose at the bridge. An Iraqi mortar round came whistling in and exploded near the group of commanders.

Fox Company had all their seven-ton trucks herringboned along the east side of the road, facing the Tykar Military Hospital. The generals and colonels all quickly moved to take cover behind the large trucks. With three generals and two colonels in the group, a lucky enemy mortar shot could have produced the most catastrophic blow ever sustained in the history of the Marine Corps. General Conway's security detail immediately manned a cordon around the commanders and began returning fire.

Mortars and direct fire erupted from the hospital and from north of the river in what seemed to be a coordinated attack. It appeared that the Iraqis did not want the Marines to come anywhere near Tykar Military Hospital on the southern bank of the Euphrates River. Dremann's 1st Platoon was still moving into position when the shooting started. He was standing in the middle of the road with Colonel Mortenson at the base of the bridge, and as soon as the shooting started, Dremann turned to his boss and said "Sir, I gotta go."[12] Dremann ran toward his Marines and moved up with his 3d Platoon. Then he told Lieutenant Southwick to leave his 1st Squad on the bridge and to attack the hospital from north to south with his remaining Marines.

Lance Corporal Joshua Menard, a young Fox Company Marine from Texas was manning a SAW position at the crest of the Euphrates River bridge when bullets started flying around his squad. When a bullet hit him in the hand one of his companions got on the radio and reported that Menard had been hit.

As 2d Platoon moved toward the hospital, they came under heavy machine gun and small arms fire from both the hospital and the north bank of the river. More enemy mortar rounds began to fall. The Marines could hear the thump of the mortars and the whistling of the rounds. They hit the deck, praying to God that the next round wouldn't land on top of them.

Fox Company was getting hit from across the river. It seemed as though there was an Iraqi behind every tree, in every window, and on every rooftop firing at the Marines from the northern bank of the Euphrates. Much of the enemy fire was coming from the "boat house."

On the west side of the road, Echo Company started receiving fire from buildings on the north side of the river, and Golf Company was being shot

---

12 Ibid. Dremann.

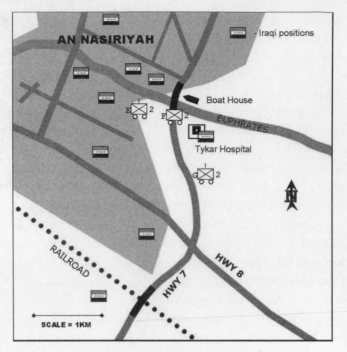

2/8 at the Euphrates River

at from the hospital and surrounding buildings to the southeast. America's Battalion was rapidly becoming involved in three separate engagements.

Upon hearing that one of his Marines had been wounded, Colonel Mortenson jumped into his soft-skinned Humvee with his driver, and Thorne and sped to the top of the bridge. As the vehicle skidded to a stop, Mortenson jumped out and raced to Menard. Seeing that his hand was badly mangled from an Iraqi bullet, he called for a LAV to come up on the bridge. Mortenson and others threw Menard into the back of the armored ambulance. The LAV raced down off the bridge and rushed him to the battalion aid station (BAS).

Bullets were hitting the guardrail and whizzing overhead, and Marines were taking cover and searching for muzzle flashes. Mortenson ordered two more LAVs up onto the bridge. Flanked by the LAVs, Mortenson stood in the middle of the road, at the topographical crest of the bridge, completely immersed in his job. He worked his radios and continually switched back and forth, talking to all of his company commanders and then to Fulford, back at his COC.

Mortenson glanced up at the gunner in the turret of the LAV that had parked next to him on the bridge. The young Marine was watching the battle below, seemingly transfixed. Mortenson got his Marine's attention and asked, "Do you see those guys shooting at *my* Marines?"[13]

"Yes, sir." The Marine responded.

"Kill them!" Mortenson commanded.

Immediately, the LAV gunner opened fire. His 25mm Bushmaster chain gun erupted; spewing a steady stream of metal at the enemy.

The enemy may have been using cell phones to coordinate their actions. All three of Mortenson's companies were under attack: Golf in the southeast, Echo on the west side of the road, and Fox at the bridge. Golf was receiving heavy fire from the military hospital compound. Echo was being attacked from the northern bank of the river, and Fox was being hit from the hospital and enemy positions across the river.

Mortenson was out of position. The battalion commander was supposed to direct his battalion from his command post. Yet, now he was in the thick of it, commanding his Marines from the vortex of the battle. It turns out that it was quite fortunate that Mortenson had ended up where he did. He could take a nine iron and hit each of his company commanders.[14]

All three company commanders were on foot, and they were using portable radios with whip antennas. They could only communicate with the TAC command post intermittently, but they all had crystal-clear communications with Mortenson. The colonel had a much more powerful vehicle-powered radio, and he was up higher than anyone else on the battlefield. Because of his position and radio power, Mortenson could also talk with the TAC command post, maintaining continuity of communications for his entire battalion. Had Mortenson been back at his command post, the company commanders would have had great difficulty maintaining clear communications with the battalion.

Standing next to the passenger door of his Humvee, Mortenson worked furiously, fighting the fight, calling in artillery and air, and keeping his company commanders updated. He had his maps spread out on the seat of his vehicle, and Sergeant Major Thorne was standing in front of the Humvee.

13 Ibid. Mortenson.

14 Personal interview with Lieutenant Colonel Mortenson.

After about fifteen minutes, Thorne got Mortenson's attention and said, "Sir, we have to get off the bridge. It's too fucking dangerous."[15]

Mortenson, who had been lost in his work, paused, looked at Thorne, and then he looked around. For the first time since he had jumped out of his vehicle, he focused on his immediate surroundings. LAVs were shooting, and Marines were shooting down from their elevated position into the buildings on both sides of the river. Bullets were hitting the guardrails and zinging over the top of his Humvee. "Yeah, you're right," Mortenson replied.

Mortenson and Thorne quickly got in the HMMWV and moved back down off the crest. They backed halfway down the bridge and stopped. Now the bridge provided some cover from the Iraqi bullets. Mortenson looked over the right railing and saw Fox Company's mortars setting up. Golf Company was defending about one kilometer to the south, and Echo lined the western flank. "My whole battalion was kind of wrapped around me."[16]

FOX COMPANY

Fox Company started pounding the hospital with 60mm mortar fire. First Sergeant Gatewood was using one of the "sixties" to lay direct fire on one of the larger two-story buildings. The Iraqis were firing on the Marines from the second-story windows, so Gatewood was firing at the side of the building. Dremann saw several mortar rounds hit the side of the building, and they were blowing large chunks out of it. Then a round exploded on the ledge of one of the windows. Shrapnel spewed into the building, silencing that enemy position.

Corporal John Friend's platoon advanced from the cover of the tree line to the north and west side of a protective berm that encircled the hospital complex. Just as they moved into position, Iraqis in the windows and on the rooftop turned their attention to Friend's squad of Marines. The Marines along the berm started exchanging fire with the Iraqis in the building. Every Marine within the line of sight of the enemy opened fire. They poured

---

15 Ibid. Mortenson.

16 Ibid. Mortenson.

deadly accurate gunfire into every window and rooftop bunker they could find. Friend and his assault team fired two SMAW[17] rockets at the enemy position. Captain Dremann showed up at Friend's position and ordered him to save his rockets. He told Friend to pull back to the tree line so that he could pound them with the battalion mortars for awhile.

As Friend was pulling back, enemy artillery began to rain down on the company. One of the artillery rounds hit a wall that three of Dremann's Marines were using for cover. All three Marines were sent flying through the air like rag dolls. They all landed, dusted themselves off, and scrambled away without a scratch.

Staff Sergeant Ricky St. John and the 1st Platoon's radio operator, Lance Corporal Clay, were also caught in the first salvo of artillery fire. When the enemy artillery started to explode around the Marines, Corporal Friend, dove for cover.

When the rounds began to fall, his first thought was, "God, I don't want to die today."[18] Friend looked up from his relatively safe spot in the tree line and saw another artillery round explode in the distance. As the smoke and dust cleared, he noticed that Staff Sergeant St. John was on his feet helping Corporal Clay up off the ground. Another round exploded, throwing both Marines into the air.

Friend was instantly on his feet, running toward his comrades. "I didn't think. I just got up and started running to help." Staff Sergeant St. John came down from his short flight through the air and landed on his feet, but Corporal Clay landed face first in a heap on the ground. Friend continued to sprint across 150 meters of open ground through small arms fire and the continuing artillery barrage, "I thought to myself, I hope I can get him out of here before I get hit."

Lance Corporal Matthew Lugo was only a step behind Friend, as they both sprinted across the battlefield with bullets whizzing all around them, and artillery rounds landing in the distance. Friend stopped at Clay, quickly checked him for wounds, then whisked him into a fireman's carry and sprinted back across the open field, carrying him to safety. As he ran, he continually reassured Clay that he was going to be okay.

Corporal Lugo grabbed Clay's radio and took off toward 1st Platoon.

---

17 Shoulder-fired, multipurpose, assault weapon.

18 Telephone interview with Corporal John Friend, 6/29/04.

Once he returned the radio, he sprinted back across the battlefield to his platoon. As Lugo and Friend ran from the spot where the previous Iraqi shells had landed, a third round fell and exploded where Clay had been lying. Had Friend not rushed to save him, Clay would surely have been killed by that third explosion.

By now, Lieutenant Southwick and his 2d Platoon were heavily engaged. Southwick moved a CAAT heavy machine gun vehicle to the eastern bank. Lance Corporal Santamaria was manning the machine gun in the armored Humvee when another artillery round landed right next to his vehicle. Santamaria took shrapnel in his shoulder, and so did Doc Cordova, who only received superficial wounds. Gunny Aubrey Hall drove to the bank of the river, loaded Santamaria in a vehicle, and got him back to a small casualty collection point near the bridge.

LIEUTENANT Greg Nolan was clearing buildings back by the battalion main command post when the battalion gunner, Nick Harris, drove up in a Humvee. He called to Nolan, "Hey, man, Santamaria got shot . . . Do you want to come help me evac him?"[19] Nolan didn't even answer. He ran over and jumped into the gunner's Humvee, and they raced north. For the first time, Nolan realized that they were really in combat. They raced past Golf Company Marines, who were all hunkered down, trying to stay out of the line of fire. "Oh, shit," Nolan thought. "This is it."

They continued to race up Highway 7 until they reached the small casualty collection point at the bridge. The corpsmen were treating Santamaria as the battle raged all around them. Gunner Harris had moved over to his battalion commander, who had taken a knee and was talking to his wounded Marine. The gunner turned and called to Nolan, "Get over here and help me provide security for the colonel." Lieutenant Haulsey, who was responsible for the TAC command post's security, drove up in his hardback Humvee. He called over to Nolan, "Nolan, do you want to roll up on the bridge with me?" For the moment, the colonel seemed to have all the protection he needed, so Nolan climbed into the CAAT HMMWV, and the two lieutenants rolled up onto the Euphrates River bridge.

They stopped short of the crest, out of the line of fire, and Nolan

---

19 Telephone interview with 1st Lieutenant Greg Nolan, 2/25/05.

hopped out of the right side of the vehicle. Down on the southern bank of the Euphrates River, a running Marine caught his eye. It was one of Nolan's men. The Marine looked up on the bridge and yelled to his lieutenant. "Sir, you gotta get down here, right now!" There was a stairway leading down to the southern bank of the river just to his right. Nolan ran down two flights of stairs and over to his sniper team.

The Iraqis were dropping knee mortars on his team from across the Euphrates. Sergeant Eric Wolfe, the sniper team leader, had jumped in a nearby ditch to take cover from the mortar explosions, nearly breaking his ankle. Nolan told Wolfe that he would take over as the team leader, and he had Wolfe moved over to the casualty collection point (CCP).

Now that they were under the bridge, they noticed a large truck parked under the bridge on the north side of the river. The first thought that came to mind was that it was probably filled with explosives and the Iraqis would ignite them at any moment, bringing the bridge crashing down. Nolan was given permission to take over as the sniper team leader, a job usually restricted to NCOs. He was ordered to not let anyone get near that truck.

Nolan and his team found cover in a line of palm trees. They set up and scanned the area with their high-powered scopes, waiting for any Iraqi to approach the truck. It was not long before three Iraqis carrying AK-47s moved toward the truck. The scout snipers took a long look at the Iraqis across the river. They all agreed that the Iraqis had weapons. Corporal Carpenter fired two .50-caliber shots in quick succession, and two of the Iraqis fell dead in their tracks. Surprised, the third guy dropped his weapon and pulled a small white flag from his pocket. He waved the flag furiously as his two comrades lay lifeless in pools of blood.

The Marine snipers held their fire. The Iraqi was surrendering, even though he had no clue where the shots had come from. The Marines had no desire to shoot an unarmed surrendering man, so they just watched him. His frantic waving soon turned to a lazy flutter. Within thirty seconds, the Iraqi had stuffed his white flag back into his pocket, and he had picked up his AK-47. Lieutenant Nolan fired. A shot rang out, and the third Iraqi lay dead under the bridge. Nolan was the first Marine Corps officer to get a sniper kill since Vietnam.

WITH the enemy artillery coming in, Mortenson told Dremann to back off from the hospital so that he could drop some of 1/10's artillery on the compound. Dremann ordered his men to pull even farther back. As Dre-mann was pulling Fox Company back and Mortenson was planning his ar-tillery barrage, a small group of civilian pickup trucks and SUVs suddenly appeared, carrying special operators of the secretive Task Force 20. There were about five of them, led by a Navy captain. The captain approached the Marines and said, "We believe that we have POWs in that hospital, and you need to let my guys take care of it."[20]

This seemed an unusual suggestion. An entire Marine infantry battalion was locked in combat with the Iraqis at the Euphrates River bridge, and two full infantry companies were assaulting the hospital. And six Navy SEALs wanted to "take care of it"? Mortenson had already started to drop artillery on the hospital when Colonel Johnson came up and told him to hold off. "We think there may be some POWs from the 507th in there. We're getting JSOF[21] to come in here."

"Why the F didn't you tell me sooner."[22] Mortenson replied, and then he immediately ceased the artillery fire.

Even without Starnes' artillery, the Iraqis in the hospital had had enough. They started putting out white flags, and the Marines ceased their fire. Two Iraqis came out of the complex dressed in white lab coats and ap-proached Dremann's 3d Platoon lines. Dremann went out to speak with the older men. One of the men told Dremann that he was the director of the hospital. He went on to tell Dremann that they did not want to fight from the hospital and that he wanted to bring his wounded out. Dremann had the two men searched, and then he sent one back in to bring out the wounded and any civilians who wanted to leave.

Soon, a dozen vehicles appeared. They drove from the complex west to-ward Highway 7, where the Marines rounded up about seventy Iraqis. Al-most every one of the seventy was a military-aged male. Only a handful of the men were wounded.

All during the fight at the hospital, "Echo Company was pummeling the snot out of the bad guys"[23] west of the road and north of the river. "The

20 Ibid. Fulford.

21 Joint Special Operations Forces.

22 Ibid. Mortenson.

23 Ibid. Mortenson.

fact of the matter is that even when they tried to attack us, we wore their asses out."[24]

Natonski stayed at the base of the bridge for most of the battle. Once things calmed down, he walked up to Colonel Mortenson, thrust out his hand, and began to vigorously shake his hand, "Great job!" Natonski exclaimed, and then he climbed back into his vehicle and drove south.

NBC NEWS

Kerry Sanders was still back in the rear with 2/8's log train, BAS and the main command post. During the day, Kerry tried to find out what was happening up north, and he watched as 2d LAR went by. He then watched as RCT-1 pulled up and parked along the road.

Eventually, casualties started showing up at the battalion aid station. Unlike the day before, Kerry Sanders was free to move around on Monday, as long as he didn't venture too far from the road. He took his film crew over to the battalion aid station, set up, and started broadcasting live for the second day of the battle for An Nasiriyah.

His backdrop this day would be a Marine ambulance with a large red cross painted on its side and American Marines being treated for their wounds. The wounded were lying out in the open, surrounded by corpsmen, doctors, and Marines dressed in surgical gloves, helmets, flak jackets, and MOPP suits. Boxes of medical supplies and discarded sterile packages were haphazardly strewn about.

Kerry stayed far enough back so that no one could tell the identity of the casualties. In fact, Kerry was filming the treatment of Josh Meynard, Corporal Clay, and Lance Corporal Santamaria. Sanders reported that none of the three young Marines was seriously wounded, and ther he continued with the rest of his story.

He reported that the Iraqis had attacked the Marines from a hospital complex. Kerry continued with a casualty report and told his viewers that there were at least nine KIA[25] and fifty WIA[26] from the two days of fighting.

---

24 Ibid. Mortenson.

25 Killed in action.

26 Wounded in action.

The Marines still did not have the correct count. There were nine known dead from Charlie Company's fight for the Saddam Canal bridge, but the number of wounded was far less than fifty. In reality, the 2d Marines had suffered less than half that number of wounded. Tragically, the number of dead would more than double to nineteen, once everything had been sorted out.

Kerry Sanders updated his previous day's report with much more accurate information. He reported that 1/2 had crossed the Euphrates River and that they had moved north of the Saddam Canal. He also reported that Royal Mortenson's Marines had moved in behind 1/2 to secure the Euphrates River bridge, but that heavy fighting had forced America's Battalion to pull back to the south side of the bridge. Then he rehashed the day's events. He talked about the Marines being attacked from the hospital and the wounded Marines.

After his first report at the battalion aid station, Sanders walked over and spoke with one of the wounded. Josh Meynard had been shot in the hand. He didn't appear to be in any pain and was willing to speak with Kerry on camera. Kerry immediately went back on the air with Josh. In one of the most compelling reports of the entire war, Kerry Sanders offered his satellite telephone to Josh so that he could call home to his mother to tell her he was okay.

Josh Meynard instantly received his fifteen minutes of fame as America watched him lay there on his litter, live from the battlefield. Meynard had "M 1330" scrawled on his forehead, indicating when he last received morphine from the corpsmen. Two Marines had to help Meynard to a sitting position, in order for the portable satellite phone to maintain its signal lock. While he was talking, one of the Marines was trying to keep the flies away from Meynard's face.

Meynard spoke with his mother in Texas. First he told of how he was wounded. ". . . some of the enemy's fire came from a nearby hospital. We were very surprised at it—it shocked everybody."[27] Then he told her that he was going to be okay, but that he had been shot in the hand. They spoke for a few moments, and television history had been made. A Marine had called home, while on live TV, to tell his mother that he had been wounded.

27 Kerry Sanders interview with Lance Corporal Joshua Menard on 3/24/03.

REGIMENTAL COMBAT TEAM-2

Major Tuggle had driven south through Ambush Alley before dawn and then returned with fuel and ammunition trucks to the Timberwolves' position north of the city. Eddie Ray had moved through Nasiriyah without firing a shot in Ambush Alley. Yet Colonel Dowdy was still hesitant about moving his regiment through the city.

All of RCT-1 was still parked along Highway 7, south of the railroad bridge. Dowdy's West Coast Marines sat waiting. They waited for hours as Dowdy kept changing the plan. Craparotta's Marines were told to get on their vehicles. Then, they were told to get off. Again, they were ordered to mount up, only to be told later to dismount. By late afternoon, Dowdy realized that his plan to move his soft-skinned vehicles around Ambush Alley would not work. So, he ordered the log trains to be reintegrated with his armored vehicles. All of RCT-1 would drive through An Nasiriyah. The 1st Marine Regiment set to work repositioning its vehicles for the move through Ambush Alley, causing another delay.

RCT-2's Marines continued to work, too. Lieutenant Colonel O'Rourke started unpacking the 2d Marines command post at the railroad bridge, and Major Fulford walked over to try to find a friend that he knew was in RCT-1. There were AMTRACs as far as one could see, waiting for orders, and Marines were sitting outside their vehicles eating chow.[28] Fulford wanted to know when the passage of lines was going to start, so he walked over to some vehicles that had 3/1 painted on them. He found his friend who was with Craparotta, but neither of them had any information on when they were supposed to advance.

So Fulford went in search of the 1st Marine Regiment's command group. He found them sitting outside Colonel Bailey's command tent. Fulford walked up to the 1st Regiment's staff and asked, "I was wondering if any of you all could tell me when the passage of lines is going to start?"[29]

One of the senior officers in the group replied, "The passage of lines will start when you finish your job."

Fulford, irritated, responded, "Sir, if you go inside RCT-2 headquarters,

---

28 Ibid. Fulford.

29 Ibid. Fulford.

you will find that the route is secure and we are prepared to do a passage of lines when you are ready."

THE BARBARIANS

Leading RCT-1 through Ambush Alley, Ray's LAR Battalion moved north of the Saddam Canal, past Colonel Grabowski and followed in trace of Captain Brook's movement to the west. Eddie Ray's LAVs passed through Alpha Company's lines and turned north at the western "T" around 1900, becoming the first MEF unit to attack north toward Baghdad on Highway 7.

Ray's Apache Company took the lead with the newly acquired platoon of tanks. He attacked north on Highway 7, under heavy fire coming from both sides of the road. The Barbarians called for air support, and Cobra gunships quickly swooped in, firing, at times, less than twenty feet in front of the leading LAVs. Apache Company, 2d LAR brought the fight to the Iraqis, using their 81s and direct fire.

Several hundred meters north of the western "T" intersection, Ray's men encountered a heavily defended military compound. The compound was only a few hundred meters north of the spot where Captain King had finally decided to turn his convoy around and retrace his steps the day before. Had King proceeded up this road, as 2d LAR was now about to do, all of the soldiers traveling in the beleaguered 507th convoy would probably have been killed or captured.

Two large-caliber antiaircraft guns protected the site. When Eddie Ray's vehicles approached, the Iraqis brought down these guns and began firing in a direct-fire mode on the Marines. Not to be outdone, Colonel Ray brought his LAV-AD forward. The LAV-AD is a new variant of the light armored vehicle. The "AD" has a radar-guided antiaircraft Gatling gun. This weapon system can be used in a direct-fire mode, too, and is capable of spewing enormous amounts of lead downrange. Ray explained later, "This is the kind of gun that will send everyone home."[30]

Suddenly, Ray noticed an enemy fuel truck driving south toward his position. He ordered his "25" gunner to place warning shots on the road in front of the vehicle. The truck quickly turned around and disappeared

---

30 Ibid. Ray.

north. About an hour later, the fuel truck returned. This time, the warning shots did not faze the driver, and he kept coming. Ray's gunner fired a quick burst directly at the truck, and a fireball appeared about a kilometer up the road. "There was a humungous explosion." Ray recalled.

The Iraqis continued to resist the LAVs, Cobras, and M1 tanks. Next, Ray called in artillery to crush the resistance. Ray remembers standing in his commander's hatch and hearing the DPICM's[31] canisters pop right over his head. For an instant, Ray believed that there had been some mistake and the bomblets would rain down on his men. Then, to his relief, the canisters burst, the bomblets dispersed, and the momentum of the projectile carried the submunitions into the nearby tree line, exactly where they wanted them.

1ST BATTALION, 10TH MARINES

Battery G, 6th Parachute Regiment, U.K. arrived at 1/10's position. The British artillery had come forward to support the parachute insertion at Qalat Sikar. Unable to move north of the city and into range of their target, they set up with Colonel Starnes' batteries and began firing.

British and American artillery pieces were lined up with military precision on both sides of the road. The guns were firing in regular succession, just hammering away as round after round was hurled toward unseen enemy positions in and around An Nasiriyah. An Nasiriyah was a city under siege.

THE BETIO BASTARDS

In the early evening, Dunahoe, Major Canfield, and Captain Day returned to RCT-2's headquarters to question the wisdom of their orders. By the time they arrived, their arguments were moot. Dowdy had finally ordered his regiment forward, and 3/2's order to move through Ambush Alley was rescinded. New orders were issued for Dunahoe's infantry battalion to pull in on the left flank of 2/8 to secure the west side of Highway 7. That whole area was still in enemy hands and rife with targets of opportunity.

The enemy refused to give up control of the intersection of highways 7

---

31 Dual-purpose, improved, conventional munitions.

and 8. They continued to harass the Marines at the crossroads with inter-mittent mortar and small arms fire. Enemy machine gun fire repeatedly ripped through the heavy palm groves west of the city. Colonel Mortenson had managed to quell the resistance at the Euphrates River, but armed Iraqis still roamed the suburban areas throughout southern Nasiriyah. With his new orders in hand, Dunahoe returned to his Marines and began to prepare to move up to the Euphrates River.

Dunahoe and his staff quickly returned to the battalion to spread the good news and to plan their movement to the Euphrates River. Major Canfield called the company commanders together and told them they would be moving in to reinforce 2/8 on the southern bank of the Eu-phrates River on March 25th. They were to bed their companies down for the night.

THE BARBARIANS

Finally, the enemy resistance subsided in the north. But now the weather started to worsen. The wind picked up, clouds rolled in, and daylight faded. Lieutenant Colonel Ray ordered the Barbarians to circle their vehi-cles at the side of the road like Conestoga wagons did in the Wild West. This provided the 2d LAR Battalion a 360-degree defense while they weathered the storm.

As soon as darkness fell, the Iraqis attacked out of the raging sand-storm. Thinking they had Ray surrounded and cut off, they attacked the Barbarians from every direction. A coiled LAR battalion can produce an enormous amount of fire. Ray's men used 25mm, TOW, tanks, and 25mm GAU[32] to decimate the enemy's massive attack with a withering hail of fire. The Iraqis were mowed down by the hundreds as they at-tacked throughout the night. Yet not a single Marine was injured in the battle.

---

32 GAU-12/U is a 25mm Gatling gun, mounted on an LAV.

AMERICA'S BATTALION

Major Mooney and Gunny Mackes had been at the bridge with Colonel Bailey during Mortenson's fight. They were told to put together a brief for the SEALs from SEAL Team 6 for the takedown of the hospital later that night. Mooney and Mackes gathered all the information they had about the hospital and the enemy's disposition inside the compound. They started presenting it to the team. In the middle of their briefing, one of the TF 20 members got a phone call and the team was told to stand down. The SEALs were told that Lynch was no longer in the hospital. The team packed up their things and disappeared as quickly as they had appeared.

Fox Company pulled back away from the hospital and consolidated its position near the bridge. Colonel Mortenson brought Rob Fulford forward, and they spent the night sleeping on the ground next to Mortenson's vehicle at the base of the bridge, right next to Fox Company's mortars.

REGIMENTAL COMBAT TEAM-2

Bailey felt much better by the end of the day. He had managed to get fuel, food, and ammunition to Grabowski in the north. Mortenson had quieted an attack at the Euphrates River, and Dunahoe was preparing to move up on Mortenson's left at the Euphrates River. By 2100, Captain Grunwald had returned to RCT-2's headquarters area with his company of LAVs. The Marines could start to deliberately expand their areas of influence in an orderly fashion the next day. Now that Bailey had his regiment back together, he felt much better about the situation. But Colonel Dowdy was still nervous. He had let Ray go north with a large part of his firepower, but he still had his three mechanized infantry battalions and his entire log train to get through Ambush Alley.

THE 1ST MARINE DIVISION

The 1st Marine Division's RCT-5 and RCT-7 continued to cross the Highway 1 bridge all night. One of the reasons that the MEF commanders were so intent on opening an eastern route through An Nasiriyah was that the Highway 1 bridge and its six-lane highway were still under construction. Steel rebar provided the only guardrail on the unfinished bridge.

The driving conditions on the bridge were so hazardous that there were several tracked vehicle accidents that night. At one point, a 1st Tank Battalion M1 tank, traveling with its turret traversed, drove through the flimsy guardrail and off the east side of the bridge. In the darkness and blowing sand, no one saw the tank go over the edge. The tank plunged its crew fifty feet to a watery death. The next morning, Marines found Staff Sergeant Donald May, Lance Corporal Patrick O'Day, and Private First Class Franeisco Martinez/Flores whose seabags had washed ashore on the northern bank of the river.

3D BATTALION, 1ST MARINES: THE THUNDERING THIRD

Colonel Dowdy was finally ready to move. At 2000, Lieutenant Colonel Craparotta was summoned to the RCT-1 headquarters. At the meeting, Craparotta was told that the entire 1st Marine Regiment would move through An Nasiriyah, starting around midnight. Dowdy told his battalion commander that he wanted him to lead the regiment and set up a picket line in the city. Once 3/1 had secured the route, Dowdy would move the rest of the regiment forward.

Craparotta returned to his battalion and called his company commanders together for a quick planning session at the hood of his Humvee. Dowdy had chopped his eight remaining tanks to Third Battalion. Craparotta would lead with the tanks, and Captain Matthew Reid's Lima Company would follow the tanks across the Euphrates River in their eleven AAVs.

Lieutenant Colonel Craparotta decided that he would follow Lima Company into the city in his soft-skinned Humvee, just as Grabowski had done on March 23rd. This would afford him maximum visibility and give him the best opportunity to communicate with, and control, his battalion. The colonel's command AMTRAC and chase vehicle would follow close behind Craparotta. The battalion 81s would follow the battalion forward command group, and then India Company would take up the rear of the armored column. Craparotta would hold Kilo Company in reserve, south of the Euphrates.

After a day and a half of fighting at the Euphrates River bridge, Craparotta ordered his Marines to, "Go in weapons tight and guns blazing."[33] They went through the plan step-by-step, and then he dismissed his officers, saying, "We are going to kick off in about thirty minutes. Let's make it happen."[34]

---

33 Personal interview with Major Matthew Reid, 5/19/05.

34 Telephone interview with Lieutenant Colonel Lou Craparotta, 3/30/04.

CHAPTER 12

The Betio Bastards

The more Marines I have around, the better I like it!
—GENERAL MARK CLARK, U.S. ARMY

THE THUNDERING THIRD

Just prior to midnight, the Code Red artillery barrage was canceled. First Marines would charge into Ambush Alley in the quiet of the night. Craparotta's eight tanks led the way across the Euphrates River bridge— clanking into Ambush Alley. The tanks were able to use their GPSs and peel off at their exact designated coordinates. Two tanks stopped near the northern bank of the Euphrates, and the other six kept plodding north. Two tanks stopped at the next major intersection, and the remaining four pushed deeper into the city. Two tanks stopped at the open field where Grabowski's Bravo Company had congregated the day before, and the final two tanks rolled up and stopped near the "Alamo."

Iraqis opened fire at the southern bridge as soon as the first tank rolled across into the city. Captain Reid's AMTRACs followed closely behind the tanks. Darkness was Reid's ally. Every one of his Marines had night-vision goggles, and all of his weapons were fitted with laser sights. They could see every Iraqi combatant as clearly as Captain Brooks's Alpha Company Marines could in the middle of the day before. The Iraqis, however, fired wildly into the dark of night, only able to hear the advancing Marines. It wasn't a fair fight, but the enemy was persistent and aggressive. They ran up and down back alleys, out of view, and repeatedly jumped out to fire at the Marines.

Lima Company lumbered forward at thirty-five kilometers per hour. Reid's Marines had been ordered to intersperse their tracks between the northern tank positions. In their excitement, the trackers raced too far forward and they all bunched up near the last tank position at the "Alamo." Reid commanded his platoon leaders to move back to the south and fan out along the road.

Colonel Craparotta raced into Ambush Alley behind Lima Company and stopped his command group nearly in the center of town. As one of his Marines was getting out of the command track, he was shot in the leg. Marines rushed to his aid and quickly bandaged his wound. The Marine was loaded back into the track, out of action for the night. He had suffered a million-dollar wound. Soon he would be on his way home with a Purple Heart pinned on his chest.

India Company rolled into the city on the heels of Craparotta's 81s. They deployed a platoon of Marines at the southernmost tank position, and began to fill in the picket line as they moved north. Their line fell well short of its intended mark. With Lima bunched up in the north and India stretched out not quite to the center of town, there was a gaping hole in the picket line in the center of the city. Two rifle companies were just not enough to secure the entire route. Lieutenant Colonel Craparotta called for Kilo Company to come up and fill in the gaps. It took Craparotta's Marines about an hour to settle into their picket line and silence the majority of the Iraqi fire.

Once they were in position, Dowdy's next battalion charged through the city. Lieutenant Colonel John Mayer's 1/4 rolled up over the Euphrates River bridge. Unlike 3/1, who had all worked together for over eighteen months, 1/4 was a new battalion, and its officers and men had not been together long. Like Dunahoe's battalion, 1/4 had filled its ranks with more than a hundred brand-new Marines before leaving for Iraq. These inexperienced young men had been spooked by rumors of ambushes and scores of dead Marines.

As soon as one Marine opened fire, they all did. Reid's Marines had to dive for cover as 1/4 raced through the city. North of the canal, Major Peeples could hear them coming, "It sounded like the gunfight at the OK Corral when they came across the Euphrates River bridge. They shot all the way through the town."[1] As they traveled through An Nasiriyah's darkness,

---

1 Ibid. Peeples.

they shot at everything that moved. Captain Blanchard heard them, too. On top of all the gunfire, Blanchard also could hear the unmistakable sound of AMTRACs racing north through the city. Blanchard also heard .50-caliber machine gun fire, and he could see little sparks and tracers lighting up the city. The noise and light show continued to draw closer, and then the lead vehicles of 1/4 came over the canal bridge. They drove north on Highway 7, screaming toward Grabowski's position.

THE TIMBERWOLVES

Somewhere between 0330 and 0400, Lieutenant Colonel Grabowski was sitting by his Humvee and his remaining C7 at the "T" intersection. The gun battle in the city had woken everyone up. Grabowski thought, "Shit! Where is this coming from?"[2] Then, 1/4 came racing through, lighting up the entire sky. Grabowski could see hundreds of tracers going east— .50-caliber tracers, small arms tracers. They were darting into the blackened night sky, some skipping off the ground into the air at strange angles. Mayer's Marines were laying down suppressive fire to the east as they traveled through Ambush Alley. They continued to fire as they moved across the canal.

Grabowski turned to Dunfee. "They are going to shoot our ass up for sure."[3] He quickly ordered Gunner Dunfee to get everyone on the radio. "Tell every company commander to light up his position with chem lights!" He ordered.

Mayer's men stopped firing as they moved north. As soon as the lead element got up to the northern "T," tracers started going off again. Then, the whole line just opened up. The gunner took off yelling and screaming. He ran toward the road, followed by Colonel Grabowski and majors Sosa and Tuggle, trying to get them to cease fire. They physically stopped the convoy.

As Dunfee and Grabowski were trying to tell the Marines at the head of 1/4's column to cease fire, their battalion XO drove up. Before looking to see who he was talking to, he yelled, "What the hell are we stopped for?"[4]

---

2 Ibid. Grabowski.

3 Ibid. Grabowski.

4 Ibid. Grabowski.

Colonel Grabowski stepped out of the darkness and snapped back, "What the hell are you shooting at?" The XO calmed a bit and offered, "They're just nervous." One of Grabowski's Marines had been shot in the shoulder in the frenzy of fire. Fortunately, his wound was not serious and he, too, would soon be on a plane home.

By now, 1st Marines' convoy had ground to a halt in Ambush Alley. The Iraqis continued to take potshots at the Marine vehicles. Brigadier General Kelly was not happy that the convoy had stopped, leaving his Marines like sitting ducks in the center of the city. He immediately got on the radio and ordered the convoy to press forward. Grabowski, Dunfee, Tuggle, and Sosa walked back down off the road, and 4/1 resumed its movement north.

THE THUNDERING THIRD

Captain Reid watched the tail end of Mayer's battalion move through the city. Then the 2d Battalion, 23d Marines followed. The seemingly endless convoy of over a thousand vehicles continued to roll through town. Soon, the sun rose, and the 1st Marines were still moving north through the city.

Reid had set his company command post up right at C201, just outside the "Alamo." With the daylight came the realization that the blackened hulk in the distance was a destroyed Marine AMTRAC—C208. Its engine was lying in the road, one hundred meters from the shattered hull.

Lima Company's maintenance guys had been working all night, and they had taken Sergeant Schaefer's MK19 grenade launcher off of C201 and installed it on one of their own tracks. Their MK19 had been damaged when the driver's side swiped a telephone pole the night before. During the night, they had scavenged all the parts that they could off C201.

They found body parts strewn around the destroyed track and noticed a body under the back ramp. Reid's Marines raised the ramp and found the burned and crushed body of one of Charlie Company's Marines. They immediately radioed to report their find and were told to leave the scene intact. RCT-2 wanted to collect their own. Reid's men covered the bodies and returned to their other work.

AT 0530, Grunwald's LAR Company moved through Ambush Alley, escorting the rest of Grabowski's log trains. Charlie Company, 2d LAR pushed north of the 23rd Brigade headquarters and filled in the line to the north and east. Grunwald sent two platoons four kilometers north and east to patrol the area outside of Grabowski's lines. They found ammunition and weapons caches in the east.

Third Platoon returned south with some of the ALOC vehicles. As soon as they returned, they were ordered to the southeast side of the city to search out and destroy four armored personnel carriers and eight artillery pieces that had been spotted earlier. In the midst of their search, they also found six antiaircraft guns. All the vehicles and weapon systems were found abandoned. This was typical. Marines throughout An Nasiriyah had seen weapons and vehicles abandoned. They also encountered unarmed military-age men. The men would move from place to place, use the weapons, and then run away. As long as the weapons remained operational, they would return, over and over again.

The Iraqis knew that the Marines would not shoot unarmed men, and they hoped that they would not destroy unmanned weapons. But, by now, the Marines had figured out the enemy's tactic. Grunwald's Marines called for engineers, who blew up all the vehicles and weapons. They would no longer threaten American troops.

TRUCK after truck continued to roll through Ambush Alley, headed north to Baghdad. Finally, around noon, the last vehicles rolled through and 3/1 was ordered to break down the picket line and follow in trace of the regiment. Craparotta's Marines moved out, starting in the south. India Company mounted up first and drove north through the city. Kilo followed with the command group and the 81s. Captain Reid waited at the southern base of the Saddam Canal bridge for his battalion to pass, and then he ordered his company to mount up and move out. As Reid drove over the canal bridge, Ambush Alley became quiet again.

THE BARBARIANS

The next morning Eddie Ray's Barbarians led RCT-1's charge to Baghdad. They had broken through the enemy's defenses north of An Nasiriyah. Now, it was on to Qalat Sikar, Al Kut, and Baghdad. Again, Eddie Ray had taken the initiative and attacked into the enemy. Task Force Tarawa had kicked the door to Baghdad open, but it was Ray's Barbarians who punched through to lead the 1st Marine Regiment to victory.

AMERICA'S BATTALION

Sergeant Wolfe's ankle was not broken; he had just sprained it severely. It was nothing a night of rest and a tightly laced boot could not fix, so, by morning, Wolfe had hobbled back to his sniper team. Lieutenant Nolan decided to stay with the team. This gave them a beefed-up, five-man team with three scoped weapons. They moved east along the tree line until they were three hundred meters from the bridge and less than two hundred meters from the hospital. From this position, they had a clear field of fire on two sides of the hospital and a view of the back.

Early in the morning, Colonel Mortenson called Dremann aside. "I want to pull the CP up here. I want to bring the engineer assets up, but I need you to clear this row of nine buildings, off to the southeast. Move all of the civilians out of there."[5]

Dremann ordered Lieutenant Southwick to take his platoon down to clear the buildings. Southwick got an interpreter and an assault section from Echo Company and moved in to methodically clear the cluster of buildings between the road and the hospital with his reinforced 2d Platoon. At each building, they told the occupants that they had thirty minutes to gather up whatever they needed, and then they would have to leave.

Clearing the first few homes was easy. But, as they got closer to the hospital, they started finding booby traps in the houses. When they found a booby trap, they left it where it sat and called for the assault team Marines, who were the demolition experts. They carefully set charges and blew each booby trap where it sat.

After pushing Southwick's patrol out, Dremann returned to the bridge. He hadn't quite made it back to 1st Platoon's position when he received a report of an Iraqi technical moving around on the road along the southern bank of the river. It was only visible for a short time before it disappeared in the tree line. Dremann sent some CAAT vehicles and a squad from 1st Platoon east to lay in wait for the technical to return. As they were moving east

---

5 Ibid. Dremann.

into position, Dremann received another report over the company net. "Hey, there is a tank in the hospital compound."[6] Dremann immediately called Major Fulford and requested air to take out the tank. Fulford told Dremann that he couldn't run air because they suspected that some of Grabowski's missing Marines might be in there.

Dremann told Fulford that he was in position to attack the hospital. Fulford asked, "How long do you need before you can step off?"[7]

"It's going to take me about twenty minutes." Dremann needed to distribute ammunition and issue a FRAGO order to his men.

"Roger. Step off as soon as you are ready," Fulford told Dremann.

Right in the middle of Dremann's preparations, an Iraqi came walking down the road, north of the hospital. At first, he didn't appear to be carrying a weapon. As Nolan and his snipers watched him head directly toward Captain Dremann's rallying point, they noticed that he was holding his arm flat against his side and that there was a weapon tucked under his clothing. Nolan fired at the man and missed. He drove another round home in his bolt-action rifle, aimed, and fired a second shot. His second shot was a direct hit.

Fox Company was moving within fifteen minutes. Dremann opened the attack with a barrage from the battalion's 81mm mortars, and then he continued with his company's 60mm mortars.

There was an open area between the tree line along the river and the hospital compound berm. The last 150 meters or so was open field. Luckily, in the fifteen minutes between Dremann's first conversation with Fulford and the time they kicked off, the weather turned from clear and sunny to the beginning of a bad sandstorm. By the time the Marines pushed out, they couldn't even see the hospital in the distance. This meant that the Iraqis in the compound couldn't see the Marines advancing, either.

Lieutenant Wong's 1st Platoon Marines moved across the open field through blowing dust and took up positions along the berm on the western perimeter of the hospital compound. They were less than fifty meters from the buildings, close enough to see the hospital through the swirling sand, which meant that the Iraqis could see them moving into attack position.

The Iraqi fighters opened fire from the upper floors. Under fire, Southwick's Marines breached the fence and rushed the first building which was

---

6 Ibid. Dremann.

7 Ibid. Dremann.

quite small. They entered the compound and cleared several sheds. Then, they moved to the hospital building. The assault team operated like a typical American SWAT team. They rushed to both sides of the doorway, stacked up along the wall, and then two Marines broke in the door with a large ram. The door flew open and Marines rushed inside, weapons at the ready. As they cleared room-to-room, the Iraqis fled out the eastern side of the hospital.

Corporal Friend and his squad were in a support-by-fire position, but they could not even see the hospital once the sand started to fill the air. Friend thought that they could not just sit there, so he moved his squad through the breach. The Iraqis had fighting holes dug all the way around the perimeter of the compound, and the positions were filled with helmets, uniforms, weapons, and gas masks. Friend moved his squad clockwise, from trench to trench. The Iraqis were all gone, but it was apparent that they had been prepared for a fight; they just had no stomach for fighting Marines.

Other Marines were moving along the walls surrounding the building, when Iraqis started firing on them from the south. Lance Corporal Hammond was hit. He took a shot to the leg and went down. Two more Marines fell with shrapnel wounds from exploding grenades. While other Marines and corpsmen rushed to help the wounded, Gunnery Sergeant Aubrey Hall ran back to the breach in the fence. He ran back across the open field to Fox Company's rear area, to get a vehicle to med-evac his Marines. Meanwhile, Staff Sergeant Ricky St. John scooped up Hammond in a fireman's carry and lugged him back through the breach. Then he returned to his men at the hospital. The Iraqi fighters were fleeing, but the compound was far from secure.

As Fox Company worked to clear the hospital grounds, Mortenson brought his TAC CP forward and tucked it into a house at the base of the bridge. He could have tossed a baseball underhanded and hit the paved road or the bridge guardrail. The main command post was still about six hundred meters south of the bridge on the east side of the road.[8]

THE BETIO BASTARDS

It was a clear and sunny morning when Colonel Dunahoe took his company commanders and his S3 on a leader's reconnaissance to the Euphrates River. By the time they met with Colonel Mortenson at the base of the bridge, the

---

8 Ibid. Mortenso.

sandstorm was starting to roll in. The entire area was very deceiving on the map. Most everything west of the road was waterlogged marsh—cut with irrigation ditches and small canals. The area wasn't really suitable for the battalion to dig into a defensive position.

Mortenson's Marines were in the middle of a fight when Dunahoe rolled up. Mortenson, Dunahoe, and his commanders were standing, with their maps spread out across the hood of a Humvee, while just five feet away a young Marine was spraying a steady stream of lead from his SAW at targets across the river. Enemy mortar rounds were exploding around the vehicle, and the two battalion commanders were trying to stay cool in front of their men. Then an enemy round exploded only feet from the two colonels. Both men decided that discretion was the better part of valor and moved to the protected side of their vehicles. They took cover and continued their discussion.

While the battalion commanders conferred, Day and Luciano carved out the battle space. Day said to Luciano, "I got from Highway Seven west and south to Highway Eight—all the way out to Route One."[9]

"Roger that," Luciano acknowledged. Then he came back with, "I'll take from the road east, down to Eight."

"Roger that," Day acknowledged.

The Marines quickly finished their discussions about where Dunahoe would place his Marines and how they would relieve Echo Company. Then Dunahoe and his officers drove south to lead their men forward.

REGIMENTAL COMBAT TEAM-2

Colonel Bailey decided that he had to go up and see for himself what the situation was north of the canal. Bailey went early on March 25th to 1/2's position. He led the remaining vehicles from 1st Marines that had been left behind when Dowdy moved through the city. "The key point was to get over to 1/2 and let them see me. I wanted to look Lieutenant Colonel Grabowski in the eye and tell him that he had done a good job."[10] Bailey called Grabowski and only told him that he was coming forward to see him.

---

9 Conversation taken from telephone interview with Major John Day, 6/5/04.

10 Ibid. Bailey.

THE TIMBERWOLVES

When Grabowski heard that Bailey was coming forward, he was certain that he would be relieved. Grabowski sent for Tuggle so that he would be there to take over command. But when Bailey arrived, it was a completely different scene. Bailey came up and grabbed Grabowski's arm and firmly shook his hand and told him that he had made Marine Corps history. He then told Grabowski, "I am responsible for everything that happens in the organization, and you did everything I told you to do."[11] Grabowski was moved by Bailey's support and encouragement.

Grabowski took a few minutes to tell Bailey of the conversation he had with Captain Santare two nights before. He told Bailey that there was a possibility that some of his Marines were killed by friendly fire. Bailey finished his short meeting with Grabowski and raced back south through Ambush Alley, to the southern bridge.

NBC NEWS

Kerry Sanders opened his report with, "Good morning. It has been a fierce two-day battle here for control of a road that leads across two bridges through An Nasiriyah." The oil tanks in southern Nasiriyah were still smoking in the background, and the wind was starting to kick up sand and loose debris. Kerry rehashed the two-day battle, but the story was still jumbled, a victim of the fog of war. The Marines still did not have an accurate accounting of Grabowski's casualties. Marines were still missing, and no one knew much about the ambush of the 507th Maintenance Company, let alone the fate of its soldiers.

Kerry really didn't have any new news to report from An Nasiriyah, other than the fact that the battle was still raging and it looked like a nasty storm was about to blow in. He concluded his report with, "It's going to be a miserable night because the rain is coming down."

---

11 Ibid. Bailey.

AMERICA'S BATTALION

As soon as Dremann's men entered the compound, Nolan ordered his team to pick up and move into the hospital. They ran into the tallest building and headed to the roof. Once on the roof, they quickly set up overwatch positions. Unfortunately, while Nolan was changing positions, most of the Iraqi fighters ran out the back and into the tree line, east of the hospital. Had Nolan and his team stayed in their original position, the retreating Iraqis would have been killed.

Friend and his Marines circled around to the east side of the compound. They found two smaller buildings. The first was an office building, and the second was the hospital morgue. When the Marines rushed the door, the smell of rotting flesh nearly knocked them over. They checked for enemy fighters and got out of there as fast as they could.

They moved up to the office building, Friend in the lead. Friend carefully looked around the corner and saw a tank main gun barrel. He jerked his head back behind the building. "Okay, we're stopping here,"[12] he told his Marines. Friend got on the radio and called to another squad leader who had deployed his Marines on the roof. They talked and exchanged hand signals.

The Marine on the roof made a V with two fingers and pointed them at his eyes, and then he pointed a single finger at the tank, indicating that he, too, could see the tank. Friend braved the corner a few more times. The tank was covered in cammo netting and appeared to be empty. Friend told the squad leader on the roof to cover him, and then he moved his squad around the corner to the tank. Friend and his platoon sergeant climbed up on the tank and cut away the netting. Friend then opened the hatch atop the turret and quickly thrust his weapon toward the opening.

The tank was clear, but the turret was full of ammunition. Strangely, it had no engine. The Iraqis must have placed it there to be used as a pillbox. Fortunately, they retreated before they ever had the chance to use it against the Marines. Once they knew that the tank was not a threat, Friend and his squad entered the building and began the tedious task of clearing each office. There were photographs of Saddam throughout the building and Republican Guard paintings on the walls. In the process, they found Chemical

---

12 Ibid. Friend.

Ali's office. It was the largest office of all, and it was evident that he had made a hasty retreat before the Marines arrived.

When Captain Dremann reached the east side of the hospital, the Iraqi fighters were sniping at the Marines from the nearby trees in the east. He assembled a line of eight 203 gunners, and he had them lob scores of grenades into the trees. Dremann's innovative use of his grenadiers as his own personal mini-artillery silenced the enemy fire in the east.

Once the hospital grounds were secure, Dremann began to search the buildings. First, he went with Friend back into the morgue. They checked the bodies to make sure that they were not American and then left to continue the search of the grounds. They found fresh body parts on the second floor, obviously victims of the deadly Marine mortar attacks. They found five dead Iraqis in various parts of the building, and it appeared obvious that they died fighting the Marines.

Then they found sets of gear from the 507th. They found MOPP suits, packs, helmets, boots, and flak vests. The clothes were bloody and torn, like they had been cut away in the emergency room. They also found a large weapons cache, NBC equipment, and enough food for a thousand people. There were huge bags of rice and dates, and the NBC equipment was everywhere. There were boxes of hundreds of chemical suits, atropine injectors, and gas masks. Nasiriyah was the home of the 11th Chemical Company and Chemical Ali. It was not unexpected to find this paraphernalia in the military hospital, as Nasiriyah was a known chemical testing area.

ONCE the complex was secure, Colonel Mortenson came to the hospital and told Dremann that he wanted him to pull back to the bridge. Mortenson did not want to overextend his lines. Dremann was not happy about having to give up the hospital compound after spending all morning fighting to secure it, but he did as he was ordered.

He had his men destroy all the weapons and ammunition in the hospital, and he called for engineers to blow up the tank in the courtyard. Once they set the charges in the tank, Dremann cleared the hospital, and then he ordered his men to pull back. The Marines went back through the breach in the fence, crossed the road, and took up positions on the west side of the berm.

First Sergeant Gatewood came up to Friend and said, "We gotta pull back farther. The charge on the tank isn't a little sissy charge. This thing's gonna make a big boom."[13] So all the Marines picked up and ran back toward the tree line and the lines that they had held the night before. They hadn't quite made it back to the trees when the charges on the tank went off. Friend felt the concussion as the invisible wave rolled across the open field. Fox Company reoccupied their previous night's fighting positions and waited for their next orders.

MARINES clearing the area around the intersection of highways 7 and 8 found Addison and Kiehl still trapped in their overturned five-ton truck. The trailer and its contents were strewn everywhere along the side of the road. Howard Johnson and Ruben Estrella's truck was right next to the overturned truck; its cab completely destroyed. The Marines found Howard Johnson's body inside the shattered cab, but Estrella was nowhere to be found. The Marines carefully righted the overturned truck, and then painstakingly removed the shattered bodies of the fallen soldiers from their destroyed vehicles.

THE BETIO BASTARDS

In the afternoon, Dunahoe's men mounted up and drove north toward the Euphrates River. As they drove up Highway 7, they encountered several busloads of clean-shaven, military-age Iraqis. The Iraqis were trying to drive north into Nasiriyah along with Dunahoe's Marines. The buses were stopped and emptied of their occupants. One hundred fifty EPWs[14] were left along the side of the road with Major Starling and a couple of corpsmen holding them at bay with their pistols. It wasn't long before a Marine sergeant helped load the Iraqis back aboard the buses and then drove them to the EPW holding area.

Then Major Starling brought the main command post forward and set it up in a farmhouse that was 150 meters off the side of the road, nearly midway between Highway 8 and the Euphrates River. The small Iraqi dwelling was perfect for the command post. It was nestled among palm trees at the edge of the grove and had a nice-size interior courtyard where Starling could

---

13 Ibid. Friend.

14 Enemy prisoner of war.

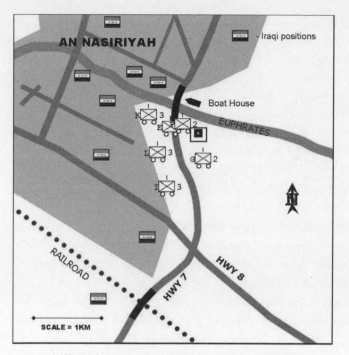

3/2's Defense Anchored on the Euphrates River

set up all of his radio antennae, out of sight of the enemy. Day set up his 81mm mortars in a clearing near the main command post. The Betio Bastards were now "good to go." They immediately started planning how they would push west.

By the time Dunahoe's Marines pulled into the line at the Euphrates River, there was a horrendous sandstorm blowing in. More civilians were also now roaming the area. In addition, there was sporadic mortar and small arms fire coming in from three sides, and it didn't seem like any of this was real. The Bastards had been in the desert for more than a month, and they had just spent nearly a week moving through Iraq's wasteland. Now, here they were in a lush date palm grove on the banks of the Euphrates River.

They were being whipped by sand and rain, potshots, and an occasional RPG. The Marines couldn't tell a thunderclap from mortar impacts. Palm trees were blowing in the wind and the sand-filled air was lighted by tracers. It was surreal. With all the blowing sand and rain, lightning and thunder, it was as if God were voicing his displeasure for this violent intrusion into His Garden of Eden.

Dunahoe's Marines moved to set a defensive line not far from their vehicles. In the pelting rain, they only moved a couple hundred meters west. They linked up with 2/8 and just kind of sat down. Kilo Company was anchored on the river, India Company was anchored on Highway 8, and Lima Company was in the middle.

Captain E. J. Healy moved into the palm groves with his Kilo Company to relieve Captain Yeo and Echo Company. When he arrived, he only found a small force. Captain Yeo had taken most of his company on patrol to investigate a military compound that sat about five hundred meters to the west. Healy warned his men to watch out for Yeo's patrol and to move up into the line. Soon, Yeo returned with his patrol, moved back through Healy's newly placed lines, collected the rest of his company, and moved to the east side of Route 7, to rejoin his battalion.

The Betio Bastards moved into the tree line. It was a surreal scene, nothing like what the Marines had expected. It was as if their seven-ton trucks had teleported them through time and space to the Vietnam War. They dug in to muddy ground, in a jungle-like scene, filled with palm trees and vegetation. All the while, artillery rounds were exploding across the river, punctuated by the constant sound of gunfire.

There was no doubt in anyone's mind; the Betio Bastards were now in combat. Healy's men quickly cleared a few nearby houses and pushed out a couple hundred meters to a small canal that ran north to south. The canal was a perfect natural defensive line, so they dug in.

Lima Company pulled in behind Kilo Company and took up positions farther south. They swept the area and pushed out to the same small canal and tied in with Kilo's southern squad. As they started digging in, it began to rain. The Marines dug their fighting positions only to have them fill with water. It was wet, muddy, and cold.

India Company was the last company in. They occupied positions in the southern portion of the battalion's area of operations. They filled in between Lima-Company on their north and Highway 8 on their south. With the weather getting worse by the minute, they settled down for the night.

While the grunts suffered in their flooded fighting holes, the battalion staff worked through the night inside the forward command post. Dunahoe's air officer, Captain Harold "Duck" Qualkinbush was sitting in the forward command post looking at satellite imagery on his laptop computer. This was the first time he had ever used Type III close air support. Type I CAS would be impossible in these weather conditions. It was impossible to see the enemy, let alone the aircraft overhead. He carefully recorded map grid coordinates from the imagery and relayed his targets to the attack aircraft overhead. Two-thousand pound bombs rained down on the suspected enemy positions, a mere thousand meters from the Marines' front lines. The explosions shook the Marines in their boots. Air Force jets, British Tornados, and Marine Harriers all took turns attacking the enemy in southern Nasiriyah, as Qualkinbush guided them in like he was playing some deadly video game on his computer.

As Qualkinbush fought the battle from his laptop and radio, Dunahoe's HET was gathering up civilians and EPWs for interrogation. One elderly man appeared willing to help the Americans. Sergeant H[15] talked with him nearly all night long. The old man helped Sergeant H mark up a map of the area, indicating the position of the local Ba'ath Party leader's house and the Ba'ath Party headquarters not far away. The Ba'ath Party headquarters compound was on Highway 8 next to a soccer stadium, less than a kilometer from the 7/8 interchange.

THE BARBARIANS

Ray had broken through the enemy's lines and was engaged in a running gunfight through a series of towns as he continued to push north up routes 7 and 17. The fighting continued in An Nasiriyah even as the 1st Marine Division raced north to the gates of Baghdad.

Now that 1st Marines had pushed through Ambush Alley, it was even more important that Task Force Tarawa establish a firm hold in the streets of An Nasiriyah. Eddie Ray would not be able to sustain his forward momentum if RCT-2 could not keep the supply routes clear. As it turned out, the Iraqi desert and the sandstorm it produced would cause the Marines to come to a grinding halt for a few days. If the supply routes couldn't be kept clear, the entire Marine charge to Baghdad could falter with disastrous results. The Marine commanders were still very concerned that if their regimental combat teams were forced to hold in place for any length of time,

---

15 The Commanding officer of the human exploitation team that was attached to 3/2 requested that the last names of his men not be used. From this point forward, I will use only the initial in their last name.

they would be vulnerable to chemical attack. Saddam's WMD threat was still frighteningly real.

TASK FORCE TARAWA

Intelligence reports started coming into the MEB headquarters that indicated that the enemy might be massing in the railroad yard—west on Route 8. If this were true, they could launch an attack into Task Force Tarawa's rear areas. The regimental headquarters could be attacked, and Glenn Starne's artillery was vulnerable, too. But the biggest problem was that all of the brigade's support and logistics units were stretched out along Highway 7, just south of Highway 8. The last thing in the world Natonski and Bailey wanted was to fight the enemy in their own rear area.

AMERICA'S BATTALION

Mortenson, Fulford, and Dupree sat knee-to-knee in the command tent for their nightly meeting, as they did every evening. The Iraqis had been fighting the Marines for three days, and Mortenson was concerned that they might try something different. Mortenson told his staff, "These sons of guns have been getting their ass handed to them for three days now. They are going to get tired of throwing themselves against frontline infantry battalions."[16]

The Marines of 2/8 had been watching the Iraqis crossing the bridges in cabs and civilian vehicles. When stopped at the checkpoints, they had no weapons. There were many military-age men who felt it necessary to get south. Others were coming across in little boats. The Marines would shoot the boats and sink them, but it was impossible to know how many others had moved south over the southwest Euphrates River bridge, which was still not in the Marines' control.

Mortenson predicted, "Rob, they're gonna walk another three thousand meters, and they're gonna turn left, and they're gonna come right into our CP group and the log trains."[17] Mortenson reasoned that the rear area

---

16 Ibid. Mortenson.

17 Ibid. Mortenson.

would provide a much more tempting target and that the enemy was probably getting tired of throwing themselves against a buzz saw.

Mortenson, Fulford, and Dupree started making plans for protecting
their rear area. In the morning, Mortenson would talk to Colonel Bailey
about his concerns.

CHAPTER 13

Blue-on-Blue

The deadliest weapon in the world is a Marine and his rifle.
—GENERAL JOHN J. "BLACK JACK" PERSHING, U.S. ARMY

THE BETIO BASTARDS

Lieutenant Brian Waite, the battalion chaplain, had spent the night with the Marines outside the forward command post. They had all dug fighting positions in the field next to the road and tried to settle in for the night. Marines do not stay in their vehicles when they are stopped—especially at night. A well-placed RPG or mortar round could prove disastrous, so they sleep on the ground, dug in.

Waite had found a large fighting position that the Marines had dug. The hole was easily ten feet in diameter. He asked the occupants if he could join them for the night. Then he climbed into his high-tech sleeping bag, pulled it up over his head, and secured it to its' most watertight condition. It rained throughout the night. Chaplain Waite had a difficult time falling asleep, trying to keep water out of his sleeping bag. He had finally drifted off to sleep but was awakened early in the morning by voices calling to him from afar. As his alertness returned, he realized that the skies had opened up like an afternoon Florida downpour. It was the kind of rain that soaks your socks in thirty seconds.

Waite could hear the company 1st Sergeant calling, "Chaplain!

Chaplain!"[1] He stuck his head out of his waterproof cocoon. Waite was the only one left in the hole, and it was filled with water. All the other Marines, disregarding procedure, had taken shelter from the rain in the trucks.

Brian Waite spent several entertaining minutes trying to get out of the water-filled hole while the Marines in the truck cheered him on. He learned that his waterproof sleeping bag held water in just as well as it held water out. By the time he had extricated himself, he was soaking wet. Waite placed his waterlogged gear under a vehicle and climbed in out of the rain to finish his night's sleep.

AMERICA'S BATTALION

First thing on the Wednesday morning, Colonel Mortenson went down and talked with Colonel Bailey about the railroad-yard report. He told Bailey that he was concerned about the rear areas and that he wanted to move his main command post forward. He gave his boss an assessment of what he thought the enemy was going to do and concluded with, "Sir, You've got to berm in."[2]

Bailey agreed with Mortenson. He knew that the rear areas were his Achilles heel. He had been siphoning off combat strength from his rear area units for days now, trying to provide an acceptable security force for the Highway 1 bridge. Bailey decided to keep a closer eye on the intel reports. Colonel Mortenson left the regimental headquarters and quickly returned to the bridge to make his own preparations.

Reports continued to come in, corroborating the earlier news of a big enemy counterattack in the making. Now I MEF was reporting that its "organic intelligence assets" were indicating an impending attack by one to two thousand enemy combatants, who were massing at Nasiriyah's railroad station.

As part of Mortenson's preparations to meet what he thought would be that night's threat, he told Major Alford, the battalion XO, to move the main command post and the log trains forward closer. He wanted all of his Marines to be tucked in closer to his infantry companies.

---

1 Ibid. Waite.

2 Ibid. Mortenson.

Alford immediately went in search of a new location for the main command post. He quickly found a perfect spot. It was southwest of the intersection highways 7 and 8. Alford radioed Mortenson, "Hey, sir, I got a great spot. It's a gas station. It's got a concrete overhang. I got the engineers with me. I can put a berm square around the whole thing, and I can get the whole log train and the main CP in here. It's perfect. I can defend it. We are good to go."[3]

"Roger—got it." Mortenson replied, and Alford started working to set up his defenses. Mortenson also sent word back to let Kerry Sanders come up to the bridge. Danny Miller and Sebastian Rich were eager to move up to the front, but Kerry was a little nervous. He asked Mortenson about the intensity of continuing enemy fire. "If they get you, it's a lucky shot." Mortenson told Sanders. "They don't know what the hell they are doing."

Mortenson did not tell Kerry Sanders about his real concern. He wanted the news crew to move north because he believed that it would be too dangerous for them to stay in the rear area. He wanted them to be out of harm's way. After their short conversation, Sanders decided to go up to Mortenson's TAC CP at the Euphrates River.

CORPORAL John Friend had been out in the open in his fighting hole all night. He had spent the most miserable night of his life lying in a foot of near-frozen muddy water. He was soaked to the bone and shivering cold. He had thanked God when the downpour subsided and the sun started to rise. After sunrise, Friend and the other Marines in his squad were sent back to the bridge to dry out and warm up. Soon they found themselves under the protective cover of the concrete girders of the bridge, on the southern bank of the Euphrates River.

They were drying their gear out and cleaning their weapons when a reporter came out of one of the seven-ton trucks. He set his satellite telephone on a folding table and announced to the Marines that they could take two minutes each and call home. A line formed quickly, and Corporal Friend ended up near the front. As he waited his turn, he decided that he would call home and talk to his mother since it was her birthday.

---

3 Ibid. Mortenson.

It wasn't long before Friend got his turn. He called home and wished his mother happy birthday. She was thrilled to hear his voice and know that he was safe. She couldn't have received a better birthday present.

After spending the previous night lying in a muddy hole, Friend was delighted to be talking to his parents. For two minutes, he was transported back to his home in New Jersey and away from the hellhole known to the Marines as "the Naz."

Right in the middle of the conversation, mortar rounds started to explode in the background and shots rang out from the hospital.

Friend's mother asked, "What was that?"[4]

"Nothing," Friend calmly answered. He did not want her to know that they were getting shot at—again. Friend quickly changed the subject. "I'm alright. I really can't tell you where I am."

She said, "I know where you are. There is a reporter with you. It's Kerry Sanders."

Friend had no idea. He turned to the man sitting next to him and asked, "You're Kerry Sanders?"

"Yeah" Kerry replied.

"Hey, Mom, I'm sitting right next to him."

Friend's mother said, "Tell him I said hi and thank him for reporting." The short two minutes were over in a flash. Friend said good-bye, hung up the phone, handed it to the next Marine in line, and went back to his squad to collect his things. Just as fast as Kerry Sanders had appeared and given him the chance to phone home, a sergeant appeared and said, "Okay, lets go. We're going back into the hospital."

※

FOR the second day in a row, Fox Company assaulted the hospital. This time the Marines knew there were no American POWs being held there, so they opened their attack with an artillery barrage. Starnes' gunners pounded the complex with concrete-piercing rounds for several minutes. When the artillery was lifted, Fox Company kicked off. They charged through the same hole in the chain-link fence that they had used the day before.

On this day, there was no enemy fire. The artillery had killed, or scared off, any snipers who had reoccupied the complex. Nolan's sniper team

---

4 Ibid. Friend.

followed the infantry into the compound on the heels of the assault and returned to their rooftop positions. Nolan was getting lazy. He wasn't being as careful as he could have been. Had he been working as he had been trained, all of the team would have moved into position without ever being detected. They say that familiarity breeds contempt. After several days of working with the team against enemy fighters that weren't very good shots, Nolan wasn't moving as fast, or crouching as low, as he could have been. As he approached his position near the edge of the roof, an enemy round took a big chunk of concrete out of a pillar that was two feet from his head. The crumbling concrete was immediately followed by a muffled report. Below his position, Dremann's infantry let lose a SMAW rocket and obliterated the small building from which the shot emanated. Nolan dove for cover, and, for the rest of the war, he was never complacent again. He remained ever vigilant.

This time, America's Battalion was here to stay at the Tykar Hospital. They moved to the east side of the compound and started digging in, while Nolan and his team started settling into their rooftop observation positions. Once the hospital was secure, the entire battalion moved to extend its lines to the east. Fox Company continued to cover the bridge and the southern bank of the river, east of the bridge. They also were responsible for the hospital itself and a security zone to the east of the buildings. Golf Company moved east, just south of the hospital and linked up with Fox Company, on its left. Echo Company moved down Highway 7, in back of Golf Company, and filled in the line, south to Highway 8.

THE BETIO BASTARDS

Dunahoe tried to be systematic and logical as he planned his attack on the city. He could have easily turned the southern portion of Nasiriyah to rubble, but this situation required a more subtle approach. He was leading a Marine infantry battalion into a major suburban battle for the first time since Vietnam. The Marine Corps had worked hard over the years preparing for military operations in urban terrain (MOUT).

Iraqi cities were a MOUT nightmare. Most buildings were made out of mud bricks with sand-based mortar. They did not provide shelter from small arms fire. Larger-caliber machine guns would send bullets screaming through wall after wall. Unless it was a government building, there were no glass windows. Iraqi homes had window-style openings to allow light to enter and to catch the breeze, but everyday Nasiriyans could not afford glass panes. City blocks were laid out haphazardly. There appeared to be neither rhyme nor reason to the layout of the city. There were frequent dead ends, out-of-place buildings, and a spiders web of power and telephone lines crisscrossing city streets.

Civilians, especially children, were a constant hazard. They seemed to have no sense of the danger they were in. They would come out of their homes to curiously watch the fighting, with no regard for the Marines' attempts to set up perimeters. They would intrude on Marine positions and intermingle with the riflemen and artillery, as if they weren't even there. Children would run up on Marine patrols. And drivers would regularly disregard roadblocks.

It was almost as if the Marines were invisible. More likely, the people of Nasiriyah believed that Americans had a deep respect for human life and that they would not fire on civilians. The enemy used this to their advantage. At every opportunity, they would feign noncombatant status or hide behind women and children. The enemy quickly discarded their uniforms and put on civilian clothes, but military boots were a giveaway. The smart ones soon switched to flip-flops. They used local businesses, mosques, hospitals, and schools as battle positions and weapons caches.

Iraqi dogs were, at times, more threatening than the enemy. Most roamed wild through the suburban sprawl of south Nasiriyah and were quite aggressive. They would bark incessantly if Marines approached, thus ruining any chance of surprise. Some would even attack the Marines.

Dunahoe knew that he had to take his MOUT training one step further. He devised a plan to first defend his men. He had already dug them in the best he could in the tree line, west of Highway 7. He sent his sniper teams forward to watch and learn. Little to no intelligence had reached Dunahoe down at the battalion level, so he set out to gather his own information about the area and the enemy he was facing. From the moment they arrived at the Euphrates River, Lieutenant D had his human exploitation team out and about interviewing civilians and EPWs. The team had been very successful the night before. Now, Colonel Dunahoe was quickly going to act on the information that Sergeant H had gathered about the Ba'ath buildings and headquarters, less than a kilometer beyond his lines.

Dunahoe ordered Healy to move his company west to investigate the military complex that Yeo had probed the day before. He ordered Captain Thomas to move out at the same time. Thomas was ordered to take a combat patrol to the Ba'ath Party leader's house and then on to the Ba'ath Party headquarters on Highway 8. Dunahoe held India Company in reserve, near his command post.

KILO COMPANY

Kilo Company started clearing to the west. Captain Healy pushed across the small canal that he had used for a defensive line the night before. Kilo Company Marines found a suburban area with more vegetation than they had seen since they left North Carolina. The neighborhood was sprinkled with small clusters of buildings and open fields. Once they crossed the canal, they came upon a densely populated north-south road. The road was cluttered with mud-brick buildings and walled compounds set back from the road. Healy's Marines methodically cleared each building. They moved down the street in a deliberate military formation, with large distances separating the Marines as they walked in two columns, one on each side of the road. The lead elements would pause and provide cover at each new building. Then, an assault team would bound forward, as all the Marines in the columns took a knee or moved to nearby cover.

The walled homes had locked metal gates opening onto interior courtyards. Some of the homes were well kept, and it was obvious that they were owned by wealthy Iraqis. If the Marines came across large, modern-looking houses, with satellite dishes or a new car in the courtyard, they could almost be certain that the inhabitants were of Saddam's privileged class or they were Ba'ath Party officials. Everyday Nasiriyans were poor and downtrodden. They were barely able to survive on the minimal sustenance the government provided, let alone able to afford modern-day luxuries, like a satellite dish or new car.

The Marines didn't bother with the locked gates. They sent Marines over the walls to search each house. Most of the time they found the occupants huddled in interior rooms, trying to let the war pass them by. All of the inhabitants were brought out and interrogated by members of Dunahoe's human exploitation team.

LIMA COMPANY

Captain Thomas led his ninety-nine man combat patrol out, just south of Captain Healy. Thomas had a specific mission. He had houses marked on his map that he had been ordered to search, and to detain their occupants. His ultimate objective for the day was to capture the Ba'ath Party headquarters on Highway 8. Thomas went out with elements of Lima Company's 1st and 2d Platoon, Lieutenant Forman, and his fire support team, a sniper team, and some machine gun teams. They came under sporadic fire within five minutes of stepping off. One or two Iraqis let loose a burst of AK-47 fire and then ran away. Thomas's patrol kept a watchful eye on all of the buildings in the area, but they headed straight for the Ba'ath Party leader's home.

The house was surrounded by a fifteen-foot wall topped with razor wire. Only the large terra-cotta roof could be seen from the street. Thomas' men quickly moved to surround the compound, which covered several acres. Once in place, they put together a plan to assault the suburban fortress.

Thomas moved an assault team to the back side of the compound and set charges along the wall. The Marines moved a safe distance away, and then the charges were detonated, crumbling a large portion of the wall to the ground. A cow was grazing inside the compound, only feet from the explosion. The wall came crashing down on the cow, killing it instantly. The Marines rushed through the breach, over the rubble and the cow's carcass.

When they entered the compound, they stopped dead in their tracks. They had entered a veritable paradise. The grounds contained an elaborate garden and zoo. Cages were arranged throughout the grounds, which contained lions, tigers, monkeys, exotic birds, chickens, and water buffalo. It was as if the owner were trying to re-create the Hanging Gardens of Babylon.

After their initial pause, the Marines returned to the business at hand. They fanned out and surrounded the house. The house itself was also something to behold. It could have easily been placed in a ritzy neighborhood in Southern California's Hollywood Hills. There were fountains leading up to the house and a luxurious swimming pool. The Marines charged the house and moved through, clearing room to room.

They swept through the house and seized more key intelligence. They also captured two uniformed Iraqis who were carrying AK-47s. Sergeant H talked with these men, and they immediately confirmed that their headquarters was just down the road.

Lima Company's Marines continued southwest toward Route 8. Soon, they came upon a four-way intersection, where they started taking fire from the north, west, and south. Lieutenant Forman broke into a three-story building on the northeast corner of the intersection with his snipers and fire support team. They cleared the building and quickly moved to the roof to provide covering fire for the Marines on the ground. Forman directed the snipers to cover the north. They detected two Iraqis shooting at the Marines. The snipers fired two quick shots, and the shooting in the north stopped.

Forman called for the battalion 81s to drop a barrage on the ten or so Iraqis who were coming at the Marines from the west. The first mortar round came whistling in and landed short, but it scared the Iraqis in the west. They scattered, and Healy's infantrymen focused their fire on the handful of enemy fighters in the south. The Iraqis were firing haphazardly; they were certainly no match for the Marines.

Forman, still perched atop the building at the intersection, could see vehicles pulling up to the Ba'ath Party headquarters, only five hundred meters south of his position. It appeared to be a hotbed of activity. After the short gunfight and the 81mm mortar barrage, the Iraqis in the building had to know that the Marines were headed toward them. Thomas continued to push south, down the dirt road. When he reached Route 8, he set his machine gun teams into blocking positions along the road.

Next, Thomas called an assault team forward. They launched two thermobaric rounds at the headquarters, using their SMAW rocket launchers. The first rocket screamed across the road and impacted on the front door. The large metal door was blown completely off its hinges. The second rocket flew through the open door and blew out every door and window in the building.

Then Thomas's men charged the building. The Marines quickly moved into the main headquarters building. Not surprisingly, the building was empty. The enemy had taken refuge in a small adjacent planning building. When the Marines moved on the smaller building, the enemy fled south into the city's train station.

Thomas and his men cleared the buildings and started their search. The smaller building had a large terrain model of the city. The model itself provided a treasure trove of information. It marked the location of defensive positions, army units, weapons and ammunition stockpiles, and other command centers. When they searched the larger building, they found a small room that had to have been a torture chamber. It was a little room with a single cot and an arc welder. The building was also full of Iraqi classified material, blackboards filled with data, and sensitive correspondence. There was actually too much information for his small team to digest, so Lieutenant D called for help from the regiment and the MEB.

One thing that Lieutenant D found that could help his battalion commander was an operations board that indicated the location of every Ba'ath Party facility in An Nasiriyah. He also found American weapons and equipment. Local civilians who were eager to thank the Americans for ridding their neighborhood of this scourge quickly gathered. They eagerly told the Marines stories of American soldiers being brought into the facility, held there for some time, and then whisked away to the west on Highway 8. The building was only a kilometer from the ambush site, so this is where the prisoners were brought and probably filmed before they were moved off to Baghdad.

Most locals were happy to see the end of this horrid place. But the enemy did not relinquish its headquarters easily. They continued to probe the Marines defenses at the headquarters. Engagements were short, yet violent. The Iraqi gunners were sloppy. They would sneak up in twos and threes and open up with an AK-47 burst or an RPG, and then the Marines would respond with everything they had. The firefights were short-lived and completely one-sided. Once the Marines opened up, any Iraqis left alive would flee. This wasn't always the case with the Fedayeen. They were undisciplined thugs, ruffians, and bullies, they were fanatically stupid. It took them a few days to realize that they were overmatched.

Throughout the day, three or four taxicabs raced up Highway 8, filled with Fedayeen fighters. Each of the attacks ended with the same result. Thomas's machine gunners would fire at the vehicle, killing everyone inside. Once the operation had been completed, Thomas left 1st Platoon at the compound and returned to the battalion command post to report to Colonel Dunahoe. Next, he picked up the rest of Lima Company and headed back toward Highway 8, filling in his defensive line as he moved southwest. As the afternoon wore on, Thomas started getting reports that the enemy was massing at the railroad station for a huge counterattack. Thomas's men were within walking distance of the rail station, holding the Ba'ath Party headquarters, so he ordered his Marines to prepare for a fight.

KILO COMPANY

As Lima Company was fighting along Highway 8, Captain Healy continued to move west along the southern bank of the Euphrates River. Iraqi fighters continued to fire on them from their bunkered positions along the northern bank of the river. Healy called for repeated artillery barrages and Cobra helicopters to silence the fire coming from across the river.

The Cobra pilots flew in close, to support Healy. This was no-nonsense CAS. They were absolutely fearless, almost to the point of it being dangerous. They would practically land on the rooftops. The Cobras would hover overhead, just slugging it out with the Iraqis on the north side of the river. Bullets were hitting the aircraft, but the Cobra pilots remained at station, unleashing everything they carried on the enemy below. The Iraqis were scared to death of the Cobras. It got to the point where they wouldn't come out when the Cobras were anywhere nearby.

South of the river, Lima Company had an urban fight on its hands. Small groups of Iraqi fighters were roaming the streets with weapons under their *dishdas*. They would fire a burst of rounds or let lose an RPG and run away. Sometimes, if the wind was right, the Marines could see the "hard edges" of the weapons under the fabric and would be able to shoot first.

The enemy was sneaky. They would plan their ambushes at night and fight during the day. They used local coordination from two or three individuals who lived on the same block. They would set a time and place to meet, and then head for the rendezvous unarmed. The small group would pick up their weapons from one of hundreds of caches located throughout the city. They would move a short distance to the predetermined ambush sight. Then they would fire on whatever enemy target they could find in the area and then quickly melt away, back into the city.

The enemy attacked during the call for prayer, when the streets were filled with civilians. They would hit quickly, and then retreat before the prayer time. During prayer time, the enemy would congregate and plan their next attacks.

Healy and his Marines countered with a deliberate movement west. Once they came across resistance, they would quickly move to isolate the enemy. Then they would use precision targeting to take them out. They called in artillery or air strikes on the enemy's command and control centers, or they used sharpshooters to kill Iraqis carrying weapons in the distance.

This technique was particularly demoralizing to the enemy. They

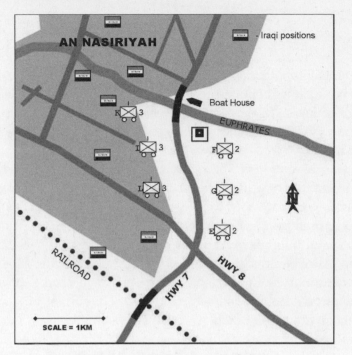

RCT-2 Expands Its Area of Influence

couldn't even get close to the Marines. They would be blocks away from the front lines when their comrade's head would explode. Quickly, the surviving enemy fighters decided to leave the city and certain death behind. But, the Saddam Fedayeen were fanatic. They had nothing to live for if Saddam were to be deposed, so most fought to the death.

They would commandeer another taxicab, pile into the vehicle, and race straight into the Marines' lines. While seemingly heroic, this tactic was exceedingly ineffective. Every Marine in sight of the rampaging vehicle would open fire before the taxi got anywhere near the Marines, and the vehicle would be peppered with well-placed gunfire. All day, there were intermittent outbreaks of extreme violence, then a return to quiet.

RAMSTEIN, GERMANY

Corporal Nick Elliot awoke with a respirator tube down his throat. He had all he could do to keep from gagging. He had been out cold for the last three days and remembered nothing since the doctors were huddled over him in the tent in Kuwait. There were no whirling helicopter blades, no .50-caliber machine gun reports, and no smell of fuel and cordite. It was as if Elliot had been magically transported back to the real world. He was in a hospital bed with clean sheets, in what appeared to be a military hospital. He could hear the wheezing respirator and the regular beep of a patient monitor next to his bed.

As soon as they noticed that Elliot had regained consciousness, a nurse was called over to remove the respirator tube. It seemed to take forever, but once the tube was removed, Elliot was much more comfortable. One of the nurses who had been caring for Elliot came to his bedside and told him that he was lucky to be alive. Apparently, the smoke damage to his lungs was much worse than anyone in the field had imagined. But now it looked like his lungs would fully recover. His leg was a different story. Skin and muscle grafts and many months of healing lay ahead for the young Marine. Thousands of questions raced through Elliot's head. What had happened to his friends? He could wait to find out. All that was important now was that he was alive and he was very tired. Elliot drifted back into a restful sleep.

REGIMENTAL COMBAT TEAM-2

Ever since Natonski had first spoken with Captain King, all of the Marines in Task Force Tarawa had the rescue of the remaining soldiers of the 507th on their mind. Many Marines' nerves were struck when Iraqis started coming to them at the Euphrates River bridge to tell them that two American women were being held captive. Rumors were flying everywhere. The women had been raped. They had been tortured. The young Marines voiced their worst fears about the fate of the two soldiers. The fears were passed from group to group throughout the brigade.

Finding the clothing in Tykar Hospital was a fact, but it only served to fuel more rumors. One thing is certain, most of the Marines were furious that American servicewomen had been put into a position where they could end up as POWs. They all feared that nothing good was happening to their sisters in arms.

More bloody clothing, boots, and a flak vest were found in a small house that was halfway between the road and Tykar Hospital. They had "Lynch" written in them in black ink and were found stuffed between the house and a courtyard wall. This discovery only led to more wild speculation but did not provide any actionable intelligence. The HET team brought the clothes to a member of the regimental intelligence shop, Staff Sergeant Joseph Muccia III. Muccia took the clothes, carefully placed them in a plastic bag, and stored them in a safe place. For some strange reason, those pieces of cloth bound him to the lost female soldier. He was now even more committed to finding her alive.

From the size of the clothes, she must have been small, five-foot-five or six. A doctor captured at Tykar Hospital said she was blonde with blue-green eyes, and she was badly hurt. Muccia's best guess was that Private First Class Jessica Lynch had probably been moved to the main hospital in the center of town.

THE TIMBERWOLVES

Alpha Company and Major Peeples' 3d Platoon was now blocking the western canal bridge. Brooks's Marines processed one hundred fifty civilians who had walked across the bridge, on March 26th. Most told the Marines that they were told by roaming bands of Fedayeen to leave the city. They were told to go north and not to stop at the Marine checkpoints. Some were told that they would be watched, and if they stopped at a Marine checkpoint, their families would be killed. With all of the foot and vehicle traffic, Captain Brooks was contemplating blowing up the bridge.

Locals begged him to leave the bridge intact. He did, but he ordered Staff Sergeant Kamper to block the bridge. Kamper used his mine plow as a bulldozer blade and pushed several abandoned cars onto the bridge, completely blocking it to vehicle traffic. Behind the blockade, Alpha Company set up a zigzag obstacle system on the road.

A group from Task Force Tarawa's staff braved the journey through Ambush Alley to visit the Timberwolves. On their way through the city, they stopped at the destroyed hulk of C208 and looked inside. Iraqis, who were in the area, told them that they had buried bodies in shallow graves in the median. The staff officers reported back to the MEB that they found what could be the remains of Marines. There was still enemy fire in the area, and that the remains could not yet be safely recovered. They climbed back into their vehicles and continued north to Grabowski's headquarters. About the same time, Grabowski got bad news from the regiment. He was told that, after an extensive search, none of the Timberwolves' missing Marines were in the rear.

1ST BATTALION, 10TH MARINES

March 26th turned out to be the busiest day for Starnes' artillerymen. UAVs swarmed over suspected enemy positions, relaying real-time pictures of enemy emplacements north and south of the city. The 1/10 gunners fired more than fifteen missions that afternoon, destroying five enemy artillery batteries in and around An Nasiriyah.

Starnes' Counter Battery Radar (CBR) continued to detect fire coming from the railroad station, south of the city. Based on the number of CBR hits, the area seemed to be an enemy stronghold. This was just one more indication that something was brewing at the railroad station. Army Special Forces and Marine HUMINT[5] were estimating that there were at least one thousand enemy combatants massing for a counterattack in the rail yard. Bailey's 2d Radio Battalion had been monitoring the enemy's radio frequencies. They reported that they believed the force to be two thousand strong.

Regardless of the number, several intelligence sources had agreed. Something was happening at the railroad station. The artillerymen quickly began planning an artillery group to drop in the enemy's lap.

The sandstorm had turned the sky yellow, and there was an adobe-colored hue to everything. It was as if the colors of blue and green had never existed. The desert was consuming everything.

NBC NEWS

Once Tykar Hospital was secured, Kerry took his crew into the compound. His Marine escorts walked him through the complex. He saw Chemical Ali's destroyed offices. He saw a cell block attached to the hospital that contained a small room with a bare metal skeleton of a cot. Blood was spattered on the walls, and there were a set of jumper cables and several car batteries on the floor next to the bed. Then Kerry saw the rooms filled with weapons, ammunition, and all of the paraphernalia of a chemical weapons company—protective clothing, gas masks, and atropine injectors. Kerry walked around

---

5 Human Intelligence.

the grounds and saw the destroyed tank and a rifle range in the courtyard. He toured the fortified positions on the roof.

Nasiriyah had long been the home of Chemical Ali, and it was well known that the 11th Infantry Division had chemical warfare capabilities. While this find was shocking and made for great video, no one was surprised to find this equipment in Nasiriyah's military hospital. The Marines and newsmen, however, were all shocked to find bloody American uniforms and what looked like a room that was used as a torture chamber.

This was the first he had heard of Jessica Lynch. Kerry was thinking, as a reporter, that this would be a great story. It had all the elements of a story with staying power. A pretty, young American female soldier had been captured behind enemy lines. It was likely that she had been tortured and raped. Most of her comrades were dead, missing, or captured. From the looks of her uniform and statements from Iraqis, she was severely injured and helpless. Her family in the back hills of West Virginia was already on the nightly news, grieving and yearning for a miracle.

Best of all, there were no other reporters around. Kerry Sanders appeared to have a big story to himself. But Marine officers whom he had come to know and trust asked him not to report on Lynch, fearing that it could cost her her life. So Kerry waited, sitting on possibly the biggest story of his career. Even with the Lynch story on hold, Kerry had plenty of news to report. He filed a story from the hospital, reporting on the weapons, explosives, chemical protection suits, and torture chamber at the hospital.

Colonel Mortenson even took a few moments to speak with Kerry on camera. Mortenson told Sanders in his colorful fashion, "There is a new sheriff in town . . . and it's America's Battalion."[6] Once Kerry finished his report, he returned to his cozy spot underneath the Euphrates River bridge.

TASK FORCE TARAWA

While Mortenson and Dunahoe were expanding their areas of control, Task Force Tarawa took the opportunity to move its headquarters from Queensland, near Jalibah, up to the southern side of An Nasiriyah. They pulled in south of Colonel Bailey's command post and began setting up the brigade

---

6 NBC News footage.

headquarters' tents and communications equipment. Cobras were making runs and Glenn Starnes' big guns were firing missions as Task Force Tarawa pounded their tents in. The MEB headquarters was up and running by late in the day.

THE TIMBERWOLVES

Around 1800, another convoy rolled north through Ambush Alley to resupply the Timberwolves. Third Platoon of Grunwald's Charlie LAR Company escorted all of Grabowski's remaining ALOC and supply trains north to the abandoned Iraqi 23rd Brigade headquarters, which Grabowski had turned into his own command post. Grunwald's LAVs immediately turned around and returned to the southern bank of the Euphrates River around 1930. Shortly after 3d Platoon's return, Grunwald's entire company was ordered back south of the Euphrates River to reinforce Mortenson's and Dunahoe's infantry in case the expected enemy counterattack materialized.

After four days of almost continuous fighting, reports of a massive enemy attack were taken very seriously. Marines throughout Task Force Tarawa were preparing for a big fight. As the word filtered down to the grunts in their fighting holes, the enemy force became two thousand strong. By the time the rumors reached Major Peeples' tankers, there were one thousand Iraqi armored vehicles massing for an attack. As the day drew to a close, everyone's nerves were on edge.

AMERICA'S BATTALION

Staff Sergeant St. John moved through the battalion's front lines, making sure his Marines were dug in and ready for whatever the night might bring. He made sure that each company knew where their neighboring company's positions were located, and he spent time with each group of Marines, calming them and building their confidence.

Ever since Mortenson's men pulled into southern Nasiriyah on March 23rd, they had taken responsibility for the intersection of highways 7 and 8. 2/8's CAAT had been hit at the intersection every day. The attacks were short-lived and usually consisted of several machine gun bursts from an industrial complex to the southwest. On this day they were hit again. At nearly the same time, another intel report came in, a SIGINT[7] hit indicating that the counterattack was massing at the train station.

. Just after sunset, an Iraqi heavy machine gun opened fire on the intersection. Then several small groups of Iraqis started spraying AK-47 rounds toward the Marines. It was a squad-size, reinforced unit with AK-47s, RPGs, and knee mortars. They attacked 2/8's main command post at the gas station. The Iraqis started lobbing RPGs and small mortar rounds into the compound, hoping to hit something—anything. The main command post was really never in danger of being overrun, but it was too soon to know that for sure.

Mortenson's CAAT section returned 'fire. So did the LAR Platoon, which had been called south to repel the large counterattack. They sprayed 25mm Bushmaster shells in the direction of the enemy. Unfortunately, their rounds also went wide to the left of the enemy position and ripped into Major Alford's ALOC at the gas station. Several trucks and HMMWVs were hit. Two seven-ton trucks were completely destroyed. One of them was loaded with ammo, and it blew sky high. Major Alford immediately called for artillery—Danger Close. The barrage broke the enemy attack but spilled over on top of the LAR unit. Fortunately, the LAR Marines raced away from the barrage before anyone was hurt.

REGIMENTAL COMBAT TEAM-2

More Iraqis had sallied out of the rail yard and moved farther south. Staff Sergeant Joe Muccia first heard two ricochets, then a third. Most everyone in the COC ran to man the perimeter. By the time Muccia had reached his spot in the line, the regimental headquarters was receiving heavy enemy machine gunfire from the north. With the turns in Highway 7, the railroad station was almost due north of Muccia.

The Marines returned fire. Then, Bailey's staff started taking enemy fire from the southwest. This had to be the anticipated enemy counterattack, but there were no where near a thousand enemy fighters. A few mortar rounds landed nearby, and a single RPG whizzed through the night sky. At 2045, RCT-2 reported to the MEB that they were under attack. They were taking

---

7 Signal Intelligence.

small arms, machine gun, and mortar fire. Marines all along the northern and western perimeter suppressed the enemy within ten minutes. Again, the battle was short but very intense.

No sooner had the first mortar round hit, than 25mm Bushmaster rounds started spilling down the road from the northeast. The large-caliber rounds looked like white glowing Coke cans flying through the air. A Marine aviation support unit, MWSS[8]-373, was parked on the road waiting to travel north with the next convoy through Ambush Alley. The large-caliber rounds started hitting the MWSS-373 trucks. Muccia ran back into the COC and announced, "We're taking friendly fire. There's twenty-five Mike Mike coming down the roadway."[9]

1ST BATTALION, 10TH MARINES

Bravo Battery started taking machine gun fire, too. Every available Marine grabbed his rifle and helmet and ran to man the perimeter. Until now, the artillerymen had been far removed from the battle on the ground. For several days, they had had to deal with Iraqi civilians roaming into their security zone and the occasional surrendering Iraqi soldier. But now they were under direct enemy fire.

One of Starnes' captains reported, "I'm seeing green tracers."[10] Every major concentration of Marines up and down Highway 7 was being attacked by small groups of Iraqis. Approximately one hundred Iraqis were attacking 2/8, RCT-2 HQ, and the artillerymen.

During the firefight, a communications officer, fearing the worst, came into Colonel Starnes' command tent and pulled several electronic boxes from a safe. The gadgets held the cryptographic codes for the regiment's secure radio nets. He gathered up all the sensitive papers in the COC, and he grabbed an empty ammo box and a book of matches. The young officer turned to Colonel Starnes, "On your command, sir,"[11] he sternly reported

---

8 Marine wing support squadron.

9 Telephone interview with Staff Sergeant Joe Muccia, 8/6/04.

10 Michael Wilson "Troops meet resistance in An Nasiriyah" (*New York Times*, no date available).

11 Ibid. Wilson.

to Colonel Starnes. Starnes nodded his head in acknowledgment. Fortunately, he never had to give the order to burn their classified materials.

THE BETIO BASTARDS

Colonel Dunahoe had turned over command of the battalion to Major Starling so that he could go get some rest. Starling was in the main command post when a report came in of enemy massing at the train station, and then there was a report of the attack. It started at the 7/8 interchange. Starling immediately got on the battalion net and ordered everyone to "get off the road. Whatever you do, stay off the road."[12] He sensed that the battle was turning into an intramural fight. In the middle of the chaos, one of 3/2's young lieutenants radioed Starling, "I'm down here taking fire."[13] Starling told Lieutenant Woods, "Hold what you got. Get your ass in a hole."

Starling was no stranger to friendly artillery fire. While serving as a platoon leader in 1st Battalion, 1st Marines during Desert Storm, his platoon was fired upon when returning from a patrol in Kuwait. Starling was right. The left-most LAVs had become disoriented on the winding road and had extended their fire too far to the left. They ended up shooting at 2/8's command post at the gas station. Thankfully, Major Alfred had had the presence of mind to berm in. Some of the fire from their long-range weapons ended up streaming down Route 7, hitting the MWSS guys, too.

By the time the battle and friendly-fire incident was over, thirty-one Marines and two Kuwaiti interpreters had been wounded. Four seven-ton trucks and several Humvees had been destroyed. America Battalion's command post and log trains suffered the most damage. Fortunately, none of the Marines were killed. Kerry Sanders had repeatedly been ignoring the Marines' pleas to stay away from his truck. He had work to do, and all his equipment was in the back of the truck. It was also a much more comfortable spot to sleep. Had Kerry been working or sleeping in his seven-ton truck that night at the gas station, he probably would have been killed. But instead, Kerry Sanders and his news crew were safely tucked under the Euphrates River bridge.

---

12 Personal interview with Major Christopher Starling, 6/14/04.

13 Ibid. Starling.

1ST BATTALION, 10TH MARINES

The battalion fired one hundred thirty-two rounds of DPICM into the railroad station at 2330. There were varying reports of the number of casualties. One thing is certain, any Iraqis who had been unfortunate enough to still be near the rail yard were either killed or scared off by the massive barrage. After nearly four days of fighting, the "King of Battle" had broken the back of the enemy forces defending Nasiriyah.

THE BETIO BASTARDS

Captain Thomas had a ringside seat for 1/10's barrage, sitting atop the Ba'ath Party headquarters building. The massive barrage was a real show. He could hear the big howitzer reports far to the south, followed by the air burst over the enemy. Each canister would shatter, and a hundred bomblets would rain down on the enemy positions. Thousands and thousands of bomblets rained down on the rail station and the surrounding area. It was an awesome display of a precision Marine artillery barrage.

Once the barrage was complete, captains Day and Qualkinbush wanted to assess the damage caused by the attack. They started looking for some aircraft to fly over the rail station and take a quick look to make sure that the Iraqis had either been killed or that they dispersed. Qualkinbush found two A-10s, and he asked them to come low and make a run over the railroad station. They refused to come below 10,000 feet because they were getting spikes on their radar. The "spikes" were a possible indication of enemy anti-aircraft guns set up in the area.

They were very nervous. "Well, you know we are getting spikes,"[14] they told Day and Qualkinbush. Day responded, slightly irritated, "Listen, man, there are no missiles around here."

The Warthog pilots were still not convinced. "Well, we're not . . ."

Day interrupted them and answered sarcastically, "Okay, thanks for the help, just keep going." No sooner than he had dismissed the A-10s, when two Marine Hornets checked on station.

---

14 Conversation with pilots taken from telephone interview with Major John Day, 5/25/04.

"We need you to check out this train station over here," Qualkinbush explained. "I need you to break five thousand feet. Do you think you could do that?"

The Marine pilot answered with no hesitation, "No problem."

"Can you give me an idea of how low you can come?" Qualkinbush asked.

"How does eight hundred sound?"

"There is nothing that high around here. You won't clip anything." Duck responded.

"Roger that. We're in from the west." Within seconds, two Hornets came screaming overhead with a bone-jarring roar. They darted over the train station and climbed back to a safe altitude. They reported seeing no activity. Qualkinbush and Day thanked them for the flyby, and the Hornets flew off into the night to find another mission.

CHAPTER 14

Phase IV

Some people spend an entire lifetime wondering if they made a difference. The Marines don't have that problem.

—RONALD REAGAN

THE BETIO BASTARDS

By March 27th, the battle for southern An Nasiriyah was shifting from full combat to a stability-and-security effort. Most of the resistance in the city had been crushed, but bands of Saddam Fedayeen still roamed the streets, and people still loyal to Saddam were hiding throughout the city. Colonel Dunahoe sent Lima Company out on a huge cordon and search of the neighborhood to their west. Lima Company went house to house; taking out the enemy's meeting places and caches. The Betio Bastards were starting to win the battle. The enemy had no place to hide.

Captain Thomas's men spent sixteen hours sealing off the neighborhood, collecting weapons, interrogating people, and searching houses and buildings. The entire company spent all day on patrol. They were carrying their weapons at the ready the entire time, not knowing if the next room they entered would have a waiting zealot who wanted to kill a Marine before he went before Allah.

Throughout the day, Lima Company's Marines would come across pockets of Fedayeen militiamen, hiding throughout the city. The small groups would launch their now-common, uncoordinated attacks with small arms and RPGs. The firefights would be short but violent, and always with the same result—more dead Iraqi fighters. In one of the larger skirmishes, the Marines killed the Ba'ath Party leader who was largely responsible for the Iraqi defenses in 3/2's sector. Once their military leader had been killed, the survivors drifted away, and the resistance disintegrated on that side of town.

During the operation, Thomas's men came across weapons and ammunition caches in buildings that had been identified by the HET team as important targets. A search of one of these buildings resulted in the capture of an Al-Quds general. The Marines' determination set the tone for the neighborhood. The residents quickly learned that Thomas's men were in control and that they were not there to hurt civilians.

KILO COMPANY

Captain Healy pushed forward with Kilo Company and a handful of Day's CAAT vehicles. They went out along the levee road and moved into a riverfront apartment complex. As they moved west, Kilo Company Marines ran into a half dozen military-age men who were just strolling down the road. Healy's men quickly rounded them up and held them for questioning.

Healy wanted to get a look at the military complex that Captain Yeo had seen a few days earlier. They spent most of the morning clearing the apartment complex. Then they took up positions on the southern buildings to get a look at the military facility that was a couple hundred meters south of their position. The complex was huge. It was easily a kilometer on each side, and there were a dozen large buildings inside its perimeter. A large fortress was close to the northern end of the grounds. It was a square building, with parapets at each corner.

While Healy's men worked their way through the apartment complex, Day's CAAT vehicles pulled off to the right side of the levee road and were scanning the buildings on the northern bank. Dunahoe's men had been receiving fire from the buildings for days, and CAAT was there to watch Healy's back. It was fortunate that they were there. An Iraqi armored vehicle, a Soviet-made BTR-60[1], showed up on the northern bank of the river. One of the CAAT Marines quickly launched a Javelin missile at the lone armored car.

---

1 Soviet-built armored car.

The Javelin dipped and then accelerated up into the sky. Then it came screaming down on the Iraqis. It was a direct hit and another kill for the CAAT team.

Once the apartment complex was secure and Healy had taken a good
long look at the military compound, he left some of his Marines at the apartment complex and returned to Colonel Dunahoe to report his findings.

TASK FORCE TRITON

A tragedy was beginning to unfold at the far-western bridge. The 1st Marine
Division's assistant operations officer, Lieutenant Colonel Lathin, had arrived
at the Highway 1 bridge during the morning of March 27th. He was searching for a tank that had been missing since the night of March 24–25. Lathin
confirmed that the names stenciled on the seabags that had washed up on the
bank of the river were, in fact, the names of the missing crewmen. Lathin sent
a recon Marine and recon corpsman out into the river. They swam to the bottom and found the tank in its watery grave. Lathin radioed in his report and
requested that Navy divers and a salvage team be sent to the Highway 1
bridge. U.S. Navy SeaBee[2] divers arrived the next morning and began recovery operations on the sunken M1 tank. Pulling a sunken seventy-ton tank
from the bottom of a river is not an easy task. The SeaBees worked for two
days to retrieve the lost vehicle. Once they managed to pull the tank out of the
water, Private First Class Francisco Martinez Flores, Staff Sergeant Donald
May, and Lance Corporal Patrick O'Day were found inside the flooded tank.
The bodies were carefully removed with the same respect accorded any fallen
Marine. Then they were loaded on a helicopter for their last journey home.

Task Force Triton, the ever-changing security force at the far-western
bridge, became Task Force Rex, with the addition of Colonel Starnes' entire
Battery B as provisional infantry. Now manned with nearly three hundred
artillerymen, the 1st Battalion, 10th Marine Regiment's executive officer
changed the name to Task Force Rex, after "the King of Battle"—artillery.
As soon as they were relieved, Colonel Bailey's Company A, 2d Recon Battalion moved north across the bridge to conduct a reconnaissance north in
preparation for RCT-2's advance.

---

2 U.S. Navy construction battalion.

TASK FORCE TARAWA

With the resistance nearly crushed, Natonski wanted to pinpoint and attack the remaining enemy strongholds. The primary job was clearing the pockets of enemy resistance and destroying any remaining command and control centers. Next, the city needed to be isolated so that the Iraqis could not reinforce and further prolong the struggle.

MEB Commanders sent SEAL Team 6 to Suq Ash Shuyukh, which was a small town, approximately fifteen kilometers downriver from An Nasiriyah, along Highway 8. The enemy had been trying to send reinforcements to Nasiriyah from Suq Ash Shuyukh since the battle had begun. With few command and control facilities left in An Nasiriyah, the enemy had shifted its command to Suq Ash Shuyukh, so General Natonski ordered all the roads in Task Force Tarawa's zone to be closed to traffic. He hoped to disrupt the enemy's lines of communication and to isolate An Nasiriyah from attempts to reinforce its beleaguered Iraqi fighters. Task Force Tarawa engineers constructed obstacles on the roads leading out of Suq Ash Shuyukh to block enemy movement into Nasiriyah from the southeast.

For the second night in a row, Qualkinbush called in precision, urban CAS on the enemy's command nodes in An Nasiriyah. He bombed the Ba'ath Party, Al-Quds, and paramilitary forces headquarters, along with 11th ID headquarters' buildings just north of the western Euphrates River bridge, near the Saddam Hospital.

The Marine commanders had set up large monitors in the MEB headquarters, and for the first time, they used high-tech systems on their Harriers to beam back real-time images. Qualkinbush would contact the aircraft, bring them in on a specific target, and then hand them off to Natonski's fires staff. The pilot would lock onto the target and beam back real-time video. General Natonski's staff would positively identify the building, and then clear the pilot hot. They went on a three-day bombing campaign. They dropped four 2,000-pound JDAMs on one building alone. The Marines also used precision artillery barrages on high-value targets in and around the city. They focused on the centers of the regime control within Nasiriyah and Suq Ash Shuyukh.

1ST BATTALION, 10TH MARINES

Colonel Starnes pulled a page from the history book and ordered the establishment of "Firebase Pokorney." The firebase concept was used extensively in Vietnam where the Marines were forced to fight from isolated strong points that were completely surrounded by enemy insurgents. Modern-day Marine doctrine presupposes that artillery battalions would support the infantry from protected positions behind the forward line of troops. The concept of firebases had not been used since Marines carved enclaves out of the jungles of Vietnam. It is designed to protect Marines while they are in hostile territory.

Starnes' artillerymen had already experienced difficulties with civilians roaming through their batteries, so he had taken the first steps toward establishing a firebase by setting security in a 360-degree circle around his guns. With the porous lines in Nasiriyah, and not wanting a repeat of the previous night's chaos, Starnes dug in. He called for engineers to build a berm around his position, and he made plans to man the walls of Firebase Pokorney with Marines from throughout his battalion.

THE TIMBERWOLVES

On March 27th, Grabowski sent out patrols hoping that they would find the rest of his missing Marines. The patrols fanned out on both sides of Highway 7, north of the canal. They combed through the spiderweb of irrigation ditches and smaller canals, hoping to find a body that may have been blown into the water. The patrols turned up nothing. After the search, Grabowski, Sosa, and Tuggle realized that their missing Marines were probably not up north, Grabowski said, "We gotta go back into the city."[3]

He knew of the previous day's report of buried Marines near C208, so he sent a patrol into the city, under heavy security. Guarded by tanks, tracks, and CAAT vehicles, the recovery team searched the area of C208's destruction. As they searched, a large crowd gathered. A few shots rang out, but for the most part the Marines were left to recover their dead.

---

3 Ibid. Grabowski.

The search detail found four or five bodies. It was difficult to really know, because none of the bodies were in one piece. They found arms, legs, and torsos. DNA testing would be required to sort things out. The fallen Marines were loaded into vehicles and driven back north. Soon a Marine helicopter showed up, the bodies were loaded, and they began their long journey home to their loved ones. But there were still Marines missing.

THE BETIO BASTARDS

Captain Healy returned to the battalion command post by early afternoon. He met with Major Canfield and told him what he had seen. Canfield wanted to sit and watch the complex for a while before he moved Marines into the area, so he sent a sniper team into the apartment complex to spend the night.

In addition to the seizure of the military complex just west of their position, Major Canfield was working on a plan for his battalion to sweep through the rest of the southern part of the city. But it was not meant to be. The Betio Bastards' attack on the 11th Infantry Division's chemical company compound would be their last action in An Nasiriyah.

AMERICA'S BATTALION

Mortenson's Marines were some of the first to conduct security and stability operations in An Nasiriyah. Now that the enemy had all but been defeated, civilians were coming out of their houses. The Marines of 2/8 started handing out food and medicine at the 7/8 intersection. They also helped the local people get their utilities turned back on.

Marine work parties were formed at Tykar Hospital. They pulled out food stockpiles, and they loaded the rice, dates, beans, and cooking oil onto one of their Osh-Kosh trucks and drove it out to the crossroads. Word spread quickly, and more people started coming out of their homes. Mortenson's men had come full circle in "the Three-Block War." They had defeated the enemy, established security and stability, and now they were conducting humanitarian operations.

The intersection of highways 7 and 8 started to look like any of the disaster relief efforts the Marines conduct on a regular basis throughout the world. Poor Iraqis waited in lines for food and medicine. Navy corpsmen and doctors held sick call for the people of Nasiriyah. They treated everything from runny noses to gunshot wounds. At the head of another line, a tired Marine filled containers with drinking water flowing from a hose attached to a large tanker truck.

All the while, children laughed and played with the Marines. In an age-old scene, Marines were giving candy to the children. One even sang and danced to entertain the kids. These fierce warriors of America's Battalion, men who had fearlessly charged a heavily fortified compound only days earlier, were now America's ambassadors.

TASK FORCE TARAWA

On March 28th, more convoys moved up Highway 7 for the fifth day in a row. The citizens of An Nasiriyah had become accustomed to the constant stream of Marine Corps vehicles moving north through the city. By now, the trip was quite calm, and the route no longer deserved the title of Ambush Alley. Marine commanders never did like the misnomer. They fought a battle to secure this route; The Marines had never been "ambushed."

General Natonski wanted to visit his old battalion and walk their lines. He knew that it was important for his Marines to see him after what they had been through. He hopped into his Humvee and traveled north on what the Marines had code named Route Moe to get north to the Timberwolves.

THE TIMBERWOLVES

Natonski spent several hours north of the canal with Lieutenant Colonel Grabowski and his Marines. He first visited the 23d Brigade headquarters building. He walked the lines and talked with as many Marines as he could. Next, he drove over to Captain Brooks's Marines at the western bridge. He climbed out of his HMMWV and talked with many more young Marines before he walked south to look at the blockaded bridge. Then he drove back around to the eastern canal bridge to retrace his path south through the city to his headquarters.

After Natonski's visit, a handful of civilian leaders from inside the city came to the bridge and wanted to speak with the commander. Colonel

Grabowski went out to see them. They asked for his permission to cross over the bridge to the water-pumping stations and to go up on the bridge itself to try to get the city's water supply turned back on. The pipe that brought fresh water into the city ran across the Saddam Canal bridge. The water main had been one of the casualties of the battle on March 23d, and it continued to spew potable water from a large hole in the pipe. Grabowski responded, "We will help you fix it, if you just tell me where my boys are."[4]

The Iraqis led Grabowski and Tuggle to a shallow grave, only feet from the shattered remains of C208. Grabowski and Tuggle both dropped to their knees and carefully began to uncover the corpses. Grabowski found two feet. He continued to carefully dig, uncovering the Marines' legs, but that was all he found. Then others unearthed a torso. While the group dug with their bare hands, 1st Sergeant Henao searched inside the charred troop compartment one last time. He found more pieces of incinerated body parts that had been missed the day before. They were barely distinguishable. In all, they found what they knew were the partial remains of four more Marines. One Marine was still missing—Sergeant Brendon Reiss.

Colonel Grabowski had the bits and pieces of his Marines loaded onto a HMMWV, and they were driven back over the bridge. When everyone was back north, they held a short memorial service for their fallen companions along the side of the road. They all bowed their heads in a moment of silence. Colonels, majors, gunnys, and privates all silently asked themselves the same questions: "Why did such good men have to die? Why wasn't it me, instead?" Then the battalion chaplain said a few words of farewell. The small group broke up and the Marines returned to their duties, but each of them left a piece of his heart on that dusty road with their fallen brothers.

THE BETIO BASTARDS

Dunahoe's snipers were watching the military compound. They reported that it appeared as if the Iraqi Army had melted away and that the complex was a ghost town. A number of civilians were looting the facility. They told of a single uniformed Iraqi who stood and helplessly watched the looting. Armed with this information, Dunahoe canceled his planned artillery preparation.

---

4 Ibid. Grabowski.

Instead, he ordered Healy to make plans to go in quickly and quietly the next morning. The entire battalion staff started planning for a two-company attack—Kilo and India, with Kilo in the lead.

INDIA COMPANY

A middle-aged Iraqi attorney, Mohammed al-Rehaief, walked south across the western Euphrates River bridge in search of the Marines' lines. It was the only bridge not in the Marines' control. To this day, it is not clear why he sought out the Marines. What is clear is that he wanted to speak with the Americans. He carefully approached India Company's lines and surrendered.

Lima Company Marines allowed him to slowly advance, and then they took him into custody and searched him for weapons. Once he was in their custody, Mohammed told the young Marines that he had important information about the Fedayeen and their locations.

He was quickly handed over to HET team members who believed enough of his story to have him sent back to the battalion main command post for further interrogation. Staff Sergeant S debriefed Mohammed for quite some time before Mohammed mentioned that he also knew the whereabouts of an American POW[5]. He had few details, but he did say that the POW's name was Jessica and that she was being held on the second floor of the hospital. He also said that the Ba'ath loyalists were using the basement of the hospital for their main headquarters. Lieutenant D thought his story credible, so he asked Mohammed if he would return to the hospital, locate the exact whereabouts of the American soldier, and collect enough information so that the Marines could map the hospital and its grounds. Mohammed was taken back to India Company's lines and released. He walked off into the darkness, toward the Euphrates River bridge.

TASK FORCE TARAWA

Just as the day before, General Natonski walked 2/8's lines. He spent most of his time at the military hospital. He toured the grounds and viewed the

5 Prisoner of war.

equipment stockpiled in the compound. As he was leaving the hospital, Kerry Sanders managed to get an on-camera interview. Natonski spoke candidly to Sanders. "We're here to give Iraq back to the people." He talked about the difficulty that Task Force Tarawa had been having while fighting to secure the road and two bridges. He told Kerry that his Marines were trying very hard to avoid civilian casualties, but the tactics employed by the enemy made that task extremely difficult. He concluded his interview with:

> *"I couldn't be more proud of these young Marines. They have lived up to every tradition of their predecessors in the Marine Corps, and they have been writing their own new history. As tough as things have gotten, their morale is high. They are in good spirits, and they meet every day with a smile on their face."*

Kerry Sanders finished his report with spectacular footage of Cobra helicopters locked in battle with Iraqis on the north bank of the Euphrates River. "Nine days into the battle of An Nasiriyah, Cobras are still firing on the north bank of the Euphrates River." Then the scene broke to Marines handing out bags of beans and rice to Iraqi civilians.

THE BETIO BASTARDS

Healy's Marines stepped off at 0100 and moved to assault positions just inside a tree line, only a couple hundred meters out from the compound. Day sent machine gun crews onto the rooftops of the apartment complex to provide covering fire. A few LAVs from Charlie Company pulled up on the levee road, just west of the Euphrates River bridge. They were ready to race west along the river and cover the operation, as CAAT had done two days before.

At 0530, Colonel Dunahoe's Marines conducted a battalion assault on the 11th Infantry Division's military complex. Captain E. J. Healy, a Citadel graduate, led the assault with his Kilo Company.

Healy's entire company attacked with the rising sun at their backs. They rushed across a small open area to a four-story building that looked just like one of the barracks at the Citadel in Charleston, South Carolina. The square fortress with parapets at each corner had a square, interior courtyard. The compound, home of an engineer and chemical battalion of the 11th Infantry Division, was quickly dubbed "the Citadel."

Healy originally planned to use a thermobaric round for an explosive breach of the eastern wall, but when the snipers reported that there was no enemy activity in the building and that civilians were roaming the compound, he opted for a mechanical breach.

The building was a couple hundred meters on each side, so when Healy reached the eastern wall and found no doors, he decided to use satchel charges to blow his way in. His Marines started setting the charges near the southeast corner. While his men set the explosives, Healy told one of his infantrymen, "Go check, just look around the corner and see if there is anything there."[6]

Just around the southeast corner, the Marine found that the southern wall was caved in and there was an entry to the compound only feet away. Healy ordered his Marines to remove the charges and move into the compound through the existing breach.

It is fortunate that they did not try to use artillery, thermobaric rounds, or satchel charges on the eastern wall. On the other side of the wall was a large room filled with tons of explosives and ammunition. Had the Marines set those explosives off, they would have taken out several city blocks, with disastrous results for the Marines and the local citizens. They could have killed hundreds of people.

The complex was enormous and stretched over acres. Healy's men cleared dozens of buildings, one at a time. As Healy moved to clear the complex, LAR moved along the levee road and screened along the river. Once the fortress had been secured, Colonel Dunahoe, Major Canfield, and a sniper team moved to the roof of the "Citadel."

Sergeant Yun of Sergeant Quinlan's sniper team spotted a squad of Fedayeen moving through the city with rifles and RPGs. They were moving along the Euphrates River, toward Kilo Company and 2d LAR from the west. Gunny Norton fired first, hitting one man before he moved behind a building. Sergeant Quinlan fired next, killing another one of the Fedayeen from 750 meters. The remaining Iraqis scattered. Soon they regrouped and began to move cautiously down a street toward the Marines again. Now they were 550 meters from Kilo's lines. Sergeant Sharon shot the next Iraqi just as he was about to let loose an RPG in the Marines' direction. The small group of fanatic Iraqis never got close to Kilo's lines. Norton's snipers reached out in the early morning light and picked off each of the Fedayeen.

---

6 Personal interview with Captain Edward Healy, 6/15/04.

Then a pickup truck drove through the western gate carrying two Iraqis. There was a tense moment when the Marines stared at the Iraqis, and the Iraqis stared at the Marines. The driver of the truck was the first to react. He slammed his truck in reverse and floored the accelerator, hoping to exit the compound through the gate he had just entered. The Marines opened fire, spraying the truck with M-16 and SAW rounds. The truck swerved, missed the exit, and crashed into the building, killing one of the truck's occupants instantly and mortally wounding the other.

On the ground, Healy could hear Colonel Dunahoe on the roof saying, "Shoot him! Shoot that guy!" The colonel was the first to notice a man in uniform, casually walking toward the "Citadel." The soldier, in his sixties, was walking to work as he probably had done every day for many years. He was carrying a briefcase and a cup of coffee. Healy's Marines saw him, too. A heartbeat before the sniper on the roof pulled his trigger, the old man saw the Marines on the ground. He dropped everything and quickly raised his hands into the air.

THE complex included offices, current maps on walls with enemy dispositions, a prison, another three or four rooms with lockers containing brand-new uniforms and equipment, and thousands of military books and documents. The complex also contained a small obstacle course. Nearby, there were warehouses filled with ammunition and nuclear, biological, and chemical masks, and equipment. The huge complex was comprised of several buildings, all of which were in poor condition. The complex itself was filthy and trashed, already picked over by looters.

The "Citadel" was the headquarters of the Iraqi 11th Infantry Division's chemical company. They found twenty-five tons of arms, explosives, and munitions. They found artillery shells, mortar rounds, and hundreds of RPGs, and close to the "Citadel" they found warehouses filled with one hundred fifty tons of food that the military had been hoarding. Once they reported that they had captured a chemical company headquarters, Task Force 20 Special Forces arrived to search for evidence of weapons of mass destruction, but none were found.

A smaller group of TF 20 soldiers arrived at the "Citadel" with a completely different mission. They had no desire to participate in the search of the compound. They were more interested in finding an approach route to the western Euphrates River bridge. They found that several hundred meters of densely populated buildings lay between the "Citadel" and the bridge. Once they had gathered this information, they quickly mounted up and headed back toward Highway 7.

THAT morning, two men claiming to be Mohammed's brothers showed up at Dunahoe's main command post. They had brought Mohammed's wife and five-year-old daughter to safety behind the American lines, asking for asylum. Mohammed's wife had worked in Saddam Hospital for nearly twenty years, and Staff Sergeant S talked with her for more than twelve hours. She provided near blueprint-quality detail of the first three floors of the hospital and the surrounding grounds. Together, they produced a set of sketches filled with the detail needed to plan a rescue mission. By now, Marines from Bailey's S-2 shop were involved. They assembled the information and sketches and went to brief the Task Force 20 staff with their intelligence findings.

RAMSTEIN, GERMANY

Corporal Nick Elliot was feeling much better after several days of rest in the U.S. military hospital in Ramstein, Germany. His leg wound would take many months to heal, and his burns had not completely healed either, but after several decent meals, he was feeling much better—especially on this day. He was going home. He was flying back to the United States.

The Air Force had organized one of the first of many air ambulance flights to come, and Elliot was going to be on the flight. When he awoke, many of the hospital staff came to say good-bye and help him prepare for the trip. Elliot was moved onto a gurney and wheeled from his hospital bed out to a waiting military bus that had been converted to a large ambulance.

Elliot was one of the first casualties loaded onto a blue Air Force bus. Then a Marine with a familiar face was brought onto the bus, Lance Corporal Samuel Velazquez. He was one of the survivors of the RPG attack on C206. While medical personnel worked quietly securing Elliot's and Velazquez's stretchers to the brackets on the bus, the wounded Marines exchanged greetings, both happy to be moving closer to home.

Next, a staff sergeant who had stepped on a land mine and lost both of his legs, was carried onto the bus. Then they brought another man on who was talking with everyone. Elliot thought he recognized the voice, so he looked over at him. The patient had nearly all of his face bandaged. He turned to Elliot and asked, "Who are you with?"[7]

"I'm with AAVs." Elliot responded.

The man with the bandaged face said, "I am, too. Who are you with?"

Elliot answered, "1/2."

The familiar voice said in astonishment, "I was with 1/2."

Then Elliot recognized the Marine. "Lieutenant Reid? You were in my track!" Reid finally realized that he was talking with C208's track commander. Elliot spent a long time telling Reid about what had happened to the track after he had last seen the lieutenant. Reid had not been told of C208's race south with casualties and its destruction in Ambush Alley. Reid, Elliot, Velazquez, and the other wounded servicemen were driven to a giant air ambulance waiting on the tarmac. They were then all carefully taken from the bus onto the giant aircraft.

Each soldier and Marine had a crew of medical personnel assigned to him to make sure the transatlantic flight would be as comfortable as possible. When all were aboard, the aircraft taxied and smoothly lifted into the air. Soon, they would be back in the United States.

AMERICA'S BATTALION

Fox Company had been taking fire from the boat house, on the northern bank of the Euphrates River, ever since they arrived at the eastern Euphrates River bridge. Lieutenant Nolan's snipers came to him with a plan. They thought they could swim across the river, under the cover of darkness, and move into the suspicious-looking building to check it out.

Nolan presented his plan to his battalion commander, who thought the plan was more than a little crazy. "Do you think your boys can do it?"[8] Mortenson asked. Nolan assured him that his men were excellent swimmers and that they knew they could make it across. Surprisingly, Mortenson approved the plan. Nolan returned to his men on the banks of the river to prepare for the mission.

---

7 Conversation taken from personal interview with Corporal Nick Elliot.

8 Telephone interview with Lieutenant Gregory Nolan.

Nolan's Marines stripped down to their underwear, stuffed their uniforms, boots, weapons, and ammo into waterproof bags and waded down into the water under the southern span of the bridge. They had planned on moving from piling to piling, under the bridge until they reached the north shore. The pilings would provide excellent cover, and they knew they would never be detected.

The two swimmers hadn't even reached the halfway mark when they realized that the current was swifter than they had anticipated. It was carrying them downstream away from the bridge. They weren't in danger of drowning, but they realized that by the time they reached the other side, they would be well south of the boat house. Worse yet, they would be out in the open as they passed the boat house. They would be sitting ducks if they were detected.

The two Marine swimmers returned to the southern bank of the river, but undaunted, they pulled open their watertight bags, dressed, collected their weapons, and ran up the stairs onto the bridge. They quickly moved across the bridge and down onto the northern bank. They ran past the picture of Saddam Hussein and up to the side of the building.

Nolan's snipers moved to the door, then disappeared inside. They searched the entire building and found it empty. Their quick search revealed that it had been a local command center of some sort. They scooped up as much material as they could and headed back to the Euphrates River bridge. The two Marines came back with maps, plot boards, RPGs, and mortars.

NBC NEWS

Mohammed was not the only Iraqi who helped free Jessica Lynch. Several Iraqis had risked their lives to warn the Marines that she was being held in the Tykar Hospital. Now, others were coming out, all around the city, to tell of her captivity at the Saddam Hospital. Many civilians took very bold steps to risk their own personal safety to help her. On the afternoon of March 31st, an Iraqi civilian walked toward Kerry Sanders and his crew as they were sitting alongside the road. Sebastian, a veteran photographer from many conflicts throughout the world was very nervous and shouted to the Iraqi to stop. The man continued to approach the news crew. He told them that a young American woman was being held in the Saddam Hospital and that she had been tortured. He went on to say that there were many people in Nasiriyah that did not approve of her treatment and that the Americans needed to go get her.

Now that several sources had indicated that Jessica Lynch was being held in the Saddam Hospital, Task Force 20 arrived at the Task Force Tarawa headquarters. They took over half of Natonski's COC tent and started setting up their state-of-the-art communications gear. Task Force 20's commanders would use Task Force Tarawa's COC to plan and orchestrate Lynch's rescue.

TASK FORCE TARAWA

By now, the Marines and Task Force 20's commanders were certain that Lynch was being held in Saddam Hospital, in the center of the city. They were faced with three immediate problems that they needed to address: How could they keep the Iraqis from moving her? How could they keep the Iraqis from killing her? And, how could they rescue her?

The Marines, with the help of Special Operations forces, had done a pretty good job of cordoning off the city, but there was always the chance that the Iraqis could spirit Lynch away, down a small trail through the swamps. The best course of action was to stay away from the hospital. Orders were given to wait until ordered to move on the western Euphrates River bridge. The hope was that if the powers that be within the hospital did not feel threatened, they would not feel compelled to move Lynch.

On the second issue, the best course was to stay away from the hospital. There was no sense in agitating the Iraqis in and around the hospital. Hopefully, they would not do something stupid. Lastly, the Task Force 20 planners started the planning for the rescue operation itself.

SEAL team and Special Operations planners traveled north to Grabowski's position to examine the western canal bridge. They boarded a Marine Huey helicopter for a nighttime aerial reconnaissance of the city. They flew all around Nasiriyah, using night-vision systems to check out the area. All the while, the Marines avoided the western Euphrates River bridge and the entire west side of the city, north of the Euphrates River.

BATTALION LANDING TEAM-2/1

The 15th Marine Expeditionary Unit's Battalion landing team arrived in An Nasiriyah on March 29th. They moved in on Dunahoe's western flank and prepared to move north on the only major road in southwestern An Nasiriyah that had yet to be cleared. They were very careful to stay away from the western bridge—less than a mile from Saddam Hospital.

CHAPTER 15

Freedom

Goodnight, Chesty, wherever you are.

TASK FORCE TARAWA

Throughout the battle, Task Force Tarawa worked closely with the Special Operations community. Army Green Beret "A" teams had collected intelligence and designated targets in the city center. They had also worked out in front of the 3d Battalion along Highway 8, south of the Euphrates River. A recon operations center (ROC) was co-located with Task Force Tarawa's command post. That way, the commanders could use the real-time intelligence that the Special Operations Forces were collecting in and around An Nasiriyah. Air Force Special Operations Command (AFSOC) AC-130 Spectre gunships were prowling the night skies over An Nasiriyah and Suq Ash Shuyukh. Navy SEALs surrounded Suq Ash Shuyukh.

With planning for the rescue of Private First Class Jessica Lynch well underway, U.S. Army Colonel Frank Kearney, a two-combat jump Ranger, took command of the operation. His men turned the Task Force Tarawa headquarters into a high-tech, state-of-the-art command center. They brought in computers and sophisticated communication equipment that would allow them to watch most of the rescue effort as it happened, on large-screen monitors.

The wheels had been set in motion for the Lynch rescue. Lieutenant Colonel Reilly's 2d Force Recon Company had moved a team into the city from the west. They snuck into a building and found a position close enough to Saddam Hospital to be able to observe the hospital grounds. A recon sniper team set up so that they could fire on any bad guys who might try to thwart the rescue. Task Force Tarawa now had eyes and ears on the hospital. The recon Marines did what they do best. They waited, undetected, and continued to watch the hospital. By the end of the month, the rescue planning was complete and TF 20 forces were running dress rehearsals at Tallil airbase.

An advance Special Forces party was sent in next. They landed near the hospital and questioned several Iraqi civilians. They asked Hassam Hamond where Saddam Hospital was and if there were any Fedayeen there. He told them that the Fedayeen had fled the day before. The soldiers believed Hassam, about as much as the Marines had believed the Iraqi doctor at Tykar Hospital, when he told them that it was a peaceful place. The next day, April 1st, a group of Fedayeen and the entire remaining Ba'ath Party leadership appeared at Saddam Hospital. They changed into civilian clothes, piled their green Army uniforms onto the lawn, and fled.[1] Nasiriyah was relinquished.

TASK Force Tarawa continued to apply pressure to the enemy, using precision air strikes and artillery barrages. Two AV-8s attacked the Ba'ath Party headquarters in An Nasiriyah, and then a circling AC-130 shot seventy-five 105mm howitzer rounds at the compound to complete the destruction. The people of Nasiriyah were overjoyed to see the destruction of the Ba'ath Party's last remaining stronghold. They started to believe that Saddam's reign of terror could finally be ending. The people of Nasiriyah started returning to their daily lives, and Saddam's few remaining death squads melted away into the back alleys of the city.

With all the roads now blocked, the Iraqis were not able to reinforce Nasiriyah from Suq Ash Shuyukh. The battle in the smaller Euphrates River town was fought with Special Forces teams, air strikes, and artillery. SEAL Team 7 had moved hunter/killer teams into Suq Ash Shuyukh and the surrounding area.

SEAL sniper teams worked the area just like the Marines had in An Nasiriyah. They hid, watched, and waited to learn who the bad guys in town were. The SEALs took out the enemy with single sniper shots or destroyed

---

1 *WorldNet Daily,* Tuesday, May 6, 2003

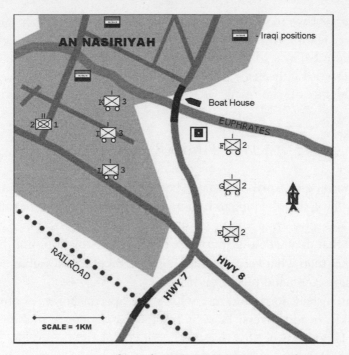

Task Force Tarawa moves the 15th MEU (BLT 2/1) into southern Nasiriyah

their command centers with precision-guided bombs. They methodically worked to corner the surviving leadership.

One at a time, the command centers in Suq Ash Shuyukh were destroyed, leaving only the Ba'ath Party headquarters building. Task Force Tarawa's planners waited just long enough for the enemy leadership to congregate in their final sanctuary, then they destroyed the building with a massive artillery barrage.

REGIMENTAL COMBAT TEAM-2

While the Task Force Commanders prepared for Lynch's rescue, Colonel Bailey began his final consolidation and preparation for the move north. Grabowski's Marines continued to patrol and man checkpoints on the roads north of the city. Mortenson's men started packing up, while Dunahoe's Marines were still fighting isolated pockets of stubborn Iraqi fighters along the banks of the Euphrates River.

In the southwest, Battalion Landing Team 2/1 was the busiest of all. They were clearing the remaining buildings of southern Nasiriyah, preparing to relieve Bailey's Marines throughout the city, and planning the attack on the western Euphrates River bridge. Their feint would be the operation that would kick off the rescue of Jessica Lynch.

THE TIMBERWOLVES

On the morning of April 1st, Major Peeples pulled Cubas and Kamper aside and said, "Hey, there's going to be a mission conducted, and they need a tank platoon. You guys are going to go into the city."[2] Both Kamper and Cubas suspected that they would be part of a POW rescue mission, but they had no details other than what Peeples had told them. Peeples told Cubas to report to the battalion command post for a briefing.

Cubas rushed north and met with some Special Forces commanders at Grabowski's headquarters. He was briefed on the entire mission and told that his platoon was needed to escort a convoy of eighteen vehicles carrying U.S. Army Rangers and Navy SEALs into the city. These Special Forces commandos would be the main ground element in a rescue mission at Saddam Hospital, in the center of An Nasiriyah.

Cubas's Third Platoon still had one tank down, but Filipkowski had now returned, so the three tank crews spent the day preparing their tanks for the mission. They set up a cammo net near C211's remains and then proceeded to remove all the gear from the outside of their tanks. They piled their rucksacks, fuel cans, and extra tread under the net and readied their tanks for one more battle. Then they waited.

TASK FORCE TARAWA

At 1245, the 24th MEU's commanding officer reported to General Natonski at the Task Force Tarawa headquarters. The MEU's Battalion Landing Team 2/2 had recently been chopped to Natonski. This visit was more than

---

2 Ibid. Kamper.

a unit reporting for duty, it was a homecoming. Lieutenant Colonel Walter Miller commanded the 2d Battalion of the 2d Marine Regiment. With his arrival, all of Colonel Bailey's 2d Marine Regiment was now part of Task Force Tarawa.

THE TIMBERWOLVES

Around mid-afternoon, eighteen vehicles drove north through Ambush Alley and crossed the canal bridge. The small convoy drove past Cubas's three tanks, pulled off the side of the road and parked in a coil. These guys were not Marines. They traveled in a handful of six-wheeled vehicles that looked like miniaturized LAVs, a dozen or so Humvees that were armed to the teeth, a couple of command Humvees, and two Marine seven-ton trucks. Navy SEALs were in the Humvees and the armored cars. The trucks carried a group of Army Rangers from the 1st Battalion of the 75th Ranger Regiment.

NBC NEWS

Kerry Sanders and his crew were still camping out at the eastern Euphrates River bridge. The battle for An Nasiriyah was winding down and the reporters were just trying to pass the time. They had been living out of their truck under the bridge for several days, but Kerry knew that something was in the making. He knew about reports of a captured soldier and a rescue attempt. He had even been told by an Iraqi that Jessica Lynch was in Saddam Hospital, in the center of the city. He was sitting on the story of a lifetime, yet he couldn't report it. If word were to get out, the entire mission would be put at risk. Lynch and some of her rescuers could be killed. Kerry had no intention of compromising this mission. The reporter in him was dying to shout to the world this historic scoop, yet he knew that he would have to keep the secret a little longer.

The military would take no chances. Early that day, all of Kerry's communications equipment stopped working. His satellite phone stopped working. He lost his computer connection. His cell phone went dead. The military had blacked out all civilian communications. But, knowing how close Kerry Sanders had been to this story, someone from Task Force Tarawa's staff showed up at his campsite and told the NBC crew, "I can't tell you what is about to happen, but at midnight tonight, have your camera trained on the southwest bridge."[3]

TASK FORCE TARAWA

The ultimate example of intra-service cooperation materialized when Task Force Tarawa's COC became the joint COC, incorporating the command of the super-secret Task Force 20. Task Force 20 had been sent in to plan and execute the rescue of Private First Class Jessica Lynch.

By sundown, all of the rescue forces were in their assembly areas. Cubas's three tanks moved up Highway 7 the short hundred yards and parked in the TF 20 coil. Filipkowski and Kamper jumped off their tanks and walked over to talk with the Rangers and SEALs. They met the unit's ground commander, an Army Ranger, who introduced himself as Chad. After the introductions were complete and the sun had set, the Rangers, SEALs, and Blue Platoon drove up to the northern "T," turned west, and proceeded to Alpha Company's position, just north of the western canal bridge.

Lieutenant Colonel Grabowski and Captain Brooks were with some Special Ops guys staged at the western bridge in one of Brooks's tracks. They had SAT COM set up to monitor the mission. Captain Brooks had readied a quick-reaction force that would move into the city if anything went wrong. Alpha Company Marines were parked alongside the road in their tracks, with some of White Platoon's tanks. When Kamper stopped, Chad came over to his tank and asked what was up on the bridge. Kamper explained that he had pushed cars up onto the bridge several days earlier to block vehicle traffic. Then he offered, "I can move the cars."[4]

"How long will that take?" Chad inquired.

"I can push a vehicle forward. It won't take me more than a minute." Kamper answered.

---

3 Personal interview with Kerry Sanders, 1/27/04.

4 Ibid. Kamper.

3D (BLUE) PLATOON, ALPHA COMPANY, 8TH TANKS

At five minutes to midnight, Staff Sergeant Alan Kamper ordered his driver to move out. Kamper's M1 tank clanked up onto the western canal bridge. The large mine plow blade hit one of the cars piled in the center of the road. Kamper's tank continued forward. He punched a hole through the automobile barricade like a tackle clearing the way for his running back. Kamper pushed one of the cars across the entire bridge, sparks flying as metal ground on pavement. He continued to push the car down off the southern end of the bridge and then off to the side of the road.

BATTALION LANDING TEAM 2/1

At midnight, the entire southwest side of the city lit up like it was the fourth of July in Middle America. Jessica Lynch's rescue opened with a diversionary attack from 15th MEU and Battery C of the 1st Battalion, 10th Marines' artillery. They mounted a noisy and violent attack on the western Euphrates River Bridge. This was the bridge that the Marines had been ignoring for the last several days. Only a short mile's drive, it was closest to the Saddam Hospital and provided the most likely rescue route. The planners hoped that any remaining enemy fighters would be drawn toward the attack.

The roof of the "Citadel" was filled with spectators. Dunahoe, Starling, Day, Vitale and even Brian Waite watched the forty-five minute diversionary attack. Kerry Sanders' cameras were rolling when artillery began to fall on the southwest side of An Nasiriyah and the Marines of Battalion Landing Team 2/1 started firing their heavy weapons across the river. M1 tanks fired round after round from their main guns, knocking big holes in buildings and making a lot of noise. Starnes' artillery leveled the downtown Ba'ath Party headquarters.

Marine jets circled high above Nasiriyah, to provide close air support for the operation. High-tech UAVs circled the hospital, beaming real-time video back into the joint command center. Black Hawk and Little Bird helicopters of the elite 160th Special Operations Aviation Regiment (SOAR) started closing on their targets. Marine Phrogs were not far behind, carrying more Army Rangers.

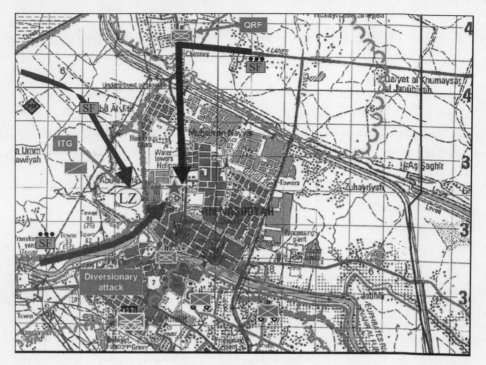

Jessica Lynch Rescue

TF 20's rescue team sped into the city from the west, feet dangling from the skids of their tiny Little Bird helicopters. Two Black Hawks followed close behind. The Little Birds dropped their passengers at exactly midnight and took back to the air to provide cover. One Black Hawk quickly disgorged its team and lifted back into the night sky. The other remained on the deck, waiting to carry Jessica to freedom. Marine helicopters ferried in a company of Army Rangers who landed to the west of the hospital and set up security for an emergency-landing zone. When the Hospital staff heard the sound of helicopters circling the upper floors, they took shelter in the windowless X-ray department.

BLUE PLATOON

Kamper's M1 led the ground assault. Cubas and Filipkowski were right behind him. Kamper remained at the southern base of the bridge while Cubas, Filipkowski, the Rangers and SEALs raced south toward the Saddam

Hospital. Kamper sat at the side of the road counting the vehicles as they passed—17, 18, 19. As soon as the last vehicle passed, he took up the rear of the lethal column.

Captain Brooks' Alpha Company stood by, north of the Saddam Canal with the Quick Reaction Force, in case something went terribly wrong. There would not be a repeat of the disaster in Mogadishu or the aborted rescue attempt of the hostages in Tehran. Every contingency had been covered. If the Iraqis were setting a trap, they would pay dearly. Jessica would be rescued no matter who was holding her.

OUTSIDE the hospital, a dozen Navy SEALs with M4 carbines, lightweight body armor and a number of shotguns for breaching, assaulted the building. They burst through the entrance and rushed inside. What would they find? Was Jessica still there? Was Jessica still alive? As they moved through the hospital toward Lynch's last known location, they scared the staff half to death. The highly experienced team calmly bypassed the terrified civilians and moved toward their objective. They methodically pressed forward, checking every room and nook along the way.

Lying in her hospital bed, Jessica heard helicopters close by. Tonight, the war seemed closer. She could hear large explosions in the night. Then there seemed to be a commotion in the hallway. She could hear voices. Outside her door, she heard, "Where is Jessica Lynch?" Terror shot through her broken body. Someone was coming for her. She thought that Iraqis were coming to take her away.

Black-clad modern-day ninjas quickly flowed down the hallway toward Jessica's closed door. The men moved as one well-trained force, moving their small, yet deadly, weapons in every direction. They assumed their choreographed assault positions, then rushed through the door.

The door flew open, and several ominous figures burst into the room. A soldier rushed to Jessica's bedside and told her, "We are American."

"We are here to take you home."

"Oh, God! This is real. I'm going home."[5] Jessica thought to herself.

One of her rescuers ripped the velcroed American flag from his shoulder and handed it to Jessica, who grabbed the flag and held onto his hand for

---

5 Rick Bragg *I am A Soldier Too* (New York: Knopf, 2003).

dear life. She did not let go. Doctors quickly checked Jessica and then the SEALs gently lifted her 70-lb. shattered body[6] onto a stretcher.

The rescue team moved out of the hospital as carefully as they had entered, constantly checking doorways and windows for any hidden threat. As she was being carried to the helicopter for her ride to safety, still in shock, she pleaded, "Don't leave me behind." Lynch was rushed aboard the waiting Black Hawk helicopter. Less than ten minutes after the SEALs had landed, Jessica was safely being whisked away.

KAMPER, Cubas, Filipkowski and the Rangers drove south for three kilometers. By the time they reached the hospital, Jessica was well on her way to safety. At the hospital, 3d Platoon dispersed and positioned themselves at three corners of the compound—Kamper took the northeast corner, Cubas parked on the southwest corner and Filipkowski took up a position in the southeast. The SEALs and Rangers dispersed around the outside of the compound and quickly established a perimeter.

Kamper watched the Rangers deploy through his night vision goggles. He could see the MH-6 Little Birds flying one to two hundred feet off the deck. It was a LASER light show. Kamper could see all different shaped LASER reticles from the SF guys' high-tech weapons, moving across buildings, all around the Hospital. Individual LASERs from each of the soldier's rifles crisscrossed in the night.

Once the hospital was secure, Task Force 20's men fanned out, searching the hospital and its grounds for more American soldiers. Members of the staff insisted that there were no more American captives and told the soldiers that several Americans had been buried on the hospital grounds. The Special Ops soldiers set about the tedious task of carefully digging in the Iraqi sand to find the remains of their American comrades.

While sitting atop his tank, Filipkowski saw what he thought were freshly covered graves nearby and the air around him smelled of death. He called out over the Special Ops TAC, "Hey, I got some mounds over here by my tank." Some of the Rangers came over and started digging with their

---

6 Bob Withers "Lynch Encourages W. Va. Educators" (Huntington, W. Virginia: *The Herald-Dispatch*, 12 Dec 2004).

hands. As soon as they realized that they had found bodies, Filipkowski threw a shovel down to the soldiers who continued to retrieve the bodies. The recovery would last for several hours. They ended up working all night.

The sun was rising by the time they had finished retrieving the bodies. Once the gruesome task was complete, the Rangers and SEALs loaded back into their vehicles. Captain Cubas and his tanks were the last to leave the hospital. They pulled out in the reverse order. Kamper led the way north, back over the Saddam Canal, followed by the Rangers and SEALs, and then Cubas and Filipkowski. The entire ground element returned safely to Alpha Company's position, north of the Saddam Canal. When Chad saw Grabowski, he paid his tank platoon commander the ultimate Ranger compliment. He told Grabowski, "Cubas is HOOAH!"[7]

MARINE Expeditionary Units undergo intensive training prior to their deployment. They train to handle many different scenarios from evacuating U.S. embassies to rescuing downed American pilots. Once they have successfully completed the training, they are designated Marine Expeditionary Unit (Special Operations Capable) or MEU(SOC). The Reserve Marines of Third (Blue) Platoon, Alpha Company, 8th Tanks were very proud of their contribution to the Jessica Lynch rescue. For the rest of their time in Iraq they called themselves "BLUE(SOC)."

NBC NEWS

After the rescue, Kerry Sanders called out on his satellite phone. "Has the president made any announcement?" He asked his producer.

"What's going on?"

"Well, I got confirmation that something big has happened here!" Kerry excitedly reported. "I don't want to give you any of the details, but has the president made any announcement?" Before New York could answer, the line went dead. Kerry couldn't get a line back until the next morning.

---

7 Ibid. Grabowski.

When Kerry Sanders finally got through to New York, he got to tell his story. Reporting from atop the Euphrates River bridge, "The good news is—Jessica Lynch has now been rescued." Kerry went on to report. "Around twelve-thirty A.M. on a moonless night, Delta Force swarmed into the Saddam Hospital."

Sanders went on to tell the entire story. He told his viewers that some of Lynch's clothes were found at the Tykar Hospital, that a doctor had told them about treating a severely injured, young American woman. While he spoke, footage of the diversionary attack showed an eerie green-and-black scene of explosions and gunfire.

LYNCH'S rescue was the first successful rescue of an American POW since World War II. The mission went off without a hitch. Jessica was safely on her way home just twenty minutes after the first shot was fired by 15th MEU. None of the rescue team was injured, no civilians at the hospital were hurt, and all but one of the remaining American bodies were recovered.

Several critics were quick to condemn the military for its overwhelming use of force. They pointed out that there were no enemy fighters in the hospital by the time the rescue force arrived. The commanders of the operation would have been remiss if they had not planned for the worst-case scenario. This operation was perfectly planned and executed. Jessica Lynch was saved, and no one from either side was hurt in the hospital.

For those who were still convinced that the rescue operation was overdone, a week later, on April 7th, a BLT 2/1 daytime patrol was attacked in the city near the hospital. Iraqi insurgents were still inside the city and willing to fight and kill Americans.

BY morning, the men of Task Force 20 had uncovered the remains of what they believed to be ten Americans. It would take military forensic specialists weeks to identify all of the remains. One was Iraqi.

It would not be until they could be identified through DNA that anyone was certain whose remains were recovered, but the Rangers collected nine Americans that night. They found George Buggs, Robert Dowdy, James Kiehl, Johnny Mata, Lori Piestewa, Brandon Sloan, Ruben Estrella-Soto, Donald Walters, and Marine Sergeant Brendon Reiss, all buried in shallow graves near the hospital.

The Rangers stopped digging that night, once they had retrieved ten bodies. They believed that they had recovered everyone. When it was determined that one of the recovered bodies was that of an Iraqi, everyone realized that there was still one missing American. Weeks after the rescue mission, a search party was sent back to Saddam Hospital, and they found Edward Anguiano buried in the same field. The soldiers had missed him on the night of Lynch's rescue. Finally, no one was left behind.

THE 507TH MAINTENANCE COMPANY

Captain King and the other uninjured survivors of the ambush would spend several weeks at Tallil Air Base, waiting for an opportunity to be reunited with the rest of their unit. Campbell, Grubb, Luten, Carista, and Tarik Johnson would all be quickly returned to hospitals in the United States to recuperate from their wounds. Hernandez, Hudson, Shoshana Johnson, and Miller would be rescued by Marines on May 13th and brought home to a hero's welcome. Jessica Lynch would spend many years recovering from her injuries and will probably never recover from the psychological injuries she suffered in An Nasiriyah.

TASK FORCE TARAWA

Before noon, General Natonski rolled across the eastern Euphrates River bridge with a small entourage accompanying his soft-skinned Humvee. The small convoy drove north slowly through Ambush Alley, as Natonski surveyed the site of the battle. They drove past the Martyrs' District and up onto the eastern Saddam Canal bridge. The general stopped for a short visit with Colonel Grabowski, and then climbed back into his vehicle to continue his tour of the city.

He drove over to the western "T" and then turned left to drive back toward Saddam Hospital, just as Cubas, Kamper, Filipkowski, and the Rangers had done the night before. The small convoy continued south, over the western canal bridge, to Saddam Hospital. The town was coming alive. People were out and about, and most of the bad guys who had survived the weeklong battle with Task Force Tarawa had left the city.

Brigadier General Richard Natonski stopped and toured the hospital for

an hour and a half. He visited Lynch's hospital room and recovered her
X rays. He talked with the medical staff and asked how the Marines could
help. They told him that they needed food, water, and IVs, which the Marines
provided. Then he left the city by driving over the western Euphrates River
bridge, south to Highway 8, back past the Ba'ath Party headquarters to
Highway 7. By the time Natonski returned to his COC, he was confident
that the city was secure. Task Force Tarawa officially declared the city of An
Nasiriyah secure at 1300.

TASK Force Tarawa had been involved in the most important battle of the
invasion, and now they would move on to provide the vital rear-area security for the 1st Marine Division, as it charged to Baghdad. Without Task
Force Tarawa, the 1st Marine Division would have had great difficulty making it to Baghdad. General Natonski's Marines kicked open the door and
kept it open for the remainder of the invasion.

Once Baghdad fell, the Marines of Task Force Tarawa assumed a much
more important mission. They were tasked with returning order to nearly
half of Iraq. Their area of responsibility stretched from Nasiriyah, north to
the southern edge of Baghdad, and from Ad Diwanyah to the Iranian border.

THE 2D MARINE REGIMENT

Of all the Marine commanders in I MEF, Colonel Ron Bailey had the great-
est challenges. He fought a determined enemy that most had thought would
fade into back alleys or surrender at the first sound of gunfire. He fought
them with limited resources, and he won decisively. Bailey's Marines fought
against fanatic fighters who were determined to kill Marines and stall the
attack toward Baghdad. He experienced the first urban resistance of Operation Iraqi Freedom, and his Marines overcame the enemy, despite their
cowardly tactic of hiding behind Iraqi civilians. Colonel Bailey and the 2d
Marine Regiment achieved the first major victory of the invasion.

Marines from Battalion Landing Team 2/1 moved to every corner of the
city and relieved Bailey's Marines at the three bridges they had been holding
for a week. The 15th MEU would remain behind in An Nasiriyah, while
Regimental Combat Team-2 moved north to secure the routes to Baghdad
behind the 1st Marine Division. No one will remember the great job Bailey's

Marines did in helping the Iraqi people over the next several months, but the 2d Marine Regiment will go down in Marine Corps history for what they accomplished in the battle for An Nasiriyah.

THE BETIO BASTARDS

The Betio Bastards had added another battle streamer to their battalion colors. Lieutenant Colonel Paul "Brent" Dunahoe had led his Marines into the first major urban fighting since Hue City. His determination and deliberate tactics defeated a fanatic enemy without suffering a single casualty in combat. In a few short days of operations, Dunahoe, Starling, Canfield, Day, Qualkinbush, Vitale, and the rest of his staff had rewritten the Marine Corps' handbook on military operations in urban terrain.

A young lieutenant, the commander of Dunahoe's human exploitation team, developed his craft to a fine art in southwestern Nasiriyah. The lessons he learned were later employed in the 1st Marine Division's attack on Fallujah and are still being successfully employed by the Marine Corps at the time of this writing.

When all was said and done, the modern-day Betio Bastards can stand tall next to their brothers who fought for a tiny wisp of coral in the Pacific. Dunahoe's Marines had defeated the enemy while upholding the traditions of the Corps and protecting each other. The Marines of 3/2 then packed up and got back in their vehicles. They retraced their route back down Highway 7, then northwest on Highway 1. This time they continued on across the Euphrates River toward Ad Diwanyah.

AMERICA'S BATTALION

America's Battalion fought from their first appearance at the intersection of highways Seven and Eight, on the afternoon of March 23rd, to the last-gasp counterattack on March 26th. Mortenson's CAAT section was engaged every single day at the 7/8 interchange from March 23rd to March 28th.

The Marines of America's Battalion handled themselves superlatively during the battle for An Nasiriyah. They charged forward when ordered, and acted with restraint when appropriate. They maintained control of the eastern Euphrates River bridge through several days of heavy fighting and finally cleared the enemy from Tykar Hospital and the southeast side of town. They defeated the enemy and then set out to help the citizens of An Nasiriyah by handing out food and water, and providing medical attention.

They had several Marines wounded during that week, but Lieutenant Colonel Royal Mortenson was extremely proud of the fact that all of his Marines survived the battle for An Nasiriyah. America's Battalion took its place in the annals of the historied 8th and 2d Marine Regiments.

THE TIMBERWOLVES

Lieutenant Colonel Rickey Grabowski and the Marines of the 1st Battalion, 2d Marine Regiment will never be the same. They will carry the memory of the battle for An Nasiriyah for the rest of their lives. The Timberwolves made the largest sacrifice of any Marine unit since the bombing of the Marine barracks in Lebanon in1980, and had suffered more losses than any combat unit since Vietnam. They lost eighteen of their comrades, and more than a dozen more were seriously wounded. Some of the Marines of Charlie Company were still in shock. Many had only the clothes on their back, and all had the battle for the eastern bridges emblazoned in their memories forever.

All of the Marines of Charlie Company now knew what it was really like to be a Marine. They had been pounded by the enemy with small arms, heavy machine guns, RPGs, mortars, and artillery. They had been mistakenly strafed by American aircraft. They had been cut off and surrounded. They had lost communications, and they had lost their ability to call in supporting arms. Yet they held on and prevailed.

They prevailed because they were Marines and they had no other option than victory. They prevailed because the entire battalion continued to absorb failures and misfortunes. They kept moving through withering enemy fire, through cesspools of mud, through broken radios, through broken-down vehicles, through swollen tank rounds, through friendly fire to press forward to victory.

They had been unstoppable. They were relentless in their attack; they overcame catastrophe after catastrophe. They grabbed hold of their enemy, and they never let him go until they had achieved their mission. The Timberwolves had truly snatched victory from the jaws of defeat, on Sunday, March 23rd, 2003.

Nine days later, Second Lieutenant David Beere, of the Timberwolves' Bravo Company, walked up on the Saddam Canal bridge and began to play his bagpipes. Most Iraqis within earshot moved toward the foreign music like children being drawn by The Pied Piper. The lieutenant stood at attention, alone on the crest of the bridge that his battalion had fought so gallantly to secure only a week earlier, playing every song he knew. Finally, after several minutes of this haunting music, Lieutenant Beere concluded his performance with the Marine Corps hymn. Then he turned north and slowly marched down off the bridge. Before the sun set, the Marines of Task Force Tarawa would be loaded up and heading north toward Baghdad, but the souls of eighteen young Marines' would forever keep watch on the eastern bridges of Nasiriyah.

The people of An Nasiriyah will not soon forget the men of Task Force Tarawa, and the Camp Lejeune Marines will never forget their battle for "the Naz," a battle that turned the tide in the invasion of Iraq and helped change the course of history. We must never forget the Marines and soldiers who died along the banks of the Euphrates River while selflessly serving their country.

APPENDIX A

American Casualties

MARCH 22, 2003

1. Sergeant Nicolas M. Hodson, 22, Killed in HMMWV traffic
   accident on Highway 1
   3d Battalion, 2d Marines
   Smithville, Missouri

MARCH 23, 2003

2. SPC Jamaal R. Addison, 22, KIA in 507th ambush
   507th Maintenance Company
   Roswell, Georgia

3. Specialist Edward J. Anguiano, 24, KIA in 507th ambush
   3d Combat Support Battalion
   Brownsville, Texas

4. Sergeant Michael E. Bitz, 31, KIA in C206
   2d Assault Amphibious Battalion
   Ventura, California

5. Lance Corporal Thomas A. Blair, 24, KIA
   2d Low Altitude Air Defense Battalion
   Broken Arrow, Oklahoma

6. Lance Corporal Brian Rory Buesing, 20, KIA north of
   Saddam Canal
   Weapons Platoon, Charlie Company, 1st Battalion, 2d Marines
   Cedar Key, Florida

7. Sergeant George Edward Buggs, 31, KIA in 507th ambush
   3d Forward Support Battalion
   Barnwell, South Carolina

8. Private First Class Tamario D. Burkett, 21, KIA
   Charlie Company, 1st Battalion, 2d Marines
   Buffalo, New York

9. Corporal Kemaphoom A. Chanawongse, 22, KIA north of
   Saddam Canal
   2d Assault Amphibious Battalion
   Waterford, Connecticut

10. Lance Corporal Donald "John" Cline Jr., 21, KIA in C208
    3d Platoon, Charlie Company, 1st Battalion, 2d Marines
    Sparks, Nevada

11. Master Sergeant Robert J. Dowdy, 38, KIA in 507th ambush
    507th Maintenance Company
    Cleveland, Ohio

12. Private Ruben Estrella-Soto, 18, KIA in 507th ambush
    507th Maintenance Company
    El Paso, Texas

13. Lance Corporal David K. Fribley, 26, KIA north of
    Saddam Canal
    Charlie Company, 1st Battalion, 2d Marines
    Lee, Florida

14. Corporal Jose A. Garibay, 21, WIA north of Saddam Canal,
    KIA in C208
    Weapons Platoon, Charlie Company, 1st Battalion, 2d Marines
    Costa Mesa, California

15. Private Jonathan L. Gifford, 20, WIA north of Saddam Canal,
    KIA in C208
    Weapons Platoon, Charlie Company, 1st Battalion, 2d Marines
    Macon, Illinois

16. Corporal Jorge A. Gonzalez, 20, WIA north of Saddam Canal,
    KIA in C208
    Weapons Platoon, Charlie Company, 1st Battalion, 2d Marines
    Los Angeles, California

17. Private Nolen R. Hutchings, 19, KIA
    Charlie Company, 1st Battalion, 2d Marines
    Boiling Springs, South Carolina

18. Private First Class Howard Johnson II, 21, KIA in 507th ambush
    507th Maintenance Company
    Mobile, Alabama

19. Staff Sergeant Phillip A. Jordan, 42, KIA north of Saddam Canal
    Weapons Platoon, Charlie Company, 1st Battalion, 2d Marines
    Brazoria, Texas

20. Specialist James M. Kiehl, 22, KIA in 507th ambush
    507th Maintenance Company
    Comfort, Texas

21. Chief Warrant Officer 2 Johnny Mata, 35, KIA in 507th ambush
    507th Maintenance Company
    El Paso, Texas

22. Corporal Patrick R. Nixon, 21, Wounded north of Saddam
    Canal, KIA in C208
    Weapons Platoon, Charlie Company, 1st Battalion, 2d Marines
    Nashville, Tennessee

23. Private First Class Lori Ann Piestewa, 23, WIA in 507th ambush,
    died as POW
    507th Maintenance Company
    Tuba City, Arizona

24. Second Lieutenant Frederick E. Pokorney Jr., 31, KIA
    north of Saddam Canal
    1st Battalion, 10th Marines, Forward Observer for Charlie Company, 1/2
    Marines
    Nye, Nevada

25. Sergeant Brendon C. Reiss, 23, KIA in C206
    Charlie Company, 1st Battalion, 2d Marines
    Casper, Wyoming

26. Corporal Randal Kent Rosacker, 21, KIA in or near C203
    Charlie Company, 1st Battalion, 2d Marines
    San Diego, California

27. Private Brandon Ulysses Sloan, 19, KIA in 507th ambush
    507th Maintenance Company
    Bedford, Ohio

28. Lance Corporal Thomas J. Slocum, 22, KIA in or near C203
Charlie Company, 1st Battalion, 2d Marines
Adams, Colorado

29. Sergeant Donald Ralph Walters, 33, captured during 507th ambush,
then murdered.
507th Maintenance Company
Salem, Oregon

30. Lance Corporal Michael J. Williams, 31, KIA in C208
Charlie Company, 1st Battalion, 2d Marines
Phoenix, Arizona

MARCH 25, 2003

31. Private First Class Francisco A. Martinez Flores, 21, KIA, tank
fell into Euphrates River
1st Tank Battalion, 1st Marine Division
Los Angeles, California

32. Staff Sergeant Donald C. May Jr., 31, KIA when tank fell
into Euphrates River
1st Tank Battalion, 1st Marine Division
Richmond, Virginia

33. Lance Corporal Patrick T. O'Day, 20, KIA when tank fell
into Euphrates River
1st Tank Battalion, 1st Marine Division
Sonoma, California

MARCH 26, 2003

34. Major Kevin G. Nave, 36, killed in accident north of An Nasiriyah
3d Battalion, 5th Marines
Union Lake, Michigan

CAPTURED
(All were eventually rescued)

1. Specialist Edgar Hernandez
507th Maintenance Company

2. Specialist Joseph Hudson
507th Maintenance Company

3. Specialist Shoshana Johnson
   507th Maintenance Company

4. Private First Class Jessica Lynch
   507th Maintenance Company

5. Private First Class Patrick Miller
   507th Maintenance Company

6. Sergeant James Riley
   507th Maintenance Company

APPENDIX B

Task Force Tarawa
Order of Battle

2d Marine Expeditionary Brigade
Brigadier General Richard F. Natonski
Commanding—"DEVIL DOG 6"

Colonel James W. Smoots
Chief of Staff

Colonel Ron Johnson
Operations Officer

Lieutenant Colonel Miner
Air Officer

2d Force Recon Company—Lieutenant Colonel James E. Reilly
    San Antonio Reserve Recon Companies
2d Light Armored Recon Battalion—Lieutenant Colonel Eddie S. Ray "Barbarian 6"
    Alpha Company—Captain Ivan I. Monclova (Attached to RCT1)
    Bravo Company—Captain William R. Speigle, II (Attached to RCT1)
    Charlie Company—Captain Gregory R. Grunwald "Gunfighter 6"
        (attached to TFT)

Regimental Combat Team 2
    Colonel Ronald L. Bailey—Commanding "Viking 6"

    Lieutenant Colonel John P. O'Rourke—Executive Officer
    Major Andy R. Kennedy—Operations Officer
    Major Michael Mooney—Intelligence Officer

Major W. P. Bair "Coco"—Air Officer
Sergeant Major E. N. Evans

    1st Battalion, 2d Marine Regiment (Mechanized)
    Lieutenant Colonel Rick Grabowski, Commanding "Timberwolf 6"

    Major Jeffrey Tuggle—Executive Officer
    Major David Sosa—Operations Officer
    Captain J. T. Greene—Air Officer
    CW04 David Dunfee—Battalion Gunner
    Sergeant Major Charles M. Arrick

2d Amphibian Battalion, Alpha Co
Captain William E. Blanchard—Commanding "Rhino 6"
1st Lieutenant Connor N. Tracy—Executive Officer and 1st Platoon Commander

Alpha Company, 8th Tank Battalion
    Major Bill Peeples—Commanding "Panzer 6"
    Captain Scott Dyer—Executive Officer
    Captain Scott Hawkins—Forward Air Controller "Hawk"
    1st Lieutenant James Carter—Forward Observer "Sprout"

    1st (RED) Platoon—Captain Jim Thompson
    2d (WHITE) Platoon—Gunney Sergeant Randy Howard "Diablo 6"
    3d (BLUE(SOC)) Platoon—Captain Romeo Cubas

    Alpha Company—Captain Michael Brooks, Commanding "Tomahawk 6"
    1st Lieutenant Matthew J. Martin—Executive Officer
    Captain Jim Jones—Forward Air Controller "Kool-Aide"
    1st Sergeant James Thompson Jr.—1st Sergeant
    Weapons Platoon—1st Lieutenant Steve Cook

    Bravo Company—Captain Tim Newland, Commanding "Mustang 6"
      1st Lieutenant Daniel—Executive Officer
      Captain Dennis Santare—Forward Air Controller "Mouth"
      1st Sergeant David M. Parker—1st Sergeant
      1st Platoon—2d Lieutenant Troy Garlock
      3d Platoon—Lieutenant David Beere

    Charlie Company—Captain Daniel J. Wittnam, Commanding
      "PALEHORSE 6"
      1st Lieutenant Eric A. Meador—Executive Officer
      1st Sergeant Jose Henao—1st Sergeant

Weapons Platoon—Lieutenant James "Ben" Reid (FiST)

1st Platoon—2d Lieutenant Scott Swantner "Palehorse 1"
 Staff Sergeant John Crosby—Platoon Sergeant

2d Platoon—1st Lieutenant Allen Lapinsky "Palehorse 2"
 Staff Sergeant Lonnie Parker—Platoon Sergeant

3d Platoon—2nd Lieutenant Michael Seely "Palehorse 3"
 SSgt Anthony Pompos—Platoon Sergeant

H&S Company—Captain Billy Ray Moore
 1st Lieutenant Gerard C. Dempster—Executive Officer

Weapons Company—Captain Karl C. Rohr
 CAAT 1—Staff Sergeant Troy Schielein
 CAAT 2—1st Lieutenant Brian S. Letendre
 81mm Mortars—Lieutenant Clayton

2d Battalion, 8th Marine Regiment (Motorized)
Lieutenant Colonel Royal P. Mortenson—Commanding "Warpath 6"
 Major Julian D. Alford—Executive Officer
 Major Robert C. Fulford—Operations Officer
 Captain John R. Dupree—Intelligence Officer
 Battalion Gunner—CWO Harris
 Sergeant Major Miles C. Thorne

Echo Company—Captain Kevin E. Yeo

Fox Company—Captain Timothy (Rich) Dremann Jr.
 1st Sergeant Gatewood—First Sergeant

 1st Platoon—1st Lieutenant Wong

 2d Platoon—1st Lieutenant Southwick

Golf Company—Captain Brian A. Ross

Weapons Company—Captain Benjamin J. Luciano

H&S Company—Captain Jim Ryan

3d Battalion, 2d Marine Regiment (Motorized)
Lieutenant Colonel Paul Brent Dunahoe—Commanding "Betio 6"

Major Christopher Starling—Executive Officer
Major Dan Canfield—Operations Officer
Captain Harold Qualkinbush—Air Officer "Duck"
Battalion Gunner—CWO Nicolas Vitale

Lima Company—Captain Gerald Thomas

Kilo Company—Captain Edward Healy

India Company—1st Lieutenant Widman

Weapons Company—Captain John L. Day

H&S Company—Captain Robert Davy

1st Battalion, 10th Marine Regiment (Artillery)
Lieutenant Colonel Glenn Starns—Commanding "Nightmare 6"

Marine Air Group 29—Colonel Robert E. Milstead
Lieutenant Colonel Darrell Thacker—Executive Officer

HMM-162
Lieutenant Colonel Robert F. Hedelund

Captain Eric Garcia
Captain Tod Schroeder
Captain Morton
Captain Eric Griggs

HML/A-269 (Cobras and Hueys)
Lieutenant Colonel Jeff M. Hewlett

Amphibious Ready Group (2)
15th MEU
24th MEU

15th Marine Expeditionary Unit

Battalion Landing Team 2/1
Lieutenant Colonel Alvah E. Ingersoll III

Echo Company
Captain Peter McAleer

Fox Company
Captain Richard J. Crevier

Golf Company
Captain Justin S. Dunne

Weapons Company
Captain Michael P McCready

Company A, 1st Light Armored Recon Battalion
Captain Donald J. Tomich

24th Marine Expeditionary Unit

Battalion Landing Team 2/2
Lieutenant Colonel Walter L. Miller Jr.—Commanding "Warlord 6"

Task Force 51

Amphibious Group 2
Amphibious Task Force—East
"Magnificent Seven"
Rear Admiral Michael P. Nowakowski, USN
Commanding

Amphibious Squadron 8
Captain Greg Jackson, USN
Commanding

USS *Kearsarge* (LHD-3)—Captain Terence E. McKnight,
USS *Bataan* (LHD-5)—Captain E. S. Yerger
USS *Saipan* (LHA-2)—Captain Chris Hase
USS *Ashland* (LSD-48)
USS *Gunston Hall* (LSD-44)—Commander John Walker
USS *Portland* (LSD-37)
USS *Ponce* (LPD-15)—Commander Andy Pachuta

Plus several USNS "Black Bottom" transports and an armed escort.

USNS *Watson*
USNS *Regulus*
USNS *Redcloud*

Amphibious Group 3
Amphibious Task Force—West
Rear Admiral W. Clyde Marsh, USN
Commanding

APPENDIX C

Acronym and Terms Glossary

81's	81mm mortar platoon
AA	Assembly area
AAA	Antiaircraft artillery
AAV	Assault amphibian vehicle
ACE	Aviation combat element—USMC
AFSOC	Air Force Special Operations Command
ALOC	Administration and Logistics Command
AMTRAC	Amphibious tracked vehicle (AAV)
AO	Air officer
AP	Armor piercing or attack position
APC	Armored personnel carrier
BAS	Battalio aid station
BDU	Battle dress uniform
BCT	Brigade combat team
BLT	Battalion landing team
Black Bottom	Nickname for a USNS transport ship
BMP	Russian-built tracked, armored personnel carrier
BP	Be prepared (to)
BTR-60	Soviet-made wheeled infantry vehicle
CAAT	Combined anti-armor team
CAS	Close air support
Cas-evac	Casualty evacuation
CAX	Combined-arms exercise
CBR	Counterbattery radar
CCP	Casualty collection point
CENTCOM	U.S. Central Command
CFLCC	Combined-force land component commander
Chop	Removing a unit from its parent unit and assigning it to another unit.
CO	Commanding officer

COB	Chief of the boat—Senior enlisted man aboard a U.S. submarine
COC	Command operations center
Comm(s)	Communications
COT	Commander of troops
CP	Command post
CSS	Confederate states ship
CW3	Chief Warrant Officer 3
DOD	Department of Defense
DPICM	Dual purpose improved conventional munitions
EAAK	External appliqué armor kit (for AAVs)
EAPU	External auxiliary power unit
EMT	Emergency medical technician
EPW	Enemy prisoner of war
FAC	Forward air controller
FARP	Forward area resupply point
FiST	Fire support team
FO	Forward observer
FOB	Forward operating base
FRAGO	Fragmentary order
FSB	Forward support battalion
GAU	Gatling gun
GCE	Gound combat element
GP	General purpose—as in GP tents
GPS	Global positioning satellite
H&S	Headquarters and support
HE	High explosive
HEMTT	Heavy expanded mobility tactical truck (HEMIT)
HET	Heavy equipment transporter or HUMINT Exploitation Team
HML/A	Marine light attack helicopter squadron
HMM	Marine medium helicopter squadron
HMMWV	High-mobility multiwheeled vehicle
HQ	Headquarters
HUMINT	Human Intelligence
I&I	Inspector and instructor
ID	Infantry division
IFAV	Infantry fast-attack vehicle
IMEF	1st Marine Expeditionary Forces
JDAM	Joint direct attack munitions
JSOF	Joint Special Operations Force
KIA	Killed in action
LAR	Light armored reconnaissance
LAV	Light armored vehicle

LAV-25	Light armored vehicle with 25mm Bushmaster automatic cannon
LAV-AT	Light armored vehicle—Antitank—TOW missile launcher
LCAC	Landing craft air cushioned
LD	Line of departure
LHA	Landing helicopter assault (Ship)
LHD	Landing helicopter dock (Ship)
LNO	Liaison officer
LPD	Landing transport dock (Ship)
LSA	Logistics support area
LSD	Landing supply dock (Ship)
LVS	Four-wheel-drive heavy-lift vehicle
LZ	Landing zone
M240G	7.62 mm machine gun
MAGTF	Marine air-ground task force
MAG	Marine air group
MEB	Marine expeditionary brigade
MEF	Marine expeditionary force
MEU	Marine expeditionary unit
MLRS	Multiple-launch rocket system
MOPP	Mission-oriented protective posture
MOUT	Military operations in urban terrain
MPAT	Multipurpose antitank
MRE	Meal-ready-to-eat
MSR	Main supply route
MWSS	Marine wing support squadron
NBC	Nuclear, biological, and chemical
NCO	Noncommissioned officer
NVGs	Night-vision goggles
ODA	Operational detachment—Alpha (Green Beret "A" Team)
PFC	Private First Class
Phrogs	Marine nickname for Sea Knight CH-46 helicopter
PL	Phase line
POW	Prisoner of war
QRF	Quick-reaction force
RCT	Regimental combat team
RIP	Relief in place
ROC	Rehearsal of concept or reconnaissance operations center
RPG	Rocket-propelled grenade
RRP	Rapid resupply point
SAM	Surface-to-air missile
SATCOM	Satellite communications
SAW	Squad automatic weapon

Scud	Russian ballistic missile
SeaBees	U.S. Navy construction battalion
SEAL	Sea, Air, and Land—U.S. Navy's elite commando unit.
SF	Special Forces
SIGINT	Signal Intelligence
Skids	Marine nickname for Cobras and Hueys
SMAW	Shoulder-fired multipurpose assault weapon
Snake	Marine nickname for a Cobra helicopter
SOAR	Special Operations Aviation Regiment
SOC	Special Operations Capable—USMC as in MEU(SOC)
SPC	Specialist
SWAT	Special weapons and tactics
TAA	Tactical assembly area
TAC	Tactical
TACP	Tactical air control party
TAD	Tactical air direction
TC	Troop commander or track commander
TCP	Tactical control point
TEWT	Tactical exercise without troops
TF	Task force
TFT	Task Force Tarawa
TOC	Tactical operations center
TOW	Tube-launched, optically tracked, wire-guided, antitank missile
UAV	Unmanned aerial vehicle
UK	United Kingdom
USS	United States ship
USMC	United States Marine Corps
USNS	United States naval ship—Ships of the military sealift command
WIA	Wounded in action
WMD	Weapon of mass destruction
XO	Executive officer
ZSU23-4	Radar-guided antiaircraft artillery

Bibliography

"Attack on the 507th Maintenance Company 23 March 2003 An Nasiriyah, Iraq: Executive Summary," U.S. Army.

Bailey, R. L. "Command Chronology For 01 January To 30 June 2003," 2d Marine Regiment, United States Marine Corps, 31 Jul 03.

Barham, D. J. "Semi-Annual Command Chronology for the period 1 January 2003 to 30 June 2003 (Operation Enduring Freedom/Iraqi Freedom)," Marine Aircraft Group 29, United States Marine Corps, 30 Jul 03.

Bolt, J. D. First Lieutenant "Summary of Actions of Surveillance and Target Acquisition (STA) Platoon 3/2 During Operation Iraqi Freedom," United States Marine Corps, 23 Apr 04.

Bonadonna, R. R. Colonel, USMCR, *A Short History of Task Force Tarawa*, USMC History Center.

Bonadonna, R. R. Colonel, USMCR, *History Deployment Journal*.

Bragg, R. *I Am a Soldier, Too: The Jessica Lynch Story*, Alfred A. Knopf, New York, 2003.

Cabell, B. "Family Honors Marines' Sacrifice," CNN, 26 May, 2003.

Cavallaro, G. "Battle for Nasiriyah," *Army Times,* 12 May, 2003.

Commanding Officer "Summary For 1st Bn 10th Marines for the period 1 January 2003–19 May 2003," 1st Battalion, 10th Marines, United States Marine Corps, Preliminary Report.

Connell, R. and Lopez, R. J. "A Deadly Day for Charlie Company," *Los Angeles Times,* 26 August, 2003.

Corvo, D., Executive Producer, *"Ambush: The Story of the 507th," Dateline NBC,* Stone Phillips, (reporting) 1 August 2003.

Davidson, O. G. "A Wrong Turn in the Desert," *Rolling Stone,* 27 May 2004.

DeFrost, R. A. "Command Chronology 01 January—30 June 2003", 2d Light Armored Reconnaissance Battalion, United States Marine Corps, 06 Aug 03.

Dunahoe, P. B. Lieutenant Colonel, USMC, *Commander's Guidance, 3rd Battalion 2nd Marines Operations in the Republic of Iraq,* 2003.

Dunahoe, P. B. Lieutenant Colonel, USMC, *Commander's Intent, Line of Departure to An Nasiriyah*, 2003.

Dunfee, D. R., "CWO3 Ambush Alley Revisited," *Marine Corps Gazette*, March 2004, pp. 44–46.

Durkin, R. T., "Command Chronology for 1 January 2003 To 30 June 2003," 1st Battalion, 2d Marines, United States Marine Corps, 04 Aug 03.

Field, W. M. Major, USMC, "Marine Artillery in the Battle for An Nasiriyah," *Field Artillery Magazine*, Nov 2003, 26–30.

Glover, H., "Command Chronology Report for Calendar Year 2003," Company A, 8th Tank Battalion, United States Marine Corps, 1 Jan 04.

Gomez, J. Sergeant, USMC, "Re:" Personal Account By E-Mail. 4 October 2004.

Grant, M., "A Tribute to Arizona War Veterans" KAET-TV/Channel 8, Arizona State University. May, 2003.

Grunwald, G. L., "Command Chronology for period of 01 Jan 03 To 30 Jun 03," Charlie Company, 2d LAR Battalion, United States Marine Corps, 30 Jun 03.

Hewlett, J. M., "Command Chronology for 1 January to 30 June 2003," Marine Light/Attack Helicopter Squadron 269, United States Marine Corps, 15 Jul 03.

Hodgkins, W. F. Brigadier General, USAF, (USCENTAF Friendly Fire Investigation Board President), "Investigation of Suspected Friendly Fire Incident Near An Nasiriyah, Iraq, 23 March 03," United States Central Command, MacDill Air Force Base, Florida, Mar 06 2004.

Ingersoll, A. E., III, "Command Chronology for the period of 01 Jan to 31 Mar 2003," 15 Marine Expeditionary Unit, United States Marine Corps, 17 Apr 03.

Livingston, G., *An Nasiriyah: The Fight for the Bridges,* Caisson Press, December 2003.

Lowry, R. S., *The Gulf War Chronicles,* iUniverse, New York, 2003.

Moore, B. R., "Command Chronology," Headquarters and Service Company, 1st Battalion, 2d Marines United States Marine Corps. Preliminary Report.

Mortenson, R. P., "Command Chronology," 2d Battalion, 8th Marines, United States Marine Corps, 30 Jun 03.

Natonski, R. F. "Command Chronology for the period 1 Jan 2003–30 Jun 2003," 2d Marine Expeditionary Brigade, United States Marine Corps, 25 Sep 03.

Natonski, R. F. Major General, USMC, "Task Force Tarawa Battle of An Nasiriyah," PowerPoint Presentation.

Natonski, R. F. Major General, USMC, "Task Force Tarawa Operation Iraqi Freedom," PowerPoint Presentation.

Officer in Charge, "Input for Command Chronology for HET 16 Support To 3/2 During Operation Iraqi Freedom," HUMINT Exploitation Team 16, USMC, 24 May 03.

Robinson, L., *Masters of Chaos: The Secret History of the Special Forces,* Public-Affairs, New York, 2004.

Rowland, J. G., "Remarks by Governor John G. Rowland," *Funeral of Gunnery Sergeant Phillip Jordan,* State of Connecticut, Hartford, 2003.

Rosenberg, H., "Nightline: The 507th Maintenance Company," ABC News, 2003.

Smith, R. and West, B., *The March Up,* Bantam, New York, September 2003.

Spears, V. H. "Shot in all four limbs, 'I could give up and die, or I could keep fighting' ", *Lexington Herald-Leader,* January 2, 2005.

Staff of 2d Force Reconnaissance Company "2d Force Reconnaissance Company at War," *Marine Corps Gazette,* July 2003, 32–35.

Stockman, J. R., Captain, USMC, *Marines in World War II Historical Monograph: The Battle for Tarawa,* Historical Section, Division of Public Information Headquarters, U.S. Marine Corps, 1947.

Thacker D. L., Jr., "Command Chronology for 1 January 2003–30 June 2003," Marine Medium Helicopter Squadron 162, United States Marine Corps, 21 Aug 03.

Toler, T., "Wound had to wait on battle," *Jacksonville Daily, News.* August 19, 2003.

Waite, B., *For God and Country,* HeartSpring Media, 2005.

Walsh, M. C. Corporal, USMC, Personal Letter.

Wentzel, J. R., USMC, "Operation Iraqi Freedom After Action Report," 1st Battalion, 2d Marines, USMC 17 May, 2003.

Wilson, M., "Troops meet resistance at An Nasiriyah," *New York Times.*

INTERVIEWS AND CORRESPONDENCE

BGen Richard Natonski	Personal Interview at Camp Lejeune	03/25/04
BGen Richard Natonski	Personal Interview at Camp Lejeune	10/27/03
Col Ron Bailey	Personal Interview at Camp Lejeune	10/27/03
Col Ron Bailey	Personal Interview at Camp Lejeune	03/25/04
Col Ron Bailey	Personal Interview at Camp Lejeune	06/14/04
Col Robert Milstead	Personal Interview at Camp Lejeune	10/27/03
Col Eddie Ray	Telephone Interview	01/22/04
Col Glenn Starnes	Telephone Interview	02/17/04
LtCol Lou Craparotta	Telephone Interview	03/30/04
LtCol P. Brent Dunahoe	Personal Interview at Camp Lejeune	10/27/03
LtCol P. Brent Dunahoe	Personal Interview at Camp Lejeune	06/15/04
LtCol Rickey Grabowski	Telephone Interview	03/01/04
LtCol Rickey Grabowski	Telephone Interview	04/01/04
LtCol Rickey Grabowski	Telephone Interview	01/05/05
LTC Glen Harp (USA)	Personal Interview at Camp Lejeune	10/27/03

LtCol Dan Kelly	Personal Interview at Camp Lejeune	03/25/04
LtCol Royal Mortenson	Personal Interview at Camp Lejeune	10/27/03
LtCol Royal Mortenson	Personal Interview at Camp Lejeune	06/15/04
LtCol James Reilly	Personal Interview at Camp Lejeune	01/13/04
LtCol Darryl Thacker	Personal Interview at New River	01/12/04
Maj Dan Canfield	Personal Interview at Camp Lejeune	10/27/03
Maj John Day	Telephone Interview	05/25/04
Maj Rich Dremann	Telephone Interview	06/05/04
Maj Rich Dremann	Personal Interview at Camp Lejeune	06/17/04
Maj Robert Fulford	Telephone Interview	04/28/04
Maj Scott Hawkins	Telephone Interview	06/04/04
Maj Ben Luciano	Telephone Interview	01/31/05
Maj John O'Neal	Personal Interview at New River	01/12/04
Maj Bill Peeples	Telephone Interview	01/29/04
Maj Bill Peeples	Telephone Interview	01/30/04
Maj Matthew Reid	Personal Interview in Orlando, FL	05/19/05
Maj Michael Mooney	Telephone Interview	11/08/04
Maj Christopher Starling	Personal Interview at Camp Lejeune	03/25/04
Maj Christopher Starling	Personal Interview at Camp Lejeune	06/14/04
Capt William Blanchard	Personal Interview at Camp Lejeune	01/13/04
Capt Michael Brooks	Personal Interview at Camp Lejeune	10/27/03
Capt Romeo Cubas	Telephone Interview	01/14/05
Capt Gerard Dempster	Telephone Interview	06/30/04
Capt Scott Dyer	Telephone Interview	05/12/05
Capt Kelly Frushour	Personal Interview at Camp Lejeune	10/27/03
Capt Eric Garcia	Telephone Interview	11/10/03
Capt Eric Griggs	Personal Interview at New River	01/12/04
Capt Tod Schroeder	Personal Interview at New River	01/12/04
Capt Edward Healy	Personal Interview at Camp Lejeune	06/15/04
Capt Timothy Newland	Telephone Interview	02/12/04
Capt Timothy Newland	Telephone Interview	02/13/04
Capt Tod Schroeder	Personal Interview at New River	01/12/04
Capt Gerald Thomas	Telephone Interview	04/28/04
Capt Jim Thompson	Telephone Interview	07/06/04
Lt Brian Waite (USN)	Telephone Interview	10/05/04
Capt Daniel Wittnam	Telephone Interview	02/18/04
Capt Daniel Wittnam	Telephone Interview	03/11/04
Capt Daniel Wittnam	Personal Interview Jacksonville, NC	03/24/04
Capt Kevin Yeo	Telephone Interview	05/04/04
1stLt Michael Dubrule	Personal Interview at Camp Lejeune	01/12/04
1stLt Melvin Euring	Telephone Interview	04/28/04
1stLt Jonathan Forman	Telephone Interview	03/30/04
1stLt Gregory Nolan	Telephone Interview	02/25/05

1stLt John Parker	Personal Interview at New River	01/12/04
1stLt James Reid	Telephone Interview	07/06/04
1stLt James Reid	Telephone Interview	02/08/05
1stLt Kris Southwick	Telephone Interview	03/26/05
Gunner David Dunfee	Personal Interview at Camp Lejeune	03/25/04
Gunner Nick Vitale	Telephone Interview	06/30/04
CW3 Marc Nash (USA)	Telephone Interview	06/13/05
SgtMaj Charles Arrick	Telephone Interview	04/06/05
1stSgt Jose Henao	Personal Interview at Orlando I&I	04/26/04
1stSgt James Thompson Jr.	Telephone Interview	08/01/04
MSgt Bragsdale	Personal Interview at Camp Lejeune	06/14/04
GySgt Kevin Barry Jr.	Telephone Interview	04/02/04
GySgt Jason Doran	Telephone Interview	09/22/04
GySgt Jason Doran	Telephone Interview	09/23/04
GySgt William Hetterscheidt	Telephone Interview	02/09/04
GySgt Alan Kamper	Telephone Interview	12/03/04
GySgt Mackes	Telephone Interview	05/20/05
SSgt Jason Cantu	Telephone Interview	10/01/04
SSgt Kevin Ellicott	Telephone Interview	02/04/04
SSgt Fowler	Telephone Interview	06/02/04
SSgt William Schaefer	Telephone Interview	03/10/04
SSgt William Schaefer	Personal Interview at Camp Lejeune	06/15/04
SSgt Troy Schielein	Telephone Interview	09/14/04
Sgt Jason Bossmeyer	Personal Interview at Camp Lejeune	06/14/04
Sgt Curtis Campbell (USA)	Telephone Interview	05/11/04
Sgt Curtis Campbell (USA)	Telephone Interview	12/22/03
Sgt James Grubb (USA)	Telephone Interview	02/19/05
Sgt Joe Muccia	Telephone Interview	08/06/04
Sgt Joe Muccia	Telephone Interview	08/16/04
Sgt Joel Petrik (USA)	Telephone Interview	05/24/05
Sgt Mark Sarmiento	Telephone Interview	09/14/04
Cpl Nicolas Elliot	Personal Interview at Camp Lejeune	06/15/04
Cpl John Friend	Telephone Interview	06/29/04
HN3 Moses Gloria (USN)	Telephone Interview	11/17/04
Cpl Jose Gomez	Personal e-mail account	10/04/04
Cpl Hensley	Personal Interview at Camp Lejeune	06/14/04
Cpl Matthew Walsh	Personal letter	04/19/04
Cpl John Wentzel	Personal Interview at Camp Lejeune	06/16/04
Cpl Randy Whidden	Telephone Interview	01/19/05
Cpl Will Bachmann	Telephone Interview	05/25/04
HN Luis Fonseca (USN)	Telephone Interview	06/04/04
Tina Cline	Telephone Interview	03/13/05
Eric and Bonnie Garcia	Personal Interview Jacksonville, NC	03/24/04

Ken Kalthoff	Personal Interview in Dallas, TX	02/23/04
Joe Raedle	Telephone Interview	11/08/04
Kerry Sanders	Personal Interview in Ft. Lauderdale, FL	01/27/04

OFFICIAL ORAL HISTORIES RECODED FOR THE MARINE CORPS HISTORY AND MUSEUMS DIVISION

Col Ron Bailey	Interviewed by Col Reed Bonadonna	01/24/03
Col Ron Bailey	Interviewed by Col Reed Bonadonna	05/08/03
LtCol P. Brent Dunahoe	Interviewed by LtCol David Walters	12/12/03
LtCol Ricky Grabowski	Interviewed by Col Reed Bonadonna	03/04/03
LtCol Ricky Grabowski	Interviewed by Col Reed Bonadonna	04/06/03
LtCol John O'Rourke	Interviewed by Col Reed Bonadonna	04/10/03
Maj John Day	Interviewed by LtCol David Walters	12/12/03
Maj Darryl Dotson	Interviewed by Col Reed Bonadonna	05/06/03
Maj Andy Kennedy	Interviewed by Col Reed Bonadonna	05/07/03
Maj David Sosa	Interviewed by Col Reed Bonadonna	03/16/03
Maj David Sosa	Interviewed by Col Reed Bonadonna	05/01/03
Capt Scott Beeson	Interviewed by Col Reed Bonadonna	03/13/03
Capt Scott Beeson	Interviewed by Col Reed Bonadonna	04/12/03
Capt Michael Brooks	Interviewed by Col Reed Bonadonna	05/01/03
Capt Thomas Campbell	Interviewed by Col Reed Bonadonna	04/12/03
Capt Timothy Hitzelberger	Interviewed by LtCol David Walters	12/12/03
Capt Timothy Newland	Interviewed by Col Reed Bonadonna	04/29/03
Capt Karl Rohr	Interviewed by Col Reed Bonadonna	05/02/03
1stLt Robert Barnhart	Interviewed by Col Reed Bonadonna	05/02/03
1stLt Jonathon Bidstrup	Interviewed by LtCol Mike Visconerez	03/26/03
1stLt Edmund Clayton	Interviewed by Col Reed Bonadonna	04/02/03
1stLt Jonathan Forman	Interviewed by LtCol David Walters	12/12/03
1stLt Michael Seely	Interviewed by Col Reed Bonadonna	05/04/03
2dLt Scott Swantner	Interviewed by Col Reed Bonadonna	05/02/03
MGySgt Mark Arnold	Interviewed by Col Reed Bonadonna	03/19/03
1stSgt Patrick Delany	Interviewed by Col Reed Bonadonna	04/12/03
GySgt Derek Leggett	Interviewed by Col Reed Bonadonna	04/02/03
GySgt Mark Pyland	Interviewed by Col Reed Bonadonna	04/12/03
SSgt Anthony Pompos	Interviewed by Col Reed Bonadonna	05/04/03
SSgt Troy Schielein	Interviewed by Col Reed Bonadonna	04/29/04
Sgt Gregory Griffin	Interviewed by Col Reed Bonadonna	03/19/03
Cpl Dana Perkins	Interviewed by LtCol David Walters	12/12/03
HM3 Robert Richie (USN)	Interviewed by Col Reed Bonadonna	05/04/03
LCpl Aaron Counts	Interviewed by LtCol David Walters	12/12/03

LCpl Christian Izaguirre   Interviewed by LtCol David Walters   12/12/03
LCpl Eric Kent   Interviewed by LtCol David Walters   12/12/03

ON THE INTERNET

http://1stbattalion3rdmarines.com
http://www.fallenheroesmemorial.com/oif/

Index